CULTURE, FORM, AND PLACE

Essays in Cultural and Historical Geography

Edited by

Kent Mathewson

GEOSCIENCE AND MAN vol. 32
Geoscience Publications • Department of Geography and Anthropology
Louisiana State University • Baton Rouge, LA 70893-6010

The Geoscience and Man series of symposia, monographs, and collections of papers in geography, anthropology and geology is published and distributed by Geoscience Publications, Department of Geography and Anthropology, Louisiana State University. A list of volumes in print, as well as other works from Geoscience Publications can be found at the back of this volume.

Editor: Kam-biu Liu.

Geoscience Publications Committee: Chair, Miles Richardson, professor of anthropology; Kam-biu Liu, associate professor of geography; M. Jill Brody, associate professor of anthropology; William V. Davidson, associate professor of geography; Barun Sen Gupta, professor of geology; and ex officio, Carville Earle, chairman of the Department of Geography and Anthropology. Managing editor: Esther Shaffer. Art director: Mary Lee Eggart, research associate.

Library of Congress Cataloging-in-Publication Data

Culture, form, and place : essays in cultural and historical geography / edited by Kent Mathewson.
      p. cm. — (Geoscience and man : v. 32)
      Includes bibliographical references.
      ISBN 0-938909-55-X
      1. America—Historical geography 2. Human geography—
America.
I. Mathewson, Kent. II. Series.
      E21.7.C85/3/   1993
      911'.73--dc20   93-37168

Cover design: Mary Lee Eggart; Artwork: Lynn Schlossberger

Contents

Introduction

Kent Mathewson

Most of the essays and articles in this volume are based on papers presented at the "Culture, Form, and Place" symposium February 20-24, 1990, "celebrating sixty years of cultural and historical geography at Louisiana State University." To set the written record straight, it should be noted that the subtitle involved a bit of circumlocution. The original idea was to celebrate Boyd Professor Emeritus Fred Bowerman Kniffen's ninetieth birthday, which fell on January 18, 1990. For a variety of reasons, not the least of which was sparing Mr. Kniffen the discomfort of having that much hoopla directed squarely at him, the event was expanded and scheduled for a month later. Accordingly, the emphasis shifted from Kniffen's longevity to celebrating the Department's record of more than six decades of cultivating geography's cultural and historical approaches.

As many readers will remember, Fred B. Kniffen arrived at L.S.U. in 1929 to help geologist and physical geographer Richard J. Russell expand the geography offerings and to teach an anthropology course or two. Like Russell, Kniffen's earlier training had been in geology, and both did their doctoral work at Berkeley. While at Berkeley, however, Kniffen's main interests had begun to shift from physical to cultural geography and anthropology. There he worked closely with both Carl O. Sauer and Alfred Kroeber and witnessed cultural geography's formal beginnings in North America. It was this formative cultural geography that Kniffen brought to L.S.U. Thus, L.S.U. geography's orientation toward cultural approaches with strong anthropological and historical inflections was established from the outset. Over the next several decades, from his base in Baton Rouge, Kniffen helped to lay cultural geography's foundations. In 1940 Carl O. Sauer (1941) delivered his presidential address "Foreword to Historical Geography" before the annual meeting of the Association of American Geographers. Appropriately enough, the meeting was hosted by Kniffen and Russell and held on the L.S.U. campus. In his talk, Sauer defended and extended the legitimacy of historical geography. By the late 1940s, when Latin Americanist cultural and historical geographer Robert C. West joined the department, both cultural and historical geography were beginning to assume a larger role in American geography. Like

Kniffen, West did his doctoral work at Berkeley under Carl Sauer's supervision. Unlike Kniffen, whose involvement with Latin American research was limited to his dissertation on the Colorado River Delta region in northern Mexico, West has spend much of his career mining the archives and studying the landscapes of Latin America. Together, these two eminent scholars have been the main architects by example and design of L.S.U.'s distinctive and distinguished record of New World cultural and historical geographic research. It was with this in mind that the symposium was organized to celebrate their contributions but also to celebrate the efforts of all those geographers and associated scholars who have drawn inspiration from their examples.

The collectivity described above is by now a rather large one. Louisiana is also justly famous for is its devotion to large scale festivities. Appropriately then, the Culture, Form, and Place symposium was held on the weekend before Mardi Gras and blessed by a spell of resplendent weather. The crew that assembled included some one hundred and fifty loyal departmental students, faculty, friends, and alumni. They came from as near as New Roads and as far away as Korea. Six distinguished "outside" speakers were invited to give 45-minute plenary-style presentations on Friday, the first day of the symposium. Departmental alumni presented shorter papers in three half-day sessions on Saturday and on Sunday morning. Entertainment included a crawfish boil and Cajun band Friday evening, a reception hosted by Rita and Jesse Walker at their home on Saturday evening, and a field trip in Acadiana on Sunday afternoon led by anthropology student Rocky Sexton.

As with all good homecomings, the "Kniffen-West Fest" as it came to be referred to by some, was a robust celebration of the semisacred and the mildly profane. Henry Glassie's homage to Kniffen and his craft offered transcendent moments while Bill Turner's Whiggish and David Stoddard's waggish self-referential tributes to two of West's concerns put the audience into the *bajo* and onto the beach with great effect. Keynoters Webb, Jordan, and Butzer saluted Kniffen and West in well measured and solidly documented presentations. The alumni papers delivered over the next two days evoked thoughts of lessons learned and mentors minded as well as glimpses of new adaptations and departures taken. As can be seen from the titles of the talks from the program as reproduced below, each reaffirmed in clear and unmistakable ways the ongoing enterprise that is easily recognized as L.S.U.-styled cultural and historical geography.

The contributions in this volume represent, though obviously do not replicate in full, the extent and the context of the symposium. All the presenters were invited to submit papers. In retrospect, an overly ambitious production schedule was announced. This may have dissuaded some. To those who met the early deadline(s), I offer my thanks for their forthrightness and my apologies for a process that extended Sauer's famous admonition that "locomotion should be slow, the slower the better" beyond what he surely intended. An editor should accept responsibility for such lags, and I do. More to the point, it is indeed unfortunate that Professor Kniffen could not see the final product. However, like Kniffen's own oak-solid productions, much of the work presented here is hardly the stuff of ephemeral scholarship. His knowing this, together with his appreciation of the oral presentations, was tribute enough I hope.

As befits a volume celebratory of cultural-historical approaches, the papers are arranged in a general historical or chronological sequence. Prehistoric (or at least pre-European) topics come first, followed by colonial themes, with modern times last. This is not meant, however, to mirror Kniffen's or West's own research trajectories. At various points in their careers, both have investigated aspects of the Americas' pre-European landscapes, colonial material culture and production, and manifestations of traditional folkways in contemporary times. In this regard, both Kniffen's and West's writings demonstrate a resistance to the constraints imposed by either narrow specialization or periodization. While certainly conscious of historical patterns and processes, and well aware of the character and constructions of particular places and regions, a profound appreciation of the morphological expressions of cultural creativity and persistence over time is what distinguishes their scholarship. For this reason, the theme of the symposium and volume was focused on culture, form, and place. Of late, much has been written on the nature of culture and place as concepts within geography and its allied disciplines. In contrast, little has been written on form or morphology in cultural and historical geography. Sauer's (1925) foundational piece for cultural geography on the "morphology of landscape" was meant more as prolegomena than as the last word on the subject. It is a topic in need of reexamination. Here, however, is not the place to extend this discussion. Future work, if it is undertaken, will perforce consider the record of cultural and historical geographers such as Fred B. Kniffen and Robert C. West, and those inspired by their examples.

All of the authors here address questions involving culture, form, and place, though none deal explicitly with these concepts. Several of the authors examine aspects of the material culture in particular places (Craig, Parsons) or in their regional distributions (Jones and Shuman, Wilhelm) and/or regional manifestations (Works, Jordan, Colten). Another author (Dixon) looks at the ethnic expressions of culture in a singular place. Several authors (Webb, Jones and Shuman, Turner, Butzer and Butzer, Meyer-Arendt, Sheldon) consider the forms that settlement and landscape modifications take at regional scales, though within quite different historical contexts. Only one author (Blaut) is primarily concerned with concepts rather than culture's material forms or culture's expressions in places or regions. Nevertheless, parts of his discussion refer to situations and circumstances in specific departments of geography.

The first section of this volume deals with the pre-European record in the Gulf South region and in the Maya lowlands of Mesoamerica. In the first chapter, Malcolm Webb uses ethnographic analogies from disparate societies to reexamine two florescent and apparently disjunct periods of aboriginal settlement and mound building and their associated subsistence activities and prestige economics to shed new light on the culture history of the lower Mississippi Valley region. At first glance Webb—schooled in the Michigan tradition of materialist anthropology—brings a more evolutionist eye to bear on these questions than one might associate with L.S.U.'s Kroeber-Sauer cultural historical groundings. Though Webb does not mention it, the Leslie White-Michigan outlook was infused into the department in the early '50s through the genial influence of William G. Haag. By then, Kniffen's active archaeological work had been supplanted by his studies of material culture in its historical and contemporary forms. Webb's piece nods in directions that not only acknowledge Kniffen's contributions to Louisiana archaeology, but also to Haag's role in planting prehistoric studies deep within the departmental agenda.

The next chapter, by Dennis Jones and Malcolm Shuman, is an unambiguous demonstration of, and statement of intent for, extending the work started by Kniffen and his W.P.A. associates James A. Ford, George I. Quimby, and Gordon R. Willey on mapping and excavating Louisiana's Indian mounds. Whether termed archaeogeography or landscape archaeology or simply solid and sane archaeology, their investigations and reconstructions are clearly in the mode favored by Kniffen and West. Rekindling the public service spirit of the W.P.A. projects while testing the latest techniques of computer graphics and analysis, Jones and Shuman's efforts point the direction for the next generation.

In the third chapter, Bill Turner reflects on the ways that geographers, archaeologists, and assorted earth scientists have reconstructed and revised our understanding of ancient Maya subsistence modes. He charts several phases of pendular swings in which an earlier orthodoxy has been knocked from its position(s) by surges of both empirical findings and theoretical reformulations. A key actor in Maya subsistence studies for the past two decades and one of the architects of the "new orthodoxy" now under attack, Turner is an able guide through the theoretical thickets and data mounds that characterize this once neglected field of Maya studies. Along the way, he accurately points out that the previous generation of field-oriented geographers, such as Robert West, cleared the way for the "new orthodoxy" with their careful attention to intensive agriculture's forms and features in Latin America.

The three chapters in the second section of the volume explore the results of Spanish colonial policies and practices in the realms of agronomy, mining, and trade. In the first of these chapters, Karl and Elisabeth Butzer demonstrate with considerable skill and detail how archival sources can be used to reconstruct colonial vegetation patterns, in this case using the Mexican Bajío region. Moreover, their paper makes an important contribution to both the methodology and our understanding of environmental history in post-Conquest Spanish America. Contrary to popularly held views concerning native land management, the authors show that the Bajío's pre-Hispanic landscapes were not without evidence of disturbance, deforestation, and degradation. In addition, the first- and second-generation Spanish settlers appear to have been better environmental stewards than has generally been thought. The Butzers' impressive handling of archival material in concert with first-hand field observation makes for a fitting tribute to Robert West's own contributions to Spanish colonial historical geography.

In the next chapter of this section, Alan Craig expertly takes the reader deep into the technology of the world's most intensive silver producing site in the 16th century. From the 1540s until a 1626 flash flood destroyed much of its capacity, Potosí and its environs in Alta Peru (Bolivia) had more hydraulic technology for milling ore than anywhere on Earth. Craig traces the mining and milling developments in this singular place, with detailed attention to two of the best preserved sites. He provides new information from archival sources and offers reconstructive documentation in drawings and photographs of what remains in the landscape. Craig's focus on mining and milling vividly recalls his mentor West's own extended interest in colonial mining in Spanish America. Two of West's best known monographs are his doctoral study *The Mining Community in Northern Mexico: The Parral Mining District* (1949) and his *Colonial Placer Mining in Colombia* (1952). Returning to the topic after many years, West along with Craig is currently co-editing a forthcoming volume on colonial mining in Latin America (Craig and West n.d.).

The third chapter in this section, by Martha Works, examines the question of New Mexico's peripheral location in colonial times in terms of its commercial articulations. It is often depicted as the Ultima Thule in the Spanish American colonial world and marginal to the point of insignificance save for its ethnic isolates, but Works challenges this image of New Mexico with evidence of far-flung trading activity. Surveying the richness of material culture production and consumption suggested in archival sources, she locates colonial New Mexico well within the global culture networks of the times. Attention to material culture items as markers of larger cultural processes, and a survey of the economic aspects New

Spain's mining and farming frontiers connects this contribution with some of Kniffen's and West's core concerns.

Proceeding toward the present, the four papers that comprise the volume's third section examine the expressions of material culture in the American South, the Midwest, and in Mexico. Terry Jordan's essay on the "Anglo-American Mestizos" and their place in southern American regional culture borders on the revelatory. Starting with a cue from Kniffen regarding graveyards as places where the past is often present, Jordan has unearthed an ensemble of traits in Southern culture that suggest Amerind origins. Recent U.S. census data on ancestry reveals a unexpectedly large number of persons reporting Amerindian forebearers. By far, the largest numbers are from the South, particularly its trans-Mississippi portions. Though Jordan's main traits are drawn from diet, speech, and folk religion, the way has been marked for others to add to his inventory. At a time when the salience and valency of ethnic identity takes on increasing if unpredictable charges, it may be helpful to blur the generative lines where possible. Demonstrating Native American bases of Anglo-Southern culture would seem to be a step in this direction. But what is not blurred in Jordan's piece is the direct link to the ethnogeographic methods that Kniffen and West pioneered in their own Southern regional studies.

If Jordan's article takes us toward frontiers, the following chapter, by Gene Wilhelm sends us back to the old home grounds, in this case in the Blue Ridge Mountain region. Tightly fitted with his own empirical findings, Wilhelm's work makes it clear that material culture studies in the Kniffen style have hardly run their course. Wilhelm takes no short cuts; statistical inferences are not even considered. He settles for nothing less than close to total survey. He put a keen morphologic eye to houses, barns, outbuildings, stores, mills, and "lesser items" and followed them through their evolution in time and space. He discerns dual origins of a distinct Blue Ridge culture complex in the Pennsylvania German-Scotch-Irish and the Chesapeake Tidewater English traditions. From these antecedents, a "mountain folk culture" style was forged. In turn, the Blue Ridge region and its material culture forms served as sources for subsequent developments in the rest of the Southern Appalachians and latterly to the Ozarks of Arkansas-Missouri.

The next chapter takes us from the Southern culture areas to the middle Mississippi Valley region. Craig Colten looks at forms of material culture associated with fishing and other extractive activities that developed along the Illinois River in concert with European settlement. He examines their origins and traces their expansions and contractions as resources were depleted or markets shifted. He suggests that a broad repertoire of techniques allowed the riverfolk to adapt to changing environmental and economic conditions. In some cases, resources declined past certain thresholds causing outmigration. As a result, Colten argues that material culture items and practices were diffused to other subregions within the Mississippi River Valley. Although neither Kniffen nor West recorded more than passing interest in this part of the country—Kniffen with house type transects and West with his work on mapping the term "bayou"—Colten's approach is clearly in the same channel.

The final paper in this section, by James Parsons, is something of a coda. It was not presented at the symposium, but was kindly contributed to the volume at the editor's invitation. Yet another vignette on Hispanic land and life by one of its foremost geographic interpreters, this contribution combines Kniffen's call to necrogeography with West's abiding interest in *todas cosas mexicanas* and most things vegetal. The result is a fine *monografita* on *Tagetes* spp., the golden flowered marigold, and its integral part in the Mexican celebrations of *"los dias de los muertos"* (All Saints' and All Souls' Days) at the beginning of November. Parsons traces the history of the flower's use in pre-Columbian Mexico, discusses its widespread diffusion from Mesoamerica, points out analogues elsewhere, comments on its popularity in the United States, and returns it to its persistent place within Mexican ceremonial and popular culture.

The fourth section takes us to three zones of landscape change with quite different settings and extents. Clifton Dixon follows one of the main paths of settlement geography—the study of agricultural colonization sites —in recounting and assessing one such example in southern Costa Rica. Among the many Europeans that immigrated to Latin America after WWII, one hundred or so Italian families were contracted to start a colony in the canton of Coto Brus, Costa Rica. They founded the town of San Vito, and as Dixon shows, made the most of the situation. Their agricultural activities have passed through several phases, each with differing landscape impacts. Expressions of their material culture such as housing and diet have contributed to the region's distinctiveness. Dixon sees this self-improving community as a possible model for sustainable colonization projects elsewhere in Latin America. His paper, with its focus on settlement sites and pioneer culture, recalls themes Kniffen and West have also pursued.

In the chapter that follows, Klaus Meyer-Arendt takes the reader to sites near home base. He discusses the historical evolution of resort development along the Gulf of Mexico shoreline. The sun-seeking Gulf tourists may be culturally distant from Kniffen's Southern pioneers or West's Latin American peasants, but the author's attention to the morphological elements and evolution of these landscapes suggests affinities with their perspectives. Moreover, Meyer-Arendt points out the significance of physical geographic processes in the cultural constructions that have come to typify these places. In analyzing the development of coastal tourist landscapes—

image strands of increasing importance to modernity's own need to sell itself—Meyer-Arendt offers some possible new directions for cultural-historical geographers.

The third paper in this section also examines changes in a sandy environment, though one quite removed from Gulf Shore beaches. Sam Sheldon, in a regional piece of environmental history, shows how Ontario's Norfolk Sand Plain was transformed from a minor dust bowl to a rich agricultural district in the course of a few decades. Sheldon sets the stage with a detailed discussion of the region's physical features and the earlier history of European settlement and subsequent deforestation, first through local use, then by commercial exploitation. By the late 19th century, it had become a zone of extreme degradation, with drifting sands and declining population. Two innovations led to the reversal: government-sponsored reforestation and the introduction of flue-cured tobacco from the southern U.S. By 1930 the transformation was completed. The large number of cultural and historical studies by L.S.U. geographers set in the American South and Latin America has somewhat obscured the record of good works done elsewhere. Sheldon's contribution, then, is two-fold. It represents this component of the whole, and it stands on its own as a study of landscape degradation and recovery.

The fifth and final section is an inspired defense of cultural geography as taught and practiced by Kniffen and his associates. Though James Blaut's intervention may not quite reveal the "*quinta essentia*" of the matter, it is not in his mind to do so. Rather, Blaut the pragmatist (pre-postmodern variety) puts Kniffen and his works in practical-philosophical perspective. The essential materialist and democratic nature of Kniffen's project *is* revealed. He also shows how this is at odds with the often dominant subjectivist outlook in geography from Kant to Hartshorne and beyond. And as for those who would claim Kniffen as a precursor of today's "pomo [postmodern] geography," Blaut would simply have them consult the "actually existing" Kniffen in pieces such as his own "Pomo Geography" (1939). As the reader will note, this chapter takes on an anecdotal-expository form. It is reproduced here, for the most part, as it was delivered. There, it served as a fitting summation and Sunday morning recessional for the symposium. Here, I would hope that it raises new questions about old traditions, and creates space for the old ways to be reconstituted within new traditions.

References

Craig, A. K. and West, R. C., eds. n.d. *Aborginal and colonial mining and metallurgy in Spanish America*. Geoscience and Man, vol. 33. Baton Rouge,

LA: Geoscience Publications, Dept. of Geography and Anthropology, Louisiana State University, forthcoming.

Kniffen, F. B. 1939. Pomo geography. *University of California Publications in American Archaeology and Ethnology* 36:353-400.

Sauer, C. O. 1925. The morphology of landscape. *University of California Publications in Geography* 2(2): 19-53.

———. 1941. Foreword to historical geography. *Annals of the Association of American Geographers* 31: 353-364.

West, R. C. 1949. *The mining community in northern New Spain: The Parral mining district.* Ibero-Americana, vol. 30. Berkeley, CA: University of California Press.

———. 1952. *Colonial placer mining in Colombia.* Louisiana State University Studies, Social Science Series, no. 2. Baton Rouge, LA: Louisiana State University Press.

Acknowledgments

I wish to thank all those that supported the symposium, helped with the tasks associated with it, and traveled from near and far to attend it. I thank David B. Harned, Pierre R. Hart, and Craig M. Cordes, Deans of the College of Arts and Sciences, for their crucial support. I extend my appreciation to Executive Vice Chancellor James M. Coleman and to Carville V. Earle, Chair of the Department of Geography and Anthropology, for their sympathetic and insightful introductory remarks. On behalf of the Department of Geography and Anthropology, I thank Boyd Professor Emeritus H. Jesse Walker for his key role in creating the Fred B. Kniffen Professorship within the Department of Geography and Anthropology, and to former Vice Chancellor for Academic Affairs and Provost Carolyn H. Hargrave for making the presentation to Professor Miles E. Richardson as the first recipient. I thank the following members of the faculty for serving as session chairs: Sam B. Hilliard, Miles E. Richardson, Carville V. Earle, Robert A. Muller, Jay D. Edwards, William V. Davidson, Richard H. Kesel, and Nigel J. R. Allan. I thank the office staff, especially Saundra Henderson, Maudrie Eldridge, and Ann Whitmer, for myriad services and suggestions offered.

Mary Lee Eggart contributed much to the layout and graphics of the volume; cover artwork is by Lynn Schlossberger. Esther Shaffer kept track of multiple drafts and made many helpful suggestions. I thank a number of students who repressed the urge to start the Mardi Gras festivities early and instead spent those three days with the assembled alums, friends, and invited guests. The following students contributed to the success of the symposium well beyond mere attendance: Ed Britton, George Castille, Chris Coggins, Mimi Fearn, Laura Hobson, Tanya Kalischer, Bob Kuhlken, Emily Lee, Rocky Sexton, Sue Smith, Joe Tuomey, Stephanie Weigel, and Mike Yoder. Special kudos go to Kathleen Kennedy, surely the occasion's *genius loci* of practical competence and incisive action. Without her help, many things from morning coffee and king cakes to crucial thoughts on how to proceed at various points in the planning and in the proceedings would not have materialized.

I also want to acknowledge the participation of departmental alumni and friends. In addition to those presenting papers, a partial list includes: Daniel Arreola, Sanford and Jolayne Bederman, Michael Camille, Janet Crane, James Curtis, Randall and Charlene Detro, Lary Dilsaver, William Doolittle, Gregory Jeane, Stephen Jett, Clarissa Kimber, Romaine and Donald Kupfer, Lawrence "Doc" L'Herisson, Jr., Chan Lee, Joann Mossa, James Parsons, Louis Seig, Philip Wagner, Eugene Wilson, John Winberry, Steven Zimrick, and the dozen or so geography students from disparate places who came to join us in this celebration.

As is customary I could offer the usual dispensations or disclaimers on the behalf of those who have assisted this publication, absolving them of any responsibility for shortcomings or errors. But I'm not so sure that I should do this here. While the initial idea for a symposium and a volume were entirely my own, as was the final editorial work, by the time it was all completed, I had received so much good advice and cheerful assistance that those standard but illusionary lines of responsibility and proprietorship had long since dissolved into that suspect category labelled collective endeavor. Therefore, I gratefully implicate and acknowledge all those that played a part.

Introductory Remarks

Culture, Form, and Place Symposium, February 23-25, 1990

Carville Earle

One of the simplest yet most powerful ideas to come from human geography in this century came from the minds of Fred Kniffen and Bob West. This was the recognition of the creativity of the folk, of ordinary people. Kniffen illustrated it through his studies of material constructions—especially houses and buildings, and West with his work on agricultural landforms. The tendrils spreading from these roots have transformed the ways we think about nature, society, and culture. I do not believe, however, that the full import of these quite revolutionary ideas has been realized. Oddly enough, it is Kniffen's ideas which I feel have fared least well. Too often, friends and foes alike have reduced them to folk houses or diffusion at the macroscale; the seminal point which has been overlooked is the creative powers of ordinary people, of folk and their culture. I suspect that when we mature as a discipline we will see the antinomy between Kniffen's folk and Hägerstrand and others' elites and "change-agents" as part of a larger dialectical whole within diffusion studies. If we step back from history, if we look attentively at the American past for example, we may indeed find this dialectical alternation between folk and elite to have been at the foundations of our experience. But of that, more at another time and place.

Bob West saw things anew, and differently, too. Tramping over much of Mexico, Central and South America, through fields and archives, he discerned agricultural landforms either forgotten or unknown to Latin American scholars, but having enormous implications for our most basic models of pre-Columbian society and culture. West's work on chinampas and related features spawned a generation of scholarship which has rewritten the agronomic and demographic history of the region. Characteristically modest in his role in anything so revolutionary as the thesis of agrarian intensification, Professor West quietly persisted in doing what he does best—searching, discerning, unfolding. The rest in a sense is denouement. One can imagine that his reaction to the interpretive structure that others have built upon his foundation would be "well of course."

I am here this morning not to praise justly famous men; of that we have had a judicious amount. Rather my intent is to praise great ideas for that, after all, is the legacy of Professors Kniffen and West.

Culture, Form, and Place

Celebrating Sixty Years of Cultural and Historical Geography

Department of Geography and Anthropology
Louisiana State University

Friday, February 23　　*Hill Memorial Library*

8:45 a. m. Welcome: **James M. Coleman**, Executive Vice-Chancellor, LSU

Invited Speakers Session I　　*Chair: Sam B. Hilliard*

9:00 a.m. **Malcolm C. Webb**, Dept. of Anthropology, University of
New Orleans
"Prehistoric Settlement, Subsistence and Social Formation in the Lower
Mississippi Valley"

10:00 a.m. **Terry G. Jordan**, Dept. of Geography, University of Texas-Austin
"The Anglo-American Mestizos and Traditional Southern Regionalism"

11:00 a.m. **Henry Glassie**, Folklore Institute, Indiana University
"The Historical Virtues of Architectural Typologies"

Invited Speakers Session II　　*Chair: Miles E. Richardson*

1:30 p.m. Opening Remarks: **H. Jesse Walker**, Boyd Professor Emeritus, LSU

1:45 pm. **B. L. Turner II**, Graduate School of Geography, Clark University
"Agricultural Landforms and the Making of the Pre-Hispanic Maya
Landscape"

2:45 pm. **Karl W. Butzer**, Dept. of Geography, University of Texas-Austin
"Spanish Settlement of the Mexican Bajío, 1540-1640"

3:45 pm. **David R. Stoddart**, Dept. of Geography, University of California,
Berkeley
"On the Beach: Space and Time in Tropical Island Biogeography"

Saturday, February 24　　*Alumni Speakers*　　*Hill Memorial Library*

I. THE SOUTH: PAST LANDSCAPES OF SETTLEMENT AND
PRODUCTION
Chair: Carville V. Earle

xvi

9:00 a. m. **Dennis C. Jones and Malcolm K. Shuman**, Geoscience Museum, LSU
"Louisiana 'Archaeogeography' Revisited: Mapping the Remaining Indian Mounds"

9:20 a. m. **Robert W. Neuman**, Geoscience Museum, LSU
"The Bison: A Missing Element in the Prehistoric Southern Landscape?"

9:40 a. m. **Gene Wilhelm**, Aves-Oikos Tours, Slippery Rock, PA
"Material Folk Culture in the Blue Ridge Mountains"

10:00 a. m. Discussion

II. THE NORTH: PAST LANDSCAPES OF SETTLEMENT AND PRODUCTIO N
Chair: Robert A. Muller

10:30 a.m. **Peter O. Wacker**, Dept. of Geography, Rutgers University
"New Englanders and English Quakers in New Jersey, 1664-1822"

10:50 a. m. **Theodore W. Kury**, Dept. of Geography and Planning, SUNY-Buffalo
"The Charcoal Iron Industry in the New York Highlands Revisited"

11:10 a. m. **Samuel R. Sheldon**, Dept. of Geography, St. Bonaventure College
"Landscape Transformation in Ontario's Norfolk Sand Plain"

11:30 a.m. Discussion

III. THE CARIBBEAN: CONTEMPORARY CULTURAL LANDSCAPES
Chair: Jay D. Edwards

2:00 p.m. **José B. Seguinot**, Dept. of Geography, University of Puerto Rico
"Folk to Urban: Puerto Rico's Cultural Landscape Transformations"

2:20 p.m. **Janet H. Gritzner**, Dept. of Geography, South Dakota State University
"Caribbean Food Ways: G.I.S. in the Service of Gastrogeography"

2:40 p.m. **Carolyn V. Prorok**, Dept. of Geography, Slippery Rock State College
"Evolution of Hindu Temples and Ethnic Identity in Trinidad"

3:00 p.m. Discussion

IV. MAINLAND LATIN AMERICAN: MATERIAL CULTURE AND SETTLEMENT
Chair: William V. Davidson

3:30 p.m. **Alan K. Craig**, Dept. of Geography, Florida Atlantic University
"The Ingenious *Ingenio*: Spanish Colonial Beneficiation Watermills at Potosí, Bolivia"

3:50 p.m. **Clifton V. Dixon, Jr.**, Dept. of Geography and Planning,
Memphis State University
"Culture in Place: Southern Costa Rica's Italian Agricultural Colony"

4:10 p.m. **Martha A. Works**, Dept. of Geography, Portland State University
"Chintz, China, Chests: Trade in Spanish Colonial New Mexico"

4:30 p.m. Discussion

Sunday, February 25   Alumni Speakers   Howe-Russell Building - Room 130

V. LOUISIANA: CONTEMPORARY TOPICS
Chair: Richard H. Kesel

9:00 am. **John B. Rehder**, Dept. of Geography, University of Tennessee
"Plantations' Progress: Louisiana's Persistent Sugar Landscapes?"

9:20 a.m. **Donald W. Davis**, Earth Sciences Dept., Nicholls State
University, Thibodeaux, La.
"Living on the Edge: Louisiana's Barrier Islands"

9:40 am. **Klaus J. Meyer-Arendt**, Dept. of Geology and Geography,
Mississippi State University
"Morphological Aspects of the Cultural Historical Evolution of Gulf
Coast Resorts"

10:00 a.m. Discussion

VI. CONTEMPORARY TOPICS IN CULTURAL GEOGRAPHY
Chair: Nigel J. R. Allan

10:30 a.m. **Craig E. Colten**, Illinois State Museum, Springfield
"Material Culture and Environment Change on the Illinois River"

10:50 a.m. **Charles F. Gritzner**, Dept. of Geography, South Dakota State
University
"Form and Place in the Landscape of Country Music"

11:10 a.m. **James M. Blaut**, Dept. of Geography, University of Illinois-Chicago
"Mind and Matter in Cultural Geography"

11:30 a.m. Discussion

There were two departures from the announced program. José Seguinot was unable to attend. Malcolm Comeaux (Ph.D., LSU, '69) Department of Geography, Arizona State University, filled in with a well illustrated and received presentation on graffiti as folk art in the
southwestern U.S. Travel plan changes prevented Charles "Fritz" Gritzner from delivering
his scheduled talk.

Contributors

James M. Blaut is Professor of Geography at the University of Illinois at Chicago. He previously taught geography at Yale and Clark Universities. A student of Fred Kniffen's in the 1950s, he received his M.Sc. ('54) and his Ph.D. ('58) from Louisiana State University following field study of Chinese market gardening in Singapore. Subsequent work has taken him repeatedly to the Caribbean and Latin America, and deep into theoretical questions ranging from children's spatial perception, cultural diffusion, colonialism, and nationalism, to cultural geography's epistemology. He is the author of numerous publications, including *The National Question: Decolonising the Theory of Nationalism* (Zed Books, 1987), *The Colonizer's Model of the World: Geographical Diffusionism and Eurocentric History* (Guilford Press, 1993), co-author of *Aspectos de la Cuestion Nacional en Puerto Rico* (Editorial Claridad, 1988), and editor of *1492: The Debate on Colonialism, Eurocentrism, and History* (Africa World Press, 1992).

Elisabeth K. Butzer is Research Associate with the Texas Archaeological Research Laboratories. She holds a B.Ed. from Bonn ('57), a B.A. in anthropology from the University of Illinois ('74) and the M.A. in geography from the University of Chicago ('77). Her research included archival documentation and demography of medieval and Christian communities in eastern Spain. Her current research is centered on Spanish settlement in Colonial Mexico. She has co-authored a monograph and several articles, and is currently completing a book documenting the human ecology of a Tlaxcalan frontier community in Northern Mexico from the 1680s to the 1820s.

Karl W. Butzer is Dickson Centennial Professor of Liberal Arts in the Departments of Geography and Anthropology at the University of Texas at Austin. He holds a M.S. ('55) from McGill and the D.Sc. ('57) from the University of Bonn where he studied with Carl Troll. He previously taught at the University of Wisconsin, the University of Chicago, and the Federal Institute of Technology in Zurich. He has conducted and directed research in a number of countries, including Egypt, Ethiopia, South Africa, Spain, and (currently) Mexico. He is the author of many articles and books in the fields of cultural ecology, geoarchaeology, and geomorphology including *Environment and Archaeology* (Aldine Press, 1964), *Early Hydraulic Civilization in Egypt* (University of Chicago Press, 1976), and *Archaeology as Human Ecology* (Cambridge University Press, 1982).

Craig E. Colten, until recently a senior research associate with the Illinois State Museum, is now affiliated with PHR environmental Consultants in Washington, D.C. He received his B.A. ('74) and M.A. ('78) in geography from Louisiana State University. His thesis, "Historical Geography of Seasonal Settlement in Henderson County, North Carolina," was directed by S. B. Hilliard. His Ph.D. ('84) in geography is from Syracuse University where he worked with D. W. Meinig. His research over the past decade has focused on human environments of the Midwest and has appeared in the *Geographical Review, Professional Geographer,* and *Environmental History Review.* He is co-editor with Lary M. Dilsaver (L.S.U. geography Ph.D. '82) of *The American Environment: Historical Geographic Interpretations of Impact and Policy.* (Rowman and Littlefield, 1992).

Alan K. Craig is Professor of Geography at Florida Atlantic University. He is a graduate of Louisiana State University in geology (B.S. '58) and in geography (Ph.D. '66). Robert C. West directed his dissertation, "The Geography of Fishing in British Honduras and Adjacent Coastal Areas." He has done field work in archaeology, geology, biogeography, and cultural and historical geography in many parts of Latin America and the Caribbean. He is also an authority on pre-Hispanic metallurgy and colonial numismatics. His work has appeared in many journals including *America Indigena, Annals of the Association of American Geographers, Caribbean Studies, Geoarchaeology, Geographical Review, The Numismatist,* and *Science.*

Clifton V. Dixon, Jr. is Associate Professor of Geography at Memphis State University. He is a Louisiana State University graduate (B.A. in zoology '76, M.A. in geography '81). His thesis, "Coconuts and Man on the North Coast of Honduras: An Historical Geographic Perspective," was directed by William Davidson. For his geography Ph.D. ('88) he studied traditional apiculture in southern Mexico under the direction of C. T. Kimber, C. Pennington and G. F. Carter at Texas A & M. His research has frequently taken him to Mexico and Central America. He is the author of articles in *Geojournal, CLAG Yearbook,* and *Journal of Developing Areas,* and book chapters on Middle American topics in cultural and historical geography.

Dennis C. Jones is Research Associate with the Center for Coastal Environmental and Energy Resources at Louisiana State University. He received his B.A. ('70) in urban studies from Washington University in St. Louis. He is a graduate of Louisiana State University (M.A. '85) in geography. His thesis, "The Crossroads Area of El Mirador: Causeways and Cityscape of a Maya Site in Guatemala," was derived from two field seasons in Guatemala's Peten region. His current research is focused on Louisiana. He is the coauthor of a number of reports on the archaeology of sites around the state.

Terry G. Jordan, Professor of Geography, holds the Walter Prescott Webb Chair in History and Ideas at the University of Texas at Austin. His

M.A. ('61) is from the University of Texas at Austin, and his Ph.D. ('65) in geography from the University of Wisconsin-Madison where he studied with A. H. Clark. Jordan has divided his extensive research on cultural-historical problems and topics between his native Texas and much of the rest of North America and Europe. He is the author of numerous books and articles. His books include *German Seed in Texas Soil* (University of Texas Press, 1966), *Texas Log Buildings* (University of Texas Press, 1978), *Texas Graveyards* (University of Texas Press, 1982), *American Log Buildings* (University of North Carolina Press, 1985), *The American Backwoods Frontier* (The Johns Hopkins University Press, 1989), *North American Cattle Ranching Frontiers* (University of New Mexico Press, 1993).

Klaus J. Meyer-Arendt is Associate Professor of Geography at Mississippi State University. Both his master's degree (M.A. '79) and doctorate (Ph.D. '87) are in geography from Louisiana State University. His thesis on "The Guava in the Upper Suárez Basin of Southern Santander and Adjacent Bocayá, Colombia: A Geographical Perspective" was chaired by William Davidson. H. Jesse Walker directed his doctoral study on "Resort Evolution Along the Gulf of Mexico Littoral: Historical, Morphological, and Environmental Aspects." His subsequent research reflects a synthesis of two L.S.U. specialties — cultural historical geography and coastal studies. His current research includes study of human adjustments to the Yucatán's storm-prone north coast. His publications have appeared in *Geojournal, Journal of Geography, Journal of Cultural Geography, and Annals of Tourism Research* among others.

James J. Parsons is Professor Emeritus of Geography at the University of California-Berkeley. A three-degree graduate of Berkeley (M.A. '38 and Ph.D. '48 in geography under Carl O. Sauer), James Parsons' wide ranging interests and research record cover much of the terrain associated with Berkeley school geography. California, Mexico, Central America, the western Caribbean, northern South America, the Iberian peninsula and associated islands have been the principle sites of his field work. He is the author of numerous publications. His books and monographs include *Antiqueño Colonization in Western Colombia* (University of California Press, 1949), *The Green Turtle and Man* (University of Florida Press, 1962), and *Antioquia's Corridor to the Sea: An Historical Geography of the Settlement of Urabá* (University of California Press, 1967).

Samuel R. Sheldon is Professor of Geography at St. Bonaventure University, St. Bonaventure, NY. He received his M.A. ('68) in geography from Eastern Michigan University and his Ph.D. ('78) from Louisiana State University in geography. His dissertation on "Ixtleros of North-Central Mexico: A Geographical Study of Man-Plant Relationships" was directed by Robert C. West. He has taught geography at a number of universities including Arkansas-Pine Bluff, Salem State, and South Carolina. He has conducted geographic research in a number of locales including Guatemala, Honduras, Mexico, and the U.S. Canadian border regions. He has published articles in journals including *Economic Botany, The Journal of Developing Areas, The Florida Geographer*, and *The American Review of Canadian Studies*.

Malcolm K. Shuman is Research Associate with the Center for Coastal Environmental and Energy Resources at Louisiana State University. He received his B.A. ('62) from Louisiana State University, his M.A. ('69) from the University of New Mexico, and his Ph.D. ('74) in anthropology from Tulane University. He has carried out archaeological work in the Gulf South region, New Mexico, Mexico, and France. His current research is centered on inventory and excavation of Louisiana's remaining Indian mounds. He is also the author of nine mystery novels, the latest of which, *The Last Man to Die*, was published by St. Martin's Press in 1992.

B. L. Turner II is Professor of Geography and Director, George Perkins Marsh Institute at Clark University. Turner's initial study of geography was at the University of Texas at Austin (BA '68, MA '69). His Ph.D. ('74) is from the University of Wisconsin-Madison where he studied with William Denevan. His research has taken him to Africa and Asia as well as Mexico and Central America. He has authored numerous articles and book chapters on Maya subsistence and cultural ecological topics in general. His books and co-edited volumes include *Pre-Hispanic Maya Agriculture* (University of New Mexico Press, 1978), *Once Beneath the Forest* (Westview Press, 1983), *Pulltrouser Swamp* (University of Texas Press, 1983), *The Earth as Transformed by Human Action* (Cambridge University Press, 1990), and *Population Growth and Agricultural Change in Africa* (University of Florida Press, 1993).

Malcolm C. Webb is Professor of Anthropology at the University of New Orleans. His graduate degrees (M.A. '58, Ph.D. '64) in archaeological anthropology are from the University of Michigan. He has taught anthropology at Louisiana State University, the University of Southwestern Louisiana, and the University of New Orleans. He has wide field experience in archaeology in the southeastern and midwestern U.S. and in Mesoamerica. His research has been focused on issues such as the origins of chiefdoms and state societies, collapse of Maya civilization and pre-Hispanic trade in the southeastern U.S. and Mesoamerica. He has published in journals such as *The American Behavioral Scientist, Journal of the Polynesian Society, American Anthropologist*, and *Current Anthropology*. He is co-editor with Miles Richardson of *The Burden of Being Civilized* (University of Georgia Press, 1986).

Gene Wilhelm is former Professor of Geography and Environmental Studies at Slippery Rock University. He received the M.A. ('61) in geography from Louisiana State University and the Ph.D. ('71) in geography from Texas A & M University. He has taught geography and environmental studies at a number of universities including DePaul, McGill, Saint Louis, and Virginia. He has been a consultant and held posts with various conservation organizations. He currently owns and operates Aves-Oikos, an eco-tourist business. He has conducted extensive research in wildlife conservation and cultural resource management and preservation in the U.S. and in South America, Central America, Africa, and Australia. His publications have appeared in many journals, including Canadian Geographer, Geographical Review, Journal of Geography, Pioneer America, and Professional Geographer. He is author of several books including The Blue Ridge: Man and Nature in Shenandoah Natural Park and Blue Ridge Parkway (University of Virginia, 1968).

Martha A. Works is Associate Professor of Geography at Portland State University. Her graduate degrees in geography are from Arizona State University (M.A. '80) and Louisiana State University (Ph.D. '84). Her dissertation, directed by Donald Vermeer, involved study of "Agricultural Change Among the Alto Mayo Aguaruna, Eastern Peru: The Effects on Culture and Environment." Her earlier research was focused on agricultural settlement and cultural change in the Andean Oriente regions of Bolivia and Peru. More recently her research and publications have centered on the colonial historical geography of New Mexico. Her publications include articles in *Geographical Review*, *Focus*, *Journal of Geography*, *Journal of Cultural Geography*, and *Amazonia Peruana*.

Prehistoric Settlement, Subsistence and Social Formation in the Lower Mississippi Valley

Malcolm C. Webb

Abstract

The aboriginal culture sequence in the Lower Mississippi Valley displays two cultural peaks: Middle Woodland or Burial Mound, and Mississippian or Temple Mound. The economic bases of these systems are examined with particular attention to reconstruction by ethnographic analogy of the possible social integrative role of the burial mound cult. An analysis of its organizational weaknesses points to its replacement by the more advanced Temple Mound system of the early second millennium A.D. It is suggested that the apparently sudden shift from one system to the other, in fact reflects a steady and protracted subsistence and prestige economics.

Key Words: Lower Mississippi Valley, mound builders, prestige economics, settlement systems

Despite its somewhat grandiose title, this paper is simply an attempt to offer comments upon the emergence of two of the generally recognized peaks of aboriginal development in the eastern United States, namely the Middle Woodland and the Mississippian horizons, as seen from the Lower Mississippi Valley and the Gulf Coast. While these may be considered ruminations or speculations, I offer them as informed and reasonable speculations. Given the space allowed, I will attempt to anchor my free balloons of theory to the local scene and the dark organic earth of archaeology. I will present various data from recent work done by the University of New Orleans Department of Anthropology and its research arm, the Archaeological and Cultural Research Program, in the Louisiana Florida Parishes, north of Lake Pontchartrain. The area, though perhaps a backwater in aboriginal times, was centrally located. As such, it reflects key developments

Culture, Form, and Place: Essays in Cultural and Historical Geography, edited by Kent Mathewson, 1993. Geoscience and Man, vol. 32, pp. 1-32. Department of Geography and Anthropology, Louisiana State University, Baton Rouge, LA 70893-6010.

1

in surrounding regions and at one critical point seems to have played a role in far-reaching social evolutionary trends.

Having alluded to social evolution, I should add that my approach here is broadly cultural ecological. That is, I see cultural systems as generally adaptive mechanisms by which human societies survive and potentially flourish in their particular circumstances. For the aboriginal peoples of the Americas, including those in Louisiana, this implies that the critical issue was largely one of adaptation to local and specific physical environments.

In light of the theme of this volume, and its tribute to Professors Fred B. Kniffen and Robert C. West, it is a pleasure to point out that they helped pioneer the cultural ecological approach, building on the rich Berkeley tradition of interaction between anthropologists and geographers. Professor Kniffen in particular, played a key role in studying the local setting. His examinations of the relationships between aboriginal sites and evolving landforms in the lower delta (Kniffen 1936) and in Iberville Parish (Kniffen 1938) were critical initial steps in the resolution of regional chronology and subsistence patterns fifty years ago. Moreover, he maintained a scholarly and humane interest in the more recent Indian population of this state throughout his life (Kniffen, Gregory and Stokes 1987).

I recall Professor Kniffen some thirty years ago, cautioning a very green, devoutly neoevolutionist instructor against reliance upon simplistic geographical explanations. Therefore, I should hasten to add that different cultures, experiencing discrete society-environment encounters, may not deal with the same environment in identical ways. Neighboring societies, however, can be expected to share much of their way of life. Useful techniques and organizational mechanisms often diffuse to the limits of their utility. Or, in the terms of our old but neglected friend: the culture area concept (elaborated perhaps most fully by Kniffen's "other" mentor, Alfred Kroeber). For everyday tasks, simple technology wielded by small-scale and organizationally non-complex kin groups would no doubt be the prime adaptive mechanism. This does not preclude the second and third levels of Leslie White's three-layered cake (social structure and ideology) from assuming primary adaptive functions from time to time. Organizational and motivational mechanisms can accomplish certain tasks, such as moving earth, as well as advanced technology. It was precisely by bringing together large groups of people and inspiring them to do the job that many ancient societies, not least the Indians of the eastern United States, carried out those monumental works which still impress and puzzle us. Finally, such monuments are expressions of considerable symbolic capital. Once constructed, they were not just the inert results of past activity but the active organizers of additional social forces. Ethnographic analogy suggests that the beholders of such works recognized those in charge as persons of power, able to bestow material and emotional benefits on those they chose.

The True Source of Iconic and Ritual Elaboration in Eastern North America

It will be evident from the above that I feel that the economics of burial mounds and mortuary enclosures, of temple mounds and of monumental ceremonial architecture in general, may be fruitfully examined not only in terms of cost, or what they imply about what the groups who constructed them could afford, but also as active mechanisms for the creation of wealth. They offer a "fossilized indicator" of ritual mechanisms for the mobilization, concentration and deployment of group resources which would otherwise remain diffuse (or even unproduced), and of the social networks along which these resources moved. If this view is correct, the roles (or presumed roles) of burial and temple mounds should provide a useful key for understanding the Hopewellian-Mississippian evolutionary succession in North America. What follows is an exploration of the outstanding material expressions of two famous ritual systems sequent in time in the same general region, not only as symbols, but as actual mechanisms of social survival. In "etic" or cultural materialist terms, mortuary ceremonialism serves the living, not the dead. Temples reflect the powers of society and its leaders which do exist, rather than of the gods who only may exist. Therefore, such an exploration should help to clarify why one social system ultimately failed (albeit after a very good run for its coppers) while the other lasted until the European conquest terminated the entire aboriginal culture sequence.

My discussion here focuses primarily on ethnographic analogy and its application to the archaeological sequence, rather than a revision of that sequence. I accept as a given the standard general syntheses worked out by Griffin (1964; 1967; 1983), Sears (1964), Willey (1966), Snow (1976), Muller (1983) and Jennings (1989). Similarly, except where noted, the standard culture sequence for the regions in question — the Lower Mississippi Valley and the eastern Gulf Coast — as elaborated by Phillips (1970), Haag (1971), Brain (1971), Walthall (1980), Milanich and Fairbanks (1980) and Neuman (1984) is accepted. The main objective of this paper will be to develop a schema of the political economy of the developed Hopewellian or Middle Woodland cult system and the reasons for its replacement by later social forms. This focus has been influenced by the wealth of material that exists on the comparative historical and ethnographic nature of chiefdoms in many parts of the world, including contact period accounts of Indians in the southeastern U.S.

Before turning to this task, it will be necessary to counter the diffusionist "explanation" of cultural development in the eastern United States that assumes contacts with or intrusions from the more advanced cultures of Mesoamerica. Since at least the early nineteenth century (Silverberg 1974; Willey and Sabloff 1974), this argument has been used to explain the origins of the Poverty Point, Hopewell/Marksville and Mississippian cultures, persisting longest for the latter. At first glance, and considered in the perspective of world culture history, the culture of the Mississippian peoples does rather resemble an incipient rural or countrified version of Mesoamerica. But it notably lacks the attributes of civilization such as writing, calendrics, Great Art styles, metallurgy, stone architecture, urbanism, and imperial expansion. It has long been recognized that Mesoamerica and the southeast U.S. share traits such as the pyramid temple complex and aspects of religious symbolism. Given the relative geographic proximity between the two regions, it is understandable that diffusion and even migration have remained popular models (Silverberg 1974; Willey and Sabloff 1974; Smith 1984). In this regard, it should be noted that the current edition of Jennings' popular text, *Prehistory of North America*, carefully leaves the question open (Jennings 1989, 254).

I have previously examined aspects of the diffusion/migration question as part of a study of Mesoamerican-Mississippian iconographic parallels (Webb 1989). Sites offered as evidence of Mesoamerican diffusion lack resemblances specific enough to demonstrate direct contact or else are so recent that the supposed southern traits are more likely to represent eastern U.S. items spreading out to the periphery. The current consensus suggests that transitional stages between Middle Woodland and Late Woodland, and emergent Mississippian are evident in key areas of the central Mississippi Valley (Morse and Morse 1983; Kelly et al. 1984a; 1984b; Griffin 1983; 1984) as well as southern Alabama (Mistovich 1988) and central Georgia (Anderson, Hally and Randolph 1986). They yield no traces of a Mesoamerican-related site-unit intrusion.

It therefore came as no great surprise to discover that the conceptual and iconographic resemblances to Mesoamerica were in fact old ideological clusters widespread throughout North America, and down into Andean South America and perhaps beyond. These appear to be of great antiquity and, in some cases, may have even entered the New World at the end of the Paleolithic, as Covarrubias (1954, 28-72) and, more recently, Davies (1979, 252-260) have suggested. These symbolic clusters — somewhat analogous to the "sacra" which Knight (1986) sees as operating in the institutional framework of Mississippian religion — will be familiar to most readers: such things as raptorial birds, felines, ophidian creatures, the solar disk and cardinal points, human skeletal fragments, and so forth.

The clear implication is that these long-standing ideological and iconic metaphors, basic to definitions of Middle Woodland/Burial Mound and Mississippian/Temple Mound, were widely dispersed by gradual and piecemeal diffusion. Some possibly did come indirectly from Mesoamerica from time to time. No doubt they combined and recombined into broadly similar conceptual clusters. They probably were dispersed in the manner of pottery decoration or tool manufacture techniques, items spread widely by down-the-line, trickle trade, and other forms of indirect and intermittent contact (Webb 1989). Since many of the supposed Mesoamerican symbols were already present in our region in Hopewellian and Poverty Point times and perhaps even before (Ford 1969; Ford and Webb 1956; C. Webb 1968; 1982; Hyde 1962, 40-50; Prufer 1964), the critical question becomes: Why did they crystallize, first, as the Middle Woodland system, shortly before the time of Christ, and later as the Mississippian, at the end of the first millennium A.D.? The answer is surely to be found in local cultural evolution rather than in changing external contacts. In other words, the symbolic vocabulary is a kind of "steady-state" background. At most it changed slowly through time in a somewhat ad hoc fashion. The origin of specific integrated ideological systems, in contrast, is to be sought in the changing political economy of the southeastern United States. What, then, were the relevant cultural ecological processes, the subsistence techniques and organizational requirements, which in turn gave rise to the Burial Mound and the Temple Mound traditions?

Subsistence and Social Development in the Mississippi Drainage 2000 B.C. - A.D. 500

It is generally agreed that the Mississippian peoples were organized in chiefdoms. Most practiced maize agriculture. For some cases, however, such as the Calusa (Goggin and Sturtevant 1964; Widmer 1988) or the Plaquemine peoples of the Louisiana gulf coast and nearby areas (Beck 1981; M. Webb 1982; Bitgood 1989, 142-145; cf. Hall 1980, 414, 430-432), little or no evidence of agriculture has been found. This suggests that groups inhabiting resource-rich environments relied largely on hunting and gathering for subsistence. In contrast, recent work portrays the Hopewellian societies as equalitarian, segmentary tribes. They were led by "big men" supported by kin followings attracted by records of success, who competed with each other for rank and power (Brose and Greber 1979; Greber 1983; Vehik 1983; Jeter 1984; Mainfort 1989). That their cultural accomplishments exceeded those typical of hunters and gatherers may be explained by highly effective wild food procurement techniques, namely Caldwell's (1958) primary forest efficiency. These techniques may have been supplemented by a well-developed horticulture (Morse and Morse

1983, 143-144; Fortier, Emerson and Finney 1984). Recent C_{14} dating of maize kernels and plant fragments from the Icehouse Bottom site in Tennessee, place them in the context of Middle Woodland (Chapman and Crites 1987), and supports Hall's (1980) suggestion that maize played a role in Middle Woodland subsistence. Nevertheless, the weight of the isotopic analysis of human skeletal populations indicates that maize was of little dietary consequence in eastern North America prior to the end of the first millennium A.D. (Lynott et al. 1986; Bender, Baerreis and Steventon 1981).

In a recent summary of the Archaic background of the Middle Woodland, Krause (1989) reminds us that for the last few millennia B.C., hunting and gathering techniques had steadily improved throughout the southeastern United States. Refinements of the procurement pattern through carefully scheduled shellfish collecting, fishing, and fowling allowed population growth, more elaborate burial ceremonialism, greater long-distance trade in exotics and ritual goods, and increased evidence of intergroup conflict. Admittedly, Poverty Point appears to present an anomaly: large and elaborate earthworks, but no agricultural evidence. The site is located at the intersection of a number of major river systems, with abundant resources for hunting, fishing, and gathering (Gibson 1974; 1980; C. Webb 1968; 1982). As Gibson (1987) has recently noted, the labor demands of the Poverty Point earthworks, while large, would not have been beyond the capacity of a hunter-gatherer population in a favorable setting, assuming sufficient time spans. Motivation, of course, is another matter.

By Woodland times, subsistence seems to have been based on the highest degree of primary forest efficiency, with nut-bearing trees being a particularly important and critical resource (Johnson 1976; 1979; Asch, Farnsworth and Asch 1979; Ford 1979). Other candidates include various techniques of resource improvement and maintenance such as controlled burning of collecting and hunting grounds, and incipient small-scale gardening involving local and tropical cultigens (Struever 1962; Yarnell 1965; 1976; Watson and Yarnell 1966; Fowler 1971; Brain 1976; Chapman and Shea 1977; Byrd 1976; Byrd and Neuman 1978; Griffin 1979). Hall (1980) notes that in central Illinois the prime locations for Hopewell settlement appear to have been the biotically rich margins of rivers and lakes, especially the points at which tributaries entered the main streams. Such zones were often subject to a kind of "soft" circumscription between less productive areas of prairie and climax forest. At the other end of the Mississippi, Gagliano (1984) and others (Weinstein and Gagliano 1985; Shenkel 1984) have long maintained that, in similar fashion, Late Archaic and Woodland populations tended to cluster along the distributary streams of deteriorating (and therefore maximally productive) delta lobes and sublobes. The midwestern workers estimate that such a base could have supported a population density of roughly 40 persons per 100 km^2 and stable long-term villages of about 50-100 (Asch, Farnsworth and Asch 1979; Buikstra 1979; Johnson 1979; Bell 1976; Robinson 1976; cf. McGregor 1952; 1958; Fowler 1952; Jefferies 1976; Milanich and Fairbanks 1980, 96-110, 131-143). Thus, populations of 1,000-2,000 could have been supported within a radius of 50-70 km.

This is an appropriate range for an equalitarian tribal society. Fried (1967, 164-174), moreover, points out that such societies are largely held together by the need of self-defense. An example that immediately comes to mind is that of the Dani of West Irian (Heider 1970; 1979). In this connection, the Hopewellian atlatl and dart may lie at the root of the historic calumet ceremonies (Hall 1977) and Hopewell trophy skulls are generally those of young adults, most commonly males (Seeman 1988). This strongly suggests that intergroup conflict was a regular and long-term, if not overwhelming, aspect of Middle Woodland culture. It might well reflect the above-mentioned circumscription. In using the term "circumscription," however, I do not wish to imply an overpopulated environment and consequent fighting for resources. Quite simply, conditions of environment and technology would fix moderately large populations so firmly in place that conflicts arising for any number of reasons could not be easily avoided. I take this to be the essential logic of the circumscription hypothesis (Carneiro 1961; 1970; Webb 1987; 1988).

The Dani conduct their everyday lives through small village life and unilineal extended kin groups. For major economic, political, ritual, and military activities they are led by competitive "big men." In this sense, they may offer a good model for Middle Woodland society. According to Swanson (1968, 100-108) there is a strong positive correlation between ancestor worship and sovereign kin groups. Those conquest period tribes most likely to represent the least modified of the northern Hopewellian peoples — the Central Algonkians such as the Shawnee, Miami, Fox, Potawatomi and Menominee (Griffin 1943, 309; Prufer 1964; Callender 1979; Hall 1979) — are characterized by a strong development of patrilineal clans (Murdock 1967, 102-103, 114-115). The ethnographic record of these kinds of societies suggests that the political system is based on a kind of *cargo* system in which the rising big men, supported by their following, seek to assume the direction of key religious activity, often through the deployment of ritual artifacts (Sahlins 1963; 1968; 1972, 221-222; Rappaport 1968, 105-109). In such circumstances, a rich elaboration of craft and exotic trade goods serves to create repositories of accumulated prestige and to facilitate exchange when the need for more mundane products is satiated. The demand for copper ear spools, Marksville incised ceramics, galena, or mica cut-outs was presumably as limitless as our desire for money.

The chief function served by these ceremonies at the community level (both inter and intra) was the ritualized distribution of goods. For distribution between communities, the best example comes from the Northwest Coast, with its famous potlatch system. Among these tribes, the Nootka may offer the closest fit. The Nootka potlatch assumed a less competitive and destructive form (Drucker 1939; 1951; 1955; Piddock 1965; Service 1978, 228-233). Distribution within the community, is well illustrated by the Plains Indians. There, leadership functioned in the context of ceremonial feasts and prestations not that different from a Melanesian big man system (Webb and Thomson 1977). In addition to the Dani, Northwest Coast and Plains Indians, such equalitarian Melanesian groups as the Siane (Salisbury 1962) and the Siuai (Oliver 1967) also serve as ethnographic analogies.

Seeman (1979) has suggested that ritual feasting was an economically significant aspect of Ohio Hopewell mortuary ceremonialism. Griffin (1979), however, questions the overall contribution of this practice to Hopewell subsistence, a point well taken. Nevertheless, Peebles and Kus (1977) argue that, even though the actual subsistence needs met by the goods typically involved in redistributive ceremonies tend to be meager, ritual exchange gatherings sponsored by prominent men do meet important survival needs. They create spatial and temporal zones of peace where craft goods and other resources can move through reciprocity and more formal barter, and occasions when manpower for self-defence can be recruited. As mentioned, the Hopewellian groups probably had to cope with hostile neighbors. Given their dependence upon nuts and other forest products, resources over which they had little or no direct control, activities that insured resource sharing must have been especially important (Brose 1979a; Ford 1979).

To be adaptive, these trade networks have to expand on their margins while previously peripheral groups reach outward to secure new kinds of goods for which already established trading partners are not yet glutted (Sahlins 1972, 285-295). They also must operate on the principle that prestige competition is necessarily a relative thing — a struggle to secure significantly more of whatever amounts (much or little) of whatever kinds of valued items (exotic or local) are available. The general tendency of such inter/intratribal exchange networks helps explain two seemingly contradictory aspects of the Middle Woodland period. They are: first, the rapid and extensive spread of the Hopewellian horizon in the broad sense — the Hopewellian ideal, so to speak; second, its subsequent maintenance in many areas in which old local traditions continued, cult practices themselves were divergent, and truly exotic goods were quite rare (Brose 1979b; Toth 1979; Goad 1979; Walthall 1979; Griffin 1979; Johnson 1979; Reid 1976; Gibson and Shenkel 1988; Brose 1988).

Burial Mounds as Memorials, Markers and Monuments

What, specifically, was the role of burial mounds and their varying associated features in all of this? As Krause (1989) points out, fairly elaborate mortuary programs as well as mound building were present by the Late Archaic. Indeed, as Gibson and Shenkel (1988) have demonstrated, mounds, at least one of which (Monte Sano) may have been involved in cremation ceremonies, were being constructed in Louisiana and Mississippi at this time, and possibly about as early as anywhere in the New World. What was needed was something to link the two activities together. Renfrew (1984, 175-188, 194-197) has recently suggested that the emergence of the megalithic tradition along the Atlantic coast of Europe was in large part due to the need to mark territorial claims through time, consequent to the initial settling in of early agricultural peoples in that environmentally rich and diverse region. Bender (1985) in similar fashion, has related emerging mortuary ceremonialism in North America at the end of the Archaic to social elaborations associated with subsistence intensification.

A mortuary cult is especially functional in a big man system, with its wheeling and dealing in ritual/exotic materials. Interring valuable ritual objects would insure continued competition by withdrawing the prestige tokens from circulation on a regular basis, thus maintaining their unique worth. Even granting regional variation in ceremonial detail (Brose 1988), the burials and associated mound construction must have functioned rather like the erection of a men's clubhouse in Melanesia or of a totem pole on the Northwest coast. They allowed leaders (especially emerging leaders) of prominent local groups to demonstrate their ability to carry out the group's social functions and the leader's claims to lead these activities (Nash 1966, 42-57). Burial mounds are particularly useful in this kind of competition. They are a localized and highly visible indication of accumulated group wealth, power, and leadership success over time.

The process has in fact been observed. Bloch (1971) has provided an ethnographic account of a contemporary equalitarian farming society, the Merina of central Madagascar. They use semi-subterranean collective tombs. The practice unites scattered communities, enables individuals and bilaterally related families to establish ties to larger and more prosperous mortuary groups, and promotes funerary patronage by men of wealth as a route to community leadership. The costs are impressive. For example, construction of a tomb costs 70 times the price of an average house or of a typical bride wealth (three times the cost of the mansions of the local elite). The periodic ceremonies of corpse cleansing and reburial (the *famadihana*) cost 20 to 50 times the price of a house, and even average funerals can cost up to six times house prices. The role of the ritual system both in the mobilization of wealth and as a leveling mechanism is clearly evident. Here is an example where an ancestral megalithic cult is the central mechanism of local social organization and control.

From the Merina and other ethnographic examples, it would appear that neither mound building nor mound burials require a long-term power hierarchy or any marked rank differences of a permanently hereditary kind. Shryock (1987) has suggested from mortuary data that the Adena might have been "simple chiefdoms" (but see Mainfort 1989). Brown (1981) and Brose (1979a), however, found no evidence of hereditary chiefly ranking in their Middle Woodland cases, a view supported by Mainfort's (1988) and Brose's (1988) recent interpretations of the situation at Pinson Mounds. Braun (1979), on the basis of a statistical reanalysis of mound materials from Illinois, argues that the well-known differentials in wealth and centrality of placement found for all ages and both sexes in Hopewell burials (e.g., Greber 1979) are as readily explained as a reflection of kin ties to men of achievement as of hereditary ranking.

Data from southern mounds or mound groups such as Crooks, Helena Crossing, Tunacunnhee and McQuorquodale tentatively support these conclusions (Ford and Willey 1940; Ford 1963; Jefferies 1976; 1979; Wimberly and Tourtelot 1941; Griffin 1979). Finally, Brose (1988) reporting on earthwork size and elaboration, and Brown (1981) on the conspicuousness and (apparent) richness of interments within these, have both pointed out that what we have tended to regard as evidence of differential societal commitment to the dead and, so, of rank differences among the dead, may often reflect nothing more than the degree of completion of the mortuary program or of relative duration of use of a mound locus.

In this context, the impressive centers such as Marksville (Toth 1974), Troyville (Walker 1936), Pinson (Mainfort 1988), and perhaps even the great Ohio sites may reflect the effect of scaling in locations where favorable circumstances permitted the long-continued operation of the system in one place. Much of the elaboration at these latter sites seems to have taken place in the middle and later Hopewell phases — perhaps A.D. 200-400 (Prufer 1964; Brown 1979; Vickery 1979; Baby and Langlois 1979; Greber 1979; Mainfort 1988; Brose 1988). The situation may resemble the manner in which the Trobriand Island chiefdoms arose within an area more generally characterized by equalitarian tribes through the simple intensification of activities (Malinowski 1922; Uberoi 1962; Belshaw 1965, 12-20). In other words, although the great size of the Ohio earthworks in particular and the richness of their associated offerings (e.g., Morehead 1922; Willoughby 1922; Greber 1979; Greber and Ruhl 1989), along with the elaboration of the contemporary ritual constructions (Baby and Langlois 1979; Brown 1979), indicate operation at the extreme upper range of the system, they are nonetheless the peaks of a basically simple and widespread pattern. Walthall (1979) has calculated the numbers required to construct centers of varying sizes and concluded that in no cases would extraordinary populations be necessary, and Greber (1979), working from reconstructed death rates, has reached similar results for the size of the community which probably maintained a typical Ohio mound.

These levels of activity seem well within the capabilities of such environmentally favored and technologically effective groups as the Plains or Northwest Coast tribes. The obvious difference is that mound building gives more permanent and, above all, cumulative results than do a Sun Dance or Potlatch (Vickery 1979; Brown 1979; Griffin 1979). One reason for the long duration of the midwestern sites, might be found in the advantages of their central location. Ohio was well situated to control or at least heavily tap into the flow of both copper and galena, two very highly valued items, for much of the east (Goad 1979; Walthall, Stow and Karson 1979; Griffin 1979). As noted, another possibility would simply be their notably rich environment, especially as the relative permanence of landform both permitted a continuous concentration of activity in any one place and also insured the survival of constructions until recent times, a situation not so prevalent in that other especially rich environment, the evolving, shifting Mississippi delta.

Macroview to Microview: The Florida Parishes of Louisiana

This is perhaps the point at which to shift from broad cultural evolutionary reconstruction to an account of our own recent departmental work of survey and small-scale excavation in the Florida Parishes, anything but environmentally rich, but an area which provides us with a few insights concerning the evolving aboriginal life ways of the delta and possibly even points further afield. The Florida Parishes lie north of the Lake Pontchartrain basin and the active delta of the Mississippi River and are bounded to the west by that river, while to the north and east lies the state of Mississippi. The region consists of rather unproductive pine-covered hills formed on the Pleistocene prairie terrace cut by a number of rivers which flow south to enter the interconnected system of (west to east) Lakes Maurepas, Pontchartrain and Borgne. More significant rivers include the Amite and Tickfaw, which flow into Lake Maurepas, the Tangipahoa and Tchefuncte, which enter Lake Pontchartrain, and, largest of all, the Pearl River system, which includes tributaries such as the Bogue Chitto, and enters Lake Borgne to form the eastern border of the region.

Interest in the region evolved, so to speak. In the late sixties and early seventies small groups from the University of New Orleans' Anthropology Department excavated at 16ST6, variously called "Indian Village," "Indian Camp" and "Indian Village Lodge." It is a small semicircular shell and earth midden just west of the West Pearl, on the first terrace north of the river's mouth. Interest increased when it was realized that the site was probably occupied as early as terminal Marksville-Early Troyville (ca. AD 350-500). The uppermost layer of earth midden had apparently been modified to form an ad hoc clay-capped mound on which several burials, unaccompanied by grave goods, had been placed (good Troyville traits). Some of the decorated sherds, although on local pastes, were characterized by motifs of surface decoration essentially identical to early Weeden Island materials (Webb 1984). In light of the possible role of a Weeden Island-Mississippi Valley connection in developments at the end of Middle Woodland times (Jennings 1952; Ford 1952; Brose 1979b), the Archaeological and Cultural Research Program took advantage of the first opportunity to explore the areas to the north and west. In 1984 and 1985, the Director of ACRP, Richard Beavers, and his associates, Teresia Lamb and John Greene, conducted site surveys along the West Pearl River, the Bogue Chitto, and the Tangipahoa from Amite to the Mississippi state line (Beavers et al. 1984; 1985a; 1985b). Most recently, the research program surveyed the area of Bayous Bonfouca and Liberty along the northeast shore of Lake Pontchartrain (Beavers, Lamb and Greene 1988). I did the laboratory analysis of the aboriginal materials from the Pearl, Bogue Chitto and Tangipahoa surveys.

Except for one badly disrupted site on the lower West Pearl, no other Troyville occupations were found in the survey. Chronology was hard to control due to the paucity of decorated sherds — indeed, of any ceramics — and the fact that lithics were for the most part those irritatingly long-lived point types such as Gary, Kent, Ellis, Yarbrough, and Williams which continue from Late Archaic into Woodland times. Three Plainview points were the earliest materials found. There were also a small number of Poverty Point period types. These tended to be atypical and poorly made, as with the lithics in general, possibly reflective of a rather unpromising source material consisting of small river cobbles. After a sparse beginning at the end of the Middle Archaic, occupation seems to have been concentrated toward the end of the Late Archaic. It tailed off (without any indication of significant participation in Poverty Point interactions) to almost nothing in Early Woodland or Tchefuncte times. In the later Marksville period, some minor reoccupation occurred along the lower Bogue Chitto and the lower West Pearl.

At the eastern end of the survey area, sites were found at the confluence of streams. The general impression is of small hunting and collecting stations, with the most notable exception being a 20 km. stretch running south along the Bogue Chitto from just north of Franklinton. Here a series of at least 13 sites with apparently complete artifact inventories and heavy concentrations of lithic debris, interspersed with a number of smaller lithic reduction stations, most located on the low but fairly sharp bluffs which line the southwestern side of the river, suggest a series of base camps. Of course it is unlikely that many were occupied simultaneously. Very minor amounts of ceramics indicate that this probably slowly-accumulating concentration lasted into the Early Woodland, while two Plainview points suggest a relatively early occupation as well.

Reasons for this long-standing attractiveness are, however, less obvious. Evidently elevation was not a factor since large sites are on both the bluff edges and the valley bottom. Perhaps the bluff edge overlooking the river and a series of moderate-sized streams which enter the river from the east at this point permitted most convenient access to the resources of the forested hills, the river bottoms (particularly including river cobbles) and the creek bottoms while still providing quick refuge from high water. Communication may have been another factor. In addition to providing a route to the southeast by way of the Pearl, the Bogue Chitto here approaches to within 12 kms of the headwaters of the Tchefuncte, where, in fact, two previously recorded Late Archaic sites, one evidently of some size, are located. From this point in turn a short traverse brings one by way of southwestward-flowing tributaries of the Tangipahoa to a section of that river — east of the town of Amite — which is also the locus of a number of Archaic sites.

Turning to the Tangipahoa, site locations, expectably, indicate a preference for points where tributaries enter the river or where minor streams join these tributaries themselves. There was no concentration of activity on the order of that south of Franklinton and, indeed, no site the size of the larger ones to the east. Taken as a whole, the sites appear to be grouped into six north-south trending clusters, suggestive of a series of (not necessarily contemporaneous) band territories. An utter lack of ceramics in all sites and collections examined indicates that occupation effectively ceased at the end of the Late Archaic.

The most economical explanation for these population shifts is that the development of primary forest efficiency by Late Archaic times motivated a small population to use the region, even though it was not very productive, especially as there was no particularly better area nearby. However, the initial formation of Lake Pontchartrain and the continued seaward growth and then initial deterioration of the Metairie lobe, the earlier stage (2000-800 B.C.) of the St. Bernard complex of the Mississippi delta (Coastal Environments 1977, 315-318, 328; Saucier 1963), created a new land mass south of the Florida Parishes sufficiently productive as to pull the population out of the latter, much poorer region. The area immediately surrounding the newly-formed lake thus became the locus of such large terminal Archaic and Poverty Point sites as Cedarland Plantation and Claiborne (Gagliano and Webb 1970; C. Webb 1982) and of the emerging coastal Tchefuncte at Big Oak Island and elsewhere (Shenkel 1984; Weinstein 1986) — would have been increasingly attractive. The evidently final abandonment of the upper Tangipahoa by this time perhaps reflects its greater distance from these resources. Then by early Marksville times the shift of major delta-building westward to the Teche lobe of the Teche complex (800 B.C. - A.D. 300) and the presence in the Barataria basin, southeast of New Orleans, of a major sublobe of the La Loutre lobe of the St. Bernard complex apparently moved the locus of coastal occupation further south and west.

In similar fashion, the modest terminal Marksville-Troyville materials east of the Bogue Chitto and just north of the West Pearl mouth may reflect the maximum expansion of the main portion of the La Loutre lobe and then its condition of greatest productivity (about A.D. 200 - 600), a time when the region immediately south of the Pearl again became the locus of considerable cultural elaboration. The extensive, at least partially late Marksville, constructions at Magnolia Mounds, in St. Bernard Parish (Gagliano et al. 1982, 20-23, 34-42; Phillips 1970, 898-899), and at Mulatto Bayou, just east of the Pearl system (Connaway 1981, 19-21; Gagliano et al.1982, 39-42; Lewis 1988; Williams 1974), are cases in point. Moderate Marksville occupations were also found along the north shore of the lake in the 1988 survey (Beavers, Lamb and Greene 1988). However, with the exception of Indian Camp and one other badly disrupted Troyville period site, occupations away from the lake shore are so minor as to imply small, temporary parties, possibly exploiting the river gravels. Moreover, the productivity of the evolving delta lobes, taken as a whole, seems to have been so great they deflected any significant inland reoccupations in later aboriginal times, unlike what took place in Temple Mound times north of the Pensacola Bay region (Bense 1983). The Florida Parishes were even more unsuited to neolithic agriculture than to hunting and gathering. Nevertheless — and even granting that the bulk of occupation in terminal Marksville-Troyville times seems to have been in the La Fouche delta to the southwest — the same eastward-extending, lobes which drew the population out of the Florida Parishes may well have also played a significant role in the western movement of traits from the Weeden Island florescence, thereby contributing to the origins of the Temple Mound cultural climax in eastern North America.

The Mississippi Delta-Gulf Role in Temple Mound Origins

Given that maize was not significant for subsistence until the Temple Mound stage was well underway, and that the colonial southeastern Indians were never fully dependent on agriculture, I would suggest that an important aspect of the evolution of the Temple Mound system was a prior need to solve critical social structural problems. A mortuary complex led by big men did not function in a tightly organized, cyclical, centralized and above all predictable fashion. Rather it operated in a somewhat random, diffuse, ad hoc manner as a changing set of local leaders accumulated varying combinations of prestige symbols. No doubt these were emically expressed as differing collections of spirit guardians, a situation perhaps expressed by the typical Hopewell monitor pipes and other status grave goods (Webb 1989). Mortuary activity is, moreover, rather socially restricted; one might therefore assume that Middle Woodland leadership had a more shamanistic, Mississippian, more priestly, even civic, role.

It would appear that the Burial Mound tradition was butting its head against the chiefdom level of organization but could not, with its organizational capacities, quite cross the line. This is compatible with the view of Braun and Plog (1982) that the end of Hopewell was not so much a simple decline, as a temporary reversion to more localized economies due to population growth and associated subsistence intensification. In other words, the process would not have been a total cultural collapse but rather a somewhat lengthy shifting of ceremonial and organizational gears. In somewhat the same way, Buikstra and her associates (Buikstra, Koningsberg and Bullington 1986) have noted that even early in the Late Woodland period populations in Illinois display fertility and mortality patterns characteristic of increased carbohydrate consumption and earlier weaning. They relate these developments initially to improved ceramic technology from the fifth century A.D. on, which allowed more effective preparation of starchy seed foods, rather than to increased maize consumption. Buikstra (1977) has also pointed out that skeletal samples from Middle to late Late Woodland times show steady trends toward larger, more genetically localized populations, increased chronic disease/nutritional stress but decreased acute disease/nutritional stress (changes characteristic of more sedentary, agriculturally oriented populations), and more evidence of violence, all of which would also support the Braun and Plog hypothesis.

In the southeast, and particularly along the Gulf Coast, the Burial Mound-Temple Mound transition seems especially smooth — little more than a social organizational clearing of the throat (Muller 1983; Knight 1989) — probably due to the especially rich subsistence provided by many of its coastal and riverine environments (Reitz and Quitmyer 1988; Lewis 1988; Bense 1983; Bitgood 1989, 142-144). With the florescence of the highly dynamic and expansive Weeden Island culture, whose ceremonialism and symbolism in many ways bridges the transition (Milanich et al. 1984, 166-174, 182-183, 197-199; Brose 1984), the Gulf Coast — as Williams and others have noted — became the diffusion route for a number of ceramic decorative techniques which characterized the evolving Temple Mound tradition (Ford 1952; Muller 1983; Belmont and Williams 1981; Williams and Brain 1983, 403-405; Brown 1984). Indian Camp, apparently dating to A.D. 350 - 500 and perched just north of where the evolving Mississippi delta temporarily created a most attractive target jutting out far to the east, seems to represent an early stage of this movement (Webb 1984). Bitgood (1989, 120-140) in fact places eastern coastal Louisiana in the western margin of the Weeden Island sphere. Further west along the Louisiana coast, the Morgan site on Pecan Island in Vermilion Parish reveals later traces of the same process (Fuller and Fuller 1987, 78-83, 153, 345-347, fig. 59; Brown 1987). In time, techniques of tempering, vessel construction and surface treatment moved into the very center of the area of Mississippian development at the onset of that tradition's emergence. No doubt this was done largely by trickle trade, down-the-line contact between adjacent regions (Bitgood 1989, 132-139, 141-144; Morse and Morse 1983, 190, 193, 216; Belmont n.d.; Stewart-Abernathy n.d.; Ensor 1978; Jenkins 1978).

Indeed, it now seems quite clear that that great hallmark of the Mississippian, the flat-topped mound (known, however, from such Middle Woodland sites as Marksville and Pinson Mounds) is well at home along the gulf and the lower Mississippi. Present in the Coles Creek and Plum Bayou cultures before the rise of Mississippian proper (Morse and Morse 1983, 195-196), the form very likely arose in large measure from the clay midden caps of Troyville and Issaquena (Belmont 1984; Webb 1984; Greengo 1964, 16-20, 65-75), the charnel platforms of Weeden Island (Milanich and Fairbanks 1980; Milanich et al. 1984; Muller 1983), and similar constructions elsewhere in the region (Belmont n.d.; Miller n.d.). The mounds at Kolomoki, now recognized as Weeden Island, were so elaborate that Sears — certainly no fool — classified the site as Temple Mound (Sears 1956).

Monumental construction also appears to have become more integrated. In the lower valley, the Coles Creek period saw the emergence of greater emphasis on astral mound orientations and standard units of mensuration, a practice also present in the formational periods at the premier site of Cahokia itself. These customs seem particularly characteristic of early Temple Mound (Sherrod and Rolingson 1987). This is of considerable significance, in light of the importance of solar symbolism for the conquest period elites. Moreover, by spatially and calendrically integrating the ritual activity of a polity, it created a widely applicable mode of unification of all of the economic and political activities of social groupings which such ritualism symbolized. Given the likely importance of the Gulf Coast and the Lower Mississippi Valley in the Middle Woodland-Mississippian transition, it is of some interest that astral orientation has been reported for the Weeden Island McKeithen site (Milanich et al. 1984, 91-92). The system of measurement common in Coles Creek, the so-called "Toltec module" (which has nothing to do with Mesoamerica; it takes its name from the Toltec Mound site in Arkansas) seems to have been in use at Marksville (Dennis Jones, personal communication). My own preliminary examination of small-scale maps indicates that astronomical orientation and the module were probably in use at Kolomoki and the module perhaps at McKeithen. This would suggest that evolving ideological mechanisms of enduring and predictable social organization and control were spreading throughout the region at this time (Cf. Williams and Brain 1983, 403-409).

The final requirement of the full emergence of the chiefdom pattern, that is, the Mississippian climax, was the introduction of improved, cold-adapted varieties of maize from the southwest which finally made temperate zone farming reasonably productive (Galinat and Gunnerson 1963; Galinat, Reinhart and Frisbie 1970; Fowler 1975). It is surely no accident that the chiefly system first emerges and also peaks in regions where good land for swidden farming, diffusion routes from the southwest, and an evolving centralized ceremonial complex from the Gulf Coast all intersect. This raises the question: Did maize move in, not only due to availability, but also because of the positive social pull of a new organizational need? In contrast, did the "collapse" of northern Hopewell reflect an earlier unavailability of a source of concentratable and expandable wealth which elites verging on chiefly status might use? While other subsistence changes, such as the introduction of the bow (Morse and Morse 1983, 210; Brain 1971, 60-62), also may have played a role, established maize agriculture would have been particularly critical. Hunting and gathering still provided a substantial portion of the food supply, but farming could now serve as a reserve, generate deployable wealth, and facilitate population concentration (M. Webb 1982). Precisely such reserves and concentrations would enable emerging chiefly dynasties, through their central role in evolving Mississippian ceremonialism, to command a disproportionate share of the social surplus in both life and death (Larson 1971; Peebles 1971; Brown 1971; Fowler 1974; 1975; Milner 1984).

Agriculture, by greatly increasing the desirability of river bottom lands and similar areas, intensified the kind of "soft circumscription," that typically gives rise to chiefdoms (Webb 1975; 1987). As Smith (1978) notes, these environments were the distinctive Mississippian adaptive niche. These processes gave rise to quite typical chieftains. These were focal entrepreneurs similar to big men, but now had the organizational and motivational capacity to carry out these characteristic tasks in a more integrated, centralized, durable (even from generation to generation) and, above all, predictable fashion. Furthermore, with the emergence of this sort of society, the ancient, long-enduring, but previously unorganized ritual vocabulary would at last come together in such a way that these symbols of power supported the rulers' claims to embody the ecological and social realities upon which society was based. All of this, I would point out in conclusion, is exactly what DeSoto and the other early European observers saw when they first penetrated the region.

References

Ames, K. E. 1981. The evolution of social ranking on the northwest coast of North America. *American Antiquity* 46:789-805.

Anderson, D. G., Hally, D. J. and Rudolph, J. L. 1986. The Mississippian occupation of the Savannah River valley. *Southeastern Archaeology* 5:32-51.

Asch, D. L., Farnsworth, K. B., and Asch, N. B. 1979. Woodland subsistence and settlement in west central Illinois. In *Hopewell archaeology: The Chillicothe conference*, eds. D. S. Brose and N. Greber, 80-85. Kent, OH: The Kent State University Press.

Baby, R. S. and Laglois, S. M. 1979. Seip Mound state memorial: Nonmortuary aspects of Hopewell. In *Hopewell archaeology: The Chillicothe conference*, eds. D. S. Brose and N. Greber, 16-18. Kent, OH: The Kent State University Press.

Beavers, R. C., Lamb, T. R. and Greene, J. R. 1988. *Preliminary archaeological survey of Bayous Liberty and Bonfouca, St. Tammany Parish, Louisiana.* Archaeological and Cultural Research Program Research Report No. 15. New Orleans: Department of Anthropology, University of New Orleans.

Beavers, R. C., Webb, M. C., Lamb, T. R., and Greene, J. R. 1984. *Preliminary archaeological survey of the lower West Pearl River, St. Tammany Parish, Louisiana.* Archaeological and Cultural Research Program, Research Report No. 9. New Orleans: Department of Anthropology, University of New Orleans.

——. 1985a. *Archaeological survey of the Bogue Chitto River drainage, Washington Parish, Louisiana.* Archaeological and Cultural Research Program, Research Report No. 10. New Orleans: Department of Anthropology, University of New Orleans.

——. 1985b. *Archaeological survey of the upper Tangipahoa River, Tangipahoa Parish, Louisiana.* Archaeological and Cultural Research Program, Research Report No. 11. New Orleans: Department of Anthropology, University of New Orleans.

Beck, C. 1981. Prehistoric settlement patterns in the Lower Mississippi Valley during the Late Mississippi period (A.D. 1200-1600). Paper presented at the annual meeting of the Society for American Archaeology, San Diego, CA, April 1981.

Bell, P. 1976. Spatial and temporal variability within the Trowbridge site, a Kansas City Hopewell village. In *Hopewellian archaeology in the lower*

Missouri River valley, ed. A. E. Johnson, 16-58. University of Kansas Publications in Anthropology No. 8. Lawrence, KS: Department of Anthropology, University of Kansas.

Belmont, J. S. 1984. The Troyville concept and the Gold Mine site. In *The Troyville-Baytown period in Lower Mississippi Valley prehistory: A memorial to Robert Stuart Neitzel*, ed. J. L. Gibson, 65-98. Louisiana Archaeology, Bulletin 9 (for 1982). Lafayette, LA: Louisiana Archaeological Society.

———. n.d. Toltec and Coles Creek: A view from the southern Lower Mississippi Valley. In *Emerging patterns of Plum Bayou culture: Preliminary investigations of the Toltec Mounds research project*, ed. M. A. Rolingson, 64-70. Arkansas Archeological Survey Research Series 18. Fayetteville, AR: Arkansas Archeological Survey.

Belmont, J. S., and Williams, S. 1981. Painted pottery horizons in the southern Mississippi valley. In *Traces of prehistory: Papers in honor of William G. Haag*, eds. F. H. West and R. W. Neuman, 19-42. Geoscience and Man, vol 22. Baton Rouge, LA: School of Geoscience, Louisiana State University

Belshaw, C. S. 1965. *Traditional exchange and modern markets*. Englewood Cliffs, NJ: Prentice-Hall.

Bender, B. 1985. Emergent tribal formations in the American midcontinent. *American Antiquity* 50:52-62.

Bender, M. M., Baerreis, D. A., and Steventon, R. L. 1981. Further light on carbon isotopes and Hopewell agriculture. *American Antiquity* 46:346-353.

Bense, J. A. 1983. Settlement patterns, climate and marine ecosystem evolution correlations in the Escambia Bay drainage system in northwest Florida. Paper presented at the annual meeting of the Southeastern Archaeological Conference, Columbia, SC, November 1983.

Bitgood, M. J. 1989. *The Baytown period in the upper Tensas basin*. Lower Mississippi Survey Bulletin No. 12. Cambridge, MA: Peabody Museum, Harvard University

Bloch, M. 1971. *Placing the dead: Tombs, ancestral villages, and kinship organization in Madagascar*. London: Seminar Press.

Brain, J. P. 1971. *The Lower Mississippi Valley in North American prehistory*. Fayetteville, AR: National Park Service, Southeast Agency and the Arkansas Archaeological Survey.

———. 1976. The question of corn agriculture in the Lower Mississippi Valley. *Southeastern Archaeological Conference Bulletin* 19:57-60.

Braun, D. P. 1979. Illinois Hopewell burial practices and social organization: A reexamination of the Klunk-Gibson mound group. In *Hopewell archaeology: The Chillicothe conference*, eds. D. S. Brose and N. Greber, 66-80. Kent, OH: The Kent State University Press.

Braun, D. P. and Plog, S. 1982. Evolution of "tribal" social networks: Theory and prehistoric North American evidence. *American Antiquity* 47:504-525.

Brose, D. S. 1979a. A speculative model of the role of exchange in the prehistory of the eastern woodlands. In *Hopewell archaeology: The Chillicothe conference*, eds. D. S. Brose and N. Greber, 3-8. Kent, OH: The Kent State University Press.

———. 1979b. An interpretation of the Hopewellian traits in Florida. In *Hopewell archaeology: The Chillicothe conference*, eds. D. S. Brose and N. Greber, 141-149. Kent, OH: The Kent State University Press.

———. 1984. Mississippian period cultures in northwestern Florida. In *Perspectives on Gulf coast prehistory*, ed. D. D. Davis, 165-198. Gainesville: The University of Florida and the Florida State Museum.

———. 1988. Seeing the Mid-South from the Southeast: Second century stasis and status. In *Middle Woodland settlement and ceremonialism in the Mid-South and Lower Mississippi Valley*, ed. R. C. Mainford, Jr., 147-157. Proceedings of the 1984 Mid-South Archaeological Conference, Pinson Mounds, Tennessee, June 1984. Mississippi Department of Archives and History Archaeological Report No. 22. Jackson, MS.

Brose, D. S., and Gerber, N., eds. 1979. *Hopewell archaeology: The Chillicothe conference*. Kent, OH: The Kent State University Press.

Brown, I. W. 1984. Late prehistory in coastal Louisiana: The Coles Creek period. In *Perspectives on Gulf Coast prehistory*, ed. D. D. Davis, 94-124. Gainesville, FL: The University of Florida Press and the Florida State Museum.

———. 1987. Afterward — The Morgan site in regional perspective. In *Excavations at Morgan: A Coles Creek mound complex in coastal Louisiana*, R. S. Fuller and D. S. Fuller. 155-164. Lower Mississippi Survey Bulletin No. 11. Cambridge, MA: Peabody Museum, Harvard University.

Brown, J. A. 1971. The dimensions of status in the burials at Spiro. In *Approaches to the social dimensions of mortuary practices*, ed. J. A. Brown, 92-112. Society for American Archaeology Memoir 25. Washington, DC.

———. 1979. Charnel houses and mortuary crypts: Disposal of the dead in the Middle Woodland period. In *Hopewell archaeology: The Chillicothe conference*, eds. D. S. Brose and N. Greber, 211-219. Kent, OH: The Kent State University Press.

———. 1981. The search for rank in prehistoric burials. In *The archaeology of death*, eds. R. Chapman, I. Kinnes and K. Randsborg, 25-37. Cambridge: Cambridge University Press.

Buikstra, J. E. 1977. Biocultural dimensions of archeological study: A regional perspective. In *Biocultural adaptation in prehistoric America*, ed. R. L. Blakely, 67-84. Southern Anthropological Society Proceedings, No. 11. Athens, GA: The University of Georgia Press.

———. 1979. Contributions of physical anthropologists to the concept of Hopewell: A historical perspective. In *Hopewell archaeology: The Chillicothe conference*, eds. D. S. Brose and N. Greber, 220-233. Kent, OH: The Kent State University Press.

Buikstra, J. E., Konigsberg, L. W., and Bullington, J. 1986. Fertility and the development of agriculture in the prehistoric Midwest. *American Antiquity* 51:528-546.

Byrd, K. M. 1976. Tchefuncte subsistence: Information obtained from the excavation of the Morton Shell Mound, Iberia Parish, Louisiana. *Southeastern Archaeological Conference Bulletin* 19:70- 75.

Byrd, K. M., and Neuman, R. W. 1978. Archaeological data relative to prehistoric subsistence in the Lower Mississippi River alluvial valley. In *Man and environment: Lower Mississippi Valley*, ed. Sam B. Hilliard, 9-21. Geoscience and Man, vol. 19. Baton Rouge, LA: School of Geoscience, Louisiana State University

Caldwell, J. R. 1958. *Trend and tradition in the prehistory of the eastern United States*. American Anthropological Association Memoir 88. Washington, DC.

Callender, C. 1979. Hopewell archaeology and American ethnology. In *Hopewell archaeology: The Chillicothe conference*, eds. D. S. Brose and N. Greber, 254-257. Kent, OH: The Kent State University Press.

Carneiro, R. L. 1961. Slash and burn civilization among the Kuikuru and its implications for cultural development in the Amazon basin. In *The evolution of horticultural systems in native South America: Causes and consequences*, ed. J. Wilbert, 47-68. Caracas: Sociedad de Ciencias Naturales La Salle.

———. 1970. A theory of the origin of the state. *Science* 1969:733-738.

Chapman, J. C., and Shea, A. B. 1977. Paleoecological and cultural interpretation of plant remains recovered from Archaic period sites in the lower Little Tennessee River valley. Paper presented at the annual meeting of the Southeastern Archaeological Conference, Lafayette, LA, October 1977.

Chapman, J. C., and Crites, G. D. 1987. Evidence for early maize (Zea mays) from the Icehouse Bottom site, Tennessee. *American Antiquity* 52:352-354.

Coastal Environments, Inc. 1977. *Prehistoric resource potential*. Vol. 1 of *Cultural resources evaluation of the northern Gulf of Mexico continental shelf*. Prepared for Interagency Archeology Services, Office of Archeology and Historical Preservation, National Park Service, U. S. Department of the Interior, Washington, DC.

Connaway, J. M. 1981. *Archaeological investigations in Mississippi 1969-1977*. Mississippi Department of Archives and History Archaeological Report No. 6. Jackson, MS.

Covarrubias, M. 1954. *The eagle, the jaguar, and the serpent; Indian art of the Americas: North America: Alaska, Canada, the United States.* New York: Knopf.

Davies, N. 1979. *Voyagers to the New World.* New York: William Morrow.

Drucker, P. 1939. Rank, wealth and kinship in Northwest Coast society. *American Anthropologist* 41:55-65.

———. 1951. *The northern and central Nootkan tribes.* Bureau of American Ethnology Bulletin 144. Washington, DC.

———. 1955. *Indians of the Northwest Coast.* New York: McGraw-Hill Book Company for the American Museum of Natural History.

Ensor, H. B. 1978. Archaeology at 1Je34, a late West Jefferson phase site. In *David L. Dejarnette: A Southeastern Archaeological Conference tribute,* organized by John A. Walthall, ed. Drexel A. Peterson, Jr., 18-20. Southeastern Archaeological Conference Special Publication 5. Memphis, TN.

Ford, J. A. 1952. *Measurements of some prehistoric design developments in the southeastern United States.* American Museum of Natural History Anthropolgical Papers 44(3). New York.

———. 1963. *Hopewell culture burial mounds near Helena, Arkansas.* The American Museum of Natural History Anthropological Papers 50(1). New York.

———. 1969. *A comparison of Formative cultures in the Americas: Diffusion or the psychic unity of man.* Washington, DC: Smithsonian Institution Press.

Ford, J. A., and Webb, C. H. 1956. *Poverty Point: A late Archaic site in Louisiana.* American Museum of Natural History Anthropological Papers 46(1). New York.

Ford, J. A., and Willey, G. R. 1940. *Crooks site: A Marksville period burial mound in La Salle Parish, Louisiana.* Louisiana Geological Survey Anthropological Study 3. New Orleans, LA: Department of Conservation.

Ford, R. I. 1979. Gathering and gardening: Trends and consequences of Hopewell subsistence strategies. In *Hopewell archaeology: The Chillicothe conference,* eds. D. S. Brose and N. Greber, 234-238. Kent, OH: The Kent State University Press.

Fortier, A. C., Emerson, T. E., and Finney, F. A. 1984. Early Woodland and Middle Woodland periods. In *American Bottom archaeology,* eds. C. J. Bareis and J. W. Porter, 59-103. Urbana, IL: The University of Illinois Press.

Fowler, M. I. 1952. The Clear Lake site: Hopewellian occupation. In *Hospewellian communities in Illinois,* ed. T. Deuel, 131-174. The Illinois State Museum Scientific Papers No. 5. Springfield, IL.

———. 1971. The origin of plant cultivation in the central Mississippi valley: A hypothesis. In *Prehistoric agriculture*, ed. S. Struever, 122-128. Garden City, NY: The Natural History Press for the American Museum of Natural History.

———. 1974. *Cahokia: Ancient capital of the Midwest*. Addison-Wesley Module in Anthropology 48. Menlo Park, CA: Cummings Publishing Co.

———. 1975. A pre-Columbian urban center on the Mississippi. *Scientific American* 233(2): 92-101.

Fried, M. H. 1967. *The evolution of political society: An essay in political anthropology*. New York: Random House.

Fuller, R. S., and Fuller, D. S. 1987. *Excavations at Morgan: A Coles Creek mound complex in coastal Louisiana*. Lower Mississippi Survey Bulletin No. 11. Cambridge, MA: Peabody Museum, Harvard University

Gagliano, S. M. 1984. Geoarchaeology of the northern Gulf shore. In *Perspectives on Gulf Coast prehistory*, ed. D. D. Davis, 1-40. Gainesville, FL: The University of Florida Press and the Florida State Museum.

Gagliano, S. M., Pearson, C. E., Weinstein, R. A., Wiseman, D. E., and McClendon, C. M. 1982. Sedimentary studies of prehistoric archaeological sites: Criteria for the identification of submerged archaeological sites of the northern Gulf of Mexico continental shelf. Report submitted to U. S. Department of the Interior, National Park Service, Division of State Plans and Grants, Contract No. C35003(79). Baton Rouge, LA: Coastal Environments, Inc.

Gaglaino, S. M., and Webb, C. H. 1970. Archaic-Poverty Point transition at the Pearl River mouth. In *The Poverty Point culture*, eds. B. J. Broyles and C. H. Webb, 47-72. Southeastern Archeological Conference Bulletin 12. Morgantown, WV.

Galinat, W. C., and Gunnerson, J. H. 1963. Spread of eight-rowed maize from the prehistoric Southwest. *Harvard University Botanical Museum Leaflets* 20:117-159.

Galinat, W. C., Reinhart, T. R., and Frisbie, T. R. 1970. Early eight-rowed maize from the middle Rio Grande valley, New Mexico. *Harvard University Botanical Museum Leaflets* 22:313-331.

Gibson, J. L. 1974. Poverty Point, the first North American chiefdom. *Archaeology* 27:96-105.

———. 1980. Speculations on the origin and development of Poverty Point. In *Caddoan and Poverty Point archaeology: Essays in honor of Clarence Hungerford Webb*, ed. J. L. Gibson, 319-348. *Louisiana Archaeology, Bulletin 6* (for 1979). Lafayette, LA: Louisiana Archaeological Society.

———. 1987. The Poverty Point earthworks reconsidered. *Mississippi Archaeology* 22(2):15-31.

Gibson, J. L., and Shenkel, J. R. 1988. Louisiana earthworks: Middle Woodland and predecesssors. In *Middle Woodland settlement and cere-*

monialism in the Mid-South and Lower Mississippi Valley, ed. R. C. Mainfort, Jr., 7-18. Proceedings of the 1984 Mid-South Archaeological Conference, Pinson Mounds, Tennessee, June 1984. Mississippi Department of Archives and History Archaeological Report No. 22. Jackson, MS.

Goad, S. I. 1979. Middle Woodland exchange in the prehistoric southeastern United States. In *Hopewell archaeology: The Chillicothe conference*, eds. D. S. Brose and N. Greber, 239-246. Kent, OH: The Kent State University Press.

Goggin, J. M., and Sturtevant, W. C. 1964. The Calusa: A stratfied, nonagricultural society (with notes on sibling marriage). In *Explorations in cultural anthropology: Essays in honor of George Peter Murdock*, ed. W. H. Goodenough, 179-219. New York: McGraw-Hill.

Greber, N. 1979. A comparative study of site morphology and burial patterns at Edwin Harness Mound and Seip mounds 1 and 2. In *Hopewell archaeology: The Chillicothe conference*, eds. D. S. Brose and N. Greber, 27-38. Kent, OH: The Kent State University Press.

———. 1983. *Recent excavations at the Edwin Harness Mound, Liberty Works, Ross County, Ohio*. Mid-Continental Journal of Archaeology, Special Paper No. 5. Kent, OH: The Kent State University Press.

Greber, N. B., and Ruhl, K. C. 1989. The *Hopewell site: A contemporary analysis based on the work of Charles C. Willoughby*. Boulder, CO: Westview Press.

Greengo, R. E. 1964. Issaquena: *An archaeological phase of the Yazoo basin of the Lower Mississippi Valley*. Society for American Archaeology Memoir 18. Washington, DC.

Griffin, J. B. 1943. *The Fort Ancient aspect: Its cultural and chronological position in Mississippi valley archaeology*. Ann Arbor, MI: University of Michigan Press.

———. 1964. The Northeast Woodlands area. In *Prehistoric man in the New World*, eds. J. D. Jennings and E. Norbeck, 223-258. Chicago: The University of Chicago Press for William Marsh Rice University

———. 1967. Eastern North American archaeology: A summary. *Science* 156:175-191.

———. 1979. An overview of the Chillicothe Hopewell conference. In *Hopewell archaeology: The Chillicothe conference*, eds. D. S. Brose and N. Greber, 266-279. Kent, OH: The Kent State University Press.

———. 1983. The Midlands. In *Ancient North Americans*, ed. J. D. Jennings, 243-301. New York: W. H. Freeman and Company.

———. 1984. Some observations on the FAI-270 Project. In *American Bottom archaeology*, eds. C. J. Bareis and J. W. Porter, 253-61. Urbana, IL: University of Illinois Press.

Haag, W. G. 1971. *Louisiana in North American prehistory.* Melanges 1. Baton Rouge, LA: Museum of Geoscience, Louisiana State University.

Hall, R. L. 1977. An anthropocentric perspective for eastern United States prehistory. *American Antiquity* 42:499-518.

——. 1979. In search of the ideology of the Adena-Hopewell climax. In *Hopewell archaeology: The Chillicothe conference,* eds. D. S. Brose and N. Greber, 258-265. Kent, OH: The Kent State University Press.

——. 1980. An interpretation of the two-climax model of Illinois prehistory. In *Early native Americans: Prehistory, demography, economy, and technology,* ed. D. L. Browman, 401-462. The Hague: Mouton Publishers.

Heider, K. G. 1970. *The Dugum Dani: A Papuan culture in the highlands of West New Guinea.* Viking Fund Publication in Anthropology 49. New York: Wenner-Gren Foundation for Anthropological Research.

——. 1979. *Grand Valley Dani: Peaceful warriors.* New York: Holt, Rinehart and Winston, Inc.

Hyde, G. C. 1962. *Indians of the Woodlands from prehistoric times to 1725.* Norman, OK: The University of Oklahoma Press.

Jefferies, R. W. 1976. *The Tunacunnhee site: Evidence of Hopewell interaction in northwest Georgia.* Anthropological Papers of the University of Georgia No. 1. Athens, GA: Department of Anthropology, University of Georgia.

——. 1979. The Tunacunnhee site: Hopewell in northwest Georgia.In *Hopewell archaeology: The Chillicothe conference,* eds. D. S. Brose and N. Greber, 162- 170. Kent, OH: The Kent State University Press.

Jenkins, N. J. 1978. Terminal Woodland-Mississippian interaction in northern Alabama: The West Jefferson phase. In *David L. Dejarnette: A Southeastern Archaeological Conference tribute,* organized by J. A. Walthall, ed. D. A. Peterson, Jr., 21-27. Southeastern Archaeological Conference Special Publication 5. Memphis, TN.

Jennings, J. G. 1952. Prehistory of the Lower Mississippi Valley. In *Archaeology of the eastern United States,* ed. J. B. Griffin, 256-271. Chicago: The University of Chicago Press.

——. 1989. *Prehistory of North America,* 3rd. ed. Mountainview, CA: Mayfield Publishing Company.

Jeter, M. D. 1984. Mound volumes, energy ratios, exotic materials, and contingency tables: Comments on some recent analyses of Copena burial practices. *Midcontinental Journal of Archaeology* 9:91-104.

Johnson, A. E. 1976. A model of the Kansas City Hopewell subsistence settlement system. In *Hopewellian archaeology in the Lower Missouri Valley,* ed A. E. Johnson, 7-15. University of Kansas Publications in Anthropology No. 8. Lawrence, KS: Department of Anthropology, University of Kansas.

———. 1979. Kansas City Hopewell. In *Hopewell archaeology: The Chillicothe conference*, eds. D. S. Brose and N. Greber, 86-93. Kent, OH: The Kent State University Press.

Kelly, J. E., Finney, F. A., McElrath, D. L., and Ozuk, S. J. 1984a. Late Woodland period. In *American Bottom archaeology*, eds. C. J. Bareis and J. W. Porter, 104-127. Urbana, IL: University of Illinois Press.

Kelly, J. E., Ozuk, S. J., Jackson, D. K., McElrath, D. L. Finney, F. A., and Esarey, D. 1984b. Emergent Mississippian period. In *American Bottom archaeology*, eds. C. J. Bareis and J. W. Porter, 128-157. Urbana, IL: University of Illinois Press.

Kniffen, F. B. 1936. A preliminary report on the Indian mounds and middens of Plaquemines and St. Bernard Parishes. In *Lower Mississippi River delta: Reports on the geology of Plaquemines and St. Bernard Parishes*, by Richard J. Russell, 407-422. Louisiana Geological Survey Geological Bulletin No. 8. New Orleans: Department of Conservation.

———. 1938. The Indian mounds of Iberville Parish. In *Report on the geology of Iberville and Ascension Parishes*, by H. V. Howe, 189-207. Louisiana Geological Survey Geological Bulletin No. 13. New Orleans: Department of Conservation.

Kniffen, F. B., Gregory, H. F. and Stokes, G. A. 1987. *The historic Indian tribes of Louisiana from 1542 to the present*. Baton Rouge, LA: Louisiana State University Press.

Knight, V. J., Jr. 1986. The institutional organization of Mississippian religion. *American Antiquity* 51:675-687.

———. 1989. Review of *The emergent Mississippian*, ed. R. A. Marshall. Proceedings of the sixth Mid-South Archaeological Conference, June 6-9, 1985. *Mississippi Archaeology* 24(1): 58-61.

Krause, R. A. 1989. The Archaic stage and the emergence of Hopewellian ceremonialism in the southeastern United States. *Mississippi Archaeology* 24(1): 1-16.

Larson, L. H. 1971. Archaeological implications of social stratification at the Etowah site. In *Approaches to the social dimensions of mortuary practice*, ed. J. A. Brown, 58-67. Society for American Archaeology Memoir 25. Washington, DC.

Lewis, R. B. 1988. Fires on the bayou: Cultural adaptations in the Mississippi Sound region. *Southeastern Archaeology* 7:109-123.

Lynott, M. J., Boutton, T. W., Price, J. E., and Nelson, D. E. 1986. Stable carbon isotopic evidence for maize agriculture in southeast Missouri and northeast Arkansas. *American Antiquity* 51:51-65.

McGregor, J. C. 1952. The Havana site. In *Hopewellian communities in Illinois*, ed. T. Deuel, 43-91. The Illinois State Museum Scientific Papers No. 5. Springfield, IL.

———. 1958. *The Pool and Irving villages: A study of Hopewell occupation in the Illinois River valley*. Urbana, IL: The University of Illinois Press.

Mainfort, R. C., Jr. 1988. Pinson Mounds: Internal chronology and external relationships. In *Middle Woodland settlement and ceremonialism in the Mid-South and Lower Mississippi Valley*, ed. R. C. Mainfort, Jr., 132-146. Proceedings of the 1984 Mid-South Archaeological Conference, Pinson Mounds, Tennessee, June 1984. Mississippi Department of Archives and History Archaeological Report No. 22. Jackson, MS.

———. 1989. Adena chiefdoms? Evidence from the Wright Mounds. *Midcontinental Journal of Archaeology* 14:164-178.

Malinowski, B. 1922. *Argonauts of the western Pacific*. London: Routledge and Kegan Paul.

Milanich, J. T., and Fairbanks, C. H. 1980. *Florida archaeology*. New York: Academic Press, Inc.

Milanich, J. T, Cordell, A. S., Knight, V. J., Jr., Kohler, T. A., and Sigler-Lavelle, B. J. 1984. *McKeithen Weeden Island: The culture of northern Florida*, A.D. 200-900. Orlando, FL: Academic Press, Inc.

Miller, J. E., III. n. d. Construction of site features; Tests of mounds C, D, E, B, and embankment. In *Emerging patterns of Plum Bayou culture: Preliminary investigations of the Toltec Mounds research project*, ed. M. A. Rolingson 30-43. Arkansas Archeological Survey Research Series 18. Fayetteville, AR.

Milner, G. R. 1984. Social and temporal implications of variations among American Bottom Mississippian cemeteries. *American Antiquity* 49:468-488.

Mistovich, T. S. 1988. Early Mississippian in the Black Warrior valley: The pace of transition. *Southeastern Archaeology* 7:21-38.

Moorehead, W. K. 1922. *The Hopewell mound group of Ohio*. Field Museum of Natural History Publication 211, Anthropological Series 6(5). Chicago.

Morse, D. F., and Morse, P. A. 1983. *Archaeology of the central Mississippi valley*. New York: The Academic Press, Inc.

Muller, J. 1983. The Southeast. In *Ancient North Americans*, ed. J. D. Jennings, 373-419. New York: W. H. Freeman and Company.

Murdock, G. P. 1967. *Ethnographic atlas*. Pittsburgh, PA: University of Pittsburgh Press.

Nash, M. 1966. *Primitive and peasant economic systems*. San Francisco, CA: Chandler Publishing Company.

Neuman, R. L. 1984. *An introduction to Louisiana archaeology*. Baton Rouge, LA: Louisiana State University Press.

Oliver, D. 1967. *A Solomon Island society: Kinship and leadership among the Siuai of Bougainville*. Boston, MA: Beacon Press.

Peebles, C. S. 1971. Moundville and surrounding sites: Some structural considerations of mortuary practices, II. In *Approaches to the social dimensions of mortuary practices*, ed. J. A. Brown, 68-91. Society for American Archaeology Memoir 25. Washington, DC.

Peebles, C. S., and Kus, S. M. 1977. Some archaeological correlates of ranked societies. *American Antiquity* 42:421-448.

Phillips, P. 1970. *Archaeological survey in the lower Yazoo basin, Mississippi, 1949-1955.* Papers of the Peabody Museum of Archaeology and Ethnology, Harvard University 60. Cambridge, MA: Harvard University

Piddock, S. 1965. The potlatch system of the southern Kwakiutl. *Southwestern Journal of Anthropology* 21:244-264.

Prufer, O. H. 1964. The Hopewell complex of Ohio. In *Hopewellian studies*, eds. J. R. Caldwell and R. L. Hall, 35-83. Illinois State Museum Scientific Papers 12. Springfield, IL.

Rappaport, R. A. 1968. *Pigs for the ancestors: Ritual in the ecology of a New Guinea people.* New Haven, CT: Yale University Press.

Reid, K. C. 1976. Prehistoric trade in the Lower Missouri River Valley: An analysis of Middle Woodland bladelets. In *Hopewellian archaeology in the Lower Missouri River Valley*, ed. A. E. Johnson, 66-99. University of Kansas Publications in Anthropology No. 8. Lawrence, KS: Department of Anthropology, University of Kansas.

Reitz, E. J., and Quitmyer, I. R. 1988. Faunal remains from two coastal Georgia Swift Creek sites. *Southeastern Archaeology* 7:95-108.

Renfrew, C. 1984. *Approaches to Social Archaeology.* Cambridge, MA: Harvard University Press.

Robinson, S. 1976. An analysis of charred seeds from a Middle Woodland occupation site in central Missouri. In *Hopewellian archaeology in the Lower Missouri River Valley*, ed. A. E. Johnson, 100-109. University of Kansas Publications in Anthropology No. 8. Lawrence, KS: Department of Anthropology, University of Kansas.

Sahlins, M. D. 1963. Poor man, rich man, big man, chief: Political types in Melanesia and Polynesia. *Comparative Studies in Society and History* 5:285-303.

——. 1968. *Tribesmen.* Englewood Cliffs, NJ: Prentice-Hall, Inc.

——. 1972. *Stone Age economics.* Chicago: Aldine-Atherton, Inc.

Salisbury, R. F. 1962. *From stone to steel: Economic consequences of a technological change in New Guinea.* New York: Cambridge University Press.

Saucier, R. T. 1963. *Recent geomorphic history of the Pontchartrain basin.* Louisiana State University Studies, Coastal Studies Series No. 9. Baton Rouge, LA: Louisiana State University Press.

Sears, W. H. 1956. *Excavations at Kolomoki: Final report.* University of Georgia Series in Anthropology No. 5. Athens, GA: The University of Georgia Press.

——. 1964. The southeastern United States. In *Prehistoric man in the New World*, eds. J. D. Jennings and E. Norbeck, pp. 259-287. Chicago: The University of Chicago Press for William Marsh Rice University

Seeman, M. F. 1979. Feasting with the dead: Ohio Hopewell charnel house ritual as a context for redistribution. In *Hopewell archaeology: The Chillicothe conference*, eds. D. S. Brose and N. Greber, 39-46. Kent, OH: The Kent State University Press.

——. 1988. Ohio Hopewell trophy-skull artifacts as evidence for competition in Middle Woodland societies circa 50 B.C.-A.D. 350. *American Antiquity* 53:565-577.

Service, E. R. 1978. *Profiles in ethnology*, 3rd. ed. New York: Harper and Row.

Shenkel, J. R. 1984. Early Woodland in coastal Louisiana. In *Perspectives on Gulf Coast prehistory*, ed. D. D. Davis, 41-71. Gainesville, FL: The University of Florida Press and the Florida State Museum.

Sherrod, P. C., and Rolingson, M. A. 1987. *Surveyors of the ancient Mississippi valley: Modules and alignments in prehistoric mound sites*. Arkansas Archeological Survey Research Series No. 28. Fayetteville, AR: Arkansas Archeological Survey.

Shryock, A. J. 1987. The Wright Mound reexamined: Generative structures and the political economy of a simple chiefdom. *Midcontinental Journal of Archaeology* 12:243-268.

Silverberg, R. 1974. *The mound builders*. New York: Ballantine Books.

Smith, B. D. 1978. Variation in Mississippian settlement patterns. In *Mississippian settlement patterns*, ed. B. D. Smith 479-503. New York: Academic Press.

——. 1984. Mississippian expansion: Tracing the historical development of an explanatory model. *Southeastern Archaeology* 3:13-32.

Snow, D. 1976. *The archaeology of North America*. New York: The Viking Press.

Stewart-Abernathy, J. C. n.d. Ceramic studies at the Toltec Mounds site: Basis for a tentative cultural sequence. In *Emerging patterns of Plum Bayou culture: Preliminary investigations of the Toltec Mounds research project*, ed. M. A. Rolingson, 44-53. Arkansas Archeological Survey Research Series 18. Fayetteville, AR: Arkansas Archeological Survey.

Struever, S. 1962. Implications of vegetal remains from an Illinois Hopewell site. *American Antiquity* 27:584-587.

Swanson, G. E. 1968. *The birth of the gods*. Ann Arbor, MI: The University of Michigan Press.

Toth, A. 1974. *Archaeology and ceramics at the Marksville site*. University of Michigan Museum of Anthropology Anthropological Papers, No. 56. Ann Arbor, MI.

———. 1979. The Marksville connection. In *Hopewell archaeology: The Chillicothe conference*, eds. D. S. Brose and N. Greber, 188-199. Kent, OH: The Kent State University Press.

Uberoi, J. P. S. 1962. *Politics of the Kula ring: An analysis of the findings of Bronislaw Malinowski*. Manchester: Manchester University Press.

Vehik, S. C. 1983. Middle Woodland mortuary practices along the northeastern periphery of the Great Plains: A consideration of Hopewellian interactions. *Midcontinental Journal of Archaeology* 8:211-255.

Vickery, K. D. 1979. "Reluctant" or "avant-garde" Hopewell? Suggestions of Middle Woodland culture change in east-central Indiana and south-central Ohio. In *Hopewell archaeology: The Chillicothe conference*, eds. D. S. Brose and N. Greber, 59-63. Kent, OH: The Kent State University Press.

Walker, W. M. 1936. *The Troyville mounds, Catahoula Parish, Louisiana*. Bureau of American Ethnology Bulletin 43. Washington, DC.

Walthall, J. A. 1979. Hopewell and the southern heartland. In *Hopewell archaeology: The Chillicothe conference*, eds. D. S. Brose and N. Greber, 200-208. Kent, OH: The Kent State University Press.

———. 1980. *Prehistoric Indians of the Southeast: Archaeology of Alabama and the Middle South*. Tuscaloosa, AL: The University of Alabama Press.

Walthall, J. A., Stow, S. H., and Karson, M. J. 1979. Ohio Hopewell trade: Galena procurement and exchange. In *Hopewell archaeology: The Chillicothe conference*, eds. D. S. Brose and N. Greber, 247-250. Kent, OH: The Kent State University Press.

Watson, P. J., and Yarnell, R. A. 1966. Archaeological and paleoethnobotanical investigations in Salts Cave, Mammoth Cave National Park, Kentucky. *American Antiquity* 31:842-849.

Webb, C. H. 1968. The extent and content of Poverty Point culture. *American Antiquity* 33:297-321.

———. 1982. *The Poverty Point culture*, 2nd ed. rev. Geoscience and Man, vol. 17. Baton Rouge, LA: School of Geoscience, Louisiana State University.

Webb, M. C. 1975. The flag follows trade: An essay on the necessary interaction of military and commercial factors in state formation. In *Ancient civilization and trade*, eds. J. A. Sabloff and C. C. Lamberg-Karlowski, 155-209. Albuquerque, NM: The University of New Mexico Press for the School of American Research.

———. 1982. The neutral calorie? On the maintenance of ranked societies in the "agriculturally deficient" environment of gulf coastal Louisiana. *Louisiana Archaeology* 8(for 1981): 1-19.

———. 1984. Preliminary report on excavations at an early Troyville period site (16ST6) on the West Pearl River, Louisiana. In *The Troyville/Baytown period in Lower Mississippi Valley prehistory: A memorial to Robert*

Stuart Neitzel, ed. J. L. Gibson, 205-250. *Louisiana Archaeology, Bulletin 9* (for 1982). Lafayette, LA: Louisiana Archaeological Society.

———. 1987. Broader perspectives on Andean state origins. In *The origins and development of the Andean state*, eds. J. Haas, S. Pozorski, and T. Pozorski, 161-167. Cambridge: Cambridge University Press.

———. 1988. The first states: How — or in what sense — did "circumscription" circumscribe? *American Behavioral Scientist* 31:449-457.

———. 1989. Functional and historical parallelisms between Mesoamerican and Mississippian cultures. In *The Southeastern ceremonial complex: Artifacts and analysis*, ed. P. Galloway, 279-293. Lincoln, NE: University of Nebraska Press.

Webb, M. C., and Thomson, L. P. 1977. Marx on the prairie? Subsistence, status and society among selected Plains Indian tribes. Paper presented at the annual meeting of the Southern Anthropological Society, Miami, March 1977.

Weinstein, R. A. 1986. Tchefuncte occupation in the lower Mississippi delta and adjacent coastal plain. In *The Tchula period in the Mid-South and Lower Mississippi Valley*. Proceedings of the 1982 Mid-South Archaeological Conference, eds. D. H. Dye and R. C. Brister, 102-127. Mississippi Department of Archives and History Archaeological Report No. 17. Jackson, MS.

Weinstein, R. A., and Gagliano, S. M. 1985. The shifting deltaic coast of the Lafourche country and its prehistoric settlement. In *The Lafourche country: The people and the land*, ed. P. D. Uzee. Lafayette, LA: Center for Louisana Studies, University of Southwestern Louisiana.

Widmer, R. J. 1988. *The evolution of the Calusa: A nonagricultural chiefdom on the southwest Florida coast*. Tuscaloosa, AL: The University of Alabama Press.

Willey, G. R. 1966. *An introduction to American archaeology*. Vol 1, *North and Middle America*. Englewood Cliffs, NJ: Prentice-Hall, Inc.

Willey, G. R., and Sabloff, J. A. 1974. *A history of American archaeology*. San Francisco, CA: W. H. Freeman and Company.

Williams, J. M. 1974. Excavations at earthworks on Mulatto Bayou. *Mississippi Archaeological Association Newsletter* 9(3): 5-9.

Williams, S., and Brain, J. P. 1983. *Excavations at the Lake George site, Yazoo County, Mississippi, 1958-1960*. Papers of the Peabody Museum of Archaeology and Ethnology, Harvard University 74. Cambridge, MA: Harvard University

Willoughby, C. C. 1922. *The Turner group of earthworks, Hamilton County, Ohio*. Papers of the Peabody Museum of American Archaeology and Ethnology, Harvard University 8(3). Cambridge, MA: Harvard University

Wimberly, S. B., and Tourtelot, H. A. 1941. *The McQuorquodale mound: A manifestation of the Hopewellian phase in south Alabama.* Geological Survey of Alabama Museum Paper 19. University, AL.

Yarnell, R. A. 1965. Early Woodland plant remains and the question of cultivation. *Florida Anthropologist* 18: 78-81.

———. 1976. Early plant husbandry in eastern North America. In *Cultural change and continuity: Essays in honor of James Bennett Griffin*, ed. C. E. Cleland, 265-273. New York: Academic Press.

Louisiana "Archaeogeography": Mapping the Remaining Indian Mounds

Dennis C. Jones and Malcolm K. Shuman

Abstract

The association of Native Americans with the many prehistoric earthen mounds and other structures in the eastern United States was often denied by scientists and the general public during the 19th century. This occurred despite the eyewitness accounts by early European explorers. The extent of the mounds in Louisiana was ignored by archaeologists until the early decades of the 20th century. Since then, the study of mound sites in the state has contributed significantly to the archaeological knowledge of North America.

Since 1986, the authors have been involved in a series of research projects to investigate mound sites in Louisiana. Over 200 sites have been investigated in 17 parishes. The projects have relocated the mounds, updated the information on the sites, computed the volume of the mound fill, noted the site's geographical setting, provided photographs, and constructed computer graphics of mounds hidden by thick vegetation. Surface collections of artifacts have been made where possible and soil probes were placed in various portions of some sites to detect cultural remains or stratigraphy. The information gathered so far has allowed the formation of a detailed data base that has provided more information and allowed further analysis of these prehistoric features.

Key Words: archaeology, cartography, Indian mounds, Kleinpeter site, Marksville site.

> *I reached the landing place of the Natchez....The brother of the chief...invited me to the village....Halfway there I met the chief....*
>
> *We repaired to his cabin, which is raised to a height of 10 feet on earth brought thither, and is 25 feet wide and 45 long. Nearby are 8 cabins. Before that of the chief is the temple mound, which forms a round, a little oval, and bounds an open space about 250 paces wide and 300 long.* (Pierre Lemoyne, Sieur d'Iberville, quoted in Swanton 1911: 190-191).

Culture, Form, and Place: Essays in Cultural and Historical Geography, edited by Kent Mathewson, 1993. Geoscience and Man, vol. 32, pp. 33-56. Department of Geography and Anthropology, Louisiana State University, Baton Rouge, LA 70893-6010.

Introduction

Iberville's visit in 1700 to the Grand Village of the Natchez is the first re-corded description of that particular Indian settlement. It was not to be the last and the ways of the Natchez were well documented by several subse-quent European visitors. Among the customs, features, and practices mentioned in these accounts was the presence of artifically constructed earthen mounds that the Natchez had built to elevate their temples and residences of their leader: the Great Sun.

These were by no means the only mounds to be found in the Lower Mississippi Valley; they were simply some of the last to be inhabited by their builders. In fact, the raising of a variety of prehistoric earthen struc-tures by Native Americans throughout the eastern United States had oc-curred for centuries before the arrival of Europeans. These earthen forms served variously as tombs, as zoomorphic or anthromorphic effigies, as ceremonial enclosures, or as the pyramidal platforms described by Iber-ville. The creation of artificial platforms, however, had become a rare oc-currence by the time of Iberville's arrival on the Mississippi River.

Despite the early accounts describing Indian peoples associated with mounds, the reports were forgotten or ignored by the Anglo-Americans as they expanded westward in the late 18th and 19th centuries. The many mounds and other structures that dotted the Ohio River Valley and the Southeast were often attributed to peoples other than the Native Ameri-cans. Both serious and pseudo scholars offered a rather diverse list of can-didates for the builders of what were often rather elaborate constructions (Silverberg 1968). Perhaps the most popular explanation was a mysteri-ous, sophisticated, and extinct race of Moundbuilders who had been anni-hilated by the ancestors of the "savages" encountered by the whites. Many found it simply inconceiveable that the Indians, with whom the whites were in frequent conflict, could have had the organization and discipline necessary to erect these mounds.

The Moundbuilder myth continued in force among the educated and general public alike until near the turn of the century. In 1894, *The Report on the Mound Explorations of the Bureau of Ethnology*, by Cyrus Thomas, was published by the Smithsonian Institution. For the scientific community this landmark publication put to rest the Moundbuilder notion. The de-sign and extent of the research was quite an accomplishment considering that Thomas had a budget of only $5000, a paltry sum even in those times.

Thomas directed his team of investigators to study a sample of known mounds throughout the various regions of the eastern United States. For what must have been a variety of reasons, few mounds were investigated in Louisiana. The report comprises some 700 pages, yet only three sites in the state were mentioned, and their descriptions are cursory. Thomas's re-port gave the impression that Louisiana had a dearth of mounds compared to other regions of the country (fig. 1). This was erroneous. The state was, and continues to be, replete with hundreds of prehistoric earthen structures.

Although Thomas and his staff apparently ignored Louisiana's mounds, this was not the case with two investigators who worked in the state soon afterward: George Beyer and Clarence Bloomfield Moore. Beyer, a zoologist on the faculty of Tulane University, traveled throughout Louisiana in the 1890s as an ad hoc archaeologist. He was called upon to investigate many reports of prehistoric discoveries (Beyer 1896; 1898).

C. B. Moore was better known than Beyer and ranged farther afield in his efforts. Moore was largely self-funded, but operated under the auspices of the Philadelphia Academy of Natural Sciences. His private steam-

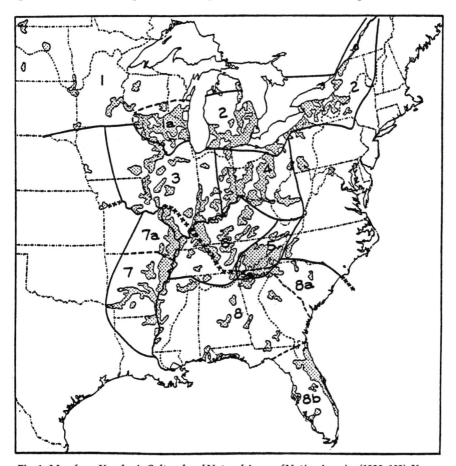

Fig. 1. Map from Kroeber's *Cultural and Natural Areas of Native America* (1939, 102). Kroeber mapped the distributions of earthen mounds from information provided in Cyrus Thomas's *Report on the Mound Explorations of the Bureau of Ethnology* (1894).

boat, the *Gopher*, traveled up and down rivers and streams throughout the southeastern United States. In Louisiana, his travels on the Mississippi, Red, Ouachita, Atchafalaya, and other drainages led him to dozens of sites. Most of these were mound sites, some of which he dug extensively. While his excavation techniques are often judged wanting by modern standards, his reports on the sites in Louisiana and other portions of the country were always finished in a timely fashion, with impressive illustrations of some of the artifacts that he discovered (Moore 1909, 1911, 1912, and 1913). His work continues to be frequently cited by archaeologists working today.

It was not until the 1930s with the advent of various federal relief projects, such as the Works Projects Administration, that scientific archaeology came into its own in Louisiana and much of the rest of the country. In those years, Louisiana State University and the Department of Geography and Anthropology were at the forefront of archaeological research. Investigators such as Fred B. Kniffen, James A. Ford, George I. Quimby, Gordon R. Willey and others all made substantial contributions to Louisiana, Lower Mississippi Valley, and North American archaeology in a variety of ways. Many of their efforts were aimed at the investigation of prehistoric sites that contained mounds and other earthen constructions. Their work established a chronology of prehistory for Louisiana and the Lower Mississippi Valley that is used to this day, although with many revisions and refinements (fig. 2).

As products of human labor, prehistoric earthen mounds can be regarded as artifacts. They can be measured, categorized, and analyzed as can other artifacts, such as projectile points and ceramics. This assumption underlay the work of investigators such as Ford and Willey (1941) and the fact that mounds seemed to differ in their shapes, functions, settings, and complexity was an important contribution to understanding North American prehistory.

Ford and Wiley proposed a temporal and functional dichotomy based on mound morphology. They argued that the earlier conical or dome-shaped mounds served as tombs or funerary monuments. In Louisiana, these conical mounds are generally associated with the Marksville period. The later mounds, which were usually flat-topped, served as platforms for temple structures or the residences of the societal elites. These mounds, of which there are a great variety, relate most frequently to the Coles Creek and Plaquemine periods. An early assumption in this analysis was that the existence of the mounds presupposed a substantial population that had a secure enough subsistence base to allow enough time to build the mounds. As a consequence, maize agriculture was often thought to be concomitant with mound construction, although there was no direct proof of its cultivation. Like many other archaeological conclusions, how-

STAGE	PERIOD	CULTURE	TIME INTERVAL
	Historic	Various Tribes	Present
	Mississippi	Natchezan	A.D. 1700
			A.D. 1600
		Mississippian	
			A.D. 1300
		Plaquemine	
Formative			A.D. 1000
	Coles Creek	Coles Creek	A.D. 850
			A.D. 700
	Baytown	Baytown/Troyville	
			A.D. 400
	Marksville	Hopewellian/Marksville	A.D. 200
			0
	Tchula	Tchefuncte	250 B.C.
			500 B.C.
	Poverty Point	Poverty Point	1000 B.C.
	Late Archaic		1500 B.C.
Archaic	Middle Archaic	Archaic	3000 B.C.
			5000 B.C.
	Early Archaic		6000 B.C.
	Late Paleo		
		Paleo-Indian	8000 B.C.
Lithic	Early Paleo		
	Pre-Projectile Point		10000 B.C.

Fig. 2. General prehistoric chronology for Louisiana and the Lower Mississippi Valley.

ever, this view of prehistory has changed and alternatives to agriculture are now being debated.

In addition to conical and platform mounds, the prehistoric Indians of Louisiana and North America built three other less common forms of earthen constructions. The first of these are earthen walls or enclosures. While these embankments may conceivably have been built for defensive purposes, they more likely served as boundaries to set a part a culturally sacred area. In Louisiana, earthen walls were used at several sites, with the Marksville and Troyville Sites most frequently noted. Another earthen construction is the effigy mound. The most often cited effigy mound in Louisiana is Mound A at the famous Poverty Point Site. This mound has been interpreted by some investigators as a bird in flight (Webb 1982).

Finally, mention should also be made of the concentric ridges at the Poverty Point Site. Measuring a half mile across, the purpose and original form of these ridges is the subject of some debate. Various excavations have shown them to consist of clay and occasional midden debris, with observable post molds. The ridges contain artifacts, and in one case may have been built over a pre-existing mound. It would appear that people lived atop these ridges, but precisely why the habitation took this peculiar configuration remains unclear (Ford and Webb 1956; Gibson 1986).

Mapping the Mounds of Louisiana

Since 1986, the authors have investigated and mapped a number of earthen mound sites throughout Louisiana. The ultimate intention is to map all extant mounds in the state, update information on them, compute the volumes of fill in the mounds, and provide computer graphics on those mounds hidden by vegetation. Surface collections of artifacts were made when possible, and soil probes were placed in various portions of the mounds and surrounding area to detect cultural remains or stratigraphy.

Computer graphics, using a combination of SYMAP and ASPEX programs on the mainframe computer at Louisiana State University, were derived from the contour maps. These images have proven to be decidedly more informative than a photograph or even a contour map. The authors and any future investigators of a particular site now have an accurate picture of how a particular mound looked when mapped and, from that, may have a better idea of the mound's original shape.

By 1991, the authors had investigated over 200 reported mound sites in 17 Louisiana parishes (Jones and Shuman 1986, 1987, 1988, 1989, 1990, 1991). Most are located in the central and southeastern portion of the state. The initial information on the mound sites was taken from the site files of the Louisiana Division of Archaeology. In some cases, however, local informants, made aware of projects through news releases, have reported previously unlisted sites. Additionally, many natural promontories such as pimple mounds or erosional remnants have been erroneously reported as Indian mounds. This project, in the course of tracking down all reported sites, attempted to correct any reporting errors.

Our mound mapping projects have accomplished several things. They have led to reinterpretations of archaeological data from some sites based on a new knowledge of mound morphology. The focus on the mounds as a form of monumental architecture has been given new impetus. Furthermore, these projects have provided the beginnings of a comprehensive data base on the geographical distribution of certain mound types during certain prehistoric periods. The sites, regions, and interpretations presented below are necessarily selective because of space limitations. However they provide representative examples of the accomplishments of the mound mapping investigations in Louisiana to date.

For those readers unfamiliar with techniques of archaeological reporting, the letter and number designations for the sites below indicate Louisiana's number (16) and abbreviations of the parishes (e.g. EBR-East Baton Rouge, AV-Avoyelles). The numbers given to the sites after the parish abbreviation reflect the order in which they were reported to the Louisiana Division of Archaeology. They do not reflect any ranking of importance based on a particular site's size or antiquity.

Problems of Mound Morphology

The Riddle Mounds (16WF4)

Situated on a terrace overlooking Thompson Creek in West Feliciana Parish, only one mound survives where five once were reported. George Beyer visited the site in the 1890s and made a sketch map which showed the plan of the site and seemingly idealized the mounds' form as square-based, truncated pyramids (fig. 3). Such a representation led to some initial suspicion during the mapping project about the accuracy of Beyer's depiction.

When the authors visited the site in 1986, the surviving mound, probably Beyer's Mound 4, was somewhat eroded and very overgrown. The contour map and computer graphic of this mound, however, seemed to indicate that Beyer's supposedly idealized drawing may have been more accurate than previously thought (fig. 4). Currently, very little is known about the Riddle Site other than the one-time existence of five mounds. Few artifacts or other data have been recovered that can give us an idea of when or by whom this interesting site was built. Further investigations at the site, including excavations, would undoubtedly reveal more.

The Clio Mound (16LV15)

The Clio Mound, on the lower Amite River in Livingston Parish, had been originally reported as a conical mound. This particular mound form, as previously noted, is generally associated with the Marksville period. The Clio mound has been heavily overgrown for decades and frequently vandalized. Richard Weinstein, then a graduate student at Louisiana State University, placed test units near the mound as part of the field work for his master's thesis. The artifacts from these units dated the site's occupation to the later Coles Creek period. This was regarded as something of an anomaly at the time (Weinstein 1974).

In 1987, the authors partially cleared the mound, and constructed the first contour map of the site. The computer graphic of this mound (fig. 5) revealed that it was a badly mauled platform mound with two corners of the base still perceptible underneath the vegetation. This morphology accorded much better with the artifacts recovered by Weinstein. The initial report of the mound's shape is understandable, however, given the heavy vegetation that covers the site.

Geographic Distribution of Mounds

The Peter Hill Site (16IV2), and other Bayou Grosse Tete Sites

At Mound A of the Peter Hill site in Iberville Parish, a photo (fig. 6) showed nothing of the mound due to heavy vegetation. The computer graphic (fig. 7), however, indicated that the mound survives beneath the vegetation as a well preserved platform mound with an adjacent borrow pit at the mound's northeast base. This configuration revealed the source of the mound's fill and indicated how little hauling was necessary during its construction. This also reflected the most common mound building technique used by the prehistoric Indians of Louisiana and other parts of North America. Quite simply, the Indians usually did not carry the fill very far in order to build up a mound.

The Peter Hill and Rosedale (16IV1) Sites, which consist of three mounds with Bayou Grosse Tete running between them, were probably a single site during the late prehistoric times (Kniffen 1938; Fredlund et al. 1982). These mounds are also part of a settlement pattern that apparently took root during Late Coles Creek and Plaquemine times in this part of Louisiana. Several mound complexes (fig. 8) seem to indicate a relatively dense prehistoric population that undoubtedly used Bayou Grosse Tete as a means of transportation. Fred Kniffen's 1938 survey of the prehistoric Indian mounds in Iberville Parish contrasted this density of mounds along Bayou Grosse Tete with the paucity of mound sites on nearby Bayou Maringouin. He found this to be somewhat enigmatic because Bayou Maringouin is at least as significant a drainage feature as Bayou Grosse Tete (Kniffen 1938).

The Eastern Edge of the Avoyelles Prairie Terrace

The famous Marksville Site (16AV1) was part of what Gerard Fowke, an investigator for the Smithsonian Institution in the 1920s, originally regarded as all one site. He located 20 earthen mounds and two enclosures with-

Fig. 3. George E. Beyer's map of the Riddle Mound (16WF4). *Source*: Beyer 1896.

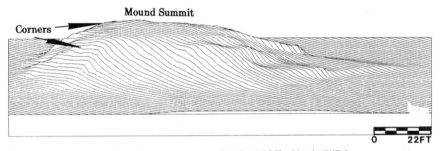

Fig. 4. Computer graphic of surviving mound at the Riddle Site (16WF4).

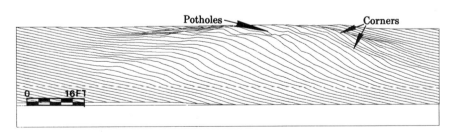

Fig. 5. Computer graphic of the mound at the Clio Site (16LV15).

Fig. 6. Photograph of Mound A at the Peter Hill Site (16IV2).

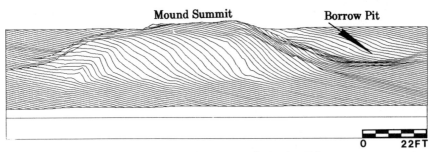

Fig. 7. Computer graphic of Mound A at the Peter Hill Site (16IV2).

in a space of less than two miles along the eastern edge of the Avoyelles Prairie terrace (fig. 9). Some of these earthen structures were on the summit of the prairie terrace, others on the floodplain at the base of the terrace, and one mound was on the slope between the base and the summit (Fowke 1928).

Later WPA investigations, however, showed that these 20 mounds were not one, but actually three separate sites. Fowke's Mound 1, a pyramidal platform mound on the edge of the terrace, was found to date from

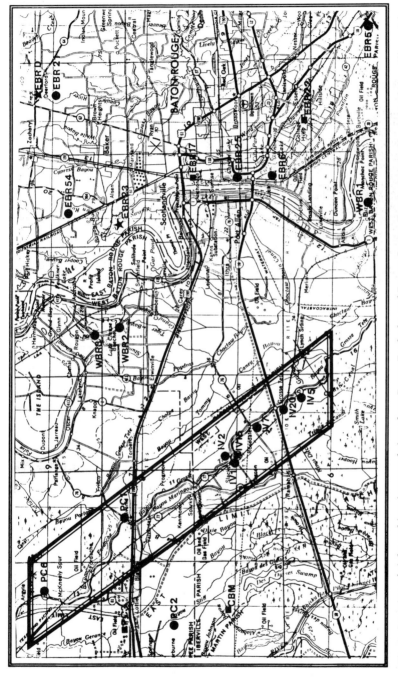

Fig. 8. Location of eight prehistoric mound sites along Bayou Fordoche and Bayou Grosse Tete in Pointe Coupee and Iberville parishes in black-bordered area.

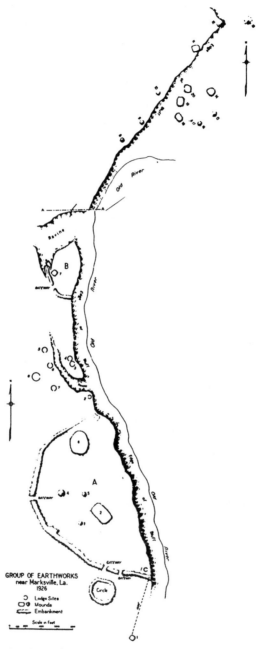

GROUP OF EARTHWORKS
near Marksville, La.
1926

Fig. 9. Gerard Fowke's map of earthen mounds and enclosures on the eastern edge of the
Avoyelles Prairie terrace in Marksville, Louisiana. *Source*: Fowke 1928.

the Plaquemine Period, A.D. 1200-1700. Mounds 2-11 and the enclosures, also on the terrace edge, were judged to date from the Marksville Period, 100 B.C. - A.D. 400. Fowke's mounds 13-20, however, were on the flood-plain and have been found to date primarily from the Coles Creek Period A.D. 500-1200 (Ford 1951).

From the several archaeological investigations that have been conducted at this concentration of mounds, it appears that very little or no re-occupation by succeeding cultures ever occurred. Separated by one thousand feet and over one thousand years, it remains a particularly interesting question as to why the Marksville Site, with its two enclosures and ten mounds, was not resettled by the later Plaquemine Culture that constructed Fowke's Mound 1. It is also worth noting that the mounds at the base of the terrace, Fowke's 13-20, are not isolated examples of floodplain occupation in eastern Avoyelles Parish during the Coles Creek Period. Rather there are several mound sites in this region that apparently flourished during the Coles Creek Period. This settlement pattern suggests that for some time throughout prehistory this portion of the state provided an attractive and stable environment that allowed prehistoric habitation without frequent inundation.

Enigmatic Characteristics of Specific Sites

The Kleinpeter Site (16EBR5)

Although no doubt known to nearby residents, the Kleinpeter Site was not reported to the scientific community until Fred Kniffen's visits to the area during his investigation of the physiography of Bayou Manchac (Kniffen 1935). He, in turn, reported the site to James A. Ford, then an archaeologist affiliated with LSU. Both Ford and Kniffen made collections and Ford made a sketch map of a portion of the site (fig. 10). The general remoteness of the site kept it in relative obscurity despite its proximity to Louisiana State University.

Several desultory scientific investigations, as well as occasional amateur efforts, were made at Klienpeter until the mid-1980s when the area became part of a golf course and residential development. At that time, the full extent of the site was realized and efforts were begun to preserve and further investigate it. These efforts eventually led to test excavations at the site in 1990 directed by the authors. This work provided evidence that the Kleinpeter Site was one of the more unique prehistoric sites in southeast Louisiana.

One of the striking discoveries during the 1990 field work was that the site appeared to be an exception to the technique of acquiring the mound fill from an adjacent borrow pit. The Kleinpeter Site's six mounds sit atop a Pleistocene terrace near the confluence of Bayous Fountain and Man-

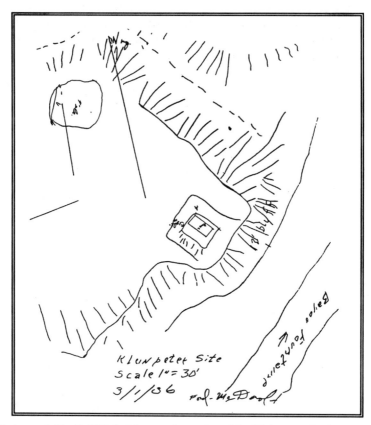

Fig. 10 . James A. Ford's 1936 sketch map of a portion of the Kleinpeter Site (16EBR5). The rectangle on the mound is a camp structure that once stood on what is now designated as Mound D at the site.

chac. This terrace, in turn, is covered by a thin mantle of loess material that covers so much of the eastern border of the Mississippi River valley. Today, no borrow pits are visible at the site, although prior to recent subdivision development, a small borrow pit may have been associated with the largest mound. In any event, this possible borrow pit could not have provided all the fill for the mounds. It appears, rather, that the fill was hauled from the banks of Bayou Fountain and up the terrace slope to be eventually formed into the mounds that exist today. Clearly, the backswamp clays on the bayou's banks provided a much more stable building material than the easily eroded loess from the top of the terrace (Jones et al. 1993)

Also, Mound D at Kleinpeter revealed a unique example of earthen architecture. As shown even by Ford's simplified sketch map of the mound, Mound D was built as a rectangular platform mound with one edge of the structure built out and over the natural slope of the terrace (figs. 11, 12). In other words, the terrace edge was sculpted to be incorporated into the truncated pyramidal form of Mound D. This produced a considerable promontory that provided a view of the confluence of Bayou Fountain with Bayou Manchac 400 feet to the east. Similarly, this same promontory was an impressive construction for any resident or visitor to the site, and could have enhanced the status of the mound's occupants.

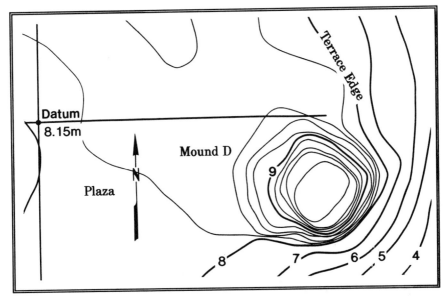

Fig. 11. Contour map of Mound D at the Kleinpeter Site (16EBR5).

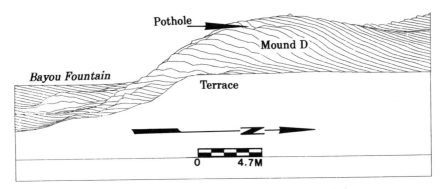

Fig. 12. Computer graphic of Mound D at the Kleinpeter Site (16EBR5).

The Marksville Site (16AV1)

As discussed earlier, one of the more impressive prehistoric sites in the Lower Mississippi Valley lies within the modern community of Marksville, Louisiana. Long noted by residents and once attributed to either the mythical Moundbuilders or Hernando De Soto's expedition, the Marksville Site is a unique group of earthworks situated along the eastern edge of the Avoyelles Prairie terrace. The most striking features of the site are the earthen embankments, with several gateways, that enclose conical and platform mounds.

The site was originally reported in a scientific context by Gerard Fowke of the Smithsonian Institute in 1927. It later became the object of more intensive archaeological investigation in 1933 by Frank Setzler of the Smithsonian who was assisted by a young James A. Ford. This project was important for several reasons. Among them, it was the first archaeological project conducted with the intent of providing work for the unemployed suffering through the Great Depression (Setzler and Strong 1936). The project was judged such a success that it served as a model for later Works Projects Administration (WPA) projects that did so much to develop archaeology throughout North America. The 1933 work also showed the Marksville Site had some sort of cultural affiliation with the Hopewell Culture of the Ohio Valley. Dating from around 100 B.C. to A.D. 400, sites of the Hopewell Culture are frequently associated with earthen enclosures such as the one at Marksville.

Until 1989, however, no detailed contour map of the entire Marksville Site was ever made. Gerard Fowke's rather generalized plan of the site was frequently used to illustrate any works concerning the site. The current mapping project spent several weeks mapping the Marksville Site, now a Louisiana State Commemorative Area. This map (fig. 13) shows that Fowke's map was accurate for the most part, except for the configuration of the southern terminus of the earthen enclosure.

This portion of the enclosure was photographed by Fowke in 1926 when it was cleared of vegetation (fig. 14). Currently, the southern portion of the Marksville Site earthworks is not on state property and is completely overgrown. The computer graphic (fig. 15) of this part of the site, however, reveals that the borrow pit for the southern part of the enclosure is still discernible and that the gateway noted by Fowke can also be relocated. The private landowners of this portion of the site have agreed not to disturb this portion of the earthworks and will allow further archaeological investigation. Perhaps some day the nature of this unusual archaeological feature will be better understood. Most archaeologists have assigned a ceremonial, rather than a defensive, function to such earthen embankments.

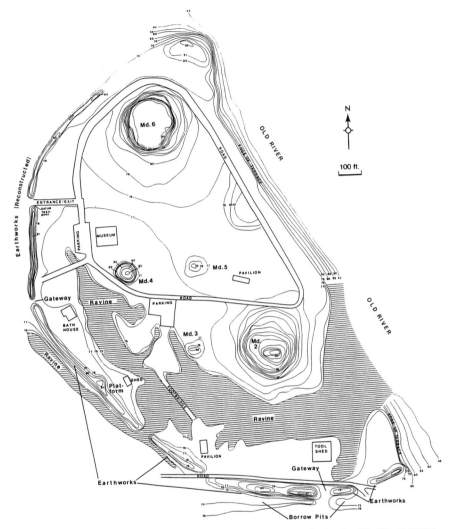

Fig. 13. Contour map of the earthen mounds and enclosure at the Marksville Site (16AV1).

Indications of Site Planning

Long a staple of Mesoamerican archaeology, large concentrations of stone architecture have been subjected to a variety of analyses to determine if there is a perceptible plan to the way various sites were originally laid out (e.g. Millon 1973). Such a program of investigation has been slow to develop in the Southeast and the Lower Mississippi Valley. Recently Clay Sherrod and Martha Rolingson (1987) of the Arkansas Archaeological Sur-

Fig. 14. Gerard Fowke's photograph of a portion of the earthen embankment at the Marksville Site (16AV1), showing the exterior moat 'at the gateway depicted at the bottom of figure 13, with Mound 2 in the background. *Source*: Fowke 1928.

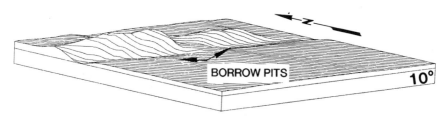

Fig. 15. Computer graphic of the southern portion of the earthen embankment at the Marksville Site, the same part as in Fowke's photograph. Note the borrow pit at the base of the feature. *Source*: Jones and Shuman 1989.

vey formulated an analysis of certain mound sites in the Lower Mississippi Valley. Based on their study of the Toltec Mound Group near Little Rock, Arkansas, planning was shown at various multi-mound sites by the distances between mounds. These distances were multiples of the so called Toltec Module: 47.5 meters. Most likely this measurement was anthropocentric, composed of measurements as simple as paces or body lengths.

Sherrod and Rolingson also noted the alignments of certain mounds in the Lower Mississippi Valley that might indicate the observations and commemoration of such celestial events as solar equinoxes and solstices. They further discussed the possibility of these alignments' having a calendric function. Sherrod and Rolingson have drawn the tentative conclusion that the use of alignments and module spacing at multi-mound sites in the Lower Mississippi Valley began during the Coles Creek period and continued into the Plaquemine period (A.D. 700/1700) (Sherrod and Rolingson 1987, 84).

During the mound mapping project, the Toltec Module has been applied to the maps of all multi-mound sites mapped. This application, however, has not yielded consistent results. The mounds at a site such as Greenhouse (16AV2) (fig. 16), appear to have been laid out in such a way as to reflect the use of the Toltec Module, while other multi-mound sites, such as the Kleinpeter Site, do not conform to the spacing module.

Another configuration of the multi-mound sites was noted by archaeologists before Sherrod and Rolingson's analysis. The seminal *Archaeological Survey of the Lower Mississippi Valley* by Philips, Ford, and Griffin (1951) noted several sites where four mounds were grouped

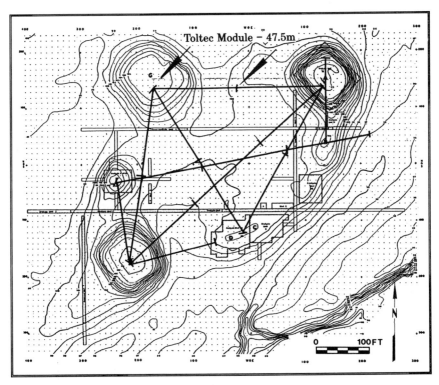

Fig. 16. Application of the Toltec Module to the Greenhouse Site (16AV2). Adapted from Ford 1951.

roughly in the cardinal directions around a plaza. Additionally, they noted that the westernmost mound was often the largest. They speculated from this that the western mound was topped by a ceremonial structure from which ritual observations were made eastward toward the rising sun across a plaza filled with the residents and visitors of the site (Philips, Ford, and Griffin 1951, 330). Examples of this mound arrangement have been noted at several sites during the mound mapping project, including the Kleinpeter Site (16EBR5) (fig. 17) and the Hoover Site (16TA5).

Conclusions

The prehistoric mounds of Louisiana have suffered a variety of fates since their prehistoric builders raised them. Many have been destroyed by agriculture, urban development, levee building, or highway construction. Ironically, others have been saved by their incorporation into the European and Black cultures of Louisiana. Many instances exist where homes, churches, and modern cemeteries have been built on or near the mounds. While these additions have obviously altered the mounds, they have also served to protect them from greater destruction.

Nevertheless, the mound mapping projects conducted by the authors have found that between a quarter and a third of mounds in Louisiana thus far investigated have already been destroyed. No laws currently exist to discourage the destruction of prehistoric mounds on private property. Therefore, there is a strong likelihood that some of the mounds studied by these projects will be destroyed in the near future. This is lamentable. Though archaeologists and geographers have been reconstructing the chronological and spatial distributions of prehistoric habitation in Louisiana over the past 50 years or so, the task is far from finished. It is a project subject to constant refinement and adjustment as more data becomes available. Clearly, archaeologists working in Louisiana and the Lower Mississippi Valley cannot study sites and discuss their significance if these sites have been destroyed. It is almost certain that the maps and reports produced during this series of investigations will be the only record of some sites.

In his report on the Indian Mounds of Iberville Parish, Fred B. Kniffen concluded with the hope that his mound investigating efforts could be extended to cover all of Louisiana's parishes (Kniffen 1938). While his hopes were not immediately realized, Dr. Kniffen's work contributed significantly to inspire the authors' efforts. It is hoped that the mound mapping investigations can continue to build a database for Louisiana archaeology and can raise the general public's interest in the state's extensive prehistoric heritage.

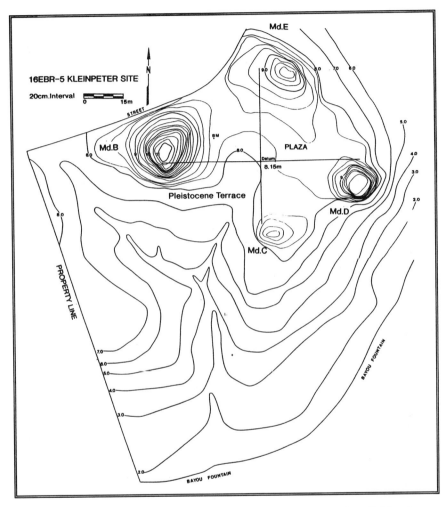

Fig. 17. Contour map of four of the six mounds at the Kleinpeter Site, where fieldwork was carried out in 1990.

Acknowledgements

Dozens of individuals and several organizations have contributed the efforts of the authors. The funding for the mapping of the prehistoric Indian mounds done thus far in Louisiana has come from the National Park Service and was administered by the Louisiana Division of Archaeology which is part of the state's Department of Culture, Recreation, and Tourism. The former Museum of Geoscience at Louisiana State University provided financial, logistical, and archival support for our projects. Several graduate students, most affiliated with the Department of Geography and Anthropology at LSU, braved the vicissitudes of field work in Louisiana and made contributions above and beyond their routine duties. Numerous volunteers, many who are members of the Louisiana Archaeological Society, also contributed their time and knowledge to our projects. Finally, and most essentially, we acknowledge the landowners of the various prehistoric mound sites we have studied.

References

Beyer, G. E. 1896. The mounds of Louisiana. *Publications of the Louisiana Historical Society* 1(4):12-32

——. 1898 The mounds of Louisiana. *Publications of the Louisiana Historical Society* 2(1):7-27

Ford, J. A. 1951. *Greenhouse: A Troyville-Coles Creek Period site in Avoyelles Parish, Louisiana.* Anthropological Papers of the American Museum of Natural History, vol. 44, pt. 1. New York.

Ford, J. A. and Wiley, G. 1941. An interpretation of the prehistory of the eastern United States. *American Anthropologist* n.s. 43(no. 3, pt. 1):325-363.

Ford, J. A. and Webb, C. H. 1956. *Poverty Point: A Late Archaic site in Louisiana.* Anthropological papers of the American Museum of Natural History, vol. 46, pt. l. New York.

Fowke, G. 1928. Archaeological investigations—II. *Forty-fourth Annual Report of the Bureau of American Ethnology,* pp. 399-450. Washington, DC.

Fredlund, R., Rivet, P., and Weinstein, R. 1982. Preliminary investigations at the Peter Hill site, 16IV2. Paper presented at the 8th annual meeting of the Louisiana Archaeological Society, Thibodaux, LA.

Gibson, J. 1986. *Earth sitting: Architectural masses at Poverty Point, northeastern Louisiana. Louisiana Archaeology, No. 13.* Bulletin of the Louisiana Archaeological Society. Lafayette, LA.

Jones, D. and Shuman, M. 1986. *East Baton Rouge, East Feliciana, and West Feliciana Parishes.* Archaeological Atlas and Report of Prehistoric Indian Mounds in Louisiana, vol. 1. Report on file with Louisiana Division of Archaeology. Baton Rouge, LA.

——. 1987. *Ascension, Iberville, Pointe Coupee, St. James and West Baton Rouge Parishes.* Archaeological Atlas and Report of Prehistoric Indian Mounds in Louisiana, vol. 2. Report on file with Louisiana Division of Archaeology. Baton Rouge, LA.

——. 1988. *Livingston, St. Helena, St. Tammany, Tangipahoa and Washington Parishes.* Archaeological Atlas and Report of Prehistoric Indian

Mounds in Louisiana, vol. 3. Report on file with Louisiana Division of Archaeology. Baton Rouge, LA.

——. 1989. *Avoyelles Parish, part I.* Archaeological Atlas and Report of Prehistoric Indian Mounds in Louisiana, vol. 4. Report on file with Louisiana Division of Archaeology. Baton Rouge, LA.

——. 1990. *Avoyelles Parish, part II.* Archaeological Atlas and Report of Prehistoric Indian Mounds in Louisiana, vol. 5. Report on file with Louisiana Division of Archaeology. Baton Rouge, LA.

——. 1991. *Acadia, Lafayette, and St. Landry Parishes.* Archaeological Atlas and Report of Prehistoric Indian Mounds in Louisiana, vol. 6. Report on file with Louisiana Division of Archaeology. Baton Rouge, LA.

Jones, D., Kuttruff, C., Shuman, M., and Stevenson, J. 1993. The Kleinpeter Site (16EBR5): The history and archaeology of a multicomponent site in East Baton Rouge Parish, Louisiana. Report submitted to the Louisiana Archaeological Conservancy, 1993. Baton Rouge, LA.

Kniffen, F. B. 1935. Bayou Manchac: A physiographic interpretation. *The Geographical Review* 25:462-466.

——. 1938. Indian mounds of Iberville Parish. *Reports on the geology of Iberville and Ascension Parishes.* Geological Bulletin No. 13, pp. 189-207. New Orleans, LA: Louisiana Geological Survey, Department of Conservation.

Kroeber, A. L. 1939. *Cultural and natural areas of North America.* Berkeley, California: University of California Press.

Millon, R. F. ed. 1973. *The Teotihuacan Map (Parts 1 and 2), Text and Maps.* Vol. 1 of *Urbanization at Teotihuacan, Mexico.* Austin, TX: University of Texas Press

Moore, C. 1909. Antiquities of the Ouachita. *Journal of the Academy of Natural Sciences of Philadelphia* 14:7-170.

——. 1911. Some aboriginal sites on the Mississippi River. *Journal of the Academy of Natural Sciences of Philadelphia* 14:365-480.

——. 1912. Some aboriginal sites on the Red River. *Journal of the Academy of Natural Sciences of Philadelphia* 14:481-664.

——. 1913. Some aboriginal sites in Louisiana and Arkansas. *Journal of the Academy of Natural Sciences of Philadelphia* 16:7-99.

Phillips, P., Ford, J. A. and Griffin, J. B. 1951. *Archaeological survey in the Lower Mississippi alluvial valley, 1940-1947.* Papers of the Peabody Museum of American Archaeology and Ethnology, Harvard University, vol. 25. Cambridge, MA.

Setzler, F. M. and Strong, W. D. 1936. Archaeology and relief. *The American Scholar* 5(1):109-117.

Sherrod, P. C. and Rolingson, M. A. 1987. *Surveyors of the ancient Mississippi valley.* Arkansas Archaeological Survey Research Series No. 28. Fayetteville.

Silverberg, R. 1968. *Mound builders of ancient America.* Greenwich, CT: New York Graphic Society, C. & O.

Swanton, J. R. 1911. Indian tribes of the Lower Mississippi Valley and adjacent coast of the Gulf of Mexico. *Bulletin of the Bureau of American Ethnology,* no. 43. Smithsonian Institute. Washington, D.C.

Thomas, C. 1985. *Report on the mound explorations of the Bureau of Ethnology.* Reprint of a 1894 publication. Washington D.C.: Smithsonian Institution.

Webb, C. H. 1982. *The Poverty Point culture.* Geoscience and Man, vol, 17. Baton Rouge, LA: School of Geoscience, Louisiana State University.

Weinstein, R. A. 1974. An archaeological survey of the lower Amite River, Louisiana. M.A. thesis, Louisiana State University, Baton Rouge, La.

Rethinking the "New Orthodoxy": Interpreting Ancient Maya Agriculture and Environment

B. L. Turner II

Abstract

Current perspectives on ancient Maya agriculture and agroecology reflect a period of intensive debate marked by claims and counterclaims that exceed the bounds of the evidence. The "swidden" or exceptionalist perspective dominated until the 1960s. It gave way to a "new orthodoxy" that envisioned the central lowland Maya as having had large populations supported by a variety of agricultures, many intensive, that utilized most of the habitats in the area. Special attention has been given to wetlands, common in the central lowlands, where vestiges of mounding and other manipulations have been found. The new orthodoxy favors anthropogenic and economic interpretations of these features, and, in some cases, made claims about their spatial significance that have yet to be adequately documented. Alternative views have also emerged, most grounded in an "ecocentric" position that ascribes a much more important role to environmental constraints and perturbations in the development of lowland Maya agriculture. Taken to extremes, these revisions suggest a revival of the exceptionalist position. These alternatives have taken three basic approaches: (i) studies of indicators of possible land degradation during Maya occupation; (ii) examinations of the distribution of wetlands for which evidence of past use is verified; and (iii) research on the origins of wetland fields and canals in northern Belize. Careful consideration of the evidence suggests that neither the new orthodoxy nor any of the alternatives has it quite right. Gaps and contradictions in the data remain.

Key Words: agricultural intensity, Maya wetlands, "new orthodoxy," swidden thesis

An orthodoxy dominates our thinking and research, directing both questions and interpretations, until it has exhausted its creativity, has been overwhelmed by anomalies, or simply has overstayed its welcome in a scholarly world that values progress and discovery. We then seek an alternative view to redirect our thinking. In the first flush of revision, both the faults of the old view and the merits of the new are exaggerated. Ultimately, though, researchers may revisit the old orthodoxy and find in it

Culture, Form, and Place: Essays in Cultural and Historical Geography, edited by Kent Mathewson, 1993. Geoscience and Man, vol. 32, pp. 57-88. Department of Geography and Anthropology, Louisiana State University, Baton Rouge, LA 70893-6010.

materials for modifying the new. Excesses of enthusiasm and rejection alike, occur as changes are proposed and resisted. This trait keeps the process of rethinking from being a purely cumulative one in which all insights of merit are preserved from the past. Often through further criticism and controversy, unjustly discarded elements of old theories are resurrected and placed within a new structure now capable of accounting for more evidence and complexity than its predecessors.

Research on ancient Maya agriculture appears to be following such a course. The past twenty years have witnessed a major change in our view of the Classic Maya civilization. No element of it has been more affected than that of its agroecological base. An environmental constraint-swidden thesis (old orthodoxy) has been replaced by an environmental opportunity-intensive agriculture thesis (new orthodoxy) with significant implications for Maya culture history in general. The new orthodoxy has been in turn questioned by a new round of studies of the environmental and agricultural base of the Maya previous to the Classic Period collapse (A.D. 800-1000). The development of the new orthodoxy may best be seen as a major shift or change — the kind that is conducive to exaggerated claims, in part because the evidence and arguments have not yet matured. The recent critiques of the new orthodoxy may be seen as part of the maturation process. Not surprisingly they too have succumbed to exaggeration.

In this paper I review the development of this new orthodoxy and the current revisions that are emerging, indicating that each has, to some degree, made claims in excess of the evidence. I also seek to demonstrate that these claims, in part, follow from the biases and predispositions of the researchers. Finally, I argue that if excessive claims can be avoided, this cyclical reconceptualizing will lead to a more sound understanding of Maya agroecology.[1]

The Old Orthodoxy

The long-held dominant view of the lowland Maya civilization, from its origins until its collapse, is best characterized as exceptionalist. Despite the ancient Maya's clear achievements in art, architecture, mathematics, calendrics, and writing, scholars resisted placing them on a par with their peers among ancient civilizations. The Classic Maya were thought to represent an exception to many theories of social, state, and agricultural development (e.g., Steward et al. 1955).[2] This exceptionalist view followed partly from the state of the evidence at that time, but also from a perspective that equated agricultural complexity with specific levels of urban and state development. The lowland Maya were thought not to have reached the level of development found in the highlands of Mexico, particularly in the Basin of Mexico.

Central to the exceptionalist position were assumptions about the agricultural and environmental base of the civilization, particularly within the central Maya lowlands of northern Petén, Guatemala, and Belize, and southern Quintana Roo and Campeche, Mexico. The civilizations elsewhere in Mesoamerica and the Andes had been sustained by a variety of intensive and sophisticated types of agriculture, including hydraulic cultivation, but the Classic Maya were thought to have relied primarily on slash-and-burn cultivation (*milpa*) and other fallow-based systems that required spatial rotation or relocation of farmland. Beyond the sparse attention given to the subject of Maya agriculture and its possible alternatives, a priori beliefs about agroecology in the lowland tropics cemented this view. It was further reified in various theories of state evolution in Mesoamerica (Turner 1981; Turner and Harrison 1978, 361). As a result, evidence for non-swidden systems in the Maya past, despite references in the earlier literature, was largely dismissed (Hammond 1978; Turner 1978, 17).

Through the 1960s, then, the Maya were viewed by some, perhaps most, as a "second class" civilization, lacking true cities and state organization, and situated in an environment that impeded the type of agricultural development capable of sustaining the kinds and level of social activities that emerged in the highlands (Mathewson 1977).

The New Orthodoxy

During the 1960s, however, some Mayanists began to turn their attention in earnest to issues of settlement and population, producing rather startling results. Repeated examinations revealed large populations sustained over long periods of time throughout the Maya realm, particularly in the central lowlands (Culbert and Rice 1990). "Rural" settlement studies produced estimates in excess of 100-150 people/km^2, and studies of "ceremonial centers" produced figures above 1,000 people/km^2.[3] These results undercut the credibility of the swidden thesis. Its dominance made it difficult to abandon, but a number of alternatives began to emerge in the literature. Some speculated that special food crops (e.g., root crops and "Maya breadnut" [*Brosimum alicastrum*]) might have provided exceptional caloric return within an overall swidden system (Bronson 1966; Puleston 1971). Others focused on cultivation techniques other than slash-and-burn that the Maya could have employed (Wilken 1971). Interestingly, earlier reports in the literature pointed to evidence of non-slash-and-burn systems (e.g., Lundell 1933), but this information was ignored as it did not conform to the then current orthodoxy.

In the early 1970s, the geographer Alfred Siemens identified ground patterns throughout the wetlands of northern Belize and southern Quintana Roo and Campeche that subsequently proved to be agricultural features (Siemens 1990). Following the leads of several members of the 1973 Río Bec Ecological Project and of Siemens, this author documented the presence of relic terraces and wetland fields in the Campeche-Quintana Roo area (Turner 1974; 1983). These same wetland fields were found also by Peter Harrison (1977). Interdisciplinary teams were formed specifically to address the wetland field issue (Siemens and Puleston 1972; Turner and Harrison 1981; 1983).[4]

These discoveries led to an explosion of research on relic agricultural features in the Maya lowlands (Harrison and Turner 1978), including terraces (Dunning 1992; Healy et al. 1983; Turner 1983) and wetland fields (Harrison 1990; Lambert and Arnason 1983), as well as documenting the possible roles of tree and shrub crops found in orchard-garden or agroforestry systems (Gómez-Pompa 1987; Turner and Miksicek 1984; Wiseman 1978). By the mid-1980s, the overall evidence of the types, distribution, and dating of ancient agricultural features in the Maya lowlands surpassed that for the Basin of Mexico (Turner 1983).

A new orthodoxy emerged from many sources, driven by a number of aims but holding as its most common thread an indifference to the old orthodoxy. Several common themes could be found within the body of this research, however.[5] The first reinterpreted the agroecological base of the central lowlands. It was recognized that region is dominated by quality soils for agriculture — the very group of soils that have historically sustained intensive cultivation elsewhere in the tropics (Sanchez and Buol 1975) — and that in its general character, this human tropical domain differed significantly from the textbook case of species diversity (forest), habitat redundancy, and the potential for the laterization process (Turner 1985; Wiseman 1978). In short, the analogue of *tierra firma* within Amazonia was not applicable to the central Maya lowlands. The second theme focused on the abundant evidence of relic agricultural features as interpreted through an emerging theory of induced intensification.

Induced intensification traces the change in systems of cultivation (and their level of output per unit area and time) to subsistence and peasant behavior. The theoretical traditions are deep and cannot be detailed here (for a review see Brush and Turner 1987). To simplify, this approach examines the behavior of farmers in socioeconomic situations not too distant from those in which the Maya apparently operated, and link this behavior to cultivation practices as a response to the demands for agricultural production placed on the farmer, but as mediated by the environmental opportunities and constraints (Brush and Turner 1987; Kates, Hyden, and Turner 1993). For the Maya, an induced intensification model indicates that as land pressures (from population growth, trade, or elites) mounted for agricultural goods, a series of intensification and expansion practices in agriculture followed, including the deforestation of uplands, the use of water, soil, and soil-nutrient retention devices, the evolution of agroforestry towards orchard-gardens, and the manipulation of wetlands to provide land for planting (Turner 1990b). The temporal sequence of these changes would, of course, vary by locale and the opportunities that each afforded.

The new orthodoxy that emerged during the 1970s generally played upon these themes and evidence, leading to a perspective in which the ancient Maya, at least in the central lowlands, were not the odd civilization out. Rather large populations over extended areas (Culbert and Rice 1990) were supported by a variety of agricultures, many intensive by any definition. To be sure, the new orthodoxy has not been monolithic, and disagreement exists as to the extent that agriculture was intensified and the function of the relic systems identified (e.g., Dunning 1992; Fedick and Ford 1990; Lambert, Siemens and Arnason 1984; Pohl 1985; Siemens 1978; 1990). But, on the whole, the new orthodoxy envisioned a central Maya lowlands considerably different from that described by the preceding orthodoxy. This new view of Maya agriculture promoted, and in turn was prompted by, a flood of revisionist thinking about the Maya. It has also been strongly supported by breakthroughs in iconography and settlement studies that provide new clues about the level of urban function and state organization that existed before the collapse of the Classic civilization (Clancy and Harrison 1990). I do not wish to enter this realm of the discussion, which is less pertinent to the roles played by geographers. The important point is that revisionist zeal extended the new orthodoxy beyond its empirical limits. Suddenly, claims were made for evidence of *chinampa* cultivation everywhere in the central lowlands, and the populations estimated for the central area became large by way of any comparison. Many of these and other claims were offered only as food for thought, but they also provided easy targets for criticism.

The New Orthodoxy Assailed

Every view begets a counter view and the new orthodoxy is no exception. The counterarguments proposed by those engaged in field work in the Maya region follow two basic paths, although both belong to a tradition in nature-society research that grants nature a very strong role. The first stems from a broader concern for reconstructing past environments, and in almost every case links environmental reconstructions to Maya prehistory — either by assigning natural (climate) change as a cause of the rise or fall of the lowland civilization, or by ascribing to the Maya some form of severe environmental degradation, with the implication that the lowlands were a particularly fragile environment or succumbed to unsustainable human pressures.[6] The second path questions the initial interpretations of Maya use of wetland fields, offering a much more limited geographical range and a different agricultural interpretation in which environmental conditions played a strong inhibiting role.[7]

Environmental Constraints

The environmental path is difficult to trace in detail because it is interwoven with the large set of paleoecological work in the Maya region. Much of this work is not aimed at the central issues examined here, although it is intended to thrust environmental considerations more to the forefront of Maya prehistory.[8] This goal is welcomed with several cautions: (i) that we not forget that environmental reconstructions are fraught with problems, as are cultural reconstructions; (ii) that we not treat them any less critically because they are the work of "natural scientists" who also carry biases and uncertainties into their interpretation; and (iii) that we remember it is extremely difficult to determine conclusively the source of environmental change for a landscape once heavily occupied for millennia, especially in the Maya area (Turner 1985).

Here I focus on the kinds of environmental interpretations that have the effect, intended or not, of questioning the suitability of the Maya lowlands or the ability of the Maya to sustain intensive cultivation over the long run (e.g., Fedick and Ford 1990), thereby promoting the view of a fragile environment that was mishandled by its users. Recent work from the Copan Valley, Honduras, is illustrative.

Copan was the major southeastern city-state of the Classic lowland Maya culture. It occupies one of the largest of a series of small pockets of highly fertile alluvial soils carved by the Río Copan into the foothills of the highlands. The environmental setting is distinct from the central Maya lowlands, including the presence of alluvial soils replenished by flooding. Despite this situation, Copan was one of the first Classic period Maya centers to collapse.

Recent palynological work there has painted a picture of Maya land use impacts that feeds into the exceptionalist perspective (Abrams and Rue 1988). The pollen interpretations are based primarily on a single core taken from the Aguada de Petapilla, a small peat bog located in the foothills to the north and west of Copan.[9] This study dated the bottom of the core to the Terminal Classic period and found the standard pollen indicators of deforestation and land disturbance, although little maize pollen was found anywhere but in the topmost or most recent segments of the core.

The conclusion that Abrams and Rue draw is consistent with virtually all other such studies from the Maya realm; viz. that the Maya significantly altered the original landscape's cover from forest to open vegetation, a change produced by all large agrarian populations inhabiting a semi-tropical forest zone for an extended period of time. From this important but conventional find, they derive a series of speculations about the relationships among the need for wood fuels, the ultimate deforestation of the upland pine forests to meet this need, and the possibility that soil erosion of the acidic pine soils followed, sufficient to diminish valley bottom agriculture and hence to precipitate the collapse of Copan.

Similar arguments have flourished throughout the history of Maya studies, largely nurtured by specialists predisposed towards environmental interpretations of human history, from perspectives that need to find either the Maya lowlands environmentally constraining or the Maya managerially and technologically incompetent, or from those who seek simple explanations for complex phenomena.[10] Of course, the mystery of the Classic Period collapse and depopulation provides a context conducive to arguments of this kind.

I am wary of arguments that give primacy to environmental causes over those of human or nature-society interactions origins for a number of reasons, including the fact that environmental change or degradation alone as a collapse agent has rarely, if ever, been demonstrated for civilizations comparable to the Maya, and the tendency of the lay community to rally around such simple explanations. All land uses alter the environment, and generally the more intensive this use, the greater the alteration, even transformation, that takes place. We should expect, then, to find evidence of human-induced environmental change — even major change — in any area once heavily occupied. Why, then, are similar land uses and pressures in similar environments associated with different cultural trajectories over the long run (e.g., collapse or sustainability)? The answer usually lies in the sociopolitical ability and willingness to manage the use-environment relationship adequately (see Whitmore et al. 1990).

There is strong evidence of significant deforestation and vegetative disturbance throughout the lowland Maya domain at very early dates, perhaps 1000 BC or earlier (see Brenner, Leyden and Binford 1990; Wiseman 1978; 1985; 1990). These changes were a fact of life with which the Maya apparently coped (successfully, in terms of the overall trajectories of material wealth and population) for some 2,000 years or more before the collapse. To implicate environmentally-induced, catastrophic consequences in the lowland Maya collapse is: (i) to conclude, as with crude Malthusianism, that the Maya surpassed their technological capacities in context of the lowland environments; or (ii) that a sudden climatic change so altered the environment that the social and technological capacity of the Maya to adjust was surpassed.

The role of climatic change cannot be adequately evaluated at this time, given the speculative nature of the evidence.[11] Environmental degradation themes are likewise difficult to evaluate, not so much because of the evidence of deforestation, soil nutrient depletion, and so forth, but because of our inability to determine the impacts of such change on Maya society. This problem arises not only because of chronological controls, but because of the paucity of comparable evidence from similar environments. The Maya were successful over the millennia, they occupied a region of quality soils, and they significantly transformed their environments, even — from a purely ecological perspective — degraded them. How we interpret this evidence probably says more about the biases of the researcher than about the status of the evidence at this time (Turner 1990b; 1991). The role of environmental problems wrought by human action or climate change cannot and should not be dismissed. Environmental problems were undoubtedly profound for the Maya, but they also appear to have been within the capacity of the Maya to manage so long as the socioeconomic and political atmosphere necessary to do so was maintained.

Wetland Agriculture

Two main issues have been raised about elements of the new orthodoxy as applied to wetland agriculture: the spatial distribution of such cultivation, and the temporal and functional components of its use.[12] The former issue is exemplified by the implications of Pope and Dahlin's (1989) assessment of the spatial and ecological context of wetland fields; the latter, by the study of wetland fields on Albion Island, Belize, by the Río Hondo project (Pohl 1990a). Both works provide important insights for interpreting Maya prehistory.

Distribution of Wetland Agriculture. Controversial evidence from remotely sensed imagery, including side-looking radar, revealed (or were perceived by some to reveal) large lines across virtually all Maya wetlands. These features have been interpreted as canals associated with wetland agriculture (Adams, Brown, and Culbert 1981). I am unaware of specific signatures in wetlands on this imagery that have been ground verified as canals, although there was a propensity for observed lines to correspond to wetlands known to have fields and canals.[13] Armed with this intriguing but speculative find and its implications, some Mayanists leaped to the conclusion that wetland agriculture dominated the Classic Maya production systems in the central lowlands or that substantial proof of its dominance everywhere had been demonstrated.[14]

The patterns of wetland fields and canals have been confirmed on the ground in an extensive arc surrounding northern Petén, from central Belize through southern Quintana Roo and on the western side of the central uplands in southwestern Campeche (Pohl 1990b; Turner 1978). With the exception of the recent discoveries at Río Azul (Culbert, Levi and Cruz 1990), no ground confirmations of wetland cultivation have been made within Petén proper or the central uplands extending into the Río Bec region.[15] Nevertheless, the spatial extent of ground patterns (probably wetland fields and canals) in northern Belize but especially in southern Quintana Roo, observed by Siemens, is significant (see Fig. 1.2 in Pohl 1990b).

Pope and Dahlin's examination of several kinds of imagery concludes that there are no "real" canals on the radar imagery and no evidence for wetland fields in Petén.[16] This study is correct, I believe, in the reading of the imagery relative to the spatial (and perhaps environmental) locations of ground confirmations (but see Adams et al. 1990). Pope and Dahlin go on, however, to make their own claims about the distribution of wetlands — grounded in a strongly environmental logic — that are likewise controversial, and they cast this work in a context that is suspect.

This context involves the manner in which the problem is set up. A simplified (and, I suggest, false) image of the new orthodoxy is presented, drawn from a definition provided by an anonymous reviewer of their paper, disregarding the more cautious and complex assessments of this orthodoxy. Indeed, this very literature is cited (p. 89) as supporting the definition used — that the new orthodoxy is based on the use of wetlands everywhere during the Classic Period.[17] The image created, therefore, is one in which the validity of the new orthodoxy hinges on the existence of wetland agriculture throughout Petén and/or acceptance of the distribution of wetland fields as interpreted from the radar imagery. This, of course, provides an image vulnerable to the very criticism that Pope and Dahlin provide.

After a discussion of the diversity of wetlands in the Maya realm, they divide those wetlands that contain relics of agriculture into two basic types that retain water (or high groundwater tables) throughout the year — riverine or floodplain wetlands and swamps (perennial) — and conclude that only these types of surface-water relationships in wetlands were suitable for cultivation by the Maya. These two types of wetlands, they argue, do not occur in Petén or the central uplands in general, presumably because wetlands at elevation (perhaps ≥ 100 m) are involved with extreme water table flux.[18] These kinds of wetlands are called seasonal swamps, while those with high water tables are called perennial swamps.[19]

The Bajo de Morocoy (about 70-85 m asl) in Quintana Roo and a small *bajo* near Río Azul in Petén are critical to the Pope-Dahlin assessment because Maya use of them has been identified, and both lie at elevations that are much higher, and may have ground water fluxes much larger, than wetlands in Belize. Morocoy has an extensive system of relic canals and fields visible from the air through vegetation and soil moisture responses. A brief trenching effort there in 1980 reached depths of 1.5 meters before exposing water (Gliessman et al. 1985), but others report even deeper water tables for the bajos of the area (see Adams et al. 1990).[20] Morocoy also experiences major seasonal fluxes in surface and ground water, although the underlying clays do not desiccate. Importantly, the vegetation (species composition) of the *bajo* seems much closer to the kind described by Pope and Dahlin for seasonal swamps (as in Petén) than for perennial swamp (as in northern Belize). The Morocoy evidence not only indicates wetland use at elevations much higher than in northern Belize, but in contexts where the seasonal fluxes in ground water were considerable.

The Río Azul case involves a recent find from an *escoba bajo* near the site of BA-20, well within the Petén upland zone, although this wetland is perhaps situated at no more than 120 m (P. Culbert, pers. com.). The Río Azul project has identified drainage networks in this wetland, interpreted as canals (Culbert, Levi, and Cruz 1990). Interestingly, these are not visible from the air, but were identified from trenches placed across the *bajo*. As in the Morocoy case, the scale of the seasonal ground water flux is not known, but it was not encountered in the trenches made by the project. This find, of course, is geographically within Petén proper, is above 100 m (msl), and clearly desiccates, but has vegetation characteristics thought to be related to perennially wet conditions.

What are we to make of this evidence and these arguments? First and foremost, few authorities doubt the geographical distribution of ground patterns confirmed thus far in the central Maya lowlands (fig. 1). Second, the Pope-Dahlin effort to relate these confirmations to wetland hydrologies is reasonable, but the evidence may be too ephemeral at this time to make strong conclusions about proposed associations; and these associations, when better understood, may reveal that a wider range of ground water conditions was used by the Maya than is implied in the perennial swamp-seasonal swamp division. And third, as the Río Azul evidence suggests, the indicators of wetland use may not always be visible from the air.

We cannot adequately typologize wetlands based on ground water characteristics at this time, owing to the paucity of the data. At best, vegetation may be used as a crude surrogate indicator, but as the Morocoy and Río Azul evidence indicates, the validity or accuracy of this surrogate is in doubt. We are not certain of the precise soil moisture characteristic to which the vegetation is responding in these wetlands. It may be the scale of the groundwater flux, as Pope and Dahlin suggest, or it may be related to the length of time that the rooting zone is inundated or desiccated. What seems clear is: (i) that seasonal swamps (wetlands) in which the water table drops well below the rooting zone of most cultivars are found outside

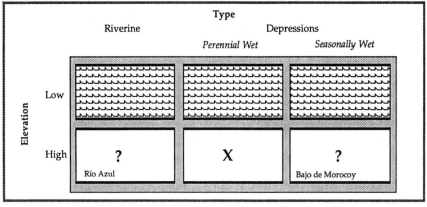

Low = between the uplands and the sea   ? = ephemeral evidence/on edges of uplands
High = within the uplands proper   x = no evidence yet

= confirmed wetland fields or patterns thereof   = no wetland fields or patterns confirmed

Fig. 1. General types of wetlands, and the evidence of wetland fields and canals in Maya lowlands.

of the Petén interior (e.g., Morocoy) and some of these contain ground patterns of fields and canals; and, (ii) ground evidence for wetland features within the Petén interior may be emerging.[21]

It is puzzling, from a human perspective, that stronger evidence for wetland use has not been found in the central uplands (and Petén). Land pressures there were simply too high to have allowed 40-60 percent of the land area under wetlands to have been unused for food production, and ancient Petén farmers were presumably well aware of wetland cultivation. Perhaps the hydrological problems were indeed too great, as Siemens (1978) and Pope and Dahlin have suggested, but perhaps, too, the use of these depressions differed in some way from those at lower elevation (and with ground patterns), precisely because of their hydrological conditions, leading to a surface signature that is not readily detectable. The Río Azul evidence provides a possible clue in this regard.

Origins and Functions of Wetland Agriculture. The final set of questions raised about the new orthodoxy centers on the proper interpretation of those Maya wetland fields that have been verified on the ground. To examine this challenge requires a brief review.

Much of the new orthodoxy in the case of Maya wetland use reflects cultural-ecological perspectives. This outlook assumes induced intensification and environmental opportunities as previously noted. Wetland fields and canals are seen primarily as a response to land pressures that made the labor investment worth it. This line of reasoning also presumes that the quality, non-inundated upland soils would have been used first over wetland soils, most of which are massive clays. This same logic implies that once wetlands were developed for use, the presence of water in canals would have allowed the cultivation of wetland fields throughout the year with the exception of extreme water levels, or most of the year save during high water. Hence, wetlands were transformed into agricultural lands of major importance, although organic fertilization and other procedures were required to cope with problems of soluble salts and aeration. The chronological evidence for the system at Pulltrouser Swamp — perhaps the most exhaustive and visible work on wetland fields associated with the new orthodoxy — indicated possible "edge of the swamp" use during the Preclassic Period. By conventional archaeological dating of artifacts within the fields and the chronology of settlement occupation around the swamp, however, the best case that could be made for complete use of the system with mature field construction was for the Late Classic Period.[22]

The interpretations of the construction of the fields and canals have been more problematic. At least two forms of fields were identified at Pulltrouser Swamp: those that occur on the shore of the swamp and those in the swamp proper. The shore fields (channelized fields) were created by the excavation of canals or channels into limestone bedrock or *sascab* of the mainland, in some cases creating "islands" where canals cut off a field from the mainland. These fields show an upland surface horizon resting on *sascab* (Turner and Harrison 1981; 1983).

In the swamp proper, however, a surface horizon rests on a mottled, gray (or upper) clay, which itself rests on a thin buried soil underlain by an old, apparently pre-Maya surface (perhaps the remains of a lake bed). Botanical indicators of vegetation disturbance and agriculture were found in the grey clay, but not in the materials below the buried soil. Importantly, this upper clay does not occur everywhere in the swamp. Large segments of the western Pulltrouser arm lack it and, significantly, lack any surface features of canals and fields; here vertisols reach to *sascab*, presumably bedrock for this segment of the swamp. As we shall see below, the interpretations of the upper clay have become central in the debate over Maya wetland agriculture.

Our original finds from the excavations in the upper clays at Pulltrouser were: that the mottling may have been created by limestone nodules (based on pH field tests); that large chunks of limestone were occasionally present; that chronologically different artifacts were vertically mixed; and, based on laboratory tests and contrary to our expectations, that the gray material was not predominantly clay. Added to our paleoecological and settlement data, we concluded that the surface patterning of fields and canals had been created by piling the soils from the canals with the addition of upland soils.

Subsequently, the Río Hondo project demonstrated that we had erred in our soil analysis. The mottling we reported was a gypsum precipitate, which, if removed before analysis, proved the material in that zone to be the massive clays expected for this environment. Revised tests based on new data for the 1981 Pulltrouser Swamp project confirmed these assessments, providing further evidence of the Río Hondo project's contention that the upper clays are likely to be a depositional material. The origin of gypsum precipitate is a bit more problematic, however. The source of gypsum lies at depth, probably associated with the development of the limestones there, and is transported in solution. The precipitate in the upper clays may have developed either in situ during the deposition or as a result of the wetland use. In the latter case, canaling increased the vertical range of the annual flux of water within the adjacent fields, providing a zone in the upper clays that desiccated enough to precipitate the gypsum. This revised evidence raises important questions about this particular wetland system, to which I shall return.

The Río Hondo project (Pohl 1990a; also Antoine, Skarie, and Bloom 1982; Bloom et al. 1983) and, to a lesser extent, work at Cobweb Swamp (Valdez, Jacob, and Gifford, 1991) have led to very different interpretations about the use of wetlands.[23] The former project focused its research on Albion Island — created by the bifurcation of the Río Hondo — and the riverine swamps located there. The main wetland-field site of study was located at the modern village of San Antonio, all of it 100 m or less from the river and within the small floodplain of its eastern branch.

Puleston (1978), who began the original excavation, reported peat at the bottom of his profile, overlain by gray clays and marls through which canals or channels had been cut. He assumed that the clays, including those near the surface, had been cultivated throughout Maya occupation of the area, although this use was an important Preclassic practice that may have significantly influenced Maya settlement decisions at that time. The later project reevaluated this work with additional evidence and a different perspective to derive a much different picture. The interpretations specific to the San Antonio fields follow.

- The area had been deforested very early during the Preclassic Period and before the beginnings of wetland cultivation.
- A peaty material or organic rich clay was present at the field site (subsequently buried by clays).
- Ditches were cut through this material, some parallel to the Hondo, others perpendicular.
- Water levels began to rise, perhaps during the Late Preclassic, owing either to sea level rise or to increased precipitation.

- Prolonged inundation deposited first marl and then soluble-salt-rich clays over this surface.
- An unidentified natural process kept the ditches cleared during the depositional period, or the depositional process retained the impression of the ditches.
- Evidence for agriculture is strong in the lower, pre-deposition material, and weaker in the clay depositional zone nearer the surface.
- The population of the island during the Late Classic and Terminal periods was extremely large.

From this, Pohl, Bloom, and Pope (1990) offer a very different interpretation from Puleston's and Pulltrouser project's work. Initial wetland cultivation at Albion Island began in the Preclassic Period, perhaps as early as 1000 BC during a period of relatively low land use pressures in which swidden cultivation dominated the uplands. The floodplain was cultivated by cutting ditches into the peat or the organically rich clays present at that time to facilitate flood recessional agriculture. Field raising was, at best, limited to a few centimeters. As water levels began to rise for whatever reasons, the wetland system had to be abandoned because of the poor quality of the deposited clays for cultivation and the deposition of marl.[24] A surface expression of the buried system was retained, largely due to the underlying ditches (one meter or more below the surface). Perhaps in the Late or Terminal Classic, the system was resurrected, apparently on the poor-quality clays that were now on the surface.

This is an intriguing thesis in which almost all the evidence is interpreted with an environmental bias — especially focusing on the quality of the depositional clays for cultivation. The evidence for Preclassic use of the buried soil is strong. What occurred above it, in the clay deposition, remains controversial. I cannot detail all the technical and interpretive issues that must be resolved to support this interpretation, but I can highlight those most important to this discussion.

First is the apparent inconsistency of positing low land use pressures in the Preclassic with evidence of major deforestation, inferring that such major disturbance indicates extensive slash-and-burn cultivation.

Second, the strong evidence for cultivation of the buried organic clay and peaty zone does not necessarily imply a flood-recessional system.[25] The river bank here has virtually no grade, so that canals could not have assisted drainage much beyond the natural flux of the river. Also, flood-recessional systems typically involve only canals or ditches aligned perpendicular to the contour to expedite drainage. The apparent network of relic ditches and canals at the Albion Island site and elsewhere in the Belize-Quintana Roo area are quite diverse in their orientation, many in fact paralleling the contour.[26]

Third, evidence from the upper clays appears to be inconsistent with the interpretations given, or can be made consistent only by stretching to the limits the capacity of natural processes to have created it. Three points are key.

(i) The marl deposition above the buried soil does not appear to exist over every field, nor is the evidence sufficient to determine if its distribution over the fields is consistent with the presumed conditions that led to its deposition (shallow water, hence its absence in the former ditches or canals).

(ii) Artifacts in the upper clays were apparently mixed chronologically (not reported in the project's published work) and, to some, the canal stratigraphy displayed a coherency different from the fields (Pohl, Bloom, and Pope 1990, 200). Mixing suggests reworking of the clay, presumably from cultivation in the wetlands as the material was deposited. The project argues, however, that the artifact mixing was a product of the depositional process — materials washing off the adjacent uplands. This interpretation requires careful consideration of the provenience and dating of the artifacts found, for if the mixing is a result of deposition alone, then those portions of the stratigraphy associated with the onset of the deposition should contain no cultural materials later than the Late Preclassic or Early Classic, and Late Classic and Terminal Classic artifacts should appear in the higher layers of the clay.[27] To my knowledge, such details have not yet been provided by the project.

(iii) The project asserts that the proposed distinction between the deposition in the canal and that on the fields is an illusion (p. 200) and that the profile and surface expressions of the canals were created by natural processes that impeded uniform deposition of the clays, leaving swales in the ditches that give an appearance of surface canals. This uneven deposition is not explained as a result of Maya clearing of the ditches as the deposition took place.

Fourth, many of these interpretations appear to follow from a belief that the Maya would have avoided the use of the poor-quality upper clays or did not have the ability to cope with the surface water conditions that led to the deposition.[28] But these same "poor"-quality clays may have been used during the very late phases of occupation, a suggestion of the project that follows from the apparent dating of a surface canal elsewhere on the island. Importantly, however, this interpretation implies that the clays were cultivable by the Maya, which they were. The question then becomes: under what conditions would the Maya have used these clays?

Finally, the entire problem of chronology is at issue, owing to the range of radiocarbon dates found throughout the various levels of the excavations at Albion Island and detailed by the project. I raise this issue not to disagree with the dates selected in the interpretations, but to re-emphasize that chronological control remains a major problem for all environmental and agricultural studies in the Maya lowlands.

The Albion Island project has extended their interpretations to a pan-northern Belize (Pohl 1990c) and, perhaps, a pan-Maya lowland (Pope and Dahlin 1989) thesis. As I understand it, this thesis holds:

- that all Maya wetlands in the region display the same basic profile (from bottom to top) consisting of a pre-Maya material, a buried soil (organically rich), and sterile clay deposition;
- that the origins of wetland agriculture are to be found in the Preclassic Period as a modification of flood recessional cultivation on the buried soils and in which excess water was drained by ditches or canals;
- that this cultivation was undertaken during periods of relatively low population pressure, perhaps guided by elite hegemony over farmers, to provide a security harvest during the dry season and to gain power and prestige over other elites;
- that rises in sea level or increased precipitation after the Preclassic but before the Late Classic "drowned" the system and deposited marl and sterile clays over it;
- that the Maya essentially abandoned wetland cultivation during this time, although much of this period was associated with very heavy occupation and the zenith of their material achievements;
- that the system was, perhaps, used again in the very Late or Terminal Classic Period; and,
- that the origins and, perhaps, development of wetland cultivation had little to do with Maya land use pressures, particularly from population.

This thesis (and its variants) must be assessed in two parts: the physical evidence and the interpretations applied to them. Both parts are founded on the basic premise that a three-layer profile (noted above) is present throughout the wetlands in northern Belize, a premise that seems supported by the work at Cobweb Swamp, the 1981 Pulltrouser work, and the recent activities of Pohl, Bloom, Pope, and Jacobs throughout northern Belize (reports forthcoming).[29] The 1981 Pulltrouser work repeatedly cored through the upper clays into a buried soils and pre-Maya surface (noted above) on numerous fields examined.[30] It seems apparent that the general profile found in those segments of the swamps with ground patterns in northern Belize is that proposed by the Río Hondo project. I am not certain that this profile is evident at Morocoy, however: a dark clay layer is present at about 70 cm depth there, but the material under this layer appears to differ from that described in Belize.

The evidence beyond this is complex and remains controversial. Below I highlight some of the major issues and problems in the proposed thesis.

(i) The pollen evidence everywhere in the Maya lowlands has been interpreted as indicating significant deforestation during the Preclassic Period, suggesting significant buildup in land use pressures. Unfortunately, chronological controls are not sufficient to determine the phasing of the general patterns of deforestation during this period. It is generally recognized that the low population levels in the earlier phases of the Preclassic probably meant relatively low levels of forest disturbance. Evidence of wetland cultivation in these phases would suggest experimentation or use of perceived optimum environments as suggested by the Pulestons (1971) and the Río Hondo project. The general population pattern by the later phases of the Preclassic, however, suggests that a significant proportion of the maximum was reached, depending on the area, of course (Rice and Culbert 1990). Evidence from Albion Island suggests an Early Classic occupational structure density of 444/km² (Pyburn 1991), indicating a large population and, perhaps, a significant population base in the Late Preclassic from which it grew (assuming no major immigration). Sometime between the Late Preclassic and the Early Classic, then, land use pressures were building in northern Belize — the very kind of pressures that would trigger the use of intensive systems of cultivation. The pollen data are typically interpreted as indicating major deforestation by this time.

(ii) The evidence of Maya use of the buried soil zone is strong and increasing with each new study. Several cautions are raised about the interpretation of the use of this zone, however. First, regardless of origins of wetland cultivation, initial evidence from Cobweb Swamp hints that the buried soil there may have been exposed and cultivated until the collapse of the Maya (Valdez, Jacob, and Gifford 1991). If this were so, then the use of wetlands by the Classic Period Maya would be supported, albeit differently from that proposed by the Pulltrouser project. Second, if the upper clays are depositional material eroded from the adjacent uplands, then the edges of depressions everywhere should contain the three-layer profile noted above. The eastern side of the western arm of Pulltrouser Swamp, however, does not have this profile and, interestingly, does not contain ground patterns.

(iii) Interpretation of the upper clays (as they appear in areas with ground patterns) remains controversial. The Río Hondo work requires reassessments of interpretations of some of the other wetlands, but recognition that the origin of the upper clays is depositional does not dismiss the multiple lines of evidence that appear incongruent with the interpretation given by that project. Several examples are noted for Pulltrouser Swamp.

- The 1981 Pulltrouser project found the upper clay on some fields adjacent to the mainland to range up to one meter above the clays on the fields around them. These "high" fields, in the northeastern corner of Pulltrouser South, adjacent to the site of Kaxob, rise to the level of mainland, which is higher here than elsewhere in the swamp. It is difficult to envision how deposition alone could account for this elevation difference; it could be explained, however, by Maya manipulation, for whatever reason.

• Evidence of artifacts and occasional large limestone chunks have been found in the upper clay zone at Pulltrouser Swamp. It is difficult to imagine how the limestone chunks could have been transported into the swamp from such a shallowly graded upland. Moreover, artifacts were chronologically mixed throughout the clay, suggesting (i) the manipulation of the clays as they were deposited, or (ii) a deposition that took place during or after the collapse (as suggested by Valdez, Jacob, and Gifford [1991]).[31]

• The preponderance of the artifacts near the surface of fields, but in the upper clays, are Late Classic and Terminal Classic materials, suggesting use at those times (not deposition of the upper clays solely in accordance with the collapse).

• Artifacts were found situated vertically in the clays, a puzzle had their provenience only followed from natural processes.

• The profiles in many trenches across field and canal revealed a distinct and sharply graded edge of the field coinciding with the upper clays, suggesting the sides of manipulated features. Indeed, many of the fields, especially those that retain water in the canals year-round, still have distinctive rectilinear shapes (and corners) on the current surface. Neither find would be expected if the surface features were merely a reflection of deposition over a lower and abandoned field system.

• No spoil heaps were found for the earth removed from the original ditching (as suggested by the Río Hondo project's interpretation) or from the subsequent canaling as the upper clays were deposited (as suggested by the revised Pulltrouser work). This would indicate that fields or planting surfaces adjacent to the canals were raised with the canal spoils, although the scale of raising would depend on the interpretation adopted. It is noteworthy that studies of labor-based wetland field and canal construction indicate that cultivators do not move earth very far, but usually incorporate it into the construction of the planting surface.

(iv) The work at Morocoy, albeit limited to one brief examination, revealed a profile somewhat different from those reported in Belize. A dark gray clay was found at about 70 cm (below the surface) through which canals had been cut, ultimately penetrating the underlying *sascab* (100 to 128 cm below the surface). The dark layer may represent the old planting surface, and the material above (which is not quite like the "upper clays" in Belize) may be deposition. Overlooked in the flurry of debate about the Belizean evidence, however, was the important discovery at Morocoy of a series of "stone structures" on the current surface of the fields (platforms) about one kilometer north of the trenching activity (Gliessman et al. 1983, 108). More than a dozen such structures were encountered, complete with cut stone and an abundance of surface sherds and lithics (as well as *manos* and *metates*). The largest structure was about 2 m in height and over 10 m in length, despite deformation by a rice development project which had cleared the *bajo* forest through the use of a large anchor chain drawn between two caterpillar tractors. Photographs of sample surface sherds on these structures were identified as probably Late Classic, but some possibly Late Preclassic.[32] Lacking excavation, we do not know how deep these structures extend. We must assume at this time that they represent surface features of significant implications. They suggest a Late Classic use of the surface or near surface of the fields, and/or a continued use from the Late Preclassic into the Late Classic. The latter raises a series of questions about the source and impacts of the materials above the dark clay zone.

(v) If wetlands were abandoned during the times proposed by the Río Hondo project, enormous, perhaps untenable, land pressures would have been created on the uplands. The apparently very large Early Classic population (e.g, 444 structures/km² at Albion Island [Pyburn 1991]) surely could not have been maintained without the use of the 40-60 percent of the terrain composed of wetlands; nor could the project's estimated 825 people/km² for Late or Terminal Classic times (Lewenstein and Dahlin 1990). An expansion of settlement along the edges of Pulltrouser Swamp during the Late Classic strongly suggests an association between the two, and, as noted, a Late Classic presence has been found for structures within the Bajo de Morocoy.

(vi) Contra Pohl (1990c), the evidence for the origins of wetland cultivation at early dates does not refute all the population-related assumptions associated with the cultural-ecological based perspectives.[33] The induced intensification theme, for example, accounts for demand from many sources, including that coerced by elites for whatever purpose. We must also recognize a difference between initial wetland cultivation — ephemeral ditches and mounding — and major forms of landesque capital, assuming that major canals and field raising were involved in the later development of the systems.

These various works and interpretations require us to probe deeper into the wetlands to reconstruct the environmental and agricultural histories of the Maya. In so doing, we may very well find, as at Pulltrouser, that many contemporary wetlands were originally open bodies of water that were affected by natural and human-induced environmental change during their use by the Maya. In contrast, Morocoy and the depressions in its vicinity may have always been a seasonally inundated depression. The variety of contemporary wetlands suggests multiple origins and human-use histories. Foremost, we must develop a better understanding of three broad issues. First, what were the possible uses of "elevated" wetlands (above 100 m asl) available to the Maya? Moreover, were they used in a manner that can only be discerned after extensive trench excavations have been made within them?[34] Second, were "low" wetlands used throughout Maya occupation? If not, how could the Maya have supported the extraordinary population and land pressures that would follow from land use restricted to the uplands? Third, what role did environmental change (natural and human-induced) play in the use of wetlands, and for that matter, all land uses employed by the Maya?

Towards a Revised Orthodoxy

A brief review is in order. Into the second half of this century, a swidden or *milpa* orthodoxy of ancient Maya agriculture dominated, lending credence to the view that the Maya constituted an unique civilization among its peers. Central to this orthodoxy, whatever unique trait was stressed (e.g., lack of warfare, long distance trade, urbanism, or large populations), was the notion that the civilization was sustained for millennia by a slash-and-burn system of production based upon land rotation with significant periods of fallow. All other ancient civilizations left unambiguous evidence of intensive agriculture. The assumption that the Maya were exceptional in this regard was challenged beginning in the late 1960s and early 1970s. The revision was based on old evidence as well as new, together with the application of revised theories of agricultural change. This challenge led to a new consensus. It was empirically demonstrated that the central lowlands contained a quality suite of soils for cultivation on which the Maya practiced a range of agricultural strategies. This range included the use of terracing on shallow and steep upland slopes, alterations of wetlands for cultivation, and orchard-gardens (perhaps walled), as well as a variety of rotational-fallow systems. Perhaps the revisionist's enthusiasm for the new consensus has stretched the evidence and implications beyond their empirical limits. Reaction to such excess, coupled with genuine alternative beliefs about the nature of Maya agriculture and the role of environmental influences on human activity, has given rise to a new round of challenges to the new orthodoxy. Foremost among the questions are the role that "natural" environmental change played in Maya land use and the character of wetland cultivation.

These challenges, if properly deployed, have the potential to move our understanding forward. Unfortunately, initial encounters been more combative than constructive. Part of this problem stems from misunderstandings among the various parties that can be overcome through cooperative contact. Another part, however, has do to the tenor of the dialogue, which, in my opinion, has bordered on the recalcitrant.

Proponents of the new orthodoxy have been too sensitive to challenges to their evidence and interpretations, failing to recognize that their work was an initial stage of research and did not necessarily "get it all right." Some have been too quick to find hidden agendas in these challenges, rather than to take them at face value. Certain challenges clearly demonstrate data or analytical errors in some works directed at wetland use, requiring revisions in the original interpretations. Some of these challenges, on the other hand, have misrepresented the range and complexity of the perspectives encompassed within the new orthodoxy, and the tenor of others borders on the dogmatic, at least in regard to primacy of environmental interpretations. In their most extreme form, these challenges bypass a range of cultural evidence and interpretations to find an environmental explanation.[35]

The ancient Maya of the central lowlands could not have supported their civilization and population solely or primarily on slash-and-burn cultivation or some intensive version of it. In fact, there is very strong evidence indicating that they did not. The Maya required and used multiple systems of food production, including a variety of agricultural strategies. It is also doubtful that the demands placed on agriculture during Classic times, including those from the apparently large populations, could have been supported by upland agriculture alone. This said, the Maya did not terrace every hill or ditch every wetland, and they were not free from the environmental impacts of their landscape transformations or from changes wrought by nature. They could and did respond to such changes, however. This response had both positive and negative outcomes on the Maya and their environments.

A new synthesis, in my opinion, will draw upon this kind of reasoning, strongly linked to the evidence but recognizing that no interpretation can resolve all the issues raised by that evidence. It will also require that we learn the lessons from well-reasoned studies of the relationships between nature and society. Perhaps the most important lesson to be learned is that socioeconomic and technological factors are as influential as natural ones in the decision to use certain types of cultivation. Neither culture nor nature dictates the relationship between the two.

Acknowledgements

The original version of this paper was prepared for the 1990 Symposium on Culture, Form, and Place, sponsored by the Department of Geography and Anthropology, Louisiana State University. Revisions have been based upon the papers presented and discussions undertaken at the 1991 Conference on Ancient Maya Agriculture and Biological Resource Management, University of California, Riverside. I am particularly grateful to Kent Mathewson who was patient with the development of this published version. I thank William B. Meyer, Heather Henderson, and Thomas M. Whitmore, who struggled with me during its preparation, and past members of the Pulltrouser Swamp projects and the Río Hondo projects whose work and commentary have influenced the final version of this paper. Most of my own data presented in this paper was developed from research supported by several grants from the National Science Foundation.

Notes

1. It is altogether fitting that we tackle this problem in a volume celebrating the achievements and contributions of Fred B. Kniffen and Robert C. West and their legacy of studies combining geography and anthropology. This is so for at least two reasons. First of all, geographers working with archaeologists have been central to the development of the new orthodoxy under review here. Second, I believe that the resolutions of the controversies must follow, in part, from the traditions of meticulous empirical standards and appreciation of nature-society relationships that are so strikingly evident in the works of Robert C. West on Latin America.

2. Throughout, I have not distinguished among theories about the development of urbanism, states, and civilization. I have not done so because, from a broad perspective, they have been intricately intertwined as applied to Mesoamerica and the Maya.

3. I do not detail here the estimation procedures and their problems. The reader is directed to Culbert and Rice (1990) and Turner (1990a).

4. It is important to recognize that, from the outset, geographers entered this arena with a different intellectual tradition from the archaeologists, and are largely free of the theoretical preconceptions that influenced most Mesoamerican archaeologists. Alfred Siemens' pathbreaking discoveries were made in the course of a truly exploratory endeavor (Siemens and Puleston 1972), although influenced by the work of Denevan (1970) and others on the ancient use of wetlands in South America. My own work followed from a strong interest in tropical agriculture and the theory of agricultural change among subsistence- and peasant-oriented farmers.

5. In this regard, the new orthodoxy has firm theoretical grounding, but not within the frames of reference of greatest interest to most Mesoamericanists. The archaeologists typically focus on questions involving social organization and societal evolution, while theorists of induced intensification turn to conceptions of decision-making as applied to agriculture per se.

6. It is one issue for experts on the Maya and Maya lowlands to make this case. It is quite another when studies by generalists with a strong taint of advocacy draw upon such work without understanding the problematic nuances. Indeed, it is not uncommon for claims to be made that there is general agreement among the experts that Maya-induced environmental

change was an important element of the Classic Period collapse (see Ponting 1990; Turner 1991).

7. The scrutiny given to wetland cultivation in the Maya lowlands is not surprising, given the place that "hydraulic" thought has held among prehistorians and the role that wetland cultivation played elsewhere in Mesoamerica. While wetland cultivation is not the kind of hydraulic agriculture to which Wittfogel (1990) and others have assigned such social importance, it plays a fundamental role in various themes about of the rise of states in the Basin of Mexico. Hence its presence in the Maya lowlands has serious implications for the highland-lowland distinctions that accompany some of these theories.

8. To my knowledge, Huntington (1917) was the first to propose that the rise and fall of Maya civilization was associated with environmental change. More recently, argument by analogy to climatic change elsewhere has been directed to the Classic Maya collapse (Gunn et al. 1985). Such themes differ from those attempts to demonstrate the significance that sea level rise might have had for the Maya (e.g., Pohl, Bloom, and Pope 1990). The impacts of sea level rise are not all-encompassing and, therefore, are rarely invoked as a cause of the origins or collapse of civilizations. They can, of course, be used to explain particular land uses.

9. We cored this same bog in 1979 (Turner et al. 1983). We did not make too much of the results owing to the compaction of the peat in the core barrel and our concern that we could not adequately measure the depth to which we had penetrated the bog. I will assume, however, that the Abrams-Rue core and analysis controlled for these problems.

10. John Jacob's work at Cobweb Swamp, Belize, and the Río Hondo project's work have provided hints that the Maya land use in northern Belize may have been associated with major sedimentation of wetlands. I do not entertain this argument here, nor the new work of King (1993), because the details of the data and arguments were not published at the time of the preparation of this paper. It is noteworthy, however, that similar arguments were posed by the Ricketsons (1937) and Harrison (1977) earlier.

11. It should be pointed out, however, that such arguments have difficulty explaining either the severity of the depopulation that ensued after the collapse or the failure of the population to increase to any significant size thereafter. Despite controversies over the precise number of Maya left in the central lowlands during the Postclassic Period, the number was extremely small relative to Classic Period occupation, far below the "carrying capacity" of swidden and orchard-garden agriculture that was in use.

12. It is interesting that with the exception of one initial flurry of responses (Sanders 1979), the part of the new orthodoxy dealing with evidence of intensive upland cultivation — the presence of terraces, boundary walls, and other stone features — has largely escaped critique.

Although this evidence has yet to be discredited the absence of such relics, even in areas known to have had extreme land pressures, is commonly interpreted as indicating that some sort of short fallow, swidden system was employed (Pohl 1990b; Sanders 1977).

13. The two features clearly seen in the radar imagery that have been observed on the ground are the canal or moat around Cerros (Belize) and a large drainage feature (origins unknown) in the middle of the eastern arm of Pulltrouser Swamp.

14. As with the environmental arguments just noted, an hegemony exercised by wetland agriculture is a possibility that cannot yet be substantiated to the degree implied by some. The induced intensification thesis supports elements of this position — primarily that the wetlands of Petén were likely used in some capacity for food production during times of peak population — but several environmental conditions may have mediated this expected outcome. Regardless, some of the leaps from the evidence to the level of the implications about Maya prehistory that followed have been as excessive as some of the attacks on the new orthodoxy. By and large, these liberal leaps have been far more common in talks and papers than in publications.

15. The work in at least one *bajo* near Río Azul confirms the presence of drainage features there. The excavators are firm in their belief at this time that the features in question were not natural and probably represent some type of Maya ditching or canaling for use of the wetland (P. Culbert, pers. com.).

16. The implications of this conclusion for the exceptionalist perspective are important. For reasons that may be invalid, Mesoamericanists have been prone to describe northeastern Petén as the "core" of the Classic Maya civilization, in part because Tikal — presumably the largest city— is located there. The spatial congruence of wetland agriculture and this "core" has been made central to several arguments about the level of sociopolitical development in the Maya area (e.g., Price 1977) and influences other arguments that are not so explicit.

17. The distribution of wetland use during the Classic Period is one issue. To use it as the base of the definition of the new orthodoxy — or the implications of the extended literature on Maya agriculture — is another.

18. In this vein, they follow a lead proposed by the geographer Alfred Siemens (1978).

19. The term "swamp" evokes an image in most minds of permanent or nearly permanent surface water with hydrophytic vegetation. Many "swamps" in the central Maya lowlands, however, desiccate seasonally for long periods of time. While we should not get bogged down in nomenclature, wetland is, perhaps, a broader and more appropriate term for all

lands in the region that are regularly inundated for some portion of time. These can be grouped into seasonally inundated and perennial wetlands.

20. Pope and Dahlin (1989) cannot be precise regarding the depths of water tables for "elevated" seasonal swamps versus "low-lying" perennial swamps, in part because the data are so sparse. They apparently consider the water table found at Bajo de Morocoy (1.5 m in 1980) to be high relative to those in *bajos* and swamps at higher elevations. The key, however, is the depth of the water table during the dry season relative to the planting surface. In this respect, I suspect that the Bajo de Morocoy probably functions (now) as a seasonal wetland, as indicated by the surface vegetation.

21. To make this evidence conform to their typological associations, Pope and Dahlin characterize Morocoy as a perennial swamp, and the *bajo* near Río Azul is referred to as transitional swamp zone.

22. For most of the fields excavated at Pulltrouser Swamp, sherds dating to various periods were found to be vertically mixed within the clays underlying the surface. In such cases, the convention holds that the date of the features from this evidence alone corresponds to the latest material in the mix. Near-surface sherds, however, displayed a different pattern (see the discussion that follows).

23. The Río Hondo Project was initiated by Alfred Siemens, who subsequently left the project, and Dennis Puleston, who died in 1978. Mathewson (1990) has written a contextual account of Puleston's place in Maya landscape archaeology. Pohl took over a second phase of the project, complete with an interdisciplinary group of researchers, but with a strong ecological focus.

24. The evidence from Laguna de Cocos (another location on the island) suggests that the wetland fields adjacent to that *laguna* were not inundated, but apparently were cultivated throughout the proposed period of high water at San Antonio (Bradbury et al. 1990:148).

25. Siemens (1990) has explored the possibility that many of the wetland systems in question were used for flood-recessional cultivation, known as *marceño* in parts of lowland Mexico where it is practiced in conjunction with relatively low land use pressures today. Some of the ancient systems may have so functioned, particularly in large floodplains where water control would have been difficult indeed. The appropriateness of this analogue for the Belize-Quintana Roo region with the land use pressures proposed is questionable, however. It should be noted that contemporary flood recessional agriculture in the lowlands typically does not involve the scale or the pattern of ditching and canaling associated with the ancient features in wetlands (see Wilken [1987] for description of modern examples).

26. The Río Hondo project uses as an analogy levee cultivation. The latter is typically practiced on rather pronounced (large and high) levees

which have sufficient grade to expose a considerable surface area with only a minor drop in the level of the surface water. The site in question does not have pronounced levees of this kind; indeed, in my opinion, it is questionable whether any levee exists at the site at all.

27. Interestingly, work at Cobweb Swamp has provided a radiocarbon date on the surface of a buried organically rich clay that is related to the Classic Period collapse. Jacobs (1990) suggests, then, that the clay deposition at Cobweb may have been associated with the collapse. In this case, the entire chronological range of artifacts might be found mixed in the clay from purely depositional processes. King (1983) provides a different interpretation of the same features.

28. The paucity of botanical remains in the clay zone is also a point favoring the project's interpretation. Unfortunately, the wet-dry environment in question is notoriously poor for preservation of organic material, especially pollen. Interestingly, the Albion Island site is so close to the adjacent upland that maize pollen should have washed or blown in — but it too would have been destroyed by the environment in question.

29. But see earlier work at Nohmul (Darch and Randall 1989) and Lamani (Lambert and Arnason 1983). None of the wetlands examined to date has the complicated upper stratigraphy found on the Río Hondo floodplain at Albion Island.

30. The 1981 Pulltrouser project took a pump into the field in order to excavate deeper into the fields and canals. Unfortunately, the pump was stolen before excavations began and attempts to obtain another were not successful. As a result, we found the buried soil only through coring.

31. Valdez, Jacob, and Jones (1991) also note dark clays "floating" in the proposed gray-clay deposition, which could have been produced by continued activity in Cobweb Swamp as the deposition began.

32. The Morocoy study was not an archaeological undertaking and the researchers did not hold a permit to excavate. As a result, excavation of the stone structures and removal of the artifacts for laboratory study was not possible. It is also noteworthy that the researchers did not excavate the fields and canals. Rather, the rice project provided the trenching as a mechanism to understand current surface hydrology in the depression.

33. I simply cannot allow Pohl's (1990c) mode of argument to pass without a comment. Intentionally or not (and similar to Pope and Dahlin [1989]), she condenses and simplifies diverse and complicated arguments into a homogeneous cultural-ecological view (or theory) of the Maya to which she takes exception (p. 408). This view is based on the role of population pressure as a driver of agricultural change and a belief in the limitations of the tropics for cultivation. Astonishingly, she attributes this view to several works that, in fact, represent long-standing disagreements about Maya agriculture, environment and cultural development, and the

relationships among them. Moreover, some of the works cited have as a major theme the quality of the Maya lowlands for cultivation — the very theme Pohl claims is absent from them.

34. Despite the significance ascribed to wetland cultivation in the Maya agriculture debates, the majority of wetland excavations has been restricted to northern Belize. Only three efforts to excavate wetlands outside northern Belize have taken place to date: a few trenches at Bajo de Morocoy; the recent work at Río Azul; and Bruce Dahlin's work at Mirador. The last claims to find no evidence of wetland use. Interestingly, no one has undertaken a trenching effort at Bajo de Santa Fe, next to Tikal, despite the apparent significance accorded by some to its use or non-use.

35. From an environmentalist position, the soils of the Great Plains of the United States should have been home to an extensive Amerindian farming populace, but they were not and the cultural evidence that informs us so cannot be ignored. Likewise, the quality of the upper clays in the wetlands fields in Belize would not have precluded cultivation, and interpretations of their use must draw on the cultural evidence as well as the socioeconomic context of the times.

References

Abrams, E. M., and Rue, D. J. 1988. The causes and consequences of deforestation among the prehistoric Maya. *Human Ecology* 16:377-95.

Adams, R. E. W., Brown, W. E. Jr., and Culbert, T. P. 1981. Radar mapping, archaeology, and ancient Maya land use. *Science* 213:1457-1463.

Adams, R. E. W., Culbert, T. P., Brown, W. E. Jr., Harrison, P. D., and Levi, J. L. 1990. Rebuttal to Pope and Dahlin: Commentary. *Journal of Field Archaeology* 17:241-244.

Antoine, P. P., Skarie, R. L., and Bloom, P. R. 1982. The origin of raised fields near San Antonio, Belize: An alternative hypothesis. In *Maya subsistence: Studies in memory of Dennis E. Puleston*, ed. K.V. Flannery, 227-236. New York: Academic Press.

Bloom, P. R., Pohl, M., Buttleman, C., Wiseman, F., Covich, A., Miksicek, C., Ball, J., and Stein, J. 1983. Prehistoric Maya wetland agriculture and the alluvial soils near San Antonio, Río Hondo, Belize. *Nature* 301:417-419.

Bradbury, J. P., Forester, R. M., Anthony Bryant, W., and Covich, A. P. 1990. Paleolimnology of Laguna de Cocos, Albion Island, Río Hondo, Belize. In *Ancient Maya wetland agriculture: Excavations on Albion Island, Northern Belize*, ed. M. D. Pohl, 119-154. Boulder: Westview.

Brenner, M., Leyden, B., and Binford, M. W. 1990. Recent sedimentary histories of shallow lakes in the Guatemalan savannas. *Journal of Paleolimnology* 4:239-252.

Bronson, B. 1966. Roots and the subsistence of the ancient Maya. *Southwestern Journal of Anthropology* 22:251-279.

Brush, S. B., and Turner II, B. L. 1987. The nature of farming systems and views of their change. In *Comparative farming systems*, eds. B. L. Turner II and S. B. Brush, 11-48. New York: Guilford Press.

Clancy, F. S., and Harrison, P. D., eds. 1990. *Vision and revision in Maya studies*. Albuquerque: University of New Mexico Press.

Culbert, T. P., Levi, L. J., and Cruz, L. 1990. Lowland Maya wetland agriculture: The Rio Azul agronomy program. In *Vision and revision in Maya studies*, eds. F. S. Clancy and P. D. Harrison, 115-124. Albuquerque: University of New Mexico Press.

Culbert, T. P., and Rice, D. S., eds. 1990. *Precolumbian population history in the Maya Lowlands*. Albuquerque: University of New Mexico Press.

Darch, J. P., and Randall, R. 1989. Maya drained field agriculture at Douglas Village, Orange Walk District, Belize. In *Advances in environmental and biogeographical research in Belize*, ed. P. A. Furley, 47-52. Biogeographical Monographs No. 3. Biogeographical Research Group, Institute of British Geographers. London.

Denevan, W. M. 1970. Aboriginal drained-field cultivation in the Americas. *Science* 169:647-54.

Dunning, N. P. 1992. *Lord of the hills: Ancient Maya settlement in the PUUC region, Yucatán, Mexico*. Monographs in World Archaeology No. 15. Madison, WI: Prehistory Press.

Fedick, S. L., and Ford, A. 1990. The prehistoric landscape of the central Maya lowlands: An examination of local variability in a regional context. *World Archaeology* 22:18-33.

Gliessman, S. R., Turner II, B. L., Rosado May, F. J., and Amador, M. F. 1983. Raised-field agriculture in the Maya lowlands of southeastern Mexico. In *Drained field agriculture in Central and South America*, ed. J.P. Darch, 91-110. British Archaeological Series, International Series 250. Oxford.

Gómez-Pompa, A. 1987. On Maya silviculture. *Mexican studies* 3:1-17.

Gunn, J., Folan, W., Eaton, J., and Patch, R. 1983. Paleoclimatic patterning in southern Mesoamerica. *Journal of Field Archaeology* 10:453-68.

Hammond, N. 1978. The myth of the Milpa: Agricultural expansion in the Maya lowlands. In *Pre-Hispanic Maya agriculture*, eds. P. D. Harrison and B. L. Turner II, 23-34. Albuquerque: University of New Mexico Press.

Harrison, P. D. 1977. The rise of the Bajos and the fall of the Maya. In *Social process in Maya prehistory*, ed. N. Hammond, 469-508. London: Academic Press.

Harrison, P. D. 1990. The revolution in ancient Maya subsistence. In *Vision and revision in Maya studies*, eds. F. S. Clancy and P. D. Harrison, 99-113. Albuquerque: University of New Mexico Press.

Harrison, P. D., and Turner II, B. L., eds. 1978. *Pre-Hispanic Maya agriculture*. Albuquerque: University of New Mexico Press.

Healy, P., Lambert, J. D., Arnason, H. J. T., and Hebda, R. J. 1983. Caracol, Belize: Evidence of ancient agricultural terraces. *Journal of Field Archaeology* 10:397-410.

Huntington, E. 1917. Maya civilization and climatic change. In *Proceedings of the Nineteenth International Congress of Americanists*. Washington, D.C.

Kates, R. W., Hyden, G., and Turner II, B. L. 1993. Theory, evidence, and study design. In *Population growth and agricultural change in Africa*, eds. B. L. Turner II, G. Hyden, and R.W. Kates, 1-39. Gainesville: University Press of Florida.

King, E. 1993. A review of the evidence for intensive agriculture at Colha, Belize. Paper presented at the 58th Annual Meetings, Society for American Archaeology, April 14-18, St. Louis, MO.

Lambert, J. D. H., and Arnason, J. T. 1983. Ancient Maya drained field agriculture: Its possible agricultural productivity at Lamanai, Belize. In *Drained field agriculture in Central and South America*, ed. J. P. Darch, 111-112. BAR International Series 189. Oxford.

Lambert, J. D., Siemens, A. H., and Arnason, J. T. 1984. Ancient Maya drained field agriculture: Its possible application today in the New River floodplain, Belize. *Agriculture, ecosystems and environment* 11:67-84.

Mathewson, K. 1977. Maya urban genesis reconsidered: Trade and intensive agriculture as primary factors. *Journal of Historical Geography* 3:203-215.

——. 1990. Río Hondo reflections: Notes on Puleston's place and the archaeology of Maya landscapes. In *Ancient Maya*, ed. M. D. Pohl, 21-51. Boulder, CO: Westview Press.

Pohl, M. D., ed. 1985. *Prehistoric lowland Maya environment and subsistence economy*. Papers of the Peabody Museum of Archaeology and Ethnology, 77. Cambridge, MA: Harvard University.

——. ed. 1990a. *Ancient Maya wetland agriculture: Excavation on Albion Island, northern Belize*. Boulder: Westview Press.

——. 1990b. The Río Hondo project in northern Belize. In *Ancient Maya wetland agriculture: Excavations on Albion Island, northern Belize*, ed. M. D. Pohl, 1-19. Boulder: Westview Press.

——. 1990c. Summary and proposals for future research. In *Ancient Maya wetland agriculture: Excavations on Albion Island, northern Belize*, ed. M. D. Pohl, 397-439. Boulder: Westview Press.

Pohl, M. D., Bloom, P. R., and Pope, K. O. 1990. Interpretation of wetland farming in northern Belize: Excavations at San Antonio, Río Hondo. In *Ancient Maya wetland agriculture: Excavations on Albion Island, northern Belize*, ed. M. D. Pohl, 187-254. Boulder: Westview Press.

Ponting, C. 1990. Historical perspective on sustainable development. *Environment* 32(9):4-9, 31-33.

Pope, K. O., and Dahlin, B. 1989. Ancient Maya wetland agriculture: New insights from ecological and remote sensing research. *Journal of Field Archaeology* 16:87-106.

Price, B. J. 1977. Shifts in production and organization: A cluster-interaction model. *Current Anthropology* 18:209-233.

Puleston, D. E. 1971. An experimental approach to the function of classic Maya chultuns. *American Antiquity* 36:322-336.

——. 1978. The art and archaeology of hydraulic agriculture in the Maya lowlands. In *Pre-Hispanic Maya agriculture*, eds. P. D. Harrison and B. L. Turner II, 225-246. Albuquerque: University of New Mexico Press.

Puleston, D. E., and Puleston, O. S. 1971. An ecological approach to the origins of Maya civilization. *Archaeology* 24: 330-337.

Pyburn, K. Anne. 1991. The political economy of ancient Maya land use. Paper delivered at the Conference on Ancient Maya Agriculture and Biological Resource Management. University of California, Riverside.

Rice, D.S., and Culbert, T. P. 1990. Historical contexts for population reconstruction in the Maya lowlands. In *Precolumbian population history in the Maya lowlands*, eds. T. P. Culbert and D. S. Rice, 1-61. Albuquerque: University of New Mexico Press.

Ricketson, O. G., and Ricketson, E. B. 1937. *Uaxactún, Guatemala, Group E, 1926-1931*. Carnegie Institution of Washington Publ. no. 477. Washington, D.C.

Sanchez, P. A., and Buol, S. W. 1975. Soils of the tropics and the world food crisis. *Science* 188:598-603.

Sanders, W. T. 1973. The cultural ecology of the lowland Maya: A reevaluation. In *The classic Maya collapse*, ed. T.P. Culbert, 325-360 Albuquerque: University of New Mexico Press.

Sanders, W. T. 1977. Environmental heterogeneity and the evolution of the lowland Maya civilization. In *The origins of Maya civilization*, ed. R. E. W. Adams, 287-297. Albuquerque: University of New Mexico Press.

Sanders, W. T. 1979. The Jolly Green Giant in tenth century Yucatan, or fact and fancy in classic Maya agriculture. *Reviews in Anthropology* 6:493-505.

Siemens, A. H. 1978. Karst and the pre-Hispanic Maya in the southern lowlands. In *Pre-Hispanic Maya agriculture*, eds. P. D. Harrison and B. L. Turner II, 117-143. Albuquerque: University of New Mexico Press.

Siemens, A. H. 1990. Reducing the risk: Some indications regarding pre-Hispanic wetland agricultural intensification from contemporary use of a wetland/terra firma boundary zone in central Veracruz. In *Agroecology: Researching the ecological basis for sustainable agriculture*, ed. S. R. Gliessman, 233-250. New York: Springer-Verlag.

Siemens, A. H., and Puleston, D. E. 1972. Ridged fields and associated features in southern Campeche: New perspective on the lowland Maya. *American Antiquity* 37:228-239.

Steward, J. H., Adams, R., Collier, M. D., Palerm, A., Wittfogel, K. A., and Beals, R. L. 1955. *Irrigation civilizations: A comparative study.* Pan American Union Social Science Monograph No. 1. Washington, D.C.: Pan American Union.

Turner II, B. L. 1974. Prehistoric intensive agriculture in the Maya lowlands. *Science* 185:118-124.

———. 1978. The development and demise of the swidden thesis. In *Pre-Hispanic Maya agriculture*, eds. P. D. Harrison and B. L. Turner II, 13-22. Albuquerque: University of New Mexico Press.

———. 1981. Agricultura y desarrollo del estado en las tierras bajas Mayas. *Estudios de Cultura Maya* 8:285-306.

———. 1983. *Once beneath the forest: Prehistoric terracing in the Rio Bec region of the Maya lowlands.* Dellplain Latin American Studies, No.13. Boulder: Westview Press.

———. 1985. Issues related to subsistence and environment among the ancient Maya. In *Prehistoric lowland Maya environment and subsistence economy*, ed. M. Pohl, 193-209. Peabody Museum of Archaeology and Ethnology, 77, Cambridge, MA: Harvard University.

———. 1990a. Population reconstruction for the central Maya lowlands: 1000 B.C. to A.D. 1500. In *Precolumbian population history in the Maya lowlands*, eds. T.P. Culbert and D.S. Rice, 301-324. Albuquerque: University of New Mexico Press.

———. 1990b. The rise and fall of population and agriculture in the central Maya lowlands: 300 B.C. to present. In *Hunger in history: Food shortage, poverty, and deprivation*, ed. L. F. Newman, 178-211. Cambridge, MA: Basil Blackwell.

———. 1991. Overview: Environmental history. *Environment* 33(4):2-3, 45.

Turner II, B. L., and Harrison, P. D. 1978. Implications from agriculture for Maya prehistory. In *Pre-Hispanic Maya agriculture*, eds. P. D. Harrison and B. L. Turner II, 337-379. Albuquerque: University of New Mexico Press.

———. 1981. Prehistoric raised-field agriculture in the Maya lowlands: Pulltrouser Swamp, northern Belize. *Science* 213:399-405.

———. eds. 1983. *Pulltrouser Swamp: Ancient Maya habitat, agriculture, and settlement in northern Belize.* Austin: University of Texas Press.

Turner II, B. L., Johnson, W., Mahood, G., Wiseman, F. M., Turner, B. L., and Poole, J. 1983. Habitat y agricultura en la region de Copan. In *Introducción a la arqueología de Copan, Honduras.* Tomo 1, Tegucigalpa, D.C.: Proyecto Arqueológico Copán y Secretaría de Estado en el Despacho de Cultura y Turismo.

Turner II, B. L. and Miksicek, C. H. 1984. Economic plant species associated with prehistoric agriculture in the Maya lowlands. *Economic Botany* 38:179-193.

Valdez, F., Jr., Jacob, J., and Jones, J. 1991. Agroecology of the ancient Maya at Colha, Belize. Paper presented at the Conference on Ancient Maya Agriculture and Biological Resource Management. University of California, Riverside.

Whitmore, T. M., Turner II, B. L., Johnson, D. L., Kates, R. W., and Gottschang, T. R. 1990. Long-term population change. In *The earth as transformed by human action*, eds. B. L. Turner II, W. C. Clark, R.W. Kates, J. F. Richards, J. T. Mathews, and W. B. Meyer, 25-39. Cambridge, U.K.: Cambridge University Press.

Wilken, G. C. 1971. Food-producing systems available to the ancient Maya. *American Antiquity* 36:432-448.

———. 1987. *Good farmers: Traditional agricultural resource management in Mexico and Central America*. Berkeley: University of California Press.

Wiseman, F. M. 1978. Agricultural and historical ecology of the Maya lowlands. In *Pre-Hispanic Maya agriculture*, eds. P. D. Harrison and B. L. Turner II, 63-115. Albuquerque: University of New Mexico Press.

Wiseman, F. M. 1985. Agriculture and vegetation dynamics of the Maya collapse in central Petén. In *Prehistoric lowland Maya environment and subsistence economy*, ed. M. Pohl, 63-71. Papers of the Peabody Museum of Archaeology and Ethnology, 77. Cambridge, MA: Harvard University.

Wiseman, F. M. 1990. San Antonio: A late Holocene record of agricultural activity in the Maya lowlands. In *Ancient Maya wetland agriculture: Excavations on Albion Island, northern Belize*, ed. M. D. Pohl, 313-337. Boulder: Westview Press.

Wittfogel, K. 1957. *Oriental despotism: A comparative study of total power*. New Haven, CT: Yale University Press

The Sixteenth-Century Environment of the Central Mexican Bajío: Archival Reconstruction from Colonial Land Grants and the Question of Spanish Ecological Impact

Karl W. Butzer and Elisabeth K. Butzer

Abstract

For some areas of Colonial New Spain, archival sources can be used to reconstruct the vegetation of the 16th century. This paper, focused on the Bajío of north central Mexico, illustrates such a methodology, based on environmental features included in the early land grant titles (*mercedes*) of 1542-91. Striking is the prevalence of open environments, and three distinctive biotic zones, similar in principle to the degraded vegetation of today. In areas with pre-Hispanic indigenous agriculture, there was evidence of disturbance, local deforestation, or even degradation at the onset of Spanish settlement. But there is no evidence that Spanish stock-raising and agriculture had an impact on the vegetation or the hydrological cycle as of about 1590. Given the large, residual tracts of land still left unsettled by both Indians and Spaniards, mobile livestock strategies appear to have been effective in limiting environmental damage. During the second phase of settlement (1592-1643), agricultural colonization of the better lands was accompanied by a deemphasis of stockraising, with sheep transhumance expanding far to the north, reducing grazing pressures in the Bajío. The documents indicate a good understanding of physical and biotic features by the first and second-generation settlers, suggesting that they were increasingly familiar with indigenous trees and shrubs, and their Indian names.

Key words: Bajío; colonial land grants; ecological impact (indigenous and Spanish); environmental history; sheep transhumance.

As the controversy over the quincentenary of the Columbian Encounter demonstrated, one of the basic questions to be addressed is what Denevan (1992) calls the myth of a pristine New World landscape. The issue has two parts: (a) whether native American peoples did or did not alter or degrade their environment, and (b) whether or not European settlers had

---

Culture, Form, and Place: Essays in Cultural and Historical Geography, edited by Kent Mathewson, 1993. Geoscience and Man, vol. 32, pp. 89-124. Department of Geography and Anthropology, Louisiana State University, Baton Rouge, LA 70893-6010.

an immediate and drastically negative impact on the environment. The first question involves matters of aboriginal technology, intensity of land use, and population levels, as well as whether indigenous peoples used conservationist strategies. The second question concerns the effect of introduced European livestock and plow technology, and the loaded issue of whether European strategies were exploitative and destructive.

Polemics can have a salutary effect if they refocus research questions and lead to pragmatic study. In the case of Mexico, a generation of research has been preoccupied with reconstruction of the aboriginal population, prior to Cortes's *entrada*, and the subsequent rate of demographic decline. But two recent papers deserve note. In the Basin of Mexico, Williams (1989) derived micro-land use data from documentary sources to argue that indigenous subsistence on marginal lands was stretched to the limit, thus placing long-term sustainability into question. In the equally marginal Valley of Mesquital, Melville (1990) used other archival sources to infer that Spanish livestock, especially sheep, may have had a disastrous impact on the environment. But her conclusions contradict the earlier work of Cook (1949), who archaeologically dated the most important evidence for soil erosion in her study area to pre-Hispanic times.

These articles serve to draw attention to the relative neglect of the wealth of archival records in New Spain, documents that might elucidate how the indigenous peoples and the Spaniards managed their resources. In North America, historians and historical geographers have made strides in this direction (for example, Cronon 1983; Butzer 1990; Doolittle 1992). In Mexico, there is a greater interest in historical studies of settlement and environmental change (see Butzer 1992a, 1992b), but West's (1949) exemplary study of the Parral mining district, as a microcosm of the interaction between technology and resources, has remained unique. West, Williams, and Melville each illustrate the immense potential of available documentary sources that invite further study.

Land Grants and Landscape Reconstruction

This paper applies the land grants awarded in the Bajío of central Mexico to environmental reconstruction of the 16th century. It is part of a long-term, comparative study of early Spanish Colonial settlement in the tropical lowlands versus the temperate central plateau of Mexico. The archival backbone for this research is the immense body of land-grant deeds, totalling some 40,000 untranscribed manuscript pages. These are primarily preserved in the 84 volumes of the section Mercedes of the Archivo General de la Nación, Mexico City, with microfilm copies in the libraries of the University of California (Berkeley) and the University of Illinois (Urbana), hereafter cited as AGNM [volume number-folio number]). Two stray volumes, representing the early 1550s, found their way into the Ayer Collection of the Newberry Library, Chicago (Ayer MS 1121), and the Kraus Collection of the Library of Congress, Washington (Kraus MS 140), the last published in slightly abbreviated form by Zavala (1982). Not all the *mercedes* ("royal awards") strictly represent land grants. They include all kinds of royal licenses, such as permits to build roadside inns or gristmills; approvals for the sale, conversion, or abandonment of land grants, as well as for rights to irrigation waters; documents of patent or survey data for deeds already rewarded; and a range of edicts related to infringements of Indian settlements by holders of land awards, including a number of revocations or fines imposed. In all, it is a very rich record of minute "events" in rural New Spain, essential to the resolution of land-use history.

The Spanish land grants specify type of grant, to whom, and where. Of particular interest is the locational information, originally provided by the applicant and recorded by the viceregal magistrate. Although often vague, such notations specify the district, any adjacent Indian settlements or Spanish holdings, and frequently include characteristic landscape features such as landforms, streams, and vegetation. With systematic regional evaluation, based on field study and the 1:50,000 maps, it is often possible to fix the location of the more specific deeds, to establish a spatial framework from which adjacent holdings can be filled in by virtue of their geometrical relationships. Our primary purpose was to reconstruct the distribution of landholdings in particular districts and their composite evolution from the 1540s to the 1640s. But this detailed procedure also brings landscape elements into synoptic view.

Our choice of the Bajío to explore this method of environmental reconstruction is predicated on two factors: (a) The percentage of land grant deeds specifying physical and biotic information is unusually good, compared with the Basin of Mexico, where a dense network of Indian toponyms and villages provided most points of reference for the Spanish settlers, or with the Gulf lowlands, where physical landmarks are usually few and the luxuriant vegetation less suitable to distinguish a particular site. (b) The Bajío was on the margins of Mesoamerican agricultural settlement (see Whitmore and Turner 1992), with long-term indigenous land use in some areas but not in others; furthermore, Spanish colonization was insignificant here before the 1550s, theoretically allowing a distinction between environmental impact before and after European intrusion.

Although this paper will focus on landscape reconstruction, some pertinent issues of Spanish Colonial land grant policy can be summarized:

(1) Land grants were awarded quasi-legally by the city council of Mexico since 1525 (see Orozco 1859), and more formally, by the viceroy, beginning in 1542 (AGNM 1). In 1642 the process of land granting came to a close (with AGNM 43), except for a few local areas and

more importantly, the developing northern periphery of New Spain. The *mercedes* include over 10,000 titles, about half of which were awarded by 1588. Some 1,100 documents were transcribed as the basis of the present study. Of these, 900 are titles, covering the period 1542-91 and constitute approximately the first half of the awards made in the Bajío.

(2) The land grants are incomplete, for several reasons. Municipal governments, particularly in Nueva Galicia and Nueva Vizcaya, competed with the viceroy in making awards. Many individual deeds were also lost, and whole collections for some of the early years have evidently disappeared. However, the granting of land was also a stop-and-go process influenced by changing policies of the viceroys and interim administrations, and sometimes a site was occupied ("homesteaded") for many years before a grant was awarded. Another factor is that many of the grantees in Mexico City usurped land, particularly during the 1530s, when the basic Mediterranean right to graze animals on the equivalent of public land (Butzer 1988) had not yet been effectively transformed into a policy of restricted land holding (Matesanz 1965), with attendant privileges and restrictions. Prem (1978, 131) suggests that less than 60 percent of the titles of grants remain on record, while Melville (1990) estimates 50 percent, arguing from cross checks with other documentary sources. Probably more important than the true number of titles is that the ranches (*estancias*) were stocked with far too many animals, ranging well beyond the nominal limits of particular landholdings. In 1555 there apparently were 60 cattle and horse *estancias* in the Valley of Toluca, with 150,000 head (Puga [1563] 1945, 153v). In fact, the number of titles corresponds roughly to our own tallies of the titles eventually formalized for Toluca by 1600, but the number of animals is five times the prescribed stocking rate used after 1567. This suggests a rough rule of thumb to assess the maximum, potential number of livestock in a particular district, a prerequisite for considering environmental impact.

(3) The sizes of land grants were definitively fixed in 1563 (AGNM 7-125), and formally spelled out in 1567 (AGNM 9-113v [verso]). The three most important categories were: (a) the *estancia de ganado mayor*, for cattle (unless specified for horses), measuring a *legua* square (4190 by 4190 m, 1756 ha or 4336 acres); (b) the *estancia de ganado menor*, for sheep (unless specified for goats or pigs), measuring two-thirds of a *legua* square (2793 by 2793 m, 780 ha or 1927 acres); and (c) the *caballería* of agricultural land, measuring 463 by 925 m (42.8 ha or 106 acres). Prior to 1563, an ordinance of 1537 appears to have been in effect, which set the *caballería* much smaller, at 161 by 322 m (5.2 ha or

13 acres) (Bentura 1787, 1:ii, 69) , although we suspect that an even earlier definition of *caballería* by the Mexico City Council, using 35.7 ha (see Fernández [1780] 1962, 1:116) was still applied in practice. Specifications for the sizes of *estancias* were first set in 1538 (Escobar 1984, 281, n. 23) and remained unchanged, although prior to the 1550s few grants distinguished between *mayores* and *menores*, although a *mayor* seems to be implied unless otherwise stated.

(4) After 1567 the prescribed stocking rate was 500 head of cattle or horses for an *estancia de ganado mayor*, and 2000 head of sheep, goats, or pigs for a *menor*. But there were many exceptions, perhaps related to proximity of Indian fields or quality of land. Rules were strict about the use of grants. The only livestock permitted on agricultural *caballerías* were draft oxen (Kraus 154v [1551]), and by 1560 it was essential to obtain formal permission to change the prescribed function of an *estancia*. Also germane is that after the formal award of a grant, title only became permanent if the required improvements were made on the land within a specified time (three months to two years) and after six (eventually four) years of appropriate use. For an *estancia*, these improvements involved stocking with the prescribed number of animals and the construction of animal sheds and a rock-walled pen or corral (AGNM 1-233 [1542]; 3-135 [1550]).

Land Use in the Bajío about 1590

The available land grants for the Bajío at the end of 50 years of awards are presented in table 1, organized according to district (see fig. 1). They comprise 1782 units of land as well as 47 gristmills, an indicator of effective local wheat production (in combination with an appropriate water source). To compensate for the lost titles, neighboring grants cited in other deeds but not registered individually are included in this total.

A *suerte* represents a quarter of a *caballería* and, in the Bajío, was awarded for domestic food production, such as vegetables and orchards, in close proximity to a town but only rarely adjacent to a house lot or *solar*. The *caballerías*, in part irrigated, were either aggregated in large alluvial areas around towns, or scattered much further out, frequently within or next to an *estancia*. The livestock *estancias* inevitably focused on some permanent water source and, in the early years or in unoccupied areas, were located next to prime pastures on floodplains or vertisolic plains. By the 1560s, they were increasingly awarded in rougher, marginal country, unattractive for agriculture.

An accurate plot of the Bajío land grants would require a publication scale of better than 1:200,000, so that figure 1 only shows their distribution in a highly generalized way, with a slight simplification of the numerical

Table 1. Land grants to Spaniards in the Bajío 1542-1591

Districts	Cattle Estancias	Sheep Estancias	Farm Land (Caballerías)	Horse Estancia	Suertes de Huerta	Gristmills
Jilotepec	5	23	57	--	--	1
Huichapan	11	42	65	--	--	1
Toliman (?)	7	--	--	--	--	--
San Juan Rio	18	1	28	--	--	1
Amascala	2	9	1	--	--	--
San Luis Paz	17	--	--	--	--	--
Querétaro	12	50	49	1	--	1
Maravatio	5	6	16	--	--	--
Acambaro	19	24	70	--	--	1
Cuitzeo Basin	11	25	49	--	--	1
Yuríria Basin	13	25	105	--	--	17
Salvatierra	8	7	35	--	--	3
Salamanca	41	6	20	--	--	2
Apaseo	29	8	39	--	--	2
Chamacuero	8	1	9	--	--	--
Celaya	19	3	153	--	24	9
Silao-Irapuato	24	--	40	--	--	--
Puruandiro	44	11	56	1	--	1
Turbío-Leon	41	3	23	--	--	1
San Miguel	18	59	101	1	32	3
San Felipe	23	25	23	1	16	3
Guanajuato	32	5	27	--	--	--
Total land units (1,829)	407	333	966	4	72	47
Total ha (1,023,570)	714,690	259,750	41,340	7,020	770	

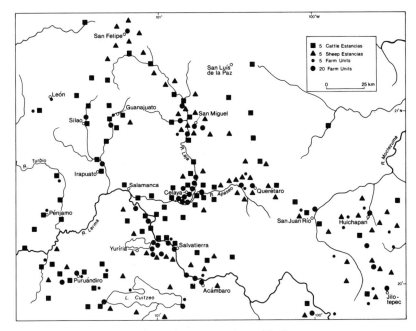

Fig. 1. Spanish land grants in the Bajío 1542-1591 (see table 1).

data. But a variable percentage of farm units or *estancias* cannot be located because no information is supplied, although in some cases later litigation records (texts or even sketch maps) do allow reconstruction. A major problem, for example, is that 75 percent of the grants for San Miguel were awarded in principle by the viceroy, but then assigned at the discretion of the town council. The situation for Celaya is not much better.

Figure 1 and table 1 serve to identify large and small clusters of land-holdings, but both underplay the large spaces with little or no settlement by 1590. Thus for figure 1 as a whole, the nominal one million ha awarded represent only 19.7 percent of a land area of 52,000 km². But within the 25-km-square municipal territory of San Miguel, we estimate that 65 percent of the land was assigned to private holders. Potential impact of Spanish land use on the environment should therefore be expected to be highest in those areas with concentrated settlement. Fortunately the density of environmental information provided by the *mercedes* is roughly proportional to the number of local land titles.

Regional Environmental Information

The environmental data gleaned from the Bajío land grants is listed in table 2, organized according to districts (fig. 2) and mainly in chronological

Table 2. Environmental References in Land Grant Deeds 1542-1591

Jilotepec
(9 references) *Sabanas* (1543 2-215); *zacatales, cienegas, montes* (1555 4-291v); *sabana de zacatales* (1582 11-215); *loma* with some small trees rising above a *sabana* (1583 12-28v); *encinal* around a stony mesa with low *palmitos*, but *encinales* and *robles* on adjacent peak (Chapantongo) (1585 13-182); extensive montes (S. Martin Tuchicuitlapilco) (1543 2-29v), later, *monte de encinas*, but mesa with cover of small *encinas* and a few wild *palmas* (1585 12-107, 1591 17-119); *sabana rasa* (Soyaniquilpan) (1590 16-89).

Huichapan
(14 references) Arroyo with *charcos de agua* (Tecozautla) (1565 8-192v); deep arroyo with *charcos de agua*, hill with *robles* and *encinas* (Huichapan) (1583 13-38); *sierra* with *monte de encinal* (Nopala = La Estancia) (1582 11-214v); dry arroyo near hill with *encinas* and another with a few small *encinas* (Sta. Maria Amealco) (1584 13-61); large *tunal* below wooded cerro (S. José Atlan) (1584 12-86); large *charco de agua* (Amealco) (1589 14-200); valley within a closed *mezquital* (Tecozautla) (1590 15-222v); spring with *maguey*, arroyo with some large *encinas*, *encinal* in valley, and flat *loma* with some *guajes, mezquites*, and *palos dulces* (Tlaxcalilla) (1590 16-5, 79v, 81); stony hill with wild *palmas*, *loma* with some large *capulín* trees, steep hills with *encinas*, and a stony cliff with tall pines south of Río S. Juan (Acazuchitlantongo) (1589 15-38v; 1591 16-25, 17-103v); isolated *encinas* and a *madroño* (Aculco) (1591 17-19).

San Juan del Río
(7 references) *Sabana* (1550 3-216v; 1552 Kraus 419v; 1554 4-77; 1560 5-33v; 1567 9-1; 1577 10-209); broad *llanos* with *laguna, encinas* on hill (El Cazadero) (1588 14-84).

Querétaro-Amascala
(21 references) *Arco de Agua* below cliff (Salto de Agua, east of Querétaro) (1563 7-140v; 1589 14-355v); hot springs and some *cardo(ne)s* (La Cañada = Villa del Marques) (1565 8-171v); *sabana*, a large *mezquital*, large *tunas*, and some small *encinas* on a peak (Valle de Amascala) (1561 5-257v; 1565 8-8); *montes* (Tlacote Bajo) (1567 9-193); *sa-ana* and dry *laguna* near rocky footslope of El Cerrito (San Francisco = Villa Corregidora) (1576 10-160v; 1585 12-131v); dry river margins full of wild mesquite trees and some large *mezquitales* (Río Pueblito, San Francisco) (1577 10-199, 10-213v; 1582 11-132; 1590 15-176); large *mezquitales* north of confluence of rivers (Río Pueblito-Querétaro) (1577 10-233; 1589 15-91); *sabana* below rough slope (S. Pedro Martir) (1584 12-83); *monte* (east of Cerro Cimatorio) (1583 13-37v); some large *tunas* and *mezquital* (road west of San Francisco) (1584 13-63v); *pinal* (between Mesa Sordo and Cerro Pinalito) (1585 12-185v); many pines and *tunales* on rocky slope (Cerro Gordo, San Francisco) (1591 16-266); *garambullo* and many *encinas* (road east of Querétaro to San Juan) (1591 17-135v); hill full of *tepeguaje* trees, wild *tunales*, and wild *magueyes* (mountain rim south of San Francisco) (1592 17-156v).

San Luis de la Paz (Sichú)
5 references) *Sabana* de San Sebastian with *charcos de agua* (S. José Iturbide) 1560 5-189, 192; 1568 9-267, 267v); some *encinas* (Sichú) and *sauces* (Manzanares)1567 9-28).

Acámbaro 18 references) Mountain *barrancas* with *charcos de agua* and *carrizal* at spring (1563 7-245; 1567 9-182); large *guajes* on mountain slopes (Tarimoro) (1581 11-40v; 1584 12-74); *cienegas* below but *tunas, zapotes,* and stands of small mesquite above (Iramuco) (1581 11-212; 1591 16-183, 248, 248v; 1592 17-183, 186v); *huizaches* and tall mesquite in hills (Jeréquaro) (1581 11-86v); large *mezquital* on hill above plain (Tarimoro) (1582 11-108v); *sauces* along river (between Acámbaro and Jerécuaro), wild *tunales* nearby (1584 12-71, 13-114; 1591 17-13v); mesquites (Paraquaro) (1584 12-77); *mezquitales* and *cienega* (between Acámbaro and Maravatio) (1590 15-291v); tall mesquites and *magueyes* (San Juan) (1591 17-32v).

Cuitzeo Lake Basin 22 references) Arroyo with running water, a large *aguacate* and isolated pines or *tunas* on hills, and shore of *cienega grande* to north (Chucandiro) (1581 11-56; 1582 11-216; 1589 14-420v; 1591 17-154v); on banks of *laguna* (Cuitzeo) (1586 13-242v); *laguna* and *cienega*, with *tunales* on hill (Araro) (1586 13-234v); *tunal grande* on *pedregal* (Cuitzeo) (1589 15-13v); *mezquital, laguna* next to a *tular,* and many wild *tunales* and *mezquitales* (Indaparapeo) (1589 15-15v, 89; 1590 15-159); river from Morelia enters *cienega* and *laguna* of Iramuco flowing across a big *llano* with *cienegas, carrizal, zacatales, mezquitales,* and *sauces,* a deserted lakeshore hamlet of fishermen, with *tunales* and small trees on hills to east (Zinepecuaro) (1590 15-183v, 208v, 263v, 268v, 275, 16-103; 1591 17-70, 132; 1592 17-167); mesquites, *tunales* and *sauz* (Copandaro) (1591 16-237v); dry arroyo with *sauces* (Uriangato) (1591 17-49).

Salvatierra-Yuríria (30 references) Many *guajes* with some *tunas, pitajayas,* and *acibuche* on lower slopes (Cerro Culiacan) (1581 11-85v; 1583 13-17; 1584 12-74, 88v); many *montes* with some *copal* (Sierra Gavia = Cerro Grande) (1583 13-16v); exit of *desaguadero* from Lake Yuríria to Río Grande (Lerma), with isolated *fresnos* and *sauces* and a village of fishermen (1581 11-72v); *llano* with *cienega* or *charcos de agua* and some *salitrales,* broken by hills with *encinal* or mesquites and *tuna,* and adjacent to *mezquital montuoso* extending to the Río Grande and Menguaro (Sta. Maria Cupareo) (1583 13-48v; 1584 13-27v, 62v; 1585 12-150v; 1588 14-74v; 1590 15-131v, 153v, 207v, 229v, 291v, 16-108v; 1591 17-105, 137); barren, stony mountains with a *bosquecillo* on slopes and *tunales,* mesquites, and a *hormiguero* below (Cerro Tetillas) (1583 11-290v; 1584 13-110v; 1590 15-215; 1591 16-153); *isla* between *brazos* of Río Grande (towards Salamanca) (1590 16-81v); large *mezquital* and Indian fishing settlement on lake, *pitajayas* and *guarumo* on or among nearby uplands (Lake Yuriria) (1590 15-202v, 216v, 222, 260); *cerros* with *encinales* (location uncertain) (1590 131v, 153v).

Apaseo 11 references) *Las cienegas de las chichimecas* at river confluence Apaseo-Laja (1544 1-237), then called *monte espeso de mezquite bravo* (1563 6-271), or *mezquital montuoso* (1564 7-388), later *mezquital grande* and *palos dulces* (1591 16-149v); large *laguna* near *mezquitales* on *camino real* to Querétaro, *sierra montuosa* and *pedregosa* beyond (El Salitre, S. Bartolomé Aguascalientes) (1560 5-11v; 1577 10-280); *huizache* and mesquite woodland (Apaseo el Alto) (1582 11-162); *cardones* next to fenced-in wheat field on a *llanada* (road to Querétaro)

(1583 11-269v); apparently barren *cerro* except for a *palma*, above road (north of Apaseo) (1584 12-57v; 1591 17-97v; 1592 17-159).

Celaya 9 references) Lands prone to flooding (*anegarse*) during the rainy season (1573 10-3); a woodland of mesquite in a watercourse forming during rainy season near a *cienega* (1573 10-168v); small to large stands of mesquite near diversion dams, canals, gristmills, or Río Laja *brazos* (between Escobedo and Celaya) (1576 10-174; 1582 11-128, 1584 12-55; 1590 15-158), but also *cardenchal* (near S. Agustin = Escobedo) (1590 15-158): *isleta* in Río Laja, with some nearby mesquites and *pitajayas* (towards Salamanca) (1582 11-200; 1584 12-95v).

Chamacuero 5 references) *Bosques* (1542 1-104v); thick *mezquital* at confluence of Río Laja and dry arroyo (A. Jalpilla) (1563 7-218v); *jaral* on island between two *brazos* of Laja below Chamacuero (1563 7-306v); *mezquital* along Laja banks (S. Geronimo = Orduña Bajo) (1564 7-388v, 390).

Silao- 18 references) Large *saucedal, alamos, mezquitales, pinos,* or *carrizal*
Irapuato along *ríos* draining south from Sierra de Guanajuato (1561 5-207v; 1563 5-3v, 6-274, 7-200v, 264v; 1565 8-7v; 1574 10-9v); scattered small or large stands of mesquite on *llanos* (1560 5-63v; 1574 10-9v; 1583 11-253v; 1584 13-97v; 1592 17-179v), local, seasonal *lagunillas* or *cienegas* (1574 10-30; 1584 13-97v; 1591 17-78), with *jarales, espinos, cardenchal* or *tunal* on low watersheds (older alluvium) (1567 9-149; 1584 13-99v; 1592 17-179v).

Puruándiro 11 references) *Cienega* and island in *río* (Guaniqueo) (1589 14-197; 1590 10-116); *cienega* on floodplain, with *fresnos* and many *sauces* along *río* and arroyo (Puruándiro) (1590 15-269; 1591 16-181, 209, 254v, 17-115; 1592 17-162v); large swampy, plains with large *tulares* (Comanja) (1591 16-191v); *robles* and *tunales* in rougher country (1591 16-235v); *encinas* on hill (Guango) (1591 16-144).

Río Turbío 5 references) *Mezquital* along river on *llano* with *cieneguilla* (1563 6-198v, 276; 1582 11-206; 1591 16-202v); *cardenchal* on mesas of headwaters (1591 16-202v).

San Miguel 8 references) *Brazo* of Río Laja with some *lagunas* near *peñas* (Tequisquiapan-S. Gabriel) (1550 3-53x; 1551 Kraus 310), below *río seco* (Río Llanito) (1565-31v); springs, *charcos de agua* near a mesquite on plains (road to Guanajuato) (1560 5-30v; 1563 6-5v); *barranco* supplying water to fulling mill above town, below *encina* (1560 5-30v); *sabanas* of S. Gabriel (1560 5-188v;); *laguna* (south of road to Nieto, at Cerritos) (1563 6-228v).

San Felipe 7 references) *Tunalejo* on *camino real* east of las Vueltas (bends of Río Laja below la Quemada) (1563 6-1v); *río de las sauces* (1563 6-25v); *charcos,* a clear blue spring (*ojo zarco*) near the large *cienega,* and beyond that the *tunal* (road to Zacatecas) (1563 6-1v, 7-120v; also 1560 5-135v); *río de alisos, robledalejo, pinal* and *lagunita* (Valle de Trinidad, to south) (1563 7-261; 1564 7-280).

Guanajuato 4 references) *Robledal* at confluence of two *ríos* below some *peñas* (1551 3-321); *vegas* and many *tunales* (Valle Potrero de Jaso) (1563 6-270v); *cienega* and *robledal* (Yerbabuena) (1564 7-272); *robledal* (1574 10-13).

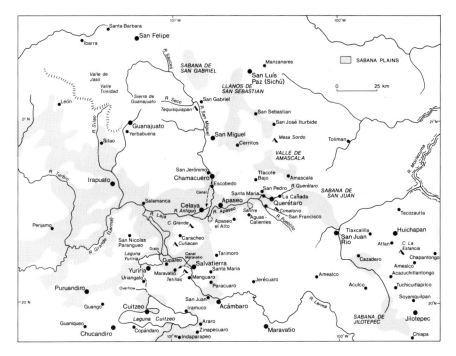

Fig. 2. The savanna-clay plains of the Bajío and locations for documentation (see table 2).

order. Locations distant from a central town or *pueblo* are given with reference to the closest modern settlement on the 1:250,000 maps. For verification of the 204 documents providing the environmental information of table 2, the year, *mercedes* volume, and first page are added to each entry. The original Spanish terms are used to avoid ambiguity, but are translated or explained in the glossary (table 3). Vegetation is the main component, but terrain elements are specified to identify the edaphic mosaic. Information on streams, standing waters, or marsh are a second key element, to elucidate local hydrology during the 50-year time span selected here.

The information in table 2 is explained and discussed in the text, within the framework of physiography, geology, soils, and the contemporary vegetation of a particular area, as based on field observation. The reader may wish to consult both the 1:250,000 topographic map series and the four state atlases (*Síntesis geográfica*) for Hidalgo, Querétaro, Michoacan, and Guanajuato, published by the *Instituto Nacional de Estadística, Geografía e Informática* during the 1980s. Pertinent aspects of the settlement history are incorporated into the discussions.

Table 3. Glossary of Spanish-Mexican Environmental Terms Used in 16th-Century Bajío Documents

Based in part on Corominas 1954; Rzedowski 1981; Santamaria 1978; Wagner 1964; and topographic maps. Note that "x" was used for "j" or "ch" at this time. Suffixes such as *-ejo*, *-illo*, or *-ito* are diminutive forms. (Mex.) denotes mexicanisms.

Physical Terms

arco de agua	waterfall
arroyo	intermittent stream, often cut into bedrock
barranca	deep valley with intermittent stream
brazo	stream channel that is curved, branching, or cut-off
cerro	isolated mountain, sometimes volcanic cone; cerrillo, hill
charco	marsh; charco de agua, marshy pool
ciénega	seasonal wetland or shallow lake (Mex.)
cúe	prehistoric mound
desaguadero	drain
laguna	lake, often small
llanada	small plain, flat land
llano	plain
llanura	large, irregular plains
loma	hill, commonly flat-topped
ojo de agua	spring
pedregal	rocky slope or ridge; pedregoso rocky
peña	cliff or peak
quebrada	small stream (Mex.)
río	stream, usually with dry-season base flow
salitral	alkali flat, seasonal salt lake (Mex.)
sierra	roup of mountains
vega	floodplain

Biotic Terms--Castilian Root

acibuche	tall, woody shrub (Celtis sp. or Forestiera sp.), similar to wild olive tree (Mex.)
alamo	cottonwood (Populus sp.), but sometimes sycamore (Acer sp.)
aliso	alder (Alnus sp.)
bosque	woods, forest
carrizal	reed stand, commonly Phragmites sp.
encina	live oak; encinal, live oak woodland
espino	thorn shrub
fresno	ash tree (Fraxinus sp.)
hormiguero	anthill
jara	thorn shrub; jaral, bushy thorn thicket
madroño	laurel tree (Arbutus sp.)
matorral	bushy vegetation, dominated by woody shrubs, in part thorny, commonly with succulents or low, deciduous trees

monte	woodland, commonly open or degraded
palma (china)	yucca palm (Yucca filifera), akin to Joshua tree (Mex.)
pinal	stand, woodland, or forest of pine
roble	deciduous oak; robledal, oak woodland
sabino	bald cypress (Taxodium mucronatum) (Mex.)
sauz	willow (Salix sp.); saucedal, willow break

Biotic Terms--Hispanic American, or Nahuatl Root

aguacate	avocado tree
capulí	wild cherry tree (Prunus serotina)
cardon	several organ-pipe Cactaceae related to garambullo and pitajaya, but may also refer to *tuna*; *cardenchal* ("*sartenxal*"), cactus thicket
copal	deciduous semitropical tree (Bursera sp.)
garambullo	tall, branching cactaceae, locally Myrtillocactus sp.
guaje	acacia with edible fruits
guarumo	evergreen, broadleaf semitropical tree (Cecropia sp.)
huizache	acacia, possibly including some mimosaceae
maguey	cultivated, feral or wild Agave sp.
mezquite	mesquite (Prosopis laevigata), adapted to deep, well-drained soils and riparian sites, unlike P. glandulosa of U.S.A. borderlands; sometimes called *algarrobe* after European carob
palo dulce	white-trunked, deciduous semitropical tree (Eysenhardtia sp.)
pitajaya	thin-stemmed, branching thorny succulent (Lemairocereus sp.)
sabana	extensive plain with open but not necessarily treeless vegetation; *sabana rasa*, flat, open plain
tepeguaje	deciduous subtropical tree (Lysiloma sp.) of acacia family
tular	reed swamp, with Typha sp. or Cyperus sp.
tuna	fruit of cultivated or wild, prickly pear or nopal (Opuntia sp.), but used to describe plant; tunal, thicket of nopal and other succulents and palmas
zacatal	grassland or grassy plain
zapote	evergreen, broadleaf semitropical tree (Manilkara zapota)

Jilotepec-Huichapan

The western margins of the Valley of Mezquital (centered on the Río Tula) are dominated by a surface of Tertiary ignimbrites and Quaternary basalt flows that slope down from 2500 m elevation at Jilotepec to 1800 m at Tecozautla. Eroded remnants of Tertiary volcanic cones rise 500 m above this undulating plain, which in some areas is mantled with sheets of volcanic ash, and in others is filled in with ancient stream and lake beds.

The modern vegetation reflects this zonation within a highly fragmented landscape. The lower plains above the rim of the Moctezuma River canyon in the north have a sparse vegetation of woody, succulent, or thorny *matorral*, while copses of live oak are found among grass and shrub on adjacent mountainous terrain. A little higher and further south, the plains have a mix of matorral and grassy acacia-mesquite parkland, depending on soil thickness; residual woodlands of live oak persist in the mountains. The foothills of the southern margin are more moist, with a good ground cover of grass, and interspersed copses or forests of mixed pine and oak, that become thick stands on mountain slopes. At Aculco, bald cypress is preserved along part of the floodplain, and dense stands of deciduous oaks intermingle with pine.

The documentation of the *mercedes* for vegetation in these districts (table 2) is fairly good, especially for the last decade of our archival study (1582-91). It verifies a mosaic environment analogous to that of today. Live oak woodlands characterized the mountains and many lower, hilly areas, but deciduous oaks were still visible in areas where they are now absent or rare (Huichapan, Chapantongo). Repeated exceptions to this were landmark hills or rocky slopes, where thin soils and rapid drainage favored xeric associations of yucca palms (an indicator for succulent matorral), scrub oak, acacia and mesquite, *palo dulce*, or even wild cherry trees. The presence of pine stands towards Aculco matches the current evidence. The now bleak landscape around the Madero Reservoir on the Río Hondo was, not surprisingly, described as a *tunal grande*. The grassy savanna documented near Jilotepec is the extensive (20 km long) grassy plain between that town and the Huapango Reservoir, an area of vertisols underlain by fine volcanic ash. These grasslands remain very lush, with much standing water during the rainy season.

Other than the repetitive mention of springs (*manantiales, fuentes, ojos de aguas*), still common in the landscape today, hydrological references are relatively scarce. But those given are significant. Streams called arroyos in the *mercedes* for this area are all cut down into hard rock, not susceptible to gullying. Notable is that some harbored marshy pools during the 1500s, while others had live oaks in them. This suggests a reasonably equitable hydrology, with seasonal runoff, but some base flow, or at least a high water table during the dry winter and spring months. The only visible features of linear or point soil erosion in the landscape today are in the Aculco district, where alfisols over duricrusts on volcanic ash are being eroded by earthflows, slumping, or gullying. But in the semiarid sectors, soils generally are thin or truncated, as a result of Pleistocene, or pre-Hispanic, or historical splash and sheet erosion. Dating of such implicit denudation must await study of the alluvial fills in the valley bottoms. Given the very coarse, Tertiary fanglomerates and interbedded sandstones widely exposed along the Moctezuma canyon, the northern part of the region has experienced a dry climate and semiarid denudation for many millions of years in the rainshadow of the Sierra Madre. At the moment, in view of persistence of bald cypress woodland along the canyon floor, we attribute the thin soil mantle of the uplands to slow pedogenesis and active slope balances over very long time spans.

The documentary sources do not indicate a marked degradation of the vegetation by about 1590. For example, matorral communities with yucca palms are very stable on rocky surfaces, linked to specific edaphic sites. They take decades or centuries to evolve, and in central Mexico do not rapidly invade less xeric locations, even if degraded. The extent, condition, and species diversity of the woodlands provide much better criteria. On that score, the region appears to have been less degraded in 1590 than it is today, despite the persistence of similar patterns of physiognomic vegetation. The evidence for subclimax arboreal vegetation on rocky strath surfaces, surrounded by woodland, underscores that oak woodland was more expansive than at present. But the references to coppiced or isolated live oaks or laurels on non-specific surfaces near Aculco do suggest some degree of human impact. Similarly, *monte* (woodland), when not qualified by adjectives such as thick, closed, or tall (*espeso, cercado, alto*) tends to imply some degree of disturbance, both in 16th-century and modern usage (see Corominas 1954, 3:425).

Melville (1983, 1990) has argued that Spanish sheep-raising in the Mezquital profoundly degraded that environment during the last third of the 16th century. Table 2 suggests that Spanish intrusion into the Jilotepec-Huichapan area was moderate as of 1590. No cattle *estancias* were awarded after 1561 and almost all the farm lands were deeded after 1574, dispersed in a half-dozen nodes. In all, the colonists were awarded 16 cattle and 65 sheep *estancias*, totalling 79,000 ha, plus 122 *caballerías* of agricultural land, another 5200 ha. That represents 16.5 percent of the 5100 km^2 area in question. Converting these numbers to animals, the nominal figures are 8,000 cattle and 130,000 sheep — for a total of 510,000 ha in the district. However, if the true numbers were twice or even five times as great, this would represent high stocking rates by most criteria — unless mobile stockraising was practiced. A more detailed review of some of Melville's assumptions is given in Butzer (1992a).

Yet our impression is that any degradation in the Jilotepec-Huichapan region in 1590 (table 2) was as much a matter of long-term Indian land use as it was of Spanish intrusion. A grant deed of 1591 near Almolonga (a lost settlement between San Martin and Soyaniquilpan) surmises rather perceptively that an open area, with a spring and a willow covered with magueys and surrounded by woodland, had once been an Indian settlement (*en el monte en una quebrada donde esta una fuente y en ella un sauz grande todo cercado de monte, donde ay muchos magueyes y parece haver avido alli poblacion de indios*) (AGNM 17-38). Such indigenous disturbance is plain on the slope above San Juan Chapantongo, where there were many agaves (*estan muchos magueyes*) in 1591 (AGNM 17-113), since feral agaves are only linked with traditional agriculture, so for example, a notation for wild agaves (*magueyes como silvestres*) around Acazuchitlan in 1586 (AGNM 13-210v).

All this is consonant with the fact that Jilotepec and Huichapan already formed part of the agricultural heartland of the Otomí nation prior to the Conquest (Wright 1988, 77-78). This does not remove the livestock from suspicion, since the viceroy had to deal with several cases of *estancieros* — and in one case an uncontrolled herd of perhaps 30,000 sheep and cattle (AGNM 4-330v [1556]) — wreaking great damage on Indian crops and settlements during the 1540s and early 1550s. But things were brought under control, and complaints were not renewed in the area until the 1590s, when Spanish settlers began to encroach on sadly depopulated Indian villages. Nonetheless, within the resolution of the available data, no case can presently be made that the Jilotepec-Huichapan area was degraded by Spanish activities as of about 1590.

San Juan del Río-Querétaro-San Luís de la Paz

To the northwest of Jilotepec-Huichapan, the focus of 16th-century settlement centered on three, semicontinuous basins that form a 170-km-long arc. These are flat-floored, late Tertiary lake basins, which maintain a remarkably consistent elevation of about 1900 m. Once known as the Sabana de San Juan, the Valle de Amascala, and the Llanos de San Sebastian, each is veneered by vertisolic sediments, over a substrate of fine ash; drainage is poorly organized, and in part internal.

These productive basins are bordered to the east by the fretted margins of the Sierra Gorda, a great block of Tertiary lavas (rhyolites), capped by younger flows. The mountains rise 500 to 1000 m or more above the several basins. The western margin of the region is defined by a similarly rough landscape, formed by eroded cones and flows of early Quaternary basalts and andesites.

Querétaro itself lies on the margin of another, major landscape unit, the Bajío, here forming an irregular, downfaulted subbasin. Vertisolic soils up to 6 or 8m thick accumulated under seasonally marshy conditions during late Quaternary time, with a ^{14}C date (calibrated for $^{12}C/^{13}C$) of 5990 years (TX-6416) at -1.2m. Below that are fine, white lake and stream beds, again derived from volcanic ash. The plain of Querétaro (at 1800 m) is linked to the longitudinally-oriented basin arc by the canyon of the Rio Querétaro, known as La Cañada, incised 200 m into basalt flows.

The entire region is semiarid; except for the higher peaks and the main Sierra Gorda, slopes and convex surfaces are dominated by an open *matorral* of succulent, woody, or spiny genera, interspersed with low, subtropical deciduous trees. Prickly pear and agaves are well developed around marginal areas of cultivation, with large cacti or rare yucca palms in rocky areas. Physiognomically this can be roughly described as an acacia-cactus parkland. Degraded remnants of live oak woodland, with intermixed laurel, occur sporadically above 2000 m. Mixed oak-pine forest is limited to extensive areas of high relief above 2500 m. The basin floors now are almost completely cultivated, with the aid of irrigation, but scattered stands of open acacia and fringing mesquite (progressively displaced by introduced pepper trees [*pirúl*]) may represent remnants of an acacia-mesquite grassland.

The archival information leaves little doubt that the vertisolic plains were open and grassy savannas during the 16th century (table 2), with localized marshes or seasonal lakes. The Sabana of San Juan was exclusively turned over to cattle *estancias* (at least 18 by 1591), and the wealth of game in this area was legendary during the early years. In 1542 the Otomí Indians demonstrated a traditional game-drive for the viceroy at El Cazadero, as a result of which more than 600 deer (browsers) and pronghorn (grazers) were killed, in addition to 100 coyotes and foxes, and uncounted rabbits and hares (Torquemada 1723, 1:611-12). This faunal assemblage, while from a marginal extension of that savanna, indicates a predominantly open environment, but one with ample bush or thickets. Based on a now-lost, detailed personal account by Fray Toríbio de Motolinía, it is significant that fire was not used in such drives.

The smaller plain of Amascala (de las Chichimecas) was mainly used for sheep (9 *estancias* versus 2 for cattle), while that of San Sebastian was only stocked with cattle (17 identified *estancias*). Yet the fertile lowland of Querétaro, whose irrigation had been pioneered by the Otomí (Super 1983, 200 ff.; Murphy 1986, 89-99; Wright 1989), was restricted to agriculture, with only two sheep grants, specifically targeted in a dry lake bed north of the Río Pueblito at San Francisco; this small area remained unique in that it was later converted to flood irrigation, judging by a map of 1830 (C.E. Davis, pers. comm.). Noteworthy on the plain of Querétaro were great riparian forests of mesquite along the seasonally-dry Pueblito river and again north of the Querétaro river at their confluence (table 2). Those forests were still shown on the 1830 map, although they have now disappeared.

Unlike the Jilotepec-Huichapan area, there are no reports of live-oak woodlands adjacent to the plains. As a composite, the documents of table 2 suggest open scrub within the broad concept of monte. Depending on substrate, exposure, and elevation, the larger elements apparently ranged from wild agaves and various Cactaceae to *tepeguajes* and scrub oak. Seemingly out of character are the pines referred to at San Francisco (1850-1900 m); this may indicate a once wider distribution of this fire-sensitive tree. The other reference to pines is from a 2700 m peak, within the present distribution of oak-pine woodland. The overall picture is therefore not incompatible with the residual vegetation of today. Nonetheless, the highly fragmented and degraded stands of oak that now survive at between 2000 and 2500 m imply more extensive oak woodland at some point during the 16th century, probably similar to the patchwork of such vegetation preserved in the mountains around Huimilpan.

The meager hydrological references are reasonably consistent with the modern picture. The Pueblito still is an intermittent stream (*río seco)* prone to periodic flash flooding that has left a trace of multiple overflow (crevasse) channels on the surface of the vertisolic plain of Querétaro; the dry *laguna* is part of this set of features. The Río Querétaro, exploited for the city's water supply, has essentially disappeared since the 1930s, except for an open sewage canal. The waterfall east of Querétaro emerged from a once-powerful spring between sheets of basalt; although now defunct, it was still active during the 1820s, when it was sketched by Berlandier, as present among his unpublished illustrations (A. Benavides, pers. comm.). For the Sabana de San Juan, other than the San Juan River, the documents mention only one water course, the Río de Galindo (AGNM 14-84 [1588]). This is the one notable stream today, under the name Río de los Zuñigas, flowing through a canyon cut deep into a basalt cap, and perennial, judging by the extensive fringing woodland of bald cypresses. A sketch map of 1584 (Murphy 1986, fig. 4.7) shows the Rio Galindo fringed by trees and continuing to join the Rio San Juan, with that river also bordered by bald cypress (see Wright 1989, 183).

There is as yet no firm archaeological evidence of Indian agricultural settlement in the region prior to the Conquest (but see Butzer 1992a), and Otomí oral tradition recorded during the seventeenth century suggests indigenous farm colonization northwestward from San Juan del Río and Aculco around 1520 (Wright 1988, 1989), with Querétaro's Cañada settled about 1530 and San Luís del Paz, the first site for Sichú, before 1560 (AGNM 5 45). The Otomí continued to control Querétaro's *huerta* into the 1600s (Murphy 1986, 95ff.; Butzer 1989a), and the *mercedes* bear this out: only four farm units of the recorded grants known to be awarded up to 1591 lay inside an ellipsoidal area of 5 by 9 km, presumably representing the enclosure (*cerca*) of Querétaro, repeatedly referred to in grants of the 1570s and 1580s. Some 45 *caballerías* were awarded outside the *cerca*, but on the alluvial plain, while 48 of 50 sheep *estancias* were relegated to the rougher scrub country round about. The available archival evidence suggests that the environment around Querétaro had not yet been degraded by the end of the 1500s. There even are hints that the most striking changes postdate the 1830s, although topsoil accumulated rapidly behind short-lived irrigation dams built during the late 18th century (Butzer 1989b, 109-111).

The 1582 *relación geográfica* of Querétaro and San Juan del Río gives estimates for Spanish livestock, but also describes the great mobility of the herds, even at that late date (see Wright 1989, 167). More than 100,000 cattle, 200,000 sheep, and 10,000 horses were allegedly pastured in these districts. The figure of 200,000 sheep, compared with 60 sheep *estancias* recorded for Querétaro, San Juan del Río, and Amascala up to 1591, suggests a theoretical stocking rate of 3300 head, reasonable in view of the transhumance strategy. For the cattle and horses, the 33 *estancias* awarded are probably far too incomplete to compare, since these titles were mainly granted during the early period, for which several key years (especially 1569-72 and 1578-80) are totally lacking.

In their search for pasture, the cattle of the region covered large distances to the limits of the Chichimecas (a vague region including the Bajío and areas northward, to beyond San Luís de la Paz or San Felipe), where there was good and extensive grazing, despite a scarcity of springs (see Wright 1989, 167). The sheep were taken by their owners on transhumance treks (*a extremo*, that is, "to the frontier") "which here are called *agostadero*," to Michoacan, with its humid climate and very good pastures, "and there they are kept until it rains" in Querétaro, when the shepherds return with their flocks (see Wright 1989, 167).

These comments indicate that cattle herds in the region were still not kept on fixed landholdings during the 1580s, and that a large-scale transhumance system, analogous to the Spanish *mesta* (Butzer, 1988, 1989a, 10-11) was already in effect. Independent verification is provided by Ciudad Real ([1589] 1976, 2:85, 128) who encountered an infinity of sheep from Querétaro on dry-season pastures near Lake Chapala as well as in central Jalisco, during the winter of 1586-87 — distances of 250 to 400 km. Such a strategy would limit grazing on assigned, home pastures to the rainy summer season, after which they would spend the other half-year far away, eliminating pressures on pasturage during the dry and cool months of minimal productivity.

The Bajío: Acámbaro

The Bajío comprises several of the districts we have studied, namely the basins of Acámbaro and Apaseo-Celaya, lakes Cuitzeo and Yuríria, the foothills of Guanajuato, and the smaller basins of Puruándiro and the Río Turbío. The linking element of the Bajío is the poorly-defined course of the Río Grande (Lerma) and its major tributaries, that zigzags its way through a maze of flat plains at 1800-1900 m. What may once have been a unified tectonic basin is interrupted by Quaternary craters, dissected late Tertiary volcanic cones, and highly irregular shields of fissure basalt, ignimbrites, and volcanic ash. These different classes of mountains rise abruptly from the plains, with a relief of 700-1200 m. Late Tertiary fanglomerates derived from volcanic materials and cut by erosional surfaces, are preserved in the Acámbaro Basin and along the Guanajuato foothills. Elsewhere, basin floors are flat, drained by underfit streams, and floored by vertisolic sediments on top of fine, white, water-laid volcanic ash.

Although most of the basin floors are intensively cultivated, the spontaneous vegetation is a grassy parkland of acacia and mesquite, with pepper trees tending to displace mesquite and willows along the riparian fringe. Bald cypress is preserved along the Rio Lerma from Acámbaro to below Salvatierra. On rougher terrain, there are thickets and parklands of low deciduous trees, as around Querétaro. But higher rainfalls and warmer temperatures support semitropical trees and a thicker mat of grasses, while the succulent understory is less developed. Oak woodlands, sometimes mixed with pine, now are limited to isolated areas on higher peaks.

The striking aspect of the Acámbaro district is that although early land grants were scattered across both the basins and intermediate uplands, no woodlands or even *monte* are indicated, and oak is not mentioned. This uncertainty can be reduced with reference to several maps attached to *mercedes* in the AGN litigation series, *tierras* (cited as AGNT below). One, dating to 1579, sketches the district south along the road to Zinapecuaro, showing pines on the mountainous watershed and live oak stands on the adjacent foothills, at perhaps 6 to 12 km distance (AGNT 2809, exp. 27-14). Two others show the area closer to Acámbaro, with riparian forest (several genera) schematically indicated along the Río Grande, and some undiagnostic woodland on the mountain directly east of the town (AGNT 2680, exp. 26-338 [1583]; AGNT 2735 [2], exp. 2-10 [1616]). Finally, a later bird's eye view of 1623 covers the area between Acámbaro and the ring of mountains some 20 km to the north: again a prominent riparian woodland gives way to mainly open vegetation on the clay plains beyond, with a few spots of open woodland suggested (AGNT 3627-182 [1623]). This corroborates the impression of an open parkland with acacia and an understory of succulents, on the plains and lower mountains, with woodland here no more extensive than today, except in the south, where it has been extensively removed and where the foothills have been converted to open pastureland.

The riparian vegetation itself included mesquite and willow, according to the *mercedes,* which curiously enough do not refer to the groves of bald cypress on the river. However, the *relación geográfica* of 1579 describes that watercourse as "a very large and deep river, full (sic) of some large tree stands called *sabinos*" (see Acuña 1987, 65). *Sabino* continues in Mexican usage for bald cypress. The *relación* also mentions good pastures, extensive clumps (*gran boscajes*) of mesquite, and woodlands of deciduous oaks and pine (*montes de robles y pinos*) that were used for construction timber (see Acuña 1987, 59-60, 66), thus filling in some notable gaps in our information for the 16th century.

Acámbaro was not an area of old settlement, apparently first colonized by 74 families of Otomí from Huichapan during the 1520s (see Acuña 1987, 60-61; Wright 1988, 78). Spanish intrusion began in 1538 but remained sporadic until 1565, and in 1579 Spanish activity was mainly focused on running 100,000 cattle between Acámbaro and Apaseo (see Acuña 1987, 66), a figure that appears realistic for 1591, although half of those animals would have been concentrated on the alluvial plain of the Apaseo and Laja rivers. The number of cattle in the rough country would have been small. Half of the 24 sheep *estancias* were awarded much later, during the decade 1582-91. This suggests insufficient time and cause to degrade the submontane vegetation, which probably still was representative of pristine conditions. The sparse references to hydrological features may imply little more surface water than today.

Interesting is that only a third of the 18 Indian villages (*pueblos*) on the 1579 pictorial map of the Acámbaro district (see Acuña 1987, facing p. 58) are replicated in the *mercedes*, but with two additional names. In part, this suggests that prime Indian lands remained off limits prior to the consolidation (*congregación*) of aboriginal settlements 1592-93; in part it reflects that Spanish settlement was still incomplete in 1591. But, more importantly, we suspect that the Indian who drew the map included settlements abandoned even before the great plague mortality of 1575.

Lake Cuitzeo

Since 1983 Lake Cuitzeo has dried out almost completely, through overexploitation of its major water source; open ponds and marshland are now limited to the eastern half. According to the *relación* of 1579, the lake was saline (*salada*) and 1.5 *varas* (1.3 m) deep, the waters leaving an efflorescence along the shores that was useful for making both soap and glass, while at the same time compatible with a lush growth of grass (see Acuña 1987, 79, 85-86). The last precludes sodium chloride, whereas common soda glass requires sodium and calcium carbonates in addition to silica sand. The waters must have been close to saturation with sodium and calcium bicarbonates, not surprising in view of the mainly basic volcanic rocks in the catchment around Morelia. The high level of alkalinity implies evaporative loss of water and would preclude a regular overflow to Lake Yuríria. Nonetheless there is a well-defined overflow channel running northward past Uriangato, that can be verified on the topographic maps. At the level of the highest lying shore marshes, water would cross this threshold (about 1835m) to run over some lava surfaces down to Lake Yuríria (now fluctuating at about 1727 m). The 1579 pictorial map for Yuríria confirms this by showing a connecting watercourse (see Acuña 1987, facing p. 66). But the soda efflorescences argue that such an overflow would have been episodic, during years with unusually heavy rains, and insufficient to maintain the level of Lake Yuríria.

The *mercedes* (table 2) provide a comprehensive picture of the environment surrounding Lake Cuitzeo (or Iramuco). A seasonally wet, grassy plain with reed swamps, mesquite thickets, and willows lay to the south. The lake margin was bordered by marshland at Iramuco (see Acámbaro) and Araro, while at Chucándiro the lake in 1589 was referred to as a large *cienega*, so that the western end would have been shallow (today that part is bone dry); the phrase *la cienega y la laguna de iramuco* also suggests less than continuous water in 1590. Lake Cuitzeo at this time evidently had poorly-defined shorelines and its water surface was probably smaller than at the time of the 1971 aerial photography. This conforms with records showing that the lake dried out 1590-91, as it had in 1543, causing great hardships by destroying the fisheries for some years (Escobar 1984, 236).

The maps from *tierras* provide more insight on fluctuations of the lake level during the late 1500s. A fairly detailed depiction of 1576 indicates that the western end of Lake Cuitzeo was shallow but too deep to be forded at any season, while the central and eastern parts also were "shallow" (*hondable*) and seven leagues in extent (also exactly 29 km from the Cuitzeo highway today); the margins of the lake are decorated with reed marsh (*tular*), while the surrounding lowlands are labelled as great, uncultivated plains (*grandes llanos eriazos* or *baldíos*) (AGNT 2764, exp. 9-97). In 1578-79 and 1587, four other sketch maps show that the lake was at least as high as and probably higher than it is today: a deep embayment of the lake, shown with fish, penetrated up to 6 km into the river from Tarímbaro, an area now filled in (1971 photography) and extended by a vast reed-swamp delta projecting another 6 km to the north (AGNT 2721, exp. 36-370, 392, 404, 416). A string of cultivated lakeshore fields would even suggest that the lake was less alkaline at the time. But in 1590 another map uses ancillary color to suggest that most of the western part of Lake Cuitzeo and broad stretches of other shorelines may have been reduced to swamp, rather than open water; this seems to be confirmed by the road from Morelia to Cuitzeo, shown running across the lake bed (AGNT 2682, exp. 19-23). By 1595 the lake seems to have been somewhat reconstituted, with an arm shown extending northward between Cuitzeo and Maya (AGNT 2721, exp. 2-19). These data indicate that Lake Cuitzeo was as high as or higher than it was c. 1971 from 1576 to 1587, shrinking markedly by 1590, before drying out 1590-91, but recovering c. 1595. Thus the documentary sources identify climatic trends over this 20-year period, for which we otherwise have little information in Central Mexico.

On higher ground, the vegetation around the Cuitzeo Basin appears to have been degraded: four references to *tunales*, one to isolated pines, one to small trees, and no mention of *monte*. Cuitzeo was a traditional part of the Tarascan agricultural world since long before the conquest, judging by a rich oral legacy (see Acuña 1987, 82). On the other hand, except at Iramuco, Spanish intrusion was incidental until 1589, when sheepherders from Querétaro began to acquire titles for winter pastures (*agostaderos*) on the grassy lowlands south of the lake (e.g. Zinapecuaro, AGNM 17-131, 132, 164 [1591-92]). But some sheep were run before that time by Indians, who had individual herds of 200-400 head (see Acuña 1987, 88). The condition of the vegetation suggests long-term degradation, and can hardly be attributed to Spaniards.

One third of the places mentioned in the list of dependencies in 1579 (see Acuña 1987, 78-79) do not come up in the *mercedes*, probably because they had long ago disappeared. The indigenous population was much reduced by the plagues of 1546 and 1576 (see Acuña 1987, 79); the abandoned fishing village of Sindo (AGNM 15-263v [1590]) is still listed among the 17 dependencies of Cuitzeo in 1579, but in 1590 there were only six or seven ruined houses and a chapel.

Lake Yuríria

Environmental information on the triangle between Salvatierra, Yuríria, and Salamanca is closely linked to Spanish settlement, which effectively began in 1581. About half the grants were in the poorly-drained lowland between the Río Grande and Lake Yuríria (also Murphy 1986, 42, note 6), described in the *mercedes* as a plain with a *cienega* and some alkali flats, next to a great forest of mesquite (table 2). Mesquites, with some ash and willow, followed the river, although bald cypress now is the dominant riparian element, raising questions as to whether the great mesquite forest was not in fact a bald cypress swamp, and whether the *mesquital* around Lake Yuríria was not composed of bald cypress, since a few such trees are still found below the monastery of that town. There also is a hint of the maze of anastomosing branches of the Río Grande (an "island between the arms of the river"), further downstream towards Salamanca (see Murphy 1986, 65-67).

Beyond the plains, the vegetation was mainly open. Cerro Tetillas, directly west of Salvatierra, had a trace of woodland, but was otherwise essentially barren, with an anthill, a feature perhaps once much more common than today. The Caracheo area near the base of Mount Culiacan had a parkland of acacia, large Cactaceae, and tall, woody shrubs (*acibuche*), presumably thicker at higher elevations. On the uplands around the lake there also were Cactaceae, with the notable presence of *guarumo*, possibly relicts in sheltered valleys. But the impression of a somewhat degraded landscape given by these examples is not corroborated by mention of several cerros with live oak woodland, one above the plain of Cupareo, and of semitropical woodlands on the lower slopes of Cerro Grande, the companion volcanic cone of Culiacan. There probably was some degradation around Yuríria about 1590, yet the evidence is mixed.

It is difficult enough today to assess whether subtropical parkland is a secondary, subclimax vegetation, or to decide whether or not thorny succulents have invaded a degraded understory. Fortunately in the case of the Yuríria district there is a pollen core, taken 15 km northwest of Lake Yuríria in the crater lake (1850 m elevation) of San Nicolas Parangueo (Brown 1985). The top 70 cm of the profile have five ^{14}C dates calibrated to 1100-1750 A.D. that are consistent but inverted, suggesting slumping and 180° rotation of a sediment slice. If this segment is accepted as valid, in reversed order, the 17 pollen spectra show a consistent increase of Chenopodiaceae and Amaranthaceae from 20 to 50 percent. Even more dramatic is the contrast between the disturbed slice and the first intact unit of 60 cm, terminated about 1000 A.D.: cheno-ams jump from almost nothing to 20 percent, high-spined compositae from 0 to 10 percent, while maize begins to make a consistent appearance, and pine drops sharply from 75 to 30 percent. Oak and grasses fluctuate in similar ranges above and below the break.

However one may interpret the details, the Parangueo profile shows that there has been unbroken agricultural settlement in the area from the late Early Postclassic (11th century) onward. In the early part of the profile, oak and grass co-vary, inversely with pine, probably carrying a climatic signal. Above the break at about 1000 A.D., the cheno-ams and Compositae increase at the cost of pine alone. This seems to suggest that oak woodlands and grass cover remained undegraded (on uplands?) until well into the Colonial era, despite intensive local disturbance due to cultivation (in the lowlands?). The minimal representation of insect-pollinated Leguminosae (such as acacia, mesquite, and some semitropical genera) or Cactaceae limits interpretation.

The Parangueo profile gives qualified support to our cautious and non-stereotypic evaluation of what provides hard evidence for degradation of subtropical parkland in the Bajío. Somewhat revolutionary is the palynological case for nine centuries of continuous agricultural occupation in the Yuríria Basin, since long before Tarascan conquest in the late 15th century (see Tudela 1977). The Spaniards were indirectly aware of long indigenous settlement here, and five different prehistoric mounds (*cués*) are identified in the *mercedes* around Cupareo (AGNM 13-109v, 110v

[1584]); 12-150v [1585]), one of *piedra antigua* ("ancient stones"), another with a zapote growing on top. Equally noteworthy is that the Colonial era did not leave an obvious mark on the grasses in this pollen profile, despite the *relacíon* map showing the hillsides of Yuríria overrun by cattle and *vaqueros* ("cowboys") in 1579 (see Acuña 1987, facing p. 66). We suspect that this represents an Indian perception of mobile intrusion into their commons since, as of 1579, we only record one cattle *estancia* near Yuríria and four near Salvatierra.

Another important question to address is Lake Yuríria itself. According to pious legend of a later century, Fray Diego de Chaves converted a marshy lowland into a permanent lake about 1550 by having the Indians cut a two-legua-long (8 km) canal from the Río Grande plain to flow into the basin, a story uncritically accepted by Murphy (1986, 42). The most proximal source is the *relacíon* of 1579 (see Acuña 1987, 70 and map facing p. 7): "The said Río Grande passes two leagues from this *pueblo* (Yuríria) and from it they made a ditch, so that the said river entered by it and filled a plain five leagues in circumference with water, making a large lake." There is no word of an Augustinian friar or an 8-km-long canal, and no period is alluded to. The map clarifies this a little.

It shows a spring-fed stream coming into the lake from the southeast, running between Maravatio (de Yuríria) and on to Casacuaran "where the Río de Maravatio enters the lake" (AGNM 13-211 [1586]), but there was no canal from Salvatierra in 1579. Instead the connection with the Río Grande is northeast of the lake, to the northwest of Santa Maria Cupareo, where the distance between the lake and river is shortest (2.5 km), in the general position of the modern "drain" to the Río Grande, the *desaguadero grande* of 1581 (AGNM 11-72v). The map twists the alignment of the drain slightly to suggest that a part of the river flowed into the lake, suggesting the possibility that a diverging channel (on what is here a convex floodplain) was merely reopened. Assuming 150 mm surface runoff with 750 mm precipitation, and 2.5 m direct evaporation over a 600 km^2 catchment (consonant with published map generalizations), a lake roughly two-thirds the size of modern Lake Yuríria could be sustained in an average year, but its level and shores would fluctuate widely, even flooding a larger area than the present 60 km^2 surface during wet years when Lake Cuitzeo overflowed. The connection to the Río Grande would consequently serve to stabilize the lake at a fairly constant level, with influx during some years, outflow during others.

To describe Lake Yuríria as artificial is misleading. The elaborate Canal Maravatio from Salvatierra was much younger than the "drain," and was not designed to fill the lake basin. The first explicit mention of an *acequia* is from August 1584, specified as coming from Salvatierra (Guasindeo), passing along the foot of Cerro Tetillas, "to irrigate . . . the plain of

Santa Maria" (AGNM 13-102). An earlier, implicit mention of the same canal is from November 1583, "irrigation with the water of the river . . . to the edge of a large *cerro* called Las Tetillas" (AGNM 12-19). From August 1583 to August 1584, a total of 105 *caballerías* of irrigated farmland, 17 grist-mills, and three sugar mills were granted between Maravatio and Santa Maria, one of the most rapid Spanish agricultural developments ever undertaken in the Bajío. This presupposes opening of the canal in the summer of 1583. A second *acequia*, the Canal San Nicolas, supplying the growing Augustinian estate, is already shown on a map of 1589 (Murphy 1986, fig. 2.3). In effect, Fray Diego did not "create" Lake Yuríria, nor was he responsible for building the Canal Maravatio.

The Bajío: Apaseo-Celaya

The modern municipalities of Apaseo, Celaya, and Chamacuero (Comonfort) were originally included in the Apaseo district, as were many other early grants subsumed under the broad category of Chichimecas. The environmental references are grouped by table 2 to focus on four sets of features.

The confluence of the Apaseo and Laja rivers evidently was a marshy, thickly forested area at the time of first settlement. From the vague *estanciero* description of the Chichimec *cienegas* in 1544, the settlers of the mid 1560s described the same area as a dense forest of wild mesquite (*monte espeso de mezquite bravo*) or a mesquite forest (*mezquital montuoso*) (table 2). By 1590 this had become a less intimidating "large mesquite woodland" with *palo dulce*, possibly reflecting some opening up and drainage. As in the case of Acámbaro, the *relación* of 1579 is quite specific, noting a "large quantity of wild trees called mesquites" as well as "many *sabinos* which are used for timber and planks for houses" (see Acuña 1987, 58). In 1579 regular, long lots are schematically shown on the pictorial map south of the river (around Mayorazgo) and a little north of Apaseo itself (around the old hacienda Jocoque) (see Acuña 1987, facing p. 58); these probably represent the first concentrations of Spanish farm plots, at a time when only irregular lots are shown at Apaseo and near Celaya. Again in 1579, 20,000 calves were branded annually within a distance of four leagues (16 km) of Celaya (see Acuña 1987, 58), at a time when 45 cattle *estancias* already were on record for the area of Apaseo-Celaya. This suggests 80,000 to 100,000 head in all, implying either that less than a quarter of the *estancia* deeds are preserved, or that stocking exceeded the prescribed rate four fold, or a combination of both. But cattle are less likely than people to have thinned out and eventually destroyed this jungle of mesquite and bald cypress; today the dry, sandy or stony river channels are mainly lined by *pirúl* and there is no trace of *Taxodium*.

Beyond the limit of the well-watered plain, the Cerro Jocoque had some yucca palms but apparently was devoid of trees, as were the rough hills further east, whereas a woodland of acacia and mesquite was present on the low mountains south of the river (see table 2). Since only eight sheep *estancias* were awarded around Apaseo before 1592, and since cattle were not normally grazed in rough mountain country, this upland vegetation would not qualify as degraded. A second feature of interest was the upstream lake, now mainly reduced to an alkali flat (El Salitre), that in 1560 was described as large and situated next to mesquite woodland. The mesquites have gone, but the flats sporadically flood with water that flows into the Río Apaseo (as in July 1991, C.E. Davis, pers. comm.). The only hint of 16th-century degradation of the alluvial lands is the record of *cardones* growing on a plain next to a wheat field—with a rock wall to protect it from livestock.

The Laja from upstream of Chamacuero down to the Apaseo confluence was apparently lined with thick, riparian mesquite woodlands. The channel island noted below Chamacuero in 1563 remains conspicuous, if only quasi-functional, today. It has shrubby vegetation, not much different from the thorny bush implied by *jaral*.

Even at the time the *relación* map of 1579 was drawn, 134 *caballerías* of farmland had already been awarded on the plain around Celaya, which was being rapidly converted into a complex, irrigated Spanish farm landscape (table 2 and Murphy 1986, 9-21), with scattered stands of mesquite, thickening towards the Río Laja. The lands prone to flooding in 1573, and the seasonal watercourse of 1576, may both refer to the abandoned course of the Laja later known as the Río Antiguo (or de los Sabinos) (see Murphy 1986, fig. 1.3). Downstream towards Salamanca the channel of the Laja may have been shallow, judging by an island and an open riparian vegetation, with thorny succulents, even in the early 1580s.

The records for Apaseo-Celaya show that the most striking, environmental differences in the Bajío between 1590 and 1990 have been the destruction of the riparian woodlands and the profound deterioration of the hydrology, due to a gradual increase in peak discharge. Since 1950, accelerating abstraction of stream and ground waters for agricultural, urban, and industrial use has dried out most smaller streams and relegated the larger ones to the removal of untreated wastewaters. But in 1590 that process had barely begun.

The Western Bajío

The *mercedes* provide only limited information for the western Bajío, in part because large areas remained unsettled until the 1600s, in part because most of these grants were made in floodplains, and in part because exact locations are difficult to identify when there are few toponymic references, such as Indian *pueblos* or adjacent *estancias*.

On the plains of Silao and Irapuato, below the escarpment of Guanajuato, rivers such as the Silao and Guanajuato (or Río Grande de Guanajuato) were probably perennial and had considerable riparian woodland. Mention is made of willow breaks, mesquite thickets, cottonwoods, and pines, with some reed breaks. The vertisolic plain of Silao had scattered small or large groups of mesquite, and there were some *cienegas* with seasonal water in this mainly open landscape. Closer to the mountain front, the fans of coarse alluvium had a variety of spiny shrubs and large Cactaceae. Although there were some prehistoric mounds (AGNM 6-274 [1563]), agricultural Indians were only then moving into the district, since the new *estancias* required a labor force for the 40 units of farm land scattered across the piedmont. Whether the cattle dominant here (perhaps 50,000 head on at least 24 *estancia* grants) had an impact on the vegetation cannot be determined from the selective information available.

The Puruándiro district includes a large area with discontinuous alluvial valleys, between the Río Grande (Lerma) and the mountain margins of Michoacan. The sparse references suggest marshy valley floors in places, with willow and ash along streams, and some reed swamps. The uplands appear to have been wooded, with live and deciduous oak, but sufficiently open or disturbed for prickly pear as well. Small farms complemented the cattle *estancias* (26 recorded, together with a horse stud) scattered about the district. Sheep had only begun to be established.

The broad valley of the Río Turbío, a major tributary catchment below León, suggests a wet, open plain with riparian thickets of mesquite (table 2). Rougher country adjacent to the floodplain has one notation of cactus bush. At least 36 cattle *estancias* were spread across this area, but many may have been rapidly abandoned, given the insecurity caused by Chichimec raiding.

The primary importance of the data for the western Bajío is that it reinforces the dichotomy of alluvial lowlands and rougher uplands, sketching — in highly summary form — patterns of mainly open vegetation similar to those more fully documented in the eastern sector.

The Basin of San Miguel and San Felipe

North of the Bajío, the great drainage basin of the Laja is bordered by a rim of mainly rhyolitic mountains. These rise 500 to 800 m above an irregular plain that falls gently from 2300 m elevation north of Guanajuato to 1900 m below San Miguel. West of the Río Laja, the plains are underlain by late Pliocene alluvium, composed of reworked sandy to gravelly volcanic materials, while to the east there are finer lake beds, derived from volcanic ash. Soils are thin and rarely qualify as vertisols. The vegetation of the lower country is a very open parkland with scattered, low and thorny deciduous trees, while thorny succulents are prominent. Mountain outliers and lower slopes have a degraded vegetation of live oak scrub, but the northern rim of mountains has pine woodlands, while the Sierra de Guanajuato preserves large tracts of deciduous oak forest.

Although the *relación* for San Miguel and San Felipe ("Chichimecas") has been lost, the pictorial map of about 1579 (see Acuña 1987, facing p. 370) replicates the panorama of modern vegetation with jarringly accurate economy, suggestively drawing unambiguous, single-trunked pines and branched oak trees at intervals among mountains outlined in olive green. The plains are left open but decorated with countless, large agave-like succulents, while the smaller basins to the northwest of San Felipe are filled with prickly pear. One tributary of the Laja, the Río de los Sauces, is fringed with a line of bushy and branched willows. This striking map provides a good backdrop for the more specific information from the *mercedes*, particularly because those data are sparse.

The deciduous oak forest of the Sierra de Guanajuato is adequately documented, as is the great *tunal* to the northwest (table 2). Whether the willows along the Río Sauces or the alder implied by the Río Alisos represented characteristic riparian vegetation elsewhere remains speculative. The *sabana* of San Gabriel, like its counterpart of San Sebastian in the northeast, suggests a prominence of open landscapes.

This limited biotic information is complemented by hydrological details: one or more cut-off channels with water in the Laja floodplain above Tequísquiapan (in 1550); a major river from the high sierra labelled as *seco* or intermittent (in 1560); another with marshy pools of water; a minor, spring-fed arroyo providing water for San Miguel's craft industries (and *huerta*); a (seasonal?) lake in the vertisolic lowland east of San Miguel (in 1563); ponds, *cienegas*, and springs in the basin of Sta. Barbara-Ibarra; and *cienegas* and small lakes on valley floors in the backcountry of Guanajuato.

All of these phenomena date within a decade of effective Spanish or Otomí settlement, and would reflect a "pristine" hydrological balance. The Río Laja appears to have been straightening its course, perhaps incising a little. Although surface water was relatively abundant, the *rio seco* cautions against assuming more than intermittent discharge in the arroyos. The overall picture is consonant with a semiarid environment.

The pictorial map also shows a landscape swarming with Spanish cattle, but only incidental horses or sheep (see Acuña 1987, facing p. 370). But there is a record of 65 cattle and 89 sheep *estancias*, almost all awarded by 1568 and implying up to 130,000 cattle and at least 200,000 sheep. This again suggests that Spanish intrusion was a matter of perception for the Indians. Perhaps the numerous vignettes of Chichimecs preying on agricultural Indians, attacking Spanish wagon trains, or hunting cattle should be seen in a similar light. A line of huts systematically follows the Río Laja to beyond modern Dolores, with the inscription "all the houses that are on the banks of this river are cattle *estancias* and some farms (*labrançae*)." This is correct except that, according to the *mercedes,* most *estancias* along the river were for sheep, with the cattle tending to be kept further out.

Unfortunately the limited and early documentation allows no inferences on possible environmental impact, but this is provided by alluvial fills. The Río Laja has deposited two sheets of flood silts across its floodplain upstream of San Miguel, as a result of "catastrophic" floods transporting soil eroded from the watershed. The older flood silts contain Indian potsherds and a hearth, with ^{14}C dates supporting a pre-Hispanic age (Charles E. Frederick, pers. comm.). The younger flood silts and terminal sands accumulated after construction of a chapel in the mid-1700s (see Butzer 1989b, 118-120); disequilibrium was probably activated by overgrazing during the late 18th or even the 19th centuries. This alluvial record does not allow for soil erosion or hydrological change from somewhat before A.D. 1500 to after 1750.

Conclusion

The results of this micro-examination of a large and diversified part of northern Central Mexico can now be summarized:

1. The land grants provide a wealth of paleo-environmental information critical to understanding land use and reconstructing the landscape of 16th-century New Spain. Acquiring and compiling such archival information is tedious, both as a procedure and in terms of its detail, but no more so than analyzing pollen cores. Interpretation, in context, is difficult but, unlike pollen counts, these documents record eyewitness testimony for a particular time and place. When the locations for land grants can be determined, they provide a potential tool to reconstruct the human and biotic landscape of the 16th century, in effect opening a new methodology for historical geography in Latin America.

2. The precision and environmental detail provided by over 200 of the land grant deeds is perhaps unexpected, with many of the applicants for *mercedes* displaying a remarkably good grasp of, and ability to describe physical and biotic features. Some descriptions are spelled out in the equivalent of two or three paragraphs. Noteworthy is that at least some of the first or second generation Spanish creoles, who put together such information for the responsible magistrates, were familiar with indigenous trees and shrubs, and their Indian names. By contrast, European travellers of the period, such as Ciudad Real

([1589]) 1976 merely identify those genera with European counterparts. Biotic elements are only mentioned in 11 percent of the land deeds before 1560, and 17 percent of those in 1560-79, but increase to 34 percent in 1580-91. Uniquely New World forms are not mentioned before 1560, when *mezquite* is first used, but after 1580 an increasing conceptual grasp of the range of succulents and subtropical hardwoods becomes apparent. This appears to document the growing familiarity of many Spanish creoles with the details of their New World environment, as part of the process of ecological re-adaptation and acculturation.

3. The information assembled here for the first 50 years of land awards in the Bajío represents approximately the halfway mark in the process of land acquisition and settlement. Primarily, it serves to delineate the environment at the time of Spanish intrusion. Secondarily, it may allow inferences about the first environmental consequences of the new forms of land use.

4. Perhaps the most striking aspects of the vegetation reconstructed here for the first decades of Spanish settlement are the prevalence of open environments, and the presence of three, distinctive biotic environments, namely: (i) the woodlands of Jilotepec, (ii) the grass-cactus-low tree associations of Querétaro and San Miguel, and (iii) the subtropical parkland of the Bajío proper. The degraded vegetation of today is similar in principle to the biotic zonation observed during the mid-16th century. But the once luxuriant, riparian forests along the major rivers have now all but disappeared, and the hydrology has been drastically changed. What the land grant records do not do is provide direct information on the immediate ground cover, e.g., whether it was grassy or not, or whether it was complete or incomplete. But palynology is little more specific, since ratios of grasses, Compositae, and Chenopodiceae represent a local composite picture that is generally skewed by variations in microtopography and substrate. Neither palynology nor any other paleoecological technique can identify shifts in grass species. We are therefore limited to the generalized evidence of biotic associations — a little more indirect and delayed in response-time with respect to possible degradation than a modern range-management expert might wish.

5. Whether 16th-century vegetation was "pristine" is not an issue in most of the region since there was no earlier agricultural settlement. But in Jilotepec-Huichapan and in the Cuitzeo and Yuríria basins, indigenous agriculture had a much longer *in situ* tradition. Here there is qualified evidence suggesting local disturbance, while the Cuitzeo Basin suggests a degree of more general, prehispanic degradation.

We should therefore refocus our attention on the impact of indigenous land-use prior to 1519, recalling the pioneer efforts of Cook (1949, 1963) in regard to pre-Hispanic soil erosion.

6. The impact of Spanish land use, particularly of grazing, is not clearly apparent as of about 1590, either in the vegetation or in the hydrological cycle. That may well be surprising, depending on one's bias. There are indeed some, but often ambiguous, suggestions that degradation had just begun in a few districts. Perhaps 1590 was too soon after settlement to expect visible changes, given the gap between impact and coherent successional response. For some districts, the data base also remains inadequate to provide a hard answer. But, in general, we cannot make a case that the first 50 years of Spanish settlement and stockraising had a tangible impact on either the land-cover or ecological equilibrium of this extensive region of north-central Mexico. Without presuming to generalize for all of Mexico, these conclusions are not necessarily limited to the Bajío. In central Veracruz Province, where we have completed a parallel study for the first century of Spanish settlement, we can verify that the stockraisers who began to exploit that region c. 1560 encountered a landscape that had already been ecologically modified, and we can identify no evidence for tangible changes in land-cover during the 16th century.

7. Such an unanticipated conclusion warrants discussion, since both the land grants and the *relaciones* imply that large numbers of domesticated stock were being run in the Bajío, overwhelmingly by Spaniards. The body of *mercedes* awarded in that region to about 1590 includes over 400 cattle *estancias*. Using the estimates available for Acámbaro and Celaya, this may represent in the order of 800,000 head. There also were almost 350 sheep *estancias*, especially in the districts of Querétaro and San Miguel. If the estimate for Querétaro in 1582 was approximately correct, there may have been an additional one million sheep in the region as a whole. These are large numbers of livestock, but cattle were allowed to roam fairly freely through much of the region, with grassy, vertisolic plains such as the Llanos de San Sebastian, providing particularly attractive pasturage. In the case of sheep, the Spaniards were evidently well aware of the dangers of overstocking on fixed, dry-season pastures, resorting to long-distance transhumance, as they were wont to do in Spain. Given the large residual tracts of land still left unsettled by both Indians and Spaniards in 1591, these mobile strategies may have been quite effective in limiting an environmental impact.

8. The land grants also provide paleo-environmental data, consonant with the interpretations offered above (item 6). Together with other

coeval documents, they show that Lake Cuitzeo was high in 1576-87 and lower in 1590-95, corroborating independent reports that the lake dried out in 1590-91. Such documentary sources establish that the lake was highly alkaline, but it did have an overflow channel that carried water down to Lake Yuríria during particularly good rainy seasons. Lake Yuríria, long claimed to be artificial, can be interpreted differently, using all available 16th-century sources, in conjunction with modern hydrological estimates. Without a link to the Río Lerma, Lake Yuríria would have averaged about two-thirds its present size, subject to strong fluctuations. But an artificial "drain," cut at some unknown time, allowed river waters to flow into the basin during some years, and excess lake waters to flow out during others, thus maintaining a relatively constant level.

9. A more conclusive verdict on the potential impact of Spanish land use might be expected for the second half of the settlement process, 1590 to 1640. Although our study of the documents for this period has not been completed, some provisional impressions can be offered as a matter of perspective. During the second 50 years, some of the districts best documented here experienced a filling-in process, while others received very few additional grants. Together with various complementary sources, evidence seems to show that Spanish land-use strategies shifted, with cattle raising increasingly limited to the western Bajío and San Felipe, and sheep raising becoming paramount in the eastern districts. A much higher proportion of the grants after 1590 was for agricultural land, implying different problems as to landscape modification. Both the de-emphasis of stockraising and the expansion of sheep transhumance northward, beyond San Luís Potosí, may have reduced pressures on pasturage in the Bajío. Our initial impressions are that there was little ecological change, and certainly no dramatic transformation. Consequently both the premises and conclusions of Melville (1990) need to be reconsidered.

In closing, it requires little emphasis that the land grants provide no substitute for further field research — specifically directed to soil erosion and valley alluviation — and palynological investigation. But until these become available — and on a comprehensive scale — the land grants and related documents will remain an inestimable source of potential information on the environments encountered, and eventually modified by Spaniards and Creoles in Mexico. Similar forms of documentation exist for several other regions of the New World, and these also need to be studied, to test current assumptions about the impacts of Spanish land-use and its temporal framework.

Acknowledgements

We are grateful to our companions in the field during the course of many trips through the study area, but particularly to William E. Doolittle, Clint E. Davis, Charles E. Frederick, Carlos Rincón, and David Wright. William M. Denevan and Philip L. Wagner provided helpful comments on a provisional manuscript, and Susan Long drafted the maps. Both the fieldwork and research were made possible by the endowment of the R.C. Dickson Professorship of Liberal Arts.

References

Acuña, R., ed. 1987. *Relaciones geográficas del siglo XVI: Michoacan.* Universidad Nacional Autónoma de México, Serie Antropólogica, 74. Mexico City.

AGNM. Archivo General de la Nación. Mercedes, 84 vols. Mexico City.

Bentura Belena, E. 1787. *Recopilación sumaria de todos los autos acordados de la Real Audiencia de Nueva España.* Mexico City: Zuñiga y Ontiveros.

Brown, R.B. 1985. A summary of late-Quaternary pollen records from Mexico west of the Isthmus of Tehuantepec. In *Pollen records from late-Quaternary North American sediments,* V.M. Bryant and R.G. Holloway, eds., 71-93. Dallas: Association of Stratigraphic Palynologists Foundation.

Butzer, K.W. 1988. Cattle and sheep from Old to New Spain: Historical antecedents. *Annals of the Association of American Geographers* 75:479-509.

——. 1989a. Historical Querétaro: Interpretation of a colonial city. *Field trip guide, Conference of Latin Americanist Geographers, Querétaro, Mexico, 1989,* pp. 3-27. Austin, TX: Department of Geography, University of Texas.

——. 1989b. Haciendas, irrigation, and livestock. *Field trip guide, Conference of Latin Americanist Geographers, Querétaro, Mexico, 1989,* pp. 91-122. Austin, TX: Department of Geography, University of Texas.

——. 1990. The Indian legacy in the American landscape. In *The making of the American landscape,* ed. M.P. Conzen, 27-50. Boston: Unwin Hyman.

——. 1992a. Ethno-agriculture and cultural ecology in Mexico: Historical vistas and modern implications. In *Benchmark 1990,* ed. T.L. Martinson, 139-152. Proceedings of the Conference of Latin Americanist Geographers , vol. 17-18. Auburn, AL.

——. 1992b. The Americas before and after 1492: An introduction to current geographical research. *Annals of the Association of American Geographers* 82:345-368.

Ciudad Real, A. de. [1589] 1976. *Tratado curioso y docto de las grandezas de la Nueva España*, 2 vol. Universidad Nacional Autónoma de México, Serie Historiadores y Cronístas de Indias, 6. Mexico City.

Cook, S.F. 1949. *The historical demography and ecology of Teotlalpan*. University of California Press, Ibero-Americana, 33. Berkeley, CA.

——. 1963. Erosion morphology and occupation history in Western Mexico. *University of California Anthropological Records* 17:281-334.

Corominas, J. 1954. *Diccionario crítico-etimológico de la lengua castellana*, 4 vol. Madrid: Editorial Gredos.

Cronon, W. 1983. *Changes in the land: Indians, colonists, and the ecology of New England*. New York: Hill and Wang.

Denevan, W. M. 1992 The pristine myth: The landscape of the Americas in 1492. *Annals of the Association of American Geographers* 82:369-385.

Doolittle, W.E. 1992. Agriculture in North America on the eve of contact: A reassessment. *Annals of the Association of American Geographers* 82:386-401.

Escobar, A.M. 1984. Las encomiendas en la cuenca lacustre de Cuitzeo. In *Michoacan en el siglo XVI*, eds. C.S. Paredos, C. Paredes Martínez, M. Piñon Floves, A. Escobar Olmedo, and M. Pulido Solís, 191-296. Colección Estudios Michoacanos, 7. Morelia: Fimax.

Fernández de Echeverría y Veytia, Mariano. [1780] 1962. *Historia de la fundación de la Ciudad de Puebla de los Angeles en la Nueva España*, 2nd printing. Puebla: Ediciones Altiplano.

Matesanz, J. 1965. Introducción de la ganadería en Nueva España, 1521-1535. *Historia Méxicana* 14:533-566.

Melville, E.G.K. 1983. *The pastoral economy and environmental degradation in highland central Mexico, 1530-1600*. Ann Arbor, MI: University Microfilms International.

——. 1990. Environmental and social change in the Valle del Mezquital, Mexico, 1521-1600. *Comparative Studies in Society and History* 32:24-53.

Murphy, M.E. 1986. *Irrigation in the Bajío region of colonial Mexico*. Dellplain Latin American Studies, 19. Boulder, CO: Westview Press.

Orozco y Berra, M., ed. 1859. *De las actas de Cabildo de la gran Ciudad de Tenuxtitan Mexico*, vols. 1-3, 1523-35. Mexico: Ignacio Bejarado.

Prem, H.J. 1978. *Milpa y Hacienda: Tenencia de la tierra indígena y española en la cuenca del Alto Atoyac, Puebla, Mexico (1520-1650)*. Wiesbaden: F. Steiner.

Puga, V. de. [1563] 1945. *Provisiones, cedulas, instrucciones para el gobierno de la Nueva España*, facsimile ed. Madrid: Ediciones Cultura Hispanica.

Rzedowski, J. 1981. *Vegetación de Mexico*. Mexico City: Limusa.

Santamaria, F.J. 1978. *Diccionario de méjicanismos*, 3rd ed. Mexico City: Porrúa.

Super, J.C. 1983. *La vida en Querétaro durante la colonia, 1531-1810.* Trans. M. Pizarro Romero. Mexico City: Fondo de Cultura Económico.

Torquemada, J. de. [1723] 1943 . *Monarquia indiana,* facsimile ed. Mexico City: Editorial S. Chavez.

Tudela de la Orden, J., ed. 1977. *Relación de las ceremonias y ritos y población y gobierno de los indios de la provincia de Michoacan (1541).* Morelia: Balsal.

Wagner, P.L. 1964. Natural vegetation of Middle America. In *Natural environment and early cultures,* ed. R.C. West, 216-264. Handbook of Middle American Indians, 1. Austin: University of Texas Press.

West, R.C. 1949. *The mining community in northern New Spain: The Parral mining district.* Ibero-Americana, 30. Berkeley: University of California Press.

Whitmore, T.M. and Turner, B.L. 1992. Landscapes of cultivation in Mesoamerica on the eve of conquest. *Annals of the Association of American Geographers* 82:402-405.

Williams, B.J. 1989. Contact period rural overpopulation in the Basin of Mexico: Carrying-capacity models tested with documentary data. *American Antiquity* 54:715-732.

Wright, D. 1988. *Conquistadores otomíes en la Guerra Chichimeca.* Gobierno del Estado de Querétaro, Colección Documentos, 6. Querétaro, Mexico.

_____. 1989. *Querétaro en el Siglo XVI: Fuentes documentales primarias.* Gobierno del Estado de Querétaro, Colección Documentos, 13. Querétaro, Mexico.

Zavala, S., ed. 1982. *Asientos de la gobernación de la Nueva España.* Mexico City: Archivo General de la Nación.

The Ingenious Ingenios: Spanish Colonial Water Mills at Potosí

Alan K. Craig

Abstract

Exceedingly rich surface veins of silver were discovered at Potosí in 1545 and a stampede of prospectors ensued. These ores were smelted directly on the Cerro Rico mountainside in simple clay furnaces of prehistoric design. Soon the richest deposits were exhausted and lower-grade ores required extensive grinding and roasting. But in this high altitude environment there were few perennial streams to supply water mills, and animal traction mills were uneconomic. At an early date (ca. 1550 ?), several small waterpowered grist mills were built near the village of Tarapaya using water from the Río San Andrés. However, the distance (10 km) from Potosí discouraged expansion and silver production from low-grade ores gradually declined until the visit of the viceroy Francisco de Toledo in 1571. Toledo promulgated many new mining regulations and the following year successfully introduced a Mexican patio amalgamation process. He also encouraged construction of an extensive reservoir system in the Kari-Kari massif above Potosí to supply water to large vertical overshot waterwheels operating multiple stamp mills. Eventually about 140 of these *ingenios* crowded the base of Cerro Rico. Known as the *Ribera*, it constituted the greatest single concentration of medieval hydraulic mill technology anywhere in the world. These improvements created a second period of prosperity that culminated in maximum silver production in 1590. A flash flood in 1626 destroyed many of these installations and Potosí never regained its former glory. Silver production declined over the next three centuries until the last waterwheel stopped turning in 1944. Today all *ingenios* are in ruins. This study examines the two best preserved sites: (1) a small, twin horizontal water mill of early design at Tarapaya, and (2) the much larger San Bartolomé complex at the downstream terminus of the *Ribera* aqueduct system where it was abandoned after the flood.

Key words: beneficiation, *ingenios*, patio amalgamation, Potosí, silver ore, Tarapaya, water mill

Potosí in Perspective

No silver deposit anywhere in the world has received more attention than the famous Cerro Rico located outside Potosí in what is now Bolivia. Hun-

---

Culture, Form, and Place: Essays in Cultural and Historical Geography, edited by Kent Mathewson, 1993. Geoscience and Man, vol. 32, pp. 125-156. Department of Geography and Anthropology, Louisiana State University, Baton Rouge, LA 70893-6010.

dreds of books and articles have been written in many languages about this incredible deposit and the fantastic events that surrounded its development.[1] Most of this literature appeared in Spanish, with few technological studies in other languages. Consequently, aspects of colonial mining and the beneficiation of silver remained poorly understood for many years. Rigorous archival research has recently uncovered a wealth of data and new understanding of these crucial processes, thanks to the pioneering scholarship of the Potosí archivist Armando Alba (1928-29, 1939, 1951).

Silver from Potosí profoundly changed the march of European history, and indeed of the entire world.[2] By 1600, Potosí had the largest population of any city in the New World.[3] The economic impact has been studied by an increasing number of scholars[4] as have the effects of the infamous *mita* (corvée labor) system.[5] On the other hand, researchers have neglected to analyze aspects of technology that evolved there as a result of the continual struggle to wring out the last ounce of silver from reluctant ores. The purpose of this paper is to investigate one facet of that technology — the waterpowered grinding and stamp mills that sprang up at the base of Cerro Rico once the problem of water supply had been solved.

Mining in one form or another has been a significant activity at Potosí for almost 450 years (with the exception of Taxco in México, this is longer than any other place in the Spanish colonial empire). There are rich archival records covering its early days as a brawling mining camp, its rapid florescence as a splendid city, and now its contemporary condition of faded decline.[6] Nowhere else do we have an equivalent record at our disposal. It is incumbent upon us as scholars to utilize these resources and recognize Potosí as an opportunity to study social institutions that often were only ephemeral at other mining communities.

Discovery and Early Events at Potosí

Spanish chroniclers agree the most important Inka silver mine was located at Colque Porco (fig. 1) in what is now central Bolivia.[7] In 1540, while a civil war between quarreling conquistadors was still in progress, a few Spaniards together with their Indian laborers established a small mining settlement to reopen the recently abandoned prehistoric silver mines. In April 1545 a Porco Indian named Gualpa discovered an outcrop of pure native silver on the slopes of a mountain about ten leagues (approx. 50 km) east of Porco. The aboriginal inhabitants of a hamlet at its base called it "*potoccsi*" in a language now extinct.[8] There are several much later romanticized versions of this discovery[9] but an archival document that has come to my attention suggests Gualpa was in fact an experienced prospector

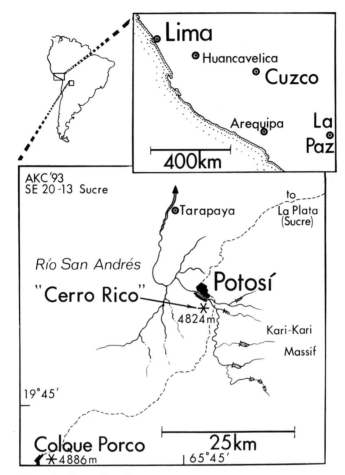

Fig. 1. Study area location map.

sent out from Porco by Captain Francisco Centeno to search for new silver deposits when his own mines began to decline.[10]

The discovery of silver at Potosí caused a stampede of Spaniards from Porco and many other parts of Peru, all of whom staked numerous claims on the choicest veins of the mountain that soon became known as Cerro Rico (fig. 2 and in the background of fig. 14). During the first year hundreds, perhaps thousands, of small clay furnaces of aboriginal design (*huayras*) were made to smelt down the silver.[11] At first such extraordinarily rich ores were simply chiseled from outcrops and smelted without any crushing or grinding.[12] These ideal conditions continued until, at the approach of winter, enslaved local Indians[13] revolted, throwing hundreds of

Fig. 2. The frost-shattered summit of Cerro Rico at Potosí.

their accumulated silver ingots into the nearby hot springs at Tarapaya (fig. 1) where they remain to this day.[14]

As Indian workers followed veins ever deeper into Cerro Rico, they soon encountered "rebellious" ore that required crushing and roasting before it could be smelted. Potosí mine owners probably first used the primitive *batán/chunga*[15] system or the two-man *quimbalete*[16] before turning to the more efficient grist mill, eventually introduced into Peru from Europe when wheat became an established crop.[17] These were small, undershot horizontal water mills (fig. 3) requiring a steady flow of water and good grindstones. Both were present 10 km north of Potosí at Tarapaya. Ten such mills eventually were built there along the eastern bank of the Río San Andrés where they became the first *ingenios* to grind silver ore from Potosí.[18]

The Tarapaya Double Horizontal Mill

The last surviving example of early mill sites at Tarapaya (figs. 4, 5 and 6) was examined in 1988. Details of the construction suggest it was originally designed as a rather ambitious double undershot horizontal mill served by an aqueduct, a holding tank and two steeply plunging raceways (fig. 5). The millstones (figs. 7, 8 and 9) were quarried from nearby outcrops of massive quartzite forming the spectacular eastern wall of the Tarapaya Valley. All of the antecedents of this European small grist mill design shown in figure 3 are represented in the Tarapaya mill site.

This unusual twin *ingenio* mill house has large basement archways for access to the horizontal waterwheels and their associated parts. Water was

Fig. 3. A small grist mill of Scandinavian design. (Printed with permission. Copyright 1983 The Johns Hopkins Press.)

Fig. 4. Western elevation of the Tarapaya mill house. Millstones were quarried from sandstone outcrops in the background. Architectural details suggest most of the structure above the double arches was rebuilt during the nineteenth century.

Fig. 5. Southern exposure of the double-horizontal Tarapaya mill house. The large cistern and double millraces fed water onto wooden blades attached to vertical shafts that rose through the floor to turn millstones inside the building. The water then flowed out through the twin archways shown in fig. 4.

Fig. 6. Rear view of the Tarapaya mill house (roofless) with the cistern in the foreground.

Fig. 7. Interior view of the Tarapaya mill house with a millstone in the corner.

Fig. 8. A *matriz* (lower millstone) in situ at the Tarapaya mill house.

Fig. 9. Detail of a *volante* (upper millstone) with shafthole and keyway inside the Tarapaya mill house.

delivered into the 3x2m two-compartment holding tank. Each compartment had simple wooden control gates allowing it to be independently filled or emptied. Water discharged from these tanks struck wooden blades of the horizontal wheel after a 3m fall. Nevertheless, the tank compartments seem to us today to be much too small for sustained ore grinding operations and in fact may prove to be a late nineteenth century special modification.[19]

When the Tarapaya mill was operational and grinding silver ore, the mill house had twin side-by-side grinding rooms, each with a square-based, round-topped millstone set firmly into the mill floor directly above the underlying waterwheel. This *matríz* millstone (fig. 8) had a circular hole in its center through which passed the vertical shaft from below. The round wooden shaft was attached to the upper millstone, referred to as the *volante* (fig. 9), by a rectangular wooden key. Anything to be ground (including grains, salt, gypsum, lime, charcoal, sulphur, and so forth) was introduced through spaces in the oversized upper shaft hole rather than in the manner shown in figure 3. Millstone grooves shown in figure 9 seem appropriate for grinding ore rather than maize or wheat but a study of diagnostic patterns for this area and era is lacking.

Other details of the mill house construction suggest it has been altered and rebuilt several times since the sixteenth century. The European-style windows are definitely an alien architectural feature, even though the walls themselves are of *tapia* (rammed earth) and adobe construction.

Unfortunately, we cannot say whether the Tarapaya mill is representative of the other nine that are known to have once been located along this same riverbank. Modern tin dredging of river bed gravels destroyed all evidence of the others and to date no archival records have been found that would be helpful in this regard.[20] Sadly, there is evidence that the mill's most recent role involved the sheltering of chickens.

Introduction of Patio Amalgamation

Although there is an extremely early archival record of Spanish mercury imported into Hispaniola in 1495,[21] it was very expensive and remained in short supply throughout most of the colonial era. A fortuitous discovery of high-grade cinnabar at Huancavelica in 1566[22] came at a time when mine owners were desperate for some means of beneficiating their "rebellious" low-grade silver ores.[23] In 1572 Francisco de Toledo became the first viceroy to visit Potosí where he consulted with mine owners at length regarding their many problems.[24] Toledo promptly promulgated a new set of mining ordinances and soon arranged for the recently perfected Mexican experts. [25] Ore samples were brought down form Potosí and the process demonstrated in front of witnesses who were amazed at the excellent results.[26]

This experiment sparked a complete resurgence in silver production that continued well into the 1590s. It was fueled by the availability of (1) large quantities of low-grade ore previously discarded in the surface tailings, (2) sufficient mercury from Huancavelica for amalgamation, and (3) a reliable supply of mill water for the stamp mills that sprang up around the base of Cerro Rico.[27] Once mine owners were convinced the new method was profitable, they rushed to install the necessary equipment and enclosed it all behind high walls to form what became known as an *ingenio*.

Reservoirs and the *Ribera*

Toledo not only stimulated miners to adopt the new amalgamation method, he also ordered them to build reservoirs sufficient to operate their new stamp mills. This was a large undertaking but not as difficult as it might seem. Once the mine owners realized they could make a profit by amalgamating masses of low-grade tailings already tipped out on the slopes of Cerro Rico, they were quite willing to participate in the community effort to construct a number of low dams across small meltwater streams originating in the nearby Kari-Kari massif. This huge eroded batholith[28] is surrounded on all sides by narrow, deeply glaciated valleys with numerous tarns and well-developed lateral and terminal moraines.[29] By damming the outlets and reenforcing the existing end moraines, it was possible to construct several large reservoirs in a matter of six months during 1572.[30]

Building a stamp mill (fig. 10) was more complicated. The first to appear at Potosí was constructed by Pedro Hernández for the mine owner Juan de Anguciana shortly after March 1572. He was granted permission to do so provided it caused no harm to the Indians by taking away their water.[31] In fact, so many mine owners applied for water mill permits it was necessary to move numerous people out of the proposed mill sites and relocate them elsewhere.[32]

These early *ingenios* with waterwheels were built along the eastern bank of a small intermittent stream of steep gradient that was normally dry most of the year. However, ample water from the new reservoirs was directed into a masonry aqueduct designed so that water from one mill passed downhill directly into the next just below it. The entire complex was connected by a tall (ca. 5 m) carefully built masonry aqueduct capable of introducing water directly into the top of the largest waterwheel. Soon this eastern stream bank area with its impressive line of stamp mills, one below the other, became known as the *Ribera*. Eventually some 200 mills were built along a 3-km distance around the base of Cerro Rico. As many as 143 operated at one time. This constitutes the harnessing of an impressive amount of hydraulic horsepower since most mills activated 8-10 vertical stamps as well as at least one set of grindstones. Taken as a whole, it seems likely the *Ribera* represented the greatest concentration of medieval hydraulic technology to be found anywhere in the world. During the eight month milling season[33] it was an anthill of activity with pack trains of llamas bringing down ore from the mountainside, charcoal from distant valleys, and food from many different sources.[34]

Mill owners soon were referred to as *azogueros*.[35] They were assigned 30-50 Indian *mitayos*[36], depending upon the size of the mill. These conscripted workers built shanties close to their assigned workplace and added to the riotous hubbub of the whole scene.

Ingenio Construction and Beneficiation

Figure 10 has been adapted from a naive sketch made circa 1700 of a Potosí *ingenio* (Arzáns 1965, I:168). This example is unusually complex and worth examining in detail. Pack trains of llamas carrying cobbles of hand-sorted ore enter through the rear gate at "A." During the winter months when no water was available for the mill, this ore was stored according to mineral type at "B." Valuable mercury and processed silver sponge were guarded at "C." Large blocks of sandstone were used for the anvil at "D" against which the stamps themselves "E" fell to crush the ore placed there. "F" represents a bank of stamps held in place by a framework (not shown) and lifted sequentially by large wooden cams (not shown) attached to the large wooden axle "G." Crushed ore was transferred to an iron mesh screen "H" for sifting with, the oversize returned for more crushing. Small ovens "J" were used to roast sulphide ores and to dry wet ore before crushing. "K" is a large bin paved with rock (see fig. 20) where standard-size batches of milled ore were mixed with reagents. "L" is a similar bin where very fine ore was mixed by treading. Low-grade ores were often given a simple assay at the mill at "M" in order to determine how they were to be beneficiated. Amalgam was separated by washing it from the remaining fines in a series of large copper basins at "N." The sponge silver was obtained by heating the amalgam in retorts under the open air shed at "O." Large *ingenios* were expected to provide a chapel "P" for the benefit of the shift workers and the overall success of the mill.

In this sketch there are two vertical waterwheels (shown with their support walls [*cárcamos*] removed). The upper wheel has only a single head (*de una cabeça*) driving a set of five *mazos* (stamps). It does not belong to the mill being illustrated but was shown to indicate that water spilling out of it passes through an aqueduct to power the double-headed wheel driving ten *mazos*. Each of these vertical stamps has a replaceable iron shoe (*amaldaneta*) that crushed the ore against a boat-shaped pillow stone (*mortero*).[37] Adjacent to this stamp mill we can see sieves of iron wire through which the crushed ore is passed. In an ordinary working day of 24 hours, a double-headed stamp mill would produce about 30 *quintales* of sieved ore (Vásquez de Espinosa 1948, 580). The women and children working at this machinery wore masks to protect themselves from the poisonous (siliceous) dust (Temple 1971, 194).

From the sieves, ore was carried in leather bags to the *buitrón*[38] pavement where the actual amalgamation took place. Here it was heaped up in a standard-sized pile (*cajón*) weighing 2 1/2 tons to which measured amounts of water, salt, and other ingredients were added according to the type of ore and the receipt of the beneficiator (usually a Spaniard). This

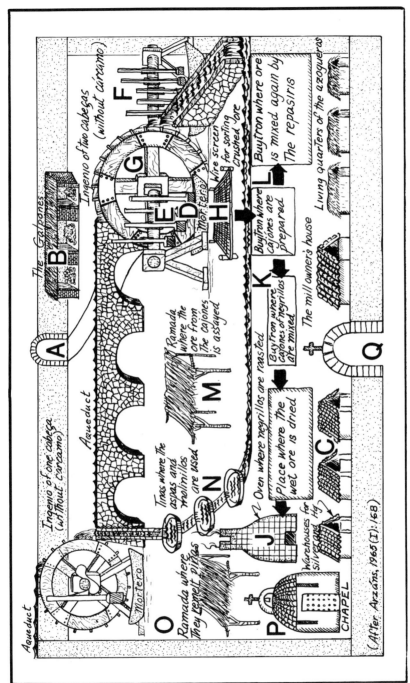

Fig. 10. Facsimile schematic sketch of a typical Potosí stamp mill ca. 1600 (after Arzans 1965).

pulp was thoroughly mixed by Indian workers (*repasiris*) using hoes and their bare feet. Mercury was carefully added to the mixture which was then stirred twice a day for as much as two weeks during which time additional water, and perhaps lime, lead, tin, copper, copper sulfate, and iron filings might be added if it seemed necessary.

When amalgamation was believed complete, the pulp was transferred to broad, circular depressions (*tinas*)[39] into which running water was directed through tubing or a spout (*chiflones*). Here a cross-brace (*aspa*) and hand mill (*molinillo*) were inserted in order to separate the lighter components (*lamas* and *relaves*[40]) from the heavier particles and amalgam. The heavier fraction then settled to the bottom of the *tina*, which was lined with a cow hide. Further careful hand washing removed the fines until the mass of amalgam (*pella*) was exposed and could be removed (Arzáns 1965, I: 170). The *pella* was placed in a linen cloth which was twisted to squeeze out and recover the excess mercury.[41] The remaining amalgam was placed in a wooden mold of triangular cross-section and pounded with a block and hammer to extract the last possible drops of mercury. The result was a *pella* shaped like a sugar loaf. This was then placed in a crucible and fired for hours until all vestiges of mercury and any other impurities were driven off. The escaping mercury vapor was condensed and recovered from a crude form of retort. The end product of all this activity was a bright, shiny *piña* of nearly pure sponge silver weighing 20-60 pounds (Temple 1971, vol. 1). *Piñas* were taken to private foundries (later to the Royal Mint itself) to be melted down and cast into bars of more or less standard size. According to law, these unassayed bars were to be submitted promptly to the mint to be assayed, valued, registered, and taxed with all prescribed marks stamped into the ingot which could then pass as legal tender.

The San Bartolomé *Ingenio* Complex

From a rough plan of what is today known as the San Bartolomé *ingenio*, sketched and measured in the field, it is found to be far more elaborate than any other ruin along the *Ribera*. In fact, it may well be the largest ever built in colonial Perú and deserves to be protected as an invaluable historic relict. The Potosí mining community has been declared a "Patrimonial Monument for all Mankind" by the United Nations.[42]

The San Bartolomé *ingenio* is located below the suburb of the same name at the final downstream left bank (west) end of the *Ribera*. On the opposite bank are the damaged remains of the much smaller San Bernabé *ingenio* (fig. 11), served by a typical Andean ditch aqueduct. The masonry west bank aqueduct terminated in a large dam and reservoir (fig. 12) built for its exclusive use. The sluiceway and aqueduct leading from the reservoir to the *ingenio* has completely disappeared. The reservoir itself has been recently filled with slimes from modern operations of the government's Pailaviri mill (fig. 13).

Inside the *ingenio* walls, another high-arched colonial aqueduct (fig. 14), of which very little remains, brought water from the reservoir to a point within the channel where it was split into two parallel streams. The principal raceway fed a large vertical, double-headed waterwheel whose wheel housing (*cárcamo*) is shown in figures 15 and 16. A secondary raceway with a steep fall powered a single-headed stamp mill built into the north side of the main aqueduct. The large broken *mortero* stone from this

Fig. 11. Principal aqueduct (width = 45 cm) of the San Bernabé *ingenio*.

Fig. 12. Colonial masonry dam and reservoir that supplied water to the San Bartolomé *ingenio*.

Fig. 13. View of the San Bartolomé reservoir filled with colonial sediments and modern slimes from the Pailaviri tin mill.

mill is still in place (fig. 17). Spent water from this wheel was channeled into an adjacent small horizontal grinding mill located immediately downslope, still on the north side of the *cárcamo*. Both of these millstones (one broken) are present, half-buried in flood deposits (fig. 18). From these remains it is quite clear that the San Bartolomé *ingenio* was indeed ingenious; it consisted of a double-headed vertical mill, a single-head vertical mill, and a single horizontal mill all built together in one structure and supplied by a single aqueduct with its own private reservoir. In addition to these milling facilities, there are various other downslope structures where large-scale roasting and other beneficiation processes occurred.

The most conspicuous of these structures is the unusually large *buitrón* shown in the background of figure 19. This 12x15m building, whose thatch roof has long since disappeared, could be used for either roasting ore in the lower unit, or gently heating pulp on the upper floor to facilitate amalgamation. In another clever arrangement, an aqueduct bringing spent water from the double-headed waterwheel, was connected to a channel built into the massive lower walls of the *buitrón* in such a way the water passed around two sides of the building and from there into a main aqueduct shown in the foreground of figure 19. This arrangement avoided the construction of a separate aqueduct to detour around the *buitrón*.

Flood damage to the San Bartolomé *ingenio* makes it impossible to reconstruct the exact nature of the lowermost buildings that were demol-

Fig. 14. Profile of the San Bartolomé *ingenio* (with Cerro Rico in the far background). Water from a large dam (fig.12) and reservoir (fig. 13) on the right was led through an aqueduct (largely torn down) with some flow diverted down the inclined raceway (center) onto a vertical waterwheel activating a stamp mill positioned at right angles in the area below the lowest arch.

Fig. 15. Main aqueduct and *cárcamo* (waterwheel housing) of the San Bartolomé *ingenio*.

Fig. 16. Skyward view of the main San Bartolomé *cárcamo*. Water issued from the aqueduct and fell with some force through the roof opening, impacting the wooden blades of the waterwheel to turn the axle fitted into a wooden bushing placed in the recesses that can be seen below on either wall. Width of the *cárcamo* = 120 cm.

Fig. 17. Remains of *mortero* stones from a subsidiary stamp mill can be seen behind this archway in the San Bartolomé ruins.

Fig. 18. Broken halves of the massive San Bartolomé grindstones probably destroyed during the 1626 mud avalanche.

Fig. 19. The San Bartolomé smelter-*buitrón* with an aqueduct bypassing the unit and de-scending into the foreground. The stamp mill complex can be seen at the upper right. Note a survey marker on the boulder in the near foreground.

ished in 1626 (described below). However, the downslope continuation of the aqueduct shown in figure 19 suggests yet another waterwheel was once housed in the rubble of the last building in this remarkable com-pound. The destructive force of the flood was sufficient to break heavy grindstones in half and fill a *cajón* (fig. 20) with flood deposits. There is nothing to be seen at the site today which suggests repairs were made after this event. San Bartolomé, as the last (and probably largest) downstream *ingenio* on the *Ribera*, was especially vulnerable to a disaster of this kind. It would have been paralyzed for lack of water until the entire aqueduct sys-tem was repaired and a new supply of water brought down to its unique reservoir.

The Great *Huayco* of 1626

The economic decline of Potosí, caused by the gradual exhaustion of high-grade silver ore, was accelerated by a disastrous avalanche of water, mud, and boulders that suddenly destroyed or damaged more than half the *in-genios* of the *Ribera* in a matter of minutes. This *huayco*[43] descended upon the unsuspecting villagers shortly after noon on March 15, 1626, wrecking many mills (figs. 21, 22 and 23) and killing at least 350 people who could not escape from its path.[44] It was caused by the sudden collapse of the

Fig. 20. Deposits from the 1626 flood and remnants of crushed ore inside a *buitrón* at the San Bartolomé *ingenio*.

principal Kari-Kari reservoir dam, releasing a wall of water that began to gouge out masses of rocks and sediment, creating a classic Andean *masamora*, inexorably engulfing everything in its path.

Waterwheels and the aqueducts supplying them were located relatively high above the stream channel being followed by the mud avalanche. The greatest damage to stamp mills took place along the narrow upper reaches of the *Ribera* before the fairly slow moving flow could spread out below on the flats around the Indian village of Cantumarca. A Spaniard caught near the headwaters was carried downhill to Cantumarca where he was found next to the *ingenio* of Pedro Zores de Ulloa.[45] He lived for 19 days before dying (with mercury pouring out of his mouth, if we may believe Arzáns!).

Evidently the dam burst at a point where it had been opened and repaired in 1599 for reasons that are not clear (Arzáns 1965, II:1). The same dam had been "repaired" during the unusually dry year of 1586 in order to make more water available [by lowering the spillway?] An investigation was made of the circumstances surrounding the 1626 disaster and there is some reason to believe the official records identifying those responsible (the *lagoneros* [lagoon keepers] and the mayor) were expunged from the archives at a later date.

Fig. 21. Ruins of a *cárcamo* and *ingenio* destroyed by the 1626 flash flood along the lower *Ribera*.

Fig. 22. Ruins of an *ingenio* recently converted into a shrine. The aqueduct supplying water to the top of this vertical waterwheel was completely destroyed by the 1626 flash flood.

Fig. 23. Rubble in the foreground represents remains of many stamp mills destroyed during the 1626 flood. Vertically dipping strata in the background are a result of thrust faulting and the Cerro Rico intrusion.

The *ingenios* of Potosí never fully recovered from the 1626 *huayco*. Silver production was steadily declining, there were serious labor problems, and the cost of replacing waterwheels was too much for many marginal operators. Only a few *ingenios* struggled on into the present century and the last wheel ceased to turn in 1944.[46]

Discussion

Potosí offers an interesting opportunity to study the long-term evolution of culture traits in a mining community. It is the only mining center in Latin America having its own archival records available on the same location. This makes it possible to practice paleographic transcriptions from colonial documents in the morning, then visit the very streets, mines, or mill ruins in the afternoon which (in the case of this writer) has a synergistic effect that is most stimulating.

There seems to be no archival documentation for the construction of vertical waterwheels driving stamp mills in the viceroyalty of Peru before 1572, when the flurry of construction began on the *Ribera*. The fully developed *ingenio* complex seems to have appeared almost without antecedents, although this is obviously improbable. First of all, we must recognize that numerous small grist mills of horizontal design, and animal-powered *trapiches* and *arrastras* were already scattered throughout the viceroyalty. They were used to grind a number of things, including silver ore in small amounts, and we know that a few were in use at or near Potosí before the hydraulic mills were built.

While easily smelted ores were mined at Potosí, medieval water mills were unnecessary. Stamp mills were introduced to crush low-grade ores after patio amalgamation was successful, and a reliable water supply was secured. This resulted in construction of a hydraulic mill complex of largely local design known as the *ingenio*. Its purpose was to use a large waterwheel to turn a massive wooden axle to which lifting cams were attached in such a way that they caused heavy iron shoes (*amaldanetas*) to be lifted and dropped onto silver ore. Many observers have remarked on the high cost of building an *ingenio*, particularly the expense of the axle. We know they were made from *soto* wood and were obtained in the distant province of Tucumán (Temple 1971, 103). Various combinations of mules, oxen, or even men were used to drag these heavy beams (6-10 *varas*, or 5-8.4 m, long) from the Chaco plains up torturous mountain trails to Potosí where they were valued in thousands of pesos.

What is left unspoken, and may not be obvious to readers unfamiliar with the workings of a stamp mill, is the fact these axles must be of large diameter in order for the cams set into them to be able to lift the individual stamp shafts as high as possible before releasing them to fall onto the ore below. The greater the axle diameter, the higher these *mazos* (the stamps) were lifted. Of course, some very careful calculations had to be made to make certain there was enough water available to power a given axle loaded down with the weight of so many stamps. Surely these details were soon worked out so that an ideal size axle could be ordered from the contractors, but so far the archives do not reveal what size was preferred. The only published photograph of a Potosí *ingenio* axle can be seen in Vignale (1944, Plate XIX).

Only the San Bartolomé ingenio, with its independent dam and water supply, could have been built without restrictions on its mill size and capacity. The fact it sprawled out over a large site, was built on a massive scale, and had extraordinary beneficiation capacity, suggests that it may in fact have been operated for the direct benefit of the King. Just as the King was entitled to the claims adjacent to any discovery claim, so it may have been that this *ingenio* was designed to process silver ore from all such claims in the region. Not even Antonio López Quiroga[47] had such a grand *ingenio* at his disposal, but it is possible it was built and operated by some as yet unidentified consortium. The answer to this and countless other fascinating facets of colonial mining at Potosí are patiently waiting in the archives for the next generation of scholars.

Conclusions

In recent years it has become possible for scholars to study many aspects of the remarkable mining community and mineral deposits at Potosí that have been actively mined longer than any other site in the New World. As a result of modern geological research, we now have a much better understanding of the regional geology, the nature of the ore bodies, and the complex mineralization of the famous Cerro Rico. Historians dealing with primary sources in a variety of archives have been able to demythologize many of the events surrounding the development of Potosí and its demography. Examples of these scholarly accomplishments include the following: (1) the role of Viceroy Francisco de Toledo in stimulating the recovery of silver production is now seen to be of the greatest importance; (2) his organization of Indian labor for the mines and its socio-political consequences have been examined in detail; and (3) the impact of Potosí silver on the economic structure of Europe, colonial Latin America, and even present day Bolivia.

All the above was dependent upon the profitable recovery of silver from what were essentially low-grade ores that required increasingly more complicated beneficiation. The *ingenio* was a remarkably successful response to these problems.

This paper identifies the important elements that contributed to success of *ingenios* whose large-scale hydraulic milling operations were based on Spanish technology cleverly adapted to local conditions encountered at this high altitude site. Control of scarce water supplies was the key to *ingenio* operations. Miners continued to convert adjacent morainal valleys into reservoirs by damming meltwater streams until the full geomorphological potential had been reached and there were no more opportunities to store water. The selection of the *Ribera* as the most appropriate location for *ingenios* represents a compromise between the necessity to distribute scarce water to as many mills as possible, while reducing the distance covered transporting ore from the mines to the mills.

The continual re-use of water by positioning waterwheels from each *ingenio* one below the other, all fed by the same aqueduct, is another locational accommodation dictated by the fundamental scarcity of water. All these arrangements required the active collaboration of the entire mining community. This was achieved and the complex projects brought to a successful conclusion by the administrative genius of the viceroy, Francisco de Toledo, who focussed his energies on solving all of the problems affecting the decline of silver production in Alto Perú.

Notes

1. A Chinese screen map circa 1582, dictated by the Jesuit Ricci, correctly locates Potosí and indicates it is an important source of silver (Giles 1919, 27). Chinese merchants of this period were faced with a chronic shortage of silver and were much interested in where it could be obtained.

2. The Spanish Armada and the many other military adventures of Felipe II during his long reign (1555-1598) were financed directly from the 20% royal tax on New World treasure, and the production of precious metals produced in large part at Potosí.

3. Maximum population figures for Potosí vary widely depending upon the author, with 160,000 serving as a mean. These demographic estimates are confused because of the variable nature of the temporary Indian population. Statements that the city's extent was once much larger at its maximum during the colonial era are incorrect. Contemporary Potosí as seen from the summit of Cerro Rico has no abandoned ruins beyond its limits. However, the colonial population was certainly vastly greater and more concentrated than the 9,000 inhabitants of today.

4. Chief among these remains Earl J. Hamilton whose 1934 doctoral dissertation is still widely cited and has been translated into Spanish as *El tesoro americano y la revolución de los precios en España, 1501-1650*. The works of Brown (1986) and Tandeter (1992) are typical of recent studies.

5. Cole (1985) has gathered together many of these data, giving an interpretation somewhat distinct from the traditional socio-anthropological view.

6. The Archivo General de Indias in Sevilla and the Archivo Nacional de Bolivia located in Sucre are the most important. The Potosí archive itself, housed in the colonial mint building, has surprising material and frustrating lacunae. Archives in Lima and Arequipa have useful copies of some important documents. Many lesser regional archives scattered throughout Spain and South America (e.g. Cuzco, Tarija, Tucuman, Arica, Codpa, etc.) are the least studied and may hold answers to many unresolved questions.

7. Porco was firmly occupied by Spaniards in 1540 in the midst of the Civil War in Alto Perú. It quickly became an official mining *asiento* (settlement with a claims official). Prospectors were required to go there in person, demonstrate the ore they had found, and receive their temporary wooden claim stakes. By 1545 the Porco mines were already in decline and relatively few Spaniards and their *yanacona* (special retainer) Indians were living there (Cañete y Domínguez [1791] 1952). Today it enjoys a modest resurgence in mining operations.

8. Neither the meaning nor language from which this word is derived have been accurately identified. It presumably was the name given to the mountain by the aboriginal Indians living at its base (it may be derived

from Puquina which is the nearest language group). We know a small group of Quechua-speaking *mitmaq* (forcibly displaced) Indians were living there at the time it was discovered by the Spanish, but the name has no meaning in either Quechua or Aymará. De Llanos (1983, 107) believed it was derived from the Aymara word *putuchini* meaning "great producer" but this is obviously forced since there is no reliable evidence of prehistoric mining activity there.

9. The apocryphal nature of the discovery is substantiated by the similarity of detail surrounding Potosí and Cerro de Pasco — for the latter see von Tschudi (1846, 256).

10. Archivo General de Indias (hereafter AGI): Charcas 134, s.f. (1603 has been written in pencil at the heading; there is no signature).

11. These crude prehistoric clay furnaces — shaped somewhat like a Spanish *buzón* (cast iron mail drop) — had numerous round air holes punched in the sides while the clay was still damp and the *huayras* itself filled with hand sorted ore and fuel. They were usually constructed in cols or mountain slopes where strong nighttime katabatic winds forced a draft into the ignited charge. Chroniclers routinely fail to mention a *huayras* must be completely destroyed in order to recover the smelted silver and, except for the base, cannot be used over again. Capoche (1959, 111) claimed exactly 6,497 of these furnaces were built on Cerro Rico, but he does not indicate how he arrived at this datum. My own efforts to find their remnants failed because the slopes of Cerro Rico are now entirely covered by colonial and modern tailings.

12. This mill site has many scattered cupellation shards and other assaying debris, some with dates of manufacture that prove the mill was used to grind ore samples for assay during the latter half of the nineteenth century. A small field behind the storage tank is filled with even earlier midden material that would be useful for excavation by an historical archaeologist. As this is the last surviving example of this very early water mill design, we can only hope that something will be done to preserve it for future study.

13. Quechua-speaking Indians living in the village of Cantumarca at the base of Cerro Rico were treated harshly by Spaniards from Porco who became frenzied at the richness of the silver veins and were desperate for workers (Quesada 1950, 24-30). The few Indians previously assigned to them had to be kept working at Porco to avoid having these claims declared abandoned and seized by claim jumpers.

14. Several attempts were made during colonial times to drain this hot spring by driving a *socavón* (adit) into its base. These attempts failed and the considerable amount of accumulated silver must remain there to this day (Arzáns 1965, I:24).

15. A *batán* and *chunga* are oversize versions of the better known Mesoamerican *metate* and *mano*. The anvil *batán* soon develops a dished surface where the pieces of ore are placed to be crushed as the *chunga* is rocked back and forth over them.

16. The *quimbalete* (or Chilean mill) was an even larger version of the prehistoric *batán/chunga* in which a long wooden pole was lashed to the rocker stone and manipulated by men on either end (Cañete y Domínguez [1791] 1952, 28).

17. Although Spanish conquistadors greatly preferred prestigious wheat bread to any other, the conquest and ensuing decade of civil war delayed the spread of European crops and the consequent need for grist mills. The earliest archival record (1550) of any sort of mill seems to be for the construction of a sugar mill (*trapiche*) at La Paz (Clemence 1932, 182). But this is curious because sugar cane was not being grown anywhere near there.

18. In all probability these were simple grinding mills using water taken from the Río San Andrés by a *bocatoma* (small check dam leading into an aqueduct). Ore had to be carried a considerable distance back and forth by llama pack trains and the location was never popular with the Potosí mine owners who do not, at first, seem to have been the owners/operators of these pioneer mills, as some later were.

19. From an analysis of cupellation shards and other surface refuse in and behind the building, I conclude it was used extensively as an assay house during the latter half of the last century.

20. According to Gunnar Mendoza (pers. com.) there is reason to be optimistic that the National Archives in Sucre contain much unused data regarding water mills and other aspects of mining in general.

21. This unusual shipment (4 *quintales*; AGI, Contratacion 3249, fol.7) can only have been for the purpose of amalgamating the placer gold then being recovered by the earliest Spaniards in the Isabella area from rivers draining the north slope of the central massif of Hispaniola.

22. For a definitive study of Peruvian mercury mining see Lohmann-Villena (1949).

23. Earlier attempts to amalgamate silver at Potosí had failed and seem puzzling. Organic impurities (perhaps ignorantly introduced) will cause mercury to "sicken and flour" (Gaudin 1939, 473-477), but Barba ([1637] 1923, 173) ascribed these same symptoms to a combination of bad practices.

24. For details, see Levillier (1925) who was indefatigable in his scholarship related to Toledo and other figures of the colonial era.

25. Pedro Fernández de Velasco and Jeronimo Piña de Zúñiga were the Mexican experts sent to Cuzco at the request of Toledo. Although their method was a success, the viceroy evidently was displeased with these in-

dividuals and only paid them a pittance for their troubles (Craig 1989, 166).

26. The silver ore samples must have been ground at Potosí and then brought down to Cuzco together with the necessary tools, reagents, and assaying equipment. The assembled mine owners were skeptical of the rather complicated process. There is no record of the receipt used, nor exactly where this demonstration took place, but the audience was galvanized by the results. Stamp mill construction began almost immediately and the first successful amalgamations took place in 1574 (Barba [1637] 1923, 82).

27. Arzáns (1965, I:157) states the first four hydraulic *ingenios* were built just below the main reservoir (variously referred to as the Chalviri or Tavacoñuño lagoon) by the men most responsible for building this key dam. All mills had special names and we know the first to begin operations was called "Agua de Castilla." According to Arzáns, a Cedula Real of 1574 offered mine owners 20,000 Indian laborers if they would agree to construct mills. However, Mendoza (in Arzáns 1965, I:n.2) states flatly that no such document exists in the sources he has consulted.

28. The geological relationships of Cerro Rico to the Kari-Kari batholith and the position of both these features with respect to the regional structure and stratigraphy can clearly be seen from outer space as evidenced in the outstanding large scale LANDSAT image 02234-098 (May 1981). Near vertical, vertical, and overturned beds near Cerro Rico (see figs. 21 and 23) are testimony to intense faulting and severe displacements that accompanied this intrusion and mineralization. Many geological aspects remain in dispute.

29. The definitive study on these features is by the engineer Rudolph (1936, 524-554) who investigated each of the 32 lagoons, the connecting canals, and construction methods of the dams involved.

30. Construction of all the dams, aqueducts, and mill sites was accomplished in the space of a few years by 66 foremen (experts?), 200 Spaniards and 400 Indians, beginning in December 1574 and continuing until mid-March 1577 when the first stamp mill operations began. By 1608 at least 132 mills had been built and there were 140 by 1610 (Arzáns 1965, I:157-8; 169). Rudolph (1936, 529-32) claims reservoir construction continued on until 1621 and that the dry season flow along the *Ribera* was reduced to 20-30 liters/sec. By his calculations the total hydraulic head amounted to 594 meters and the left bank aqueduct carried about 250 liters/sec which would provide a steady 600 hp at the mills.

31. Arzáns 1965, I:145, note 2, by Gunnar Mendoza.

32. This collaborative community effort is another of many such examples that occurred at Potosí where mutual cooperation was imperative in matters related to mining and beneficiation.

33. During the four harsh winter months (June-September) no stamp mills operated at Potosí because the water in the reservoirs and the moistened crushed ore was frozen. Mining from the interior of Cerro Rico continued however, with the accumulated ore stockpiled in locked storage rooms (*galpones*) inside the security walls of the *ingenio* (see fig. 10, "B").

34. Thousands of pack llamas were necessary for transport of ore and the logistical supply of Potosí. Food in the form of dried fish (*congrio*) was brought in from the Pacific port of Cobija 200 leagues away in Chile. Widespread deforestation around the mining center itself resulted in charcoal being carried in by llamas from a distance of as far as 80 leagues (approximately 446 km). Charcoal, in fact, was the basis for promptly moving the mint briefly established in La Plata in 1574, to Potosí. It was easier to transport relatively light charcoal from the eastern Andean foothills up to Potosí, than to bring the heavy ore down to La Plata for grinding where there were few, if any, *ingenios* in place and inappropriate water supplies available for powering the grinding mills. (AGI Charcas 16, leg.55; Dr. Barros to the crown, 8/9/1572). For further details see Cobb (1972).

35. The word "*azoguero*" (mercury user) does not seem to appear before 1580 in archival records relating to Potosí. Presumably it was intended to mean the owner of an *ingenio*, they being the only individuals allowed to purchase the scarce mercury. Later it came to include mine owners as well, many of whom also owned mills. As the number of mill owners slowly declined during the seventeenth century, the term finally became synonymous with mine owner (Cañete y Domínguez [1791] 1952, 637).

36. The *mita* was a widespread system of forced, tribute Indian labor institutionalized by the viceroy, Francisco de Toledo. It was the most important of his many efforts to stimulate mining and, as a consequence, increase the amount of the King's 20% royalty tax charged for "permitting" his serfs to dig up silver that legally belonged to him (as did all valuable natural resources in the New World). A voluminous literature exists on the *mita* (Ballesteros Gaibrois 1950; Basadre 1939; Cole 1985; Tandeter 1981; Weidner 1959-60).

37. These quartzite anvil stones positioned beneath the vertical stamps were indeed canoe-shaped and hollowed out to some extent in order to allow wet crushing which reduced the hazardous silica dust. Broken remains of such a *mortero* can be seen behind the broad arch in figure 17.

38. This term makes reference to the early practice of building a shed under which small fires (in braziers?) gently heated the pulp to improve amalgamation. It was soon abandoned as too costly and the *cajónes* were merely covered with cowhides to prevent nighttime freezing (de Llanos

1983, 17). Eventually the word *buitrón* came to mean the walled patio itself where amalgamation took place in the *cajónes*.

39. Evidently in some installations the *tinas* were merely depressions dug into the patio surface (and stone lined?) where hand washing could take place. But Barba ([1637] 1923) makes it clear that large metal cauldrons were to be preferred for recovering the amalgam. However, wooden tubs were probably more common as seen in the realistic watercolor sketch held by the Hispanic Society of New York and best illustrated in Prieto (1973, op. 44).

40. *Lamas* were slimes of fine sediment washed out of crushed ore. If from a rich mineral, the slimes were carefully collected and either sold or reprocessed at a profit. *Relaves* were the coarser fractions remaining after cleanup of the amalgam. They were routinely assayed for residual silver content and beneficiated again if practical.

41. The amalgam is an imperfect mixture of mercury and silver. There is always some liquid mercury remaining unamalgamated and trapped within the pasty mass from which it can be mechanically expressed.

42. Nevertheless, the ruins of San Bartolomé are not effectively protected under this manifesto. Abundant survey markings on the remains (fig. 19) suggest it is destined to be demolished to make room for a new roadway.

43. The Quechua word *huayco* is used throughout the central Andes to designate a variety of sudden mass wasting events that take the form of avalanches, landslides, or in the case described, a rather slow moving mudslide. The 1626 *huayco* was notable for the loud rumble (caused by impacts of boulders contained in the mudflow against bedrock) that developed from the initial wall of water.

44. Some sources claim thousands were killed but the most reliable estimate seems to be that of Arzáns (1965) even though he actually wrote about the events 80 years after they happened.

45. This penultimate mill site presumably was located not far from the present day ruins of San Bartolomé. The dry river bed of the *Ribera* is still being worked by artisanal miners in its lower reaches who hope to recover ore, amalgam, mercury and other valuables carried downhill by the 1626 and subsequent floods.

46. Vignale (1944) contains an evocative photograph (Lamina XVIII) of the last waterwheel at Potosí encased in its *cárcamo*.

47. For a fascinating account of the career of Potosí's leading silver miner, mill owner, merchant, and farmer, see Bakewell's (1988) *Silver and Entrepreneurship in Seventeenth-Century Potosí: The Life and Times of Antonio López Quiroga*.

Acknowledgements

Following my inadvisable high altitude honeymoon at Potosí in 1959, my anoxia and chronic headache were replaced by another desire: to capture the significance and essence of this great colonial mining city. Since that time I have gained motivation from the examples of field work and scholarship provided by my mentor, Robert C. West who, together with Fred B. Kniffen (deceased), is being honored with this *festschrift*. Archival work was facilitated by Ing. Soux at Potosí and Gunnar Mendoza, Director of the Archivo General de Bolivia at Sucre. Travel to, and within, Bolivia was partially supported by the Bolivian Geological Survey and a modest travel grant from Florida Atlantic University. William Watkins of the Florida Atlantic University photography laboratory processed the figures and Susan Wilde of the geography department aided in solving computer puzzles.

References

Alba, A. 1928-1929. Indice general del Archivo Municipal (de Potosí). *Boletín de estadistica municipal de la ciudad de Potosí*. Nos. 1-19.

——. 1939. Los archivos coloniales de Potosí. *Kollasuyo* Año I: 13-30.

——. 1951. Archivo de documentos de la Casa Real de Moneda, Indice analítico, Parte Primera: Siglo XVII. *Boletín de la Sociedad Geográfica y de Historia Potosí*. Año 39(11): 156-159.

Arzáns de Orsúa y Vela, B. 1965. *Historia de la Villa Imperial de Potosí*. Tomo I-III. Edición de Lewis Hanke y Gunnar Mendoza. Providence, Rhode Island: Brown University Press.

Bakewell, P. 1988. *Silver and entrepreneurship in seventeenth century Potosí: The life and times of Antonio López de Quiroga*. Albuquerque: University of New Mexico Press.

Ballesteros Gaibrois, M. 1950. *Descubrimiento y fundación de Potosí*. Zaragoza.

Barba, A. A. [1637] 1923. *El arte de los metales*. Translation by Ross E. Douglas and E. P. Mathewson. New York: John Wiley and Sons.

Basadre, J. 1939. El régimen de la mita. In *El Virreinato del Perú*, J. M. Valega, 187-203. Lima: Universidad de San Marcos.

Brown, K. W. 1986. *Bourbons and brandy*. Albuquerque: University of New Mexico Press.

Cañete y Domínguez, P. V. [1791] 1952. *Guia histórica, geográfica, física, política, civil y legal del Gobierno e Intendencia de Potosí*. Colección Primera; Los escritores de la Colonia. No. 1. Potosí: Editorial "POTOSI."

Capoche, L. 1959. *Relación general de la Villa Imperial de Potosí*. Edicíon y estudio preliminar por Lewis Hanke. Biblioteca de Autores Españoles, vol. 122. Madrid: Editorial Atlas.

Clemence, S. R. 1932. *The Harkness Collection in the Library of Congress: Calendar of Spanish manuscripts concerning Peru 1531-1651*. 2 vols. Washington, DC: U.S. Government Printing Office.

Cobb, G. B. 1972. *Potosí y Huancavelica: Bases económicos 1545-1640*. La Paz: Academia Boliviana de la Historia.

Cole, J. A. 1985. *The Potosí mita 1573-1700: Compulsory Indian labor in the Andes*. Stanford, CA: Stanford University Press.

Craig, A. K. 1989. Mining ordenanzas and silver production at Potosí: The Toledo reforms. In *Precious metals, coinage and the changes in monetary structures in Latin-America, Europe and Asia (late middle ages-early modern times)*. Ed. Eddy H. G. Van Cauwenberghe, 159-183. Brussels: Leuven University Press.

de Llanos, G. 1983. *Diccionario y maneras de hablar que se usan en las minas y sus labores en los ingenios y beneficios de los metales [1609]*. Con un estudio de Gunnar Mendoza L. y un comentario de Thierry Saignes. Serie Fuentes Primarias No.1, Museo Nacional de Etnografía y Folklore. La Paz: MUSEF editores.

Escalona, G. de. 1775. *Gazophilacium regium Perubicum*. Madrid.

Gade, D. W. 1971. Grist milling with the horizontal waterwheel in the central Andes. *Technology and Culture* 12:43-51.

Gaudin, A. M. 1939. *Principles of mineral dressing*. New York: McGraw-Hill Book Co.

Giles, L. 1919. Translations from the Chinese world map of Father Ricci. *Geographical Journal* 53 (Jan. 19-30): 19-30.

Gritzner, C. F. 1974. Hispano gristmills in New Mexico. *Annals of the Association of American Geographers* 64(4): 514-524.

Levillier, R. 1925. *Gobernantes del Perú, cartas y papeles siglo XVI*. Tomo VIII. Madrid.

Lohmann-Villema, G. 1949. Las minas de Huancavelica en los siglos XVI y XVII. Sevilla: Escuela de Estudios Hispano-Americanos.

Mendieta Pacheco, W. 1988. *Potosí: Patrimonio de la humanidad*. Potosí: Editora "El Siglo."

Prieto, C. 1973. *Mining in the New World*. New York: McGraw Hill Book Co.

Quesada, V. G. 1950. *Crónicas Potosinas*. Tomo I. Potosí: Sociedad Geográfica y de Historia Potosí.

Rudolph, W. E. 1936. The lakes of Potosí. *The Geographical Review* 26(4): 529-554.

Tandeter, E. 1981. Forced and free labor in late colonial Potosí. *Past and Present* 93:98-136.

——. 1992. *Coacción y mercado: La minería de la plata en el Potosí colonial, 1629-1826*. Archivos de Historia Andina 15. Cusco: Centro de Estudios Regionales Andino "Bartolomé de Las Casas."

Temple, E. [1833] 1971. *Travels in various parts of Peru: Including a year's residence in Potosí*. 2 vols. New York: AMS Press. First American printing by E. L. Carey of Philadelphia.

Vásquez de Espinosa, A. 1948. *Compendio y descripción de las Indias Occidentales*. The Smithsonian Institution Publication 3898, Vol. 108, Smithsonian Miscellaneous Collections. Washington D.C.

Vignale, P. J. 1944. *La casa real de moneda de Potosí*. Buenos Aires: Ediciones de arte "Albatross."

von Tschudi, J. J. 1846. *Peru: Reiseskizzen aus den Jahren 1838-1842*. St. Gallen. Also published in 1966 as *Testimonio del Peru*. Lima: Talleres Gráficos P. L. Villanueva.

Weidner, D. L. 1959-60. Forced labor in colonial Peru. *The Americas*, 16:357-83

Trade and the Emergence of Global Culture in Spanish Colonial New Mexico

Martha A. Works

Abstract

Trade from Mexico City, through the silver mining towns of northern Mexico to the frontier colony of New Mexico brought silks, lace and porcelain from the Far East, linen from Europe, and finely executed crafts — carved chests, textiles and pottery — from Mexico proper. Although colonial New Mexico (1598-1821) is commonly regarded as isolated and impoverished, it was connected through an inticate web of trade relations to the rest of the world. Items and techniques of workmanship came to Mexico from the far reaches of Spain's empire where they were redistributed to the outlying provinces. Philippine carved chests, Majolica pottery, Oriental rugs and religious icons inspired cottage and guild industries throughout the New World. In New Mexico, colonial material culture — imported and domestic — reflects this myriad of influence. Archival sources from the colonial era (decrees, supply lists, wills and inventories) indicate the relative richness of New Mexico's material culture and the impact of trade in the development of a distinctive regional culture.

Key words: colonial New Mexico, global culture, trade

Northern New Mexico was the far northern frontier of New Spain for most of the colonial era. As such the region is often characterized as isolated and impoverished, and no doubt it was when compared to the glittering colonial capital of Mexico City. However, a look at the domestic material culture of colonial New Mexico reveals an extensive web of trade connections from the earliest days of exploration and settlement. What was in New Mexico homes in the seventeenth, eighteenth and early nineteenth centuries? What does this tell about patterns of trade, production and industry, and the emerging material culture of provincial New Mexico?

This paper draws on many sources for general information. However, specific observations are culled from the wills and inventories in Series I of the Spanish Archives of New Mexico, commonly called the Land

Culture, Form, and Place: Essays in Cultural and Historical Geography, edited by Kent Mathewson, 1993. Geoscience and Man, vol. 32, pp. 157-173. Department of Geography and Anthropology, Louisiana State University, Baton Rouge, LA 70893-6010.

Grant Records.[1] These documents were originally assembled to help law-yers sort out problems of land ownership. Most of the documents relate to transfers of land, but the collection includes over 140 wills and inventories of possessions that make reference to holdings of land and livestock, and have extensive lists of items to be divided amongst the relatives and associates of the deceased. There are many other sources of information about colonial material culture and trade: church inventories, supply lists for settler caravans and mission supply trains, customs house reports, and reports from royal inspections.

Trade and material culture in colonial New Mexico have been sub-jects of interest to art historians and historians, but the geographical di-mension is often missing. Existing work does not focus on questions of origin, distribution and interaction. Also, while various elements of mate-rial culture have been studied in great detail —notably New Mexican tex-tiles (Fisher 1979), iron (Simmons and Turley 1980), silver (Boylan 1974), and furniture (Taylor and Bokides 1987) — little has been done on the web of trade relations that connected New Mexico to the rest of the world in the colonial era. Max Moorhead's excellent book, *New Mexico's Royal Road* (1958), has a good chapter on the colonial trade, but the focus of the book is the post-1821 Santa Fe Trail trade.

This paper also addresses some of the ongoing debates about the de-velopment of regional culture in northern New Mexico. Was the region isolated from outside influences and poverty-stricken? Did it exist as an enclave of Spanish colonial culture peripheral to an emerging world sys-tem (Hall 1986)? Does the area, today isolated by political boundaries and modern transportation from its cultural history, represent an historic relic of the Spanish colonial era (Nostrand 1970, 1975, 1980)?

Blaut and Ríos-Bustamante (1984, 57) refute an isolationist viewpoint and argue against the existence of a "distinctive, Spanish-derived, non-Mexican subculture" in northern New Mexico. They counter that the Span-ish-speaking population in the area represents an ongoing process of im-migration from Mexico and that the communities of northern New Mexico are not known to be significantly different from Hispanic or mestizo com-munities of northern Mexico. They see northern New Mexico, not as a dis-junct enclave, but as a contiguous part of an Hispanic culture region.

Ahlborn (1983) addresses the common perception of isolation and poverty, and makes a case for an abundance of possessions and hence rel-ative wealth in colonial New Mexico. Ahlborn does not put his evidence in social or demographic perspective, however, and draws on examples from several particularly opulent wills, inventories, and supply lists.

I will argue that, despite a location peripheral to emerging industrial and commercial centers, northern New Mexico experienced an influx of items and ideas from various parts of the world. The result of trade was not a materially wealthy province, as one might infer from Ahlborn's work (1983), for New Mexico had little to offer in return that might drive trade. The result instead was a province that was exposed, however intermittently, to outside influences which significantly affected items that were produced and consumed in New Mexico homes.

New Mexico's and specifically Santa Fe's importance as a terminus of trade during the Spanish era (1598-1821) and as a pivot for trade in the Mexican (1821-1847) and United States eras (1847 until the coming of railroads in 1880s) was due to strategic location and not to the natural wealth of the region. Therefore the benefits of trade, particularly in the colonial era, accrued to a very small number of people, and these people in turn were heavily indebted to merchants in Chihuahua (Ríos-Bustamante 1976). Trade enriched northern New Mexico only marginally in a material sense (i.e., the inhabitants did not become richer), but more importantly through association with a global community.

Spanish Settlement of New Mexico

The first Spaniards to enter the upper Rio Grande valley accompanied Francisco Vásquez de Coronado's 1540 expedition. They were spurred by Father Marcos de Niza's vision of gilded cities, but returned to Mexico City disappointed and disgraced by their failure to vindicate the province as a "new" Mexico, full of fabulous cities and exotic riches. Despite several smaller expeditions in the intervening years, it was not until 1598 that Don Juan de Oñate entered the area with families, livestock, soldiers, priests, and the intent to settle. Impetus for exploration and settlement was based on a lingering hope of riches. Equally important, the region had in abundance that other great motivator of Spanish settlement: Indian souls to convert to Christianity. The Pueblo Indians of the valley found themselves the target of an aggressive conversion campaign which involved destruction of native religious structures and symbols and suppression of traditional beliefs.[2]

The missionary motive proved the prevailing force for continued occupation in the seventeenth century as the Spanish failed in their efforts to find mineral riches. However, zealous tactics of the priests, combined with repressive labor conditions for Indians under tribute-obsessed governors, and several decades of drought and famine led the loosely organized Pueblos to pool their strengths and rebel against the Spanish. The Pueblo Revolt of 1680 resulted in several hundred slain colonists and the retreat of the surviving colonists (some 2,000) south to El Paso.

The abandonment of the New Mexico colony was a bitter blow to New Spain and the Spanish crown. Determination to resettle the area, something effected by General Diego de Vargas in 1693, was prompted by growing Spanish concern over the possibility of French incursions from the east. New Mexico became a defensive frontier in the 1700s, now peopled by settlers without illusions of great and imminent wealth and with a military presence, the Santa Fe Company.

Scattered farms and ranches and several nuclei of settlement (Santa Cruz, Santa Fe, Albuquerque, and distant El Paso) now formed a permanent community on the far northern frontier of Spain's New World empire (fig. 1). A distinctive pattern of settlement and economy emerged during this time, with the Río Arriba area around Santa Fe, Santa Cruz and Taos specializing in agriculture and trade, and the more affluent Río Abajo area around Albuquerque with emphasis on cottage industry and ranching.

The 1700s in New Mexico were characterized by a time of peace with the Pueblo Indians. Repressive labor regimes and zealous missionary tactics were replaced with an understanding of the necessity for conciliatory and cooperative relations to insure survival of the colony. In fact, the Pueblos and Spanish became allies against increasing raids by the Utes, Comanches, Apaches, and Navajo. Swift and devastating raids by the nomadic tribes wreaked havoc on Hispanics and Pueblo Indians alike until late in the eighteenth century when a peace was established through a combination of military retaliation by the Spanish and trading concessions to the tribes. The century was also a time of increasing illegal trade with the French. Several parties of Frenchmen surreptitiously made their way to Santa Fe where they found a population eager for manufactured goods (Simmons 1988, 80-81).

Spain always tried to monopolize trade amongst her colonies and pressure had been building in New Mexico as well as in other Spanish colonies for a more liberal exchange of goods. Mexican independence in 1821 finally opened the way for free trade between Mexico, New Mexico and the newly-independent Americans. The legendary era of the Santa Fe Trail trade now began, as Mexico welcomed trade with the United States, and American traders were eager for the famous silver coins from Mexican mines. The name Santa Fe Trail is something of a misnomer, however, for, as had been true throughout the colonial era, goods from northern and central Mexico, not Santa Fe, were the focus of trade. In 1847 New Mexico became part of the United States, and by 1880 the railroad came through northern New Mexico, bypassing Santa Fe, and issuing the final blow to colonial patterns of trade.

An Overview of Colonial Trade

For most of the colonial era, and particularly during the first 100 years of settlement, the major thrust of trade from Spain and central Mexico to New Mexico was toward supplying the colony. After disappointment over the absence of mineral riches, there was little expectation of lucrative

Fig. 1. Northern New Mexico and regional trade routes.

return from economic activity in the region. Missionary activity, then the defensive frontier justified this drain on the crown's coffer.

Don Juan de Oñate entered the region in 1598 with several hundred settlers, 83 wagons and carts, and over 4,000 head of livestock. The wagons were filled with items to sustain the colony: wheat, flour, sugar, unworked iron, tools, fabric, medicine, articles for barter, and artillery and arms (Hammond and Rey 1953, 1:199-308). Another caravan with soldiers, settlers, friars, and supplies reached the area in late 1600 and in 1610 a caravan carrying supplies and a new governor arrived in New Mexico (Oñate was dismissed in 1607). By this time, the crown was committed to full support of the New Mexico missions.

A regular supply service was to be sent every three years, but for the next two decades there is firm record of only 3 mission caravans (Scholes 1930, 94). By 1631 the government turned responsibility for the caravans over to the friars and the supply trains ran regularly every 3 or 4 years for the next 30 years. By the early 1660s maintenance of the supply caravans was delegated to a lay administrator, and efficiency of service declined, perhaps contributing to the fall of the colony during the Pueblo Revolt (Scholes 1930, 386).

Little documentation on trade or any other aspects of New Mexico life remains for the seventeenth century, as any paperwork in the province at the time was destroyed in the Revolt of 1680. It is known that this was a long, dusty trip of some 1,500 miles which roughly follows the route of Mexican highways 49 and 45 through Zacatecas, Parral and Chihuahua, and Interstate 25 in New Mexico. The round trip took 18 months: 6 months out, 6 months in Santa Fe and 6 months for the return to Mexico City.[3] From the contract of 1631 it is known that the missions were regularly supplied with food (including dried fish, beans, oil, vinegar, sugar, jams, and cheese), nails, latches, tools, livestock, fabric, shoes, kitchenware, and medicine as well as vestments, wine, candles, and vessels for religious services (Scholes 1930, 100-113).

No provisions were made for any sort of exchange of goods on the return trip, although, the governors of New Mexico would frequently fill the wagons with cloth, salt, hides and piñon nuts at considerable profit to themselves. Governor Luis de Rosas in 1639 sent a shipment to Parral, Mexico, which included 1,900 *varas* (one *vara* equals approximately 33 inches) of woolen cloth, 5 bales of painted buffalo hides, several bales of chamois skins, 2 boxes containing 900 candles, nearly 500 blankets, and several other boxes of drapes, hangings, overskirts, and doublets (Bloom 1935, 244-45). Other governors profited from similarly supplied caravans. That much of the labor to produce these woven goods, hides and candles came from Pueblo and Apache slaves did nothing to improve Spanish-Indian relations — another factor contributing to the Pueblo Revolt of 1680.

When trade resumed after the Reconquest in 1693, supply was a factor, this time of military installations as well as missions, but of growing importance was true exchange. New Mexican governors proved that a profit could be made in the mining towns of northern Mexico on goods from the province. More important, traders from northern Mexico realized that New Mexico settlers were desperate for goods: the colonists often had gone without while friars and governors scrambled for goods from the supply trains of the seventeenth century. Government supply trains continued to bring goods into the area in the 1800s, and by at least mid-century ran on a yearly basis on regularly scheduled excursions. Smaller caravans left during other times of year to carry mail or special decrees to and from Mexico City. The establishment of Chihuahua as a mining town in 1697 had a major impact on the New Mexico colony. Closer than Parral, it became the staging ground for trade and communication for the northern frontier. As early as 1721 Chihuahua merchants had a presence in Santa Fe as evidenced by the will of Juan de Archiveque, a Santa Fe trader already indebted to Chihuahua merchants (SANM I, 8:007).[4]

The influence of Chihuahua merchants grew over the eighteenth century as did illegal trade with Plains Indians (forbidden because they were not Christians), French, and eventually Americans. Spain's monopolistic trading practices, the low value of New Mexico's goods relative to imported goods from Europe and manufactured items from central Mexico, and the complicated currency system in use on the frontier frustrated the colonists.[5] They, along with a succession of New Mexican governors, petitioned the viceroy and crown repeatedly for measures to enhance their trading advantage. In 1737 the citizens of Albuquerque petitioned the governor to revoke a decree prohibiting the sale of wool, grain or cattle (SANM II, 7:969). Plans were made in 1788 and 1789 to improve the quality of woven and leather goods in New Mexico in an effort to improve economic conditions (SANM II, 12:90, 12:238). The *alcabala*, or sales tax, on goods from New Mexico was temporarily lifted for ten years in 1796 to further encourage trade.

Trade fairs were established to provide an outlet for New Mexican goods and an arena for trade. As early as 1723 Spanish royal decrees established annual fairs at Taos and Pecos, partly to attract Indian trade away from the French (Simmons 1983a, 78). Later, in the early 1800s, fairs were established in San Juan de los Lagos, south of Aguascalientes; San Juan del Río, near present-day Torreon; in Saltillo; and in the Valle de San Bartolomé (Allende), near Hidalgo de Parral. To encourage participation, collection of sales and consumption taxes was suspended during the official days of the fair (Simmons 1983a, 84).

Given the growing emphasis on trade and material goods in the 1700s and 1800s, what was actually traded? Since some trade was illegal and not documented and many official reports documenting trade were falsified or destroyed, the wills and inventories of Series I of the Spanish Archives of New Mexico give a good picture of what type of domestic material culture was in New Mexican homes and in many instances where items originated, and the extent of the colonial trading network. Supply lists and customs reports indicate what was brought into New Mexico, not how it was distributed, and hence the wills also indicate a social hierarchy based on the division of goods.

Trade Goods in New Mexican Homes

While cottage industries developed in New Mexico, particularly textile work, carpentry and metalworking, the colony remained dependent on imported goods from central Mexico, Europe, and even the Far East. Of central concern to this study are: the items of trade that were brought into the New Mexican province, what these items reveal about the extent of the colonial trading network, and the impact of imported goods on the development of regional culture.

Fabric comprised the bulk of imported goods throughout the colonial era and was a possession of high value to individuals. Indicative of its high value are the thorough descriptions of fabric whenever mentioned on supply lists or in wills: documents specify the type of weave, its color and origin, and whether it was new or used. The inventory of Antonio Durán de Armijo, a Taos resident who died intestate in 1748, includes "2 *varas* of wine-colored Castilian cloth of second quality," "10 *varas* of red China silk," and "a new red scarf from Solomonica (sic) with a flounce and a fringe of silver" (SANM I, 8:618). Another inventory from 1736 lists "a red Puebla cloth jacket, new with hand braided edge and back buttons" (SANM I, 8:362). The trader Archeveque, who was killed in a foray into Indian territory in 1720, had as part of his estate "60 *varas* of flowered Rouen linen," "2 very large pieces of unbleached muslin from La Puebla," and "12 *varas* of flannel from Castile" (SANM I, 8:007).

Fabric imported into New Mexico came from 3 sources: Europe, central Mexico and the Far East. The rarest of fabrics, mentioned only in a handful of documents, came from the Far East: silks, ribbons and lace from Asia via the Manila galleons. More common among the imported fabrics were European goods from Spain (or Castile), France (Rouen, Brittany, Lorraine), and England. European fabrics included linens, silks, velvets, flannels, ribbons, and lace. Serge or twill weaves were common as were flowered or calico prints.

Woolen and cotton fabric from central Mexico came chiefly from Mexico City, Tlaxcala, Puebla and the Bajío. Fabric from New Spain was manufactured in *obrajes*, small factory-like arrangements organized around the Iberian guild system, or in *telares sueltos* (independent looms), where pre-Hispanic weaving traditions were continued (Salvucci 1987). Spain tolerated and encouraged textile production in New Spain both to build on existing indigenous manufactures and to meet New World demand which exceeded Iberian productivity.

New Mexico settlers wore mostly locally-made, roughly woven wool or hide clothes. Everyday clothes were rarely considered valuable enough to mention in wills. Instead, the documents mostly record imported fabric and clothing used for special events and the occasional trip to town. The wills indicate relative wealth by amount and kind of fabric that was left to heirs. Some wills, for instance, list a few agricultural tools and riding equipment (saddle, bridle) as the only possessions of the deceased and no fabric. Other wills list a few woolen stockings that were to be used for barter; a blue serge cape, old and worn, or a bolt of unbleached muslin from Puebla as among the few possessions worthy of note. At the other extreme, wealthy merchants would have bolt after bolt of imported fabric (*indianilla* [South Asian inspired calico prints], silks, linen from Rouen, lace from Brittany) and wealthy citizens would leave behind velvet capes, satin dresses and silk topcoats.

Part of the reason for New Mexicans' heavy reliance on imported fabric was the lack of technology and raw materials for production of the finer fabrics in the region, and Spanish protection of Iberian and colonial textile industries. There was, however, a weaving tradition of longstanding among Pueblo Indians, early Spanish settlers and, by the mid-1600s, among Navajo Indians (Fisher 1979; Kent 1983; 1985). Hispanic weaving tradition using a treadle loom (instead of the Pueblo vertical loom) developed in the early 1600s to meet local need for everyday clothes and demand for tribute to the governor and *encomenderos* (Minge 1979). However, local weaving did not develop beyond cotton blankets and rough woolen goods for everyday use until the post colonial era when both Hispanic and Navajo weaving traditions become quite sophisticated.

Another major item of trade was iron. Spain carefully controlled trade in iron from mines in northern Spain to the colonies (Simmons and Turley 1980, 7). Iron was imported from Spain in the colonial era or was contraband from Germany, despite known iron deposits in New Spain. Oñate brought substantial quantities of unworked iron to New Mexico in 1598 in anticipation of finding silver. Most of this iron was no doubt eventually reworked into agricultural tools, iron griddles, latches and locks, fireplace spits, and other domestic items that are mentioned in many wills. Subsequent supply caravans and traders carried both raw iron and worked tools. The mission supply caravans of the 1600s were to include for every friar "10 axes from la Calle de Tacuba, Mexico City, three adzes, three spits, 10 hoes, 1 large latch for the church door, 10 pounds of steel," several other tools, and several thousand nails (Scholes 1930, 103-104).

Virtually every will includes some iron tool, whether only a hoe and an iron griddle, or a more extensive inventory of iron goods. Iron goods cut across economic boundaries in the documents. They were a critical commodity for colonial survival and very much in demand. A Santa Fe resident left in his will of 1727 "2 large boxes from a foreign country trimmed with iron, an iron pot and griddle, an axe, [and] one iron spit" (SANM I, 1: 586). The inventory of a contested will of 1739 includes "an iron tablespoon, 2 hoes, an iron ploughshare, an adze, an ax, one *arroba* (25 pounds), of old iron, an iron mortar [and] an iron griddle" (SANM I, 1:637). A smith shop of 1748 had a mold for nailheads, chisels, files, augers, vices, forge bellows, anvils, tongs, hammers, and 36 pounds of old iron (SANM I, 8:618).

Iron smiths were scattered in ranches, pueblos and military garrisons throughout the province, with a concentration of shops in Santa Fe (Simmons and Turley 1980, 31). Since iron was scarce on the frontier, much of the smith's work involved reworking old tools or forging scrap iron. Traders continued to bring new tools and unworked iron into the province, however, as the 1815 inventory of a Chihuahua merchant includes "25 hammers, 11 axes, 8 adzes, 7 chisels, 11 pounds of scrap iron, 3 pieces of 3 pound steel, [and] 14 pieces of 6 pound iron" (SANM I, 2:365).

Items made of other metals such as tin, brass, bronze, copper and silver were also present in New Mexican homes. Silver coins are mentioned in a few wills (usually those of traders) and worked silver appears occasionally as buttons, buckles, rosaries, spoon sets, and salt cellars in the wills of apparently wealthy citizens. Silver was clearly a marker of wealth and status, and only the people with abundant possessions include worked silver goods as part of their property. Silver goods were brought into New Mexico by Oñate and the pretentious first settlers who accompanied him, as well as by the provincial governors, and they were an important element of ecclesiastical material culture. Some silver was worked in New Mexico, either from silver coin or bullion imported from northern Mexico mines (Boylan 1974). There is no indication of origin on any of the silver items in New Mexican wills, and it is not clear whether the silver was worked in New Mexico, Mexico or Spain.

Items of copper and other "yellow metals" (bronze and brass), on the other hand, appear frequently in the wills. Reference to copper cups, kettles, basins and pitchers are numerous. Only occasionally are these items designated as to place of origin, but it is clear from other evidence (West 1948; Barrett 1987) that domestic copperware was manufactured in Michoacán (Santa Clara and Pátzcuaro) and distributed widely in New Spain. By the late 1700s copper was mined and worked in New Mexico and perhaps even exported (Simmons 1983a, 75).

Furniture was uncommon in New Mexican homes during the colonial era, but one type of furniture was more common than any other and appears with surprising frequency in the wills: the wooden chest. This item further reveals specific trade connections with Mexico as many of the chests were from Michoacán. Taylor and Bokides's inventory of New Mexican furniture in SANM I wills found mention of 150 chests, 1/3 of them specifically designated as from Michoacán (Taylor 1983; Taylor and Bokides 1987).

Chests were highly valued items, used to transport goods on the supply caravans, and to store valuables, particularly fabric, chocolate, tobacco, sugar, silver coins, and important papers. Chests were painted, plain, or carved with low relief. The most valuable boxes came with locks, a feature that was often noted in the wills.

Wooden boxes were concentrated in the hands of traders and wealthy citizens and were a definite marker of status. The 1748 inventory of Taos resident Armijo mentions "seven chests, 3 large, 4 small, 2 from Michoacán with keys, 2 of the country without locks," and goes on to list the bolts of fabric and imported clothing within the trunks (SANM I, 8:618). The 1762 will of a Santa Fe resident of more modest means includes what was certainly a prized possession: "a locked chest with one jug and 2 flasks of brandy [from El Paso]" (SANM I, 1:776). It is not yet possible to determine by wood analysis the origin of boxes — all were made of pine, and some were made in New Mexico— but there is abundant documentary evidence of the Michoacán origin.

Other items frequently found in northern New Mexican homes included leather goods, shoes and riding gear from Michoacán, Mexico City and sometimes from Spain. Arms, both guns and swords of all types, were imported from Spain. Agricultural goods brought from Mexico included chocolate, sugar, indigo, cochineal and tobacco.

The Trading Network

The general pattern of things brought into New Mexico included fabric, raw iron, and arms from Europe and Spain, as well as the five and dime items such as buttons, mirrors, scissors, and thread. From central Mexico came shoes, iron goods, and fabric from Mexico City; fabric and blankets from Campeche, Tlaxcala, and Queretaro; *majolica* (tiles and dishes) and muslin from Puebla; and leather goods, furniture, and copperware from Michoacán.

From the Far East came some fabrics and some stylistic influences on wooden boxes. Floral and rosette designs of Asian origin carved on massive mahogany chests from the Philippines (which had been introduced by the Spanish) appear in much simpler form on wooden chests carved in Michoacán and New Mexico (Ahlborn 1961). Some china ware was probably traded as far as New Mexico, but the generic use of "china" for cups and plates obscures a definite origin. In some cases it is not clear from the wills whether references are to *"tipo chino"* (chinese type), to items specifically from China, or to items more generally Asian in origin. China cups and plates and buttons were expensive, valuable items, difficult to transport on cart or mule back. Only the most materially wealthy citizens list items of specifically "Chinese" origin.

Trade was not entirely one sided. Cotton blankets, woolen blankets, wool flooring, stockings, and raw wool were traded from New Mexico into the mining areas, to Sonora, and possibly as far as Mexico City (Simmons 1983a). Sheep were driven to Chihuahua and Parral. Hides were common and were used as a means of exchange for imported items. Chamois (sheep) skins, and elk, antelope and buffalo hides were listed in great numbers in the wills of both Santa Fe merchants and common folk. Wheat and corn were also traded. The upper Río Grande gained a reputation as a source for wool, meat (mutton), and eventually for woolen blankets and rough woolen goods such as stockings and *jerga* (a rough twill weave flooring). While the people of New Mexico did have items to trade — hides, wheat, corn, salt, woolen stockings and blankets — and the means of exchange was fairly equally accessible, these items were of low value compared to imported goods (Moorhead 1958, 49).

There was also considerable trade with Plains Indians and at least some trade with the French via Louisiana. Pecos, east of Santa Fe, had long been a trading center between Plains and Pueblo Indians, and Taos to the north emerged around 1700 as a major center for Indian and European traders. Merchants from Chihuahua, Parral and Mexico City joined French traders from the Mississippi Valley, Comanches, Utes, and Apaches for the Taos fair. Indians traded meat, hides and captives for arms, horses and exotica from New Spain. A "Truce of God" or "peace of the market" prevailed even during the height of violence between Spanish and Plains Indians in the eighteenth century (Simmons 1983b; 1988, 86).

Trade with the French occurred on a fairly regular basis through the eighteenth century even though the first French traders to formally approach New Mexico's governor in 1739 were summarily dismissed by a subsequent viceregal decree. There is documentary evidence of trade with the French through the records of those traders who were caught and arrested and had their goods confiscated (cf: SANM II, 8:1021). However, many Frenchmen were able to make their way to Santa Fe, exchange their manufactured trinkets and cloth, and return east with some hides and silver coins for their effort (Simmons 1988, 81).

By the late 1700s the economy and social structure of New Mexico were undergoing rapid change. This was a time of peace with the Comanches and Apaches and increasing prosperity for the province. Bourbon reforms in opening commerce and streamlining the bureaucracy had an impact on the frontier, beginning in the late eighteenth century. Population in New Mexico increased and trade flourished (Hall 1989, 143). Trade fairs in northern Mexico became the focus of economic activity and there was increasing trade between New Mexico, Mexico City and other parts of New Spain. The increasing pace of economic life in New Mexico paralleled the pace of global economic activity. New Mexico's world of trade and interaction gradually expanded as the isolated and embattled outpost, connected by slender link to the colonial heartland, became the hub in the wheel of frontier commerce.

Concluding Remarks

This overview of trade and material culture helps address some of the perennial questions about colonial New Mexico. Was it culturally and economically isolated with minimal contact outside the region? Was it poverty-stricken and disadvantaged by trading relations with the rest of the colonial world?

While Santa Fe was at the end of a 6 month journey from Mexico City, a remarkable diversity of goods reached the region: linens, lace, china, crystal, even books by the 1800s. These goods were not evenly distributed amongst the population by any means, but the goods represented a glimpse of the outside world for the predominantly agricultural communities on the edge of the Spanish empire.

It is easy to dwell on the apparent abundance represented by a few wills but this evidence must be put into perspective. Evidence from the wills and inventories can give a distorted view of the nature of existence in the colonial era. There are some 140 wills and inventories in the Spanish Archives of New Mexico, Series I from 1695-1850. During that time population of the province increased from around 10,000 to 34,000.[6] Therefore, only a fraction of the total population is represented in the wills and this writer assumes that most of those people without wills in the series did not have much in the way of material goods. For most of the wills in Series I, the bulk of the value of the estate was in land and livestock, not in goods. Northern New Mexico in the colonial era can not be considered materially wealthy. Despite an impressive array of goods that reached the region, the bulk of the population did not directly experience the material benefits of trade. In fact, most observers of the time note the abject poverty of the area (cf: Domínguez 1956; Simmons 1985). However, power and money from ranching, governing and trade attracted some luxury goods into the area and revealed the web of material connections that helped shape the regional character.

One of the major repercussions of trade in terms of material forms is reflected in the cottage industries that developed in northern New Mexico to meet domestic needs: textiles such as the embroidered Colcha coverlets which imitated flowered calicos and block prints from Europe and India; Río Grande blankets in Saltillo serape style, with a design based probably on oriental rugs; indigo and white ikat-dyed textiles characteristic of those of central Mexico, Ecuador and Perú, the ikat technique being of possible Asian origin; and furniture, religious art, and ironwork that reflects Asian and European influence.

The material culture of colonial New Mexico represented a blend of influences from Spain and other parts of Europe, from western and central Mexico, from the Far East, and from Plains and Pueblo Indians — a blend of native and imported ideas and workmanship. Domestic industry represented the wide range of ideas and styles that filtered in to affect life in New Mexico. This array of materials, designs and forms from several parts of the world is still apparent today in some Indian work and in "revival" Hispanic crafts.

Events and exchanges in colonial New Mexico symbolize not only the emerging global economy that resulted from industrialization and capitalism, but also an emerging world or global culture. Colonial New Mexico was an isolated outpost on the far northern frontier of New Spain, but it was also a place connected economically as well as culturally and materially to the rest of the world.

Notes

1. The Spanish Archives of New Mexico (SANM) are housed in the State Records Center and Archives in Santa Fe, New Mexico. Both Series I and Series II (which includes official correspondence and royal decrees) are available to the public on microfilm. There are 9 rolls of microfilm for Series I and 23 rolls in Series II. See footnote 4 for guide to referencing the series entries.

2. I am indebted to Simmons's (1988) concise and lively overview of New Mexico's history for insight into this early period.

3. The route of the supply caravans as pioneered by Oñate in 1598 is described in detail in Moorhead (1958, 12-26).

4. Reference to documents in the Spanish Archives of New Mexico will specify whether they are from Series I or Series II, followed by a number indicating the microfilm roll number for the document, and by the frame number containing the initial page of the document. This will mean that (SANM I, 8:007), for instance, can be found in Series I, roll 8, frame 007.

5. Moorhead (1958, 50) describes the currencies in use on the frontier during the colonial era:

The real monetary unit was the peso, but there were four concepts of its value in New Mexico during the eighteenth century. The official *peso de plata*, a silver coin which was practically nonexistent there, had a value of eight *reales* and was the standard later adopted by the United States for its silver dollar. As a substitution for it in New Mexico, there were three imaginary coins which were employed only in bookkeeping. The *peso a precios de proyecto* was worth only six *reales*; the *peso a precios antiguos*, only four *reales*; and the *peso de la tierra*, only two *reales*.

6. Hispanic population increased from a few hundred to nearly 25,000 between 1600 and 1800; Pueblo Indian population remained at about 10,000 throughout the colonial period, due in large part to a smallpox epidemic in 1780-81 which killed more than 5,000 Indians and Hispanics (Scurlock 1986, 101).

References

Ahlborn, R. E. 1961. Two colonial variations in the Spanish carved chest. *El Palacio* 68(2): 106-22.

———. 1983. Frontier possessions: The evidence from colonial documents. In *Colonial frontiers: Art and life in Spanish New Mexico*, ed. Christine Mather, 35-57. Santa Fe, NM: Ancient City Press.

Barrett, E. 1987. *The Mexican colonial copper industry.* Albuquerque: University of New Mexico Press.

Blaut, J. and Ríos-Bustamante, J. A. 1984. Commentary on Nostrand's "Hispanos" and their "Homeland." *Annals of the Association of American Geographers* 74: 157-184.

Bloom, L. 1935. A trade invoice of 1638. *New Mexico Historical Review* 10(3): 242-248.

Boylan, L. D. 1974. *Spanish colonial silver.* Santa Fe, NM: Museum of New Mexico Press.

Domínguez, F. A. 1956. *The missions of New Mexico, 1776.* Translated and annotated by E. B. Adams and F. A. Chavez. Albuquerque: University of New Mexico Press.

Fisher, N., ed. 1979. *Spanish textile tradition of New Mexico and Colorado.* Santa Fe, NM: Museum of New Mexico Press.

Hall, T. D. 1986. Incorporation in the world system: Toward a critique. *American Sociological Review* 5: 390-402.

———. 1989. *Social change in the Southwest.* Lawrence, KS: University Press of Kansas.

Hammond, G. P. and Rey A., eds. and trans. 1953. *Don Juan de Oñate, colonizer of New Mexico, 1595-1628*, 2 vols. Albuquerque: University of New Mexico Press.

Kent, K. P. 1983. *Pueblo Indian textiles: A living tradition.* Santa Fe, NM: School of American Research Press.

———. 1985. *Navajo weaving: Three centuries of change.* Santa Fe, NM: School of American Research Press.

Minge, W. A. 1979. Efectos del pais: A history of weaving along the Río Grande. In: *Spanish textile tradition of New Mexico and Colorado*, ed. N. Fisher, 8-28. Santa Fe, NM: Museum of New Mexico Press.

Moorhead, M. L. 1958. *New Mexico's royal road: Trade and travel on the Chihuahua Trail.* Norman, OK: University of Oklahoma Press.

Nostrand, R. 1970. The Hispanic-American borderland: Delimitation of an American culture region. *Annals of the Association of American Geographers* 60:638-661.

———. 1975. Mexican-Americans circa 1850. *Annals of the Association of American Geographers* 65:378-390.

———. 1980. The Hispano homeland in 1900. *Annals of the Association of American Geographers* 70:382-396.

Ríos-Bustamante, J. A. 1976. New Mexico in the eighteenth century: Life, labor and trade in la Villa de San Felipe de Albuquerque, 1706-1790. *Aztlan* 7(3): 357-389.

Salvucci, R. 1987. *Textiles and capitalism in Mexico: An economic history of the Obrajes, 1539-1840.* Princeton, NJ: Princeton University Press.

SANM. The Spanish Archives of New Mexico, series I and II. Santa Fe, NM: State Records Center and Archives.

Scholes, F. 1930. The supply service of the New Mexican missions in the seventeenth century. *New Mexico Historical Review* 5: 93-115, 186-210, 386-404.

Scurlock, D. 1986. Spanish expansion, 1710-1821. In *New Mexico in maps*, ed. J. Williams, 100-101. Albuquerque: University of New Mexico Press.

Simmons, M. 1983a. Colonial New Mexico and Mexico: The historical relationship. In: *Colonial frontiers: Art and life in Spanish New Mexico*, ed. Christine Mather, 71-89. Santa Fe, NM: Ancient City Press.

———. 1983b. The great Taos trade fair. *New Mexico Magazine* 61(9): 30-33, 50-51.

———. 1985. The Chacón economic report of 1803. *New Mexico Historical Review* 60(1): 81-88.

———. 1988. *New Mexico: An interpretive history.* Albuquerque, NM: University of New Mexico Press. (Originally published: 1977. New York: Norton.)

Simmons, M. and Turley, F. 1980. *Southwestern colonial iron work: Spanish blacksmithing tradition from Texas to California.* Santa Fe, NM: Museum of New Mexico Press.

Taylor, L. 1983. New Mexican chests: A comparative look. *El Palacio* 89(2): 32-41.

Taylor, L. and Bokides D. 1987. *New Mexican furniture, 1600-1940: The origins, survival, and revival of furniture making in the Hispanic Southwest.* Santa Fe, NM: Museum of New Mexico Press.

West, R. C. 1948. *Cultural geography of the modern Tarascan area.* Smithsonian Institution, Institute of Social Anthropology, Publication no. 7. Washington, DC: U.S. Government Printing Office.

The Anglo-American Mestizos
and Traditional Southern Regionalism

Terry G. Jordan

Abstract

Almost five million persons in the United States reported partial Amerindian ancestry in the 1980 census. Numerically and proportionally, these mixed bloods were more important in the South, where most lived without stigma or notice as part of the old-stock Anglo-American population. The author proposes that the greater genetic survival of Amerindians in the South is accompanied by notable retention of Indian cultural traits in the population at large, contributing significantly to southern regionalism. Examples, based on field data for diet, dialect, and folk religion, are offered as supporting evidence.

Key words: Amerindians, dialects, diet, folk culture, racial mixing, regionalism, religion, South

Introduction

The principal lesson I learned, vicariously, from Fred Kniffen was that the greater artifacts of traditional culture, the folk landscape, contained diagnostic clues valuable in reconstructing past geographies (Kniffen 1965). Such landscapes were well worth learning to read, quite aside from their intrinsic aesthetic value. Kniffen's methodology, with roots traceable to the likes of August Meitzen and Paul Vidal de la Blache, found in his work an inspired application to the American scene. Along the way, Kniffen often dropped hints and suggestions about some neglected facet or another of folk landscapes in the United States that held particular promise.

Precisely such a hint, deposited on my intellectual path some twenty years ago, led to my writing this paper. Kniffen suggested, in a brief, tantalizing article, that we might learn a great deal from the landscapes of the

Culture, Form, and Place: Essays in Cultural and Historical Geography, edited by Kent Mathewson, 1993. Geoscience and Man, vol. 32, pp. 175-195. Department of Geography and Anthropology, Louisiana State University, Baton Rouge, LA 70893-6010.

dead, from what he called necrogeography (Kniffen 1967). At that time I already haunted graveyards, gathering data for the compilation of an ethnic map of rural Texas. Because of the article on necrogeography, I became more curious about the many strange items of cemetery material culture observed in acquiring my ethnic data, and I began studying the subject. One such item, found in the southern Anglo-American graveyards of Texas, subsequently proved, to my satisfaction at least, to be of American Indian origin (Jordan 1982, 37). I will elaborate on this, but for now, suffice it to say that the discovery led me to wonder how much of the southern culture at large might contain Indian influence, since I had come to regard the graveyard as a microcosm of the region.

Busy with other projects, I set the question aside for some years, only to be reminded of it when the 1980 United States census, the first ever to include a question on remote ancestry, startlingly revealed the presence of a sizable, previously unrecognized element in the population. Almost five million Americans reported that they were of partial Amerindian origin (table 1) (fig. 1). These self-professed mixed bloods were not Mexican-Americans, very few of whom acknowledged their mestizo status, nor were very many Afro-Americans, even though perhaps a quarter or more of all blacks claim some Indian ancestry (McIntosh 1968, 93, 104; Ashley-Montagu 1944, 63; Flint 1828, v. 1, 470-71). Residents of the Hispanic borderland in the Southwest and the "black belt" of the South both reported

Table 1. Leading Ten States in Number of Persons Reporting
Partial American Indian Ancestry, 1980

State	Number of Persons Reporting Partial Indian Ancestry	As a % of Total Responding Population
California	564,221	2.7%
Texas	513,781	4.5%
Ohio	249,259	2.8%
Oklahoma	213,451	9.4%
Florida	210,073	2.7%
Missouri	204,745	5.2%
Michigan	195,200	2.4%
Illinois	183,561	1.9%
New York	160,499	1.1%
Indiana	158,325	3.7%
United States	4,794,995	2.5%

Source: U.S. Bureau of the Census 1983a, 63-68

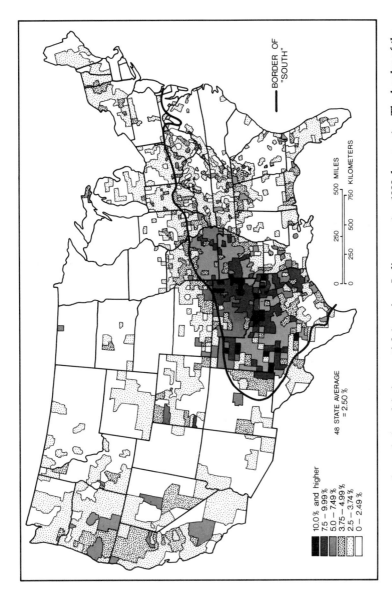

Fig. 1. Percentage of population claiming partial American Indian ancestry, 1980, by county. The border of the cultural South is based largely upon Zelinsky (1973, 118), with modifications for Texas and New Mexico. Note that the Lumbees (Croatans) of North Carolina (see fig. 3) claimed unmixed Indian ancestry. *Source:* U.S. Bureau of the Census 1983b.

relatively low admixtures of Indian blood. Similarly, relatively few Louisiana "Cajuns" claimed partial Indian ancestry, ignoring a mixing achieved early in colonial Nova Scotia (Griffiths 1973, 5; Clark 1968, 68, 89, 128, 361, 377). Not many of the mixed bloods professed to be Indians or lived on reservations. Instead, the large majority apparently belonged without stigma or distinction to the old-stock Anglo-American population.

The number of self-described Anglo mixed bloods, combined with the mestizos of Latin-, Franco-, and Afro-American origin and with the ethnic Indian population, adds up to well over twenty-five million persons, at least double the number of Amerindians living in the United States at the time of European contact in 1500. Perhaps the stereotyped view of the United States as a land where Indians suffered extermination, with only a few remnants clinging to reservations, should be discarded (Paz 1979, 140; Dobyns 1983).

Proportionally, claims of mixed blood by Anglo-Americans are far more common in the South, particularly the trans-Mississippi portion (fig. 1). In terms of actual numbers, the southern dominance is less striking, given the larger total population of the North, but the states south of the Mason-Dixon line and Ohio River still reported fifty percent more mixed bloods than did the North (fig. 2). Considering the fact that southern cultural influences reach well north of the Ohio in the Midwest, the regional concentration of self-professed mixed bloods can only be described as substantial. Cultural geographers and scholars from a variety of other disciplines have long sought to explain the special character of the American South, that highly distinctive, enigmatic, and rebellious section of the United States. In some of the most fruitful explanatory efforts, various writers interpreted the South in terms of the particular Old World origins of its people. One highly controversial thesis depicted the South as a transplanted Celtic stronghold and the Civil War as another rising of the Celts against their English oppressors (McWhiney 1988). Others, belatedly, acknowledged the substantial African contributions to traditional southern culture (Wood 1974). I propose, additionally, that some of the distinctiveness of the South, a consequential part of its traditional regional identity and sense of place, may derive from the disproportionate strength of the residual Amerindian genetic and cultural presence there. The claim of Indian blood seems to strengthen the southerners' sectional attachment and allows them to say, in effect, "our people have always been here."

Validity of the 1980 Census Response

The claim of mestizo status by numerous southerners cannot be proven, and a conclusive answer concerning the magnitude of Indian genetic sur-

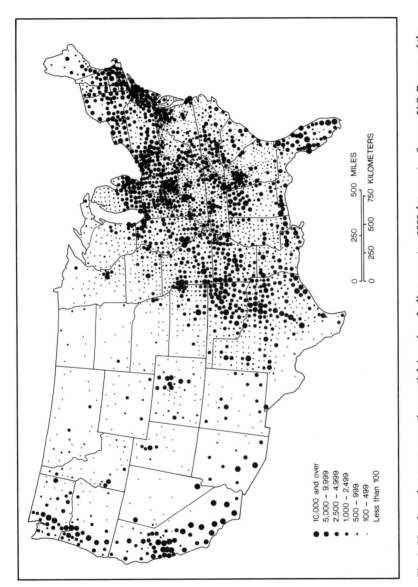

Fig. 2. Number of persons reporting partial American Indian ancestry, 1980, by county. *Source:* U.S. Bureau of the Census 1983b.

vival in the region is unattainable. I have chosen to believe the census respondents but at the same time know that the statistical base must remain unverifiable. In my opinion, white southerners are unlikely to claim racial mixing in their families if none in fact exists, given the regional attitude toward miscegenation. The census does not record the degree of Indian admixture in the Anglo mestizo population, or the time when the mixing occurred, but my own experience in the South suggests that the typical respondent would comfortably, even proudly, admit having one temporally remote female Indian ancestor.

Reports of cohabitation and intermarriage on the frontier, particularly in the South, are common over a span of two centuries, beginning in the 1600s. For example, records survive of the cohabitation of a Dutchman and an Indian woman near Burlington, New Jersey, in 1679; of an Indian man with a white wife near the site of Pittsburgh in 1761; of the two earliest white residents of Cherokee County, North Carolina, having part-Indian wives in 1817; and of a half-blood cattle raiser near Savannah, Georgia in 1734 (Danckaerts 1913, 149; Kenny 1913, 7; Williams and Dockery 1984, 14; Merrens 1977, 120). Such unions were apparently not much stigmatized on the frontier. In 1861, for instance, a white man and his Indian wife living on the Red River border of Texas and Oklahoma held a "get acquainted" dance for people from both banks, and those in attendance included many members of each race (Jordan and Kaups 1989, 87-88). Opportunities for miscegenation abounded, as in Shelby County, Texas, where the population in 1835 consisted of 687 Anglos, 29 blacks, and 217 Indians (Jordan 1986, 421). Only the Puritan frontier in New England seems not to have produced much racial mixing. Moreover, the mathematics of demography are such that the sizable number of Anglo mestizos in 1980 could have been produced by a relatively small number of interracial marriages in frontier times. Early mixture with the Cherokees and Choctaws alone, groups occasionally mentioned in southern genealogies and family reminiscences, could have provided much or most of the present mixed blood population (Owens 1966, 80-85). Earlier interracial unions would have had an immense genealogical ripple effect. The descendants of Pocahontas alone must today be in the hundreds of thousands, if not millions. I am inclined to believe that the mixing was an ongoing southern frontier phenomenon, from colonial times to the middle nineteenth century, though it may have been most common in the Cherokee region in the late 1700s and early 1800s, particularly in eastern Tennessee. In sum, I find no compelling reason to doubt the claim of the self-professed mestizos (Wright 1989, 408). Indeed, the 1980 census may have undercounted the number of white southerners having Indian ancestry, given the numerous people who are ignorant of their remote ancestry and the huge potential for multiplication from very early miscegenation.

The Ethnicity Issue

Three possible fates awaited the mestizo offspring of interracial marriages. Perhaps most commonly, they were absorbed into the remnant Indian tribes of the eastern woodlands, to the extent that few if any full-blood Indians any longer exist in these populations (Nash 1988, 28; Hewes 1940, 106, 112, 113, 121, 127). The second possibility was for the mixed bloods to be stigmatized by a special ethnic status, forming the so-called "little races." The Melungeons of the southern Appalachians, the Lumbees (or Croatans) of the eastern Carolinas, the Métis of the Great Plains, and the Redbones of the lower Mississippi Valley provide examples. Most such groups live in the American South, again emphasizing that region as the principal zone of racial mixing (fig. 3). Scholars from a variety of disciplines have studied these ethnic groups in considerable detail (Beale 1957; Berry 1963; Price 1953; Thompson 1972). Special ethnic status apparently occurred when too much Indian blood was present, when some African

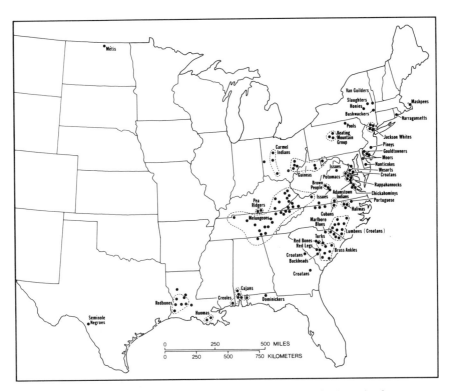

Fig. 3. **Ethnic racial isolates of reputed partial Indian origin.** Such stigmatized groups are concentrated in the eastern half of the American South. Some are triracial in origin. *Sources*: Price 1953; Beale 1957, 193–196; Porter 1952.

ancestry was known or suspected, and/or when the group remained in the East, rather than moving westward with the frontier. Indian-white-mixing bore little or no stigma on the outer margin of Euroamerican settlement, but less tolerance existed behind the frontier. To remain back East was to run the risk of ethnic status. In the South as a whole, figures 1 and 3 accordingly reveal complementary patterns, with the highest percentages of non-ethnic mixed bloods in the western part of the region and the "little races" concentrated in the eastern section.

The third possible fate of the later generations of Anglo mestizos involved non-ethnic absorption, without stigma or notice, into the old-stock white population, best achieved when the Indian admixture was small, when no African ancestry was suspected, and when the mestizos continued to migrate with the frontier. In recent times, some members of the previously-mentioned ethnic isolates have passed unnoticed into southern white society, and traditionally numerous others achieved such release by moving west or north (Thompson 1972, 1302). Mixed bloods continued their westward shift well into the present century, as "Okies," "Arkies," Anglo-Texans, and other southerners, and moved into parts of New Mexico, the Central Valley of California, the lumber towns of Oregon, and the Washington Cascades, leaving vivid traces on the map of mixed bloods (figs. 1 and 2) (Clevinger 1942). It is these non-ethnic Anglo mestizos who provide the focus of the present paper, both because such people have previously been ignored and because they could most easily have introduced Indian elements into southern white culture at large.

Cultural Consequences of the Mixing

When two sizable groups meet and mix, the genetic exchange is normally, perhaps inevitably, accompanied by acculturation on both sides. For the eastern woodland tribes, such acculturation has already received considerable attention, and the same is true of the mixed-blood ethnic isolates (Hewes 1940, 67; Pillsbury 1983; Porter 1983). By contrast, little has been written concerning white adoption of Indian ways and particularly whether such borrowings displayed durable regional variations. We have not progressed beyond a few general introductory statements and suggestions (Hallowell 1957; Jessee 1983).

This slow progress may rest partly upon a reluctance to make historical inferences from contemporary data. Reliance upon both the 1980 census and surviving material culture places me in that precarious position. However, historical data are by no means lacking. Contemporary observers, for example, often pointed to the partially Indian character of the white backwoods folk who formed the vanguard of Euroamerican agricultural settlement in the forested East. The pioneers "live very much like the

Indian and acquire similar ways of thinking" or "a strong tincture of Indian ways" (Harpster 1938, 134, 195-97). "Nearly allied in disposition and manners to an Indian," they displayed "a half Indian appearance" and often took scalps in warfare (Hazard 1853, vol. 2, 772; Baily 1969, 116; Guillet 1963, vol.1, 246).

Indian cultural and genetic influence, I feel, proceeded differently in the Upland and Lowland South. The former culture region, based originally in Pennsylvania, spread with the remarkably successful forest colonization culture it spawned. The upland southern backwoods way of life took shape, I suggest, in the Delaware Valley hearth area of the Middle Atlantic colonies in the latter half of the seventeenth century, and part of the merger of Indian and European ways, producing the prototypical pioneers, was accomplished by the Finns and Swedes of the New Sweden colony in their interaction with the local Delaware Indians (Jordan and Kaups 1989, 88-92, 249). By the time William Penn arrived on the Delaware in the early 1680s, "the Swedes themselves are accused that they were already half-Indians" (Kalm 1972, 217). The abundant Indian influence upon the upland southern pioneer adaptive system can be seen in the plowless mound cultivation of corn, intertillage with beans and squash, deerskin clothing, selection of field site, and deadening of trees by ringbarking (Wilson and Ferris 1989, 568; Wright 1989, 407, 408).

In the Lowland South, by contrast, the major absorption of Indian genes and culture was apparently accomplished within the slave population (Wright 1989, 408). Both Africans and Indians labored as slaves in the early coastal plantation districts. For two generations, blacks and native Americans lived as fellow slaves in the South Carolina lowlands, enabling widespread racial mixing and extensive cultural exchange. For example, the basketry tradition in the Charleston area apparently draws upon both African and Indian contributions (Wood 1974, 164-165).

Implicit in my argument is the assumption that cultural borrowing is more profound when accompanied by intermarriage. I do not deny that diffusion can proceed unaccompanied by miscegenation, especially when immigrants arrive in a new land and encounter a native population possessing successful and useful adaptive strategies. Planting corn does not imply that an Iowa farmer has Indian ancestry. I maintain, however, that racial mixing is more likely to yield cultural borrowings that are nonadaptive in character and unrelated to survival in the new habitat. Southern culture reveals abundant examples of both adaptive and incidental borrowings from the Indians, running the gamut from folk tales to necrogeography. It is precisely this profundity of borrowing that permits Indian culture to help shape southern regionalism. Let me now present a few examples suggesting the vivid regional survival of Indian-white acculturation.

Foodways

One of the most revealing facets of any culture lies in the choice of foods. The distinctiveness of southern fare has been widely proclaimed, and the contributions of the Africans and French duly noted (Hilliard 1972). Indian gifts, however, provide perhaps the most characteristic elements of southern diet, including the fondness for cornmeal and grits products, squash, squirrel, roasted or baked raccoon and opossum, catfish, pokeweed salad, and the addition of hickory nuts to stews (Taylor 1982, 3-9, 32; Wright 1989, 407-408; Wilson and Ferris 1989, 688, 689)).

For some decades, the United States Department of Agriculture (1956, 1968) has carried out a food consumption field survey. The published results, unfortunately lumped into only four multistate regions, nevertheless permit a comparison of the South to the rest of the country. Rather startling dietary contrasts exist. In the farm population in 1955, for example, eighteen times as much grits and cornmeal products were consumed in the South as in the next highest section, and 82 percent of the southern households reported using such foods, far ahead of the 19 percent in the second-ranking region (fig. 4). Considering grits alone, we find that one-fourth of all southern rural households reported consumption during the 1965 survey week, as contrasted to only 1.4 percent in the West, the second-ranking area.

The South also ranked highest in consumption of roasting ear corn and of corn-derived whiskey. In both 1955 and 1965, southern farm households reported consuming 70 percent more fresh corn than farmers in the next highest region (U.S. Department of Agriculture 1956, 1968). Maize in the more thoroughly Germanic North serves principally as a livestock feed. Regrettably, however, very little place-specific dietary data have ever been collected, rendering conclusions concerning foodways largely intuitive and speculative. Restaurant chains carefully guard information concerning regional differences in their menus.

Speechways

American English dialects have been subjected to far more intensive field research than have foodways. At first glance, the traditional division of the South into two major dialects — Midland (Hill Southern) and Plantation Southern — would seem to negate any unifying regional speech traits that might demonstrate Indian influence. Loanwords, however, reveal a different pattern (Wilson and Ferris 1989, 763; Wright 1989, 408). In recent years, publication of a comprehensive, field-derived dictionary of American regional English has begun, and the first volume, including A through C, is now available (Cassidy 1985). By mapping from that volume words of acknowledged Amerindian origin, a pattern of southern concentration

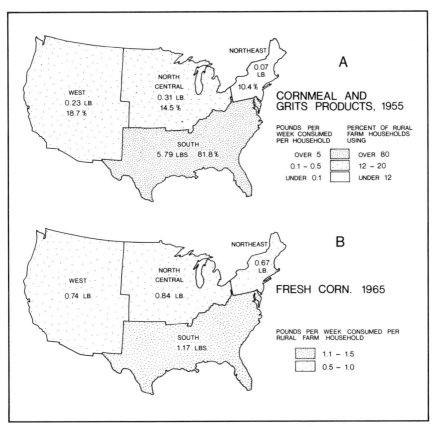

Fig. 4. Consumption of cornmeal and grits products and fresh corn by the rural farm population. Data were available only for the four multistate regions shown. *Source:* U.S. Dept. of Agriculture 1956, 1968.

is revealed, coincident with the zone of above-average proportional mestizo presence (fig. 5). Southern words such as *atamasco* (lily), *bobbasheely* (close friend or to associate with socially), *chinquapin* (nut tree), and *cushaw* (squash) are representative. Future volumes will likely reveal the southern concentration of other loanwords such as *pone, hominy, tawkee* (arrow arum), and *pecan* (nut tree).

Some Indian loanwords acquired generic toponymic status. Perhaps *bayou* achieved the widest acceptance of any Indian-derived generic name, but it, in common with most others, remains solidly southern in distribution (West 1954). Other such generic forms include *pocosin*, a coastal Virginia-North Carolina place name for swamp, and *bogue*, a central Gulf Coast term for stream (Rooney 1982, 133, 137). Even more common are Indian-based specific toponyms employing loan words, such as Catalpa

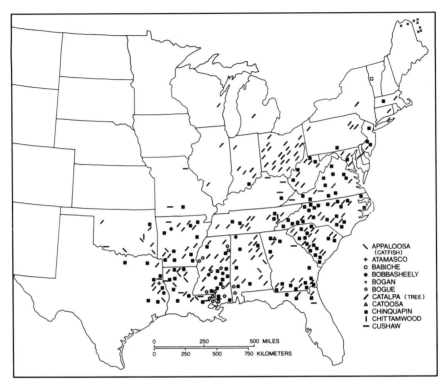

Fig. 5. Selected Indian loanwords in regional American English. The southern concentration is evident at a glance. *Sources:* Cassidy 1985; U.S. Geological Survey, various dates; and personal field observations.

Creek. Occasionally, especially in the South, a place name consists of both Indian-derived specific and generic components, as in the central Texas stream called Pecan Bayou.

Folk Religion

The emotional, fundamentalist Protestantism of the American South owes a primary formative debt to hill Britons, especially the Scotch-Irish. Celtic Christianity became more exuberant on the southern frontier, but the shaping influence of the British highlands is unmistakable. Yet one finds aspects of southern folk Christianity that seem difficult to explain in Celtic or any other European terms (Wilson and Ferris 1989, 1275). Snake handling by certain Appalachian sects, among both Anglo-Americans and Melungeons, comes to mind (Holliday 1966; Carden and Pelton 1976; Bible 1975, 54). Too, a deep streak of fatalism colors the Anglo-southern world view, as in the response to natural hazards and disasters. For exam-

ple, Alabamians reportedly reacted to the threat of tornadoes rather pas-
sively, relying on God to see them through, while a northern control group
of Illinoisans, adherents of a liberal, lower-intensity Protestantism, felt
more in control of their destiny and took greater measures to protect themselves from storms (Sims and Baumann 1972). Perhaps southern fatalism
represents, in minor measure at least, a regional heritage of the Amerindian.

More convincing evidence of Indian influence in southern folk Christianity comes from field studies of traditional religious material culture.
As I suggested earlier, my own field research on this topic, inspired by
Fred Kniffen's work, led me originally to the thesis of Indian cultural imprint in the South, before the appearance of the 1980 census (Jordan 1982,
39). Two elements of religious material culture, in particular, offer evidence of borrowing from the Indians: traditional camp meeting grounds
and gravesheds.

Across most of the South, from northern Florida through the Carolinas, from Georgia to Texas, a particular type of revival camp meeting
ground occurs widely in the rural cultural landscape (fig. 6) (Baugh 1953;
Clements 1973). Usually standing in sequestered, deeply rural places, the
camp meeting grounds consist of a central, open-sided tabernacle, successor to an earlier brush arbor, around which cabins or tents belonging to individual participating families often form a square, circle, or semicircle. A
remarkable consistency of this form occurs across most of the South. In the

Fig. 6. Noonday Camp Meeting ground, near Hallsville, Harrison County, Texas. Typical
of such grounds in the South, Noonday has a large tabernacle and adjacent cabins. Photo
by the author, 1980.

early summer, a slack period in the agricultural labor calendar, families gathered at the camp grounds for a week or so of revival preaching, emotional exclamations, and socializing. Many still do so today.

No adequate European or African prototype for the southern camp meeting ground exists. Instead, its older brush arbor form "is identical--not merely similar, but identical--with structures of similar function used by the Creeks, Alabamas, Seminoles, and other Indian groups belonging to the Southeastern Culture Complex" (Zelinsky 1953, 280). Indian towns in the southeast often featured dwellings grouped around a public place containing a ceremonial brush arbor, and periodically used council grounds displayed the same configuration. Such places often provided the setting for Indian conversions to Christianity. While the southeastern tribes generally dispersed their houses as acculturation progressed, the older, traditional clustered settlement form survived to serve a ceremonial function. When the great religious revival swept across the South about 1800, the Indian meeting ground proved nicely preadapted for the mass gatherings. In these early revivals, Indians and whites often attended the same meetings.

Perhaps no aspect of folk religion remains as conservative and revealing as the practices associated with disposal of the dead. The traditional southern graveyard houses a bewildering abundance of traditional material culture. If some individual form elements can be identified as Indian in origin, in these most conservative of places, then the probability of major native American influence upon southern culture would take on much added strength. The graveshed or gravehouse is such an item (fig. 7) (Ball 1977). These diminutive roofed structures, their sides either open or par-

Fig. 7. Gravesheds in a cemetery in Garland, Dallas County, Texas. Though the cemetery is for whites, the gravesheds are apparently an Indian legacy. These retain much of the form and appearance of the pre-Christian prototype, including a suggestion of palisading to keep out scavengers. Photo by the author, 1977.

Fig. 8. A more acculturated version of the southern graveshed, covering multiple burials, in the white Eagle Springs Baptist churchyard, Tallapoosa County, Alabama. Photo by the author, 1988.

tially enclosed by pickets, lattices, or wire, cover normal in-ground burials. Some older examples consist of wide-chink notched-log construction. Usually gravesheds protect individual burials, but not infrequently the structure covers a husband/wife grouping or even an entire family plot (fig. 8). Years of patient field research, by the present author and others, have revealed the distribution of gravesheds to be distinctly and almost exclusively southern, coinciding with the zone of highest mixed blood percentages (fig. 9) (Jordan 1982, 37).

While gravesheds appear in white, black, Indian, and Melungeon cemeteries, they are clearly most common among eastern Indian groups and occur least frequently among blacks. Further, in the Oklahoma Cherokee country, gravesheds are found most often among the "full bloods," who also better retain the ancestral language (Hewes 1940). The custom is almost certainly of Indian origin, though not all scholars agree on this point (Jordan 1982, 34; Zelinsky 1953, 286; Jeane 1989, 126). Many Amerindian groups of the eastern United States, northern and southern alike, built similar sheds in the disposal of their dead, but only in the South did the practice pass to the white population (Voegelin 1944, 341). A Choctaw custom possibly explains the original function of such shelters. Some

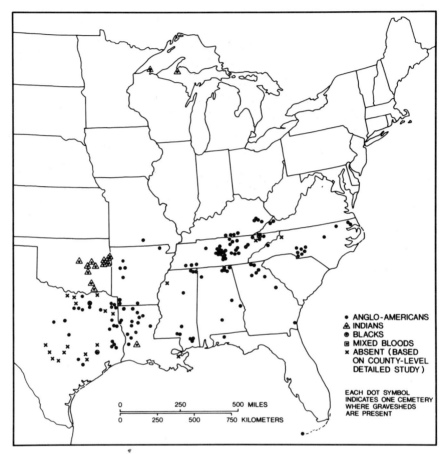

ANGLO-AMERICANS
△ INDIANS
⊙ BLACKS
⊞ MIXED BLOODS
× ABSENT (BASED
  ON COUNTY-LEVEL
  DETAILED STUDY)

EACH DOT SYMBOL
INDICATES ONE CEMETERY
WHERE GRAVESHEDS
ARE PRESENT

Fig. 9. Gravesheds observed through field research. The distribution shown is surely fragmentary. *Sources*: personal field research; Jordan 1982, 37; Ball 1977; Hewes 1940, plate 18a; Jeane 1989; Milbauer 1989, 178-179; Pitchford 1979; Jeane and Purcell 1978, 244-261; and unpublished data generously provided by Alice Little; James E. Price for Arkansas; Tadashi Nakagawa for Louisiana; Lynn Morrow for Missouri; Richard C. Finch for Tennessee and Kentucky; Goodloe Stuck for Louisiana; Merilyn Osterlund for Alabama; Mary Ruth Winchell for North Carolina; Richard Pillsbury and Alice Andrews for Georgia; Charles L. Sullivan for Mississippi; and Douglas Helm for North Carolina.

Choctaws formerly placed the dead on top of the ground in the yard of the dwelling and erected a small structure over the body while it decomposed, to keep predators away, after which the cleaned bones were collected and buried (Swanton 1931, 185). Conversion to Christianity subsequently obliged the Choctaws to bury the dead at once, but the custom of the little houses persisted and gravesheds still remain a highly visible aspect of their cemeteries in Oklahoma today (fig. 10) (Jordan 1982, 37).

Fig. 10. Choctaw Indian graveshed, Homer Chapel, Choctaw County, Oklahoma. This low structure lacks the lattice or palisade sides, but otherwise fits the ancestral Choctaw prototype rather well. The cemetery contains multiple gravesheds. (Photo by the author, 1979).

Conclusion

These examples drawn from diet, speech, and folk religion--three basic attributes of any culture--by no means exhaust the possible Indian influences in the South. Folklore, in particular music, "buck" dancing, legends, and tales, have much to offer, as does the southern hunting complex, with its abundant forest lore, the gathering of wild plants, and herbal medicine (Aldrich, de Blieux and Kniffen 1943; Kniffen 1949; Rafferty 1973; Price 1960; Wilhelm 1974, 247, 250; Wilson and Ferris 1989, 352, 496, 998, 1034, 1275; Wright 1989, 408; Eaton 1937, 133-146). The lack of concern for permanence, order, and rigid geometry in the cultural landscape, as evidenced by the casual southern attitude toward paint, vertical fenceposts, and straight furrows in the field could derive in part from Indian attitudes. Indeed, Hewes (1940, 218-19) concluded as much concerning the use of paint in rural eastern Oklahoma. Many items of lesser material folk culture and handicrafts such as clay tobacco pipes, gourd water dippers, and basketry seem at least partially Indian-derived (Wilson and Ferris 1989, 352; Wright 1989, 308; Eaton 1937, 166-167, 234).

The Indian imprint on the South would seem most vivid in traditional, rural, archaic elements. As the South becomes increasingly urban and industrial, its Indian heritage grows fainter. Regional distinctiveness fades, and with it the reminders of the mixing of races and cultures that define the Old South. Indian loanwords now seem old fashioned, camp meeting grounds and gravesheds dwindle in number, and foodways gradually change. Even so, much remains to remind us of the substantial native contributions to the regional culture, and many southerners, clearly, remember and value their mestizo heritage.

References

Aldrich, C. C., de Blieux, M.W. and Kniffen, F. B. 1943. The Spanish moss industry of Louisiana. *Economic Geography* 19:347-357.

Ashley-Montagu, M. F. 1944. The African origins of the American negro and his ethnic composition. *Scientific Monthly* 58:58-65.

Baily, F. 1969. *Journal of a tour in unsettled parts of North America in 1796 and 1797*. Carbondale and Edwardsville, IL: Southern Illinois University Press.

Ball, D. B. 1977. Observations on the form and function of middle Tennessee gravehouses. *Tennessee Anthropologist* 2(1, Spring): 29-62.

Baugh, S. T. ca. 1953. *Camp grounds and camp meetings in south Arkansas.* Little Rock, AR: Epworth Press.

Beale, C. L. 1957. American triracial isolates. *Eugenics Quarterly* 4:187-196.

Berry, B. 1963. *Almost white.* New York, NY: Macmillan.

Bible, J. P. 1975. *Melungeons yesterday and today.* Rogersville, TN: East Tennessee Printing Co.

Carden, K. W. and R. W. Pelton. 1976. *The persecuted prophets.* New York, NY: A. S. Barnes.

Cassidy, F. G. 1985. *Dictionary of American regional English*. Vol. 1. Cambridge, MA: Harvard University Press.

Clark, A. H. 1968. *Acadia: The geography of early Nova Scotia to 1760.* Madison, WI: University of Wisconsin Press.

Clements, W. M. 1973. The physical layout of the Methodist camp meeting. *Pioneer America* 5(1): 9-15.

Clevinger, W. R. 1942. Southern Appalachian highlanders in western Washington. *Pacific Northwest Quarterly* 33:3-25.

Danckaerts, J. 1913. *Journal of Jasper Danckaerts, 1679-1680.* New York: Charles Scribner's Sons.

Dobyns, H. F. 1983. *Their numbers become thinned: Native American population dynamics in eastern North America.* Knoxville, TN: University of Tennessee Press.

Eaton, A. H. 1937. *Handicrafts of the Southern Highlands.* New York: Russell Sage Foundation.

Flint, T. 1828. *A condensed geography and history of the western states, or the Mississippi Valley.* 2 vols. Cincinnati, OH: E. H. Flint.

Griffiths, N. 1973. *The Acadians: Creation of a people.* Toronto: McGraw-Hill Ryerson.

Guillet, E. C. 1963. *The pioneer farmer and backwoodsman*. 2 vols. Toronto: Ontario Publishing Co.

Hallowell, A. I. 1957. The impact of the American Indian on American culture. *American Anthropologist* 59:201-217.

Harpster, J. W., ed. 1938. *Pen pictures of early western Pennsylvania*. Pittsburgh, PA: University of Pittsburgh Press.

Hazard, S., ed. 1853. *Pennsylvania archives*. Ser. 1, vol. 2. Philadelphia, PA: Joseph Severns Co.

Hewes, L. 1940. The geography of the Cherokee country of Oklahoma. Ph.D. diss., University of California, Berkeley, CA.

Hilliard, S. B. 1972. *Hog meat and hoe cake: Food supply in the old South*. Carbondale, IL: Southern Illinois University Press.

Holliday, R. K. 1966. *Tests of faith*. Oak Hill, WV: Fayette Tribune.

Jeane, D. G. 1989. The Upland South folk cemetery complex: Some suggestions of origin. In *Cemeteries and gravemarkers: Voices of American culture*, ed. R. E. Meyer, 107-136. Ann Arbor, MI: U.M.I. Research Press.

Jeane, D. G., and Purcell, D. C. 1978. *The architectural legacy of the lower Chattahoochee Valley*. Tuscaloosa, AL: University of Alabama Press.

Jessee, G. J. 1983. Culture contact and acculturation in New Sweden. M.A. thesis, William and Mary College, Williamsburg, VA.

Jordan, T. G. 1982. *Texas graveyards: A cultural legacy*. Austin, TX: University of Texas Press.

——. 1986. A century and a half of ethnic change in Texas, 1836-1986. *Southwestern Historical Quarterly* 89:385-422.

Jordan, T. G., and Kaups, M. 1989. *The American backwoods frontier: An ethnic and ecological interpretation*. Baltimore, MD: Johns Hopkins University Press.

Kalm, P. 1972. *Travels into North America*. Barre, MA: Imprint Society.

Kenny, J. 1913. Journal of James Kenny, 1761-1763. *Pennsylvania Magazine of History and Biography* 37:1-47, 152-201.

Kniffen, F. B. 1949. The deer-hunt complex in Louisiana. *Journal of American Folklore* 62:187-188.

——. 1965. Folk housing: Key to diffusion. *Annals of the Association of American Geographers* 55:549-577.

——. 1967. Necrogeography in the United States. *Geographical Review* 57:426-427.

McIntosh, J. H. 1968. *The official history of Elbert County, 1790-1935*. Atlanta, GA: Cherokee Publishing Co.

McWhiney, G. 1988. *Cracker culture: Celtic ways in the old South*. University, AL: University of Alabama Press.

Merrens, H. R. 1977. *The colonial South Carolina scene: Contemporary views, 1697-1774*. Columbia, SC: University of South Carolina Press.

Milbauer, J. A. 1989. Southern folk traits in the cemeteries of northeastern Oklahoma. *Southern Folklore* 46:175-185.

Nash, A. E. 1988. Demographic regimes in the American South and Caribbean, 1620-1820. In *The American South*, eds. R. L. Nostrand and S. B. Hilliard, 25-40. Geoscience and Man, vol. 25. Baton Rouge, LA: Geoscience Publications, Department of Geography and Anthropology, Louisiana State University.

Owens, W. A. 1966. *This stubborn soil.* New York, NY: Scribner.

Paz, O. 1979. Reflections: Mexico and the United States. *New Yorker* 55(31): 136-153.

Pillsbury, R. 1983. The Europeanization of the Cherokee settlement landscape prior to removal: A Georgia case study. In *Historical Archaeology of the Eastern United States*, ed. R. W. Neuman, 59-69. Geoscience and Man, vol. 23. Baton Rouge, LA: School of Geoscience, Louisiana State University.

Pitchford, A. 1979. The material culture of the traditional East Texas graveyard. *Southern Folklore Quarterly* 43:277-290.

Porter, F. W. III. 1983. Material acculturation among Indian survivals in the middle Atlantic region. *Pioneer America Society Transactions* 6:37-48.

Porter, K. W. 1952. The Seminole Negro-Indian scouts, 1870-1881. *Southwestern Historical Quarterly* 55:358-377.

Price, E. T. 1953. A geographic analysis of white-negro-Indian racial mixtures in eastern United States. *Annals of the Association of American Geographers* 43:138-155.

———. 1960. Root digging in the Appalachians: The geography of botanical drugs. *Geographical Review* 50:1-20.

Rafferty, M. D. 1973. The black walnut industry: The modernization of a pioneer custom. *Pioneer America* 5(1): 23-32.

Rooney, J. F., Zelinsky, W., and Louder, D. R., gen'l eds. 1982. *This remarkable continent: An atlas of United States and Canadian society and cultures.* College Station, TX: Texas A&M University Press.

Sims, J. H. and Baumann, D. D. 1972. The tornado threat: Coping styles of the North and South. *Science* 176:1386-1392.

Swanton, J. R. 1931. *Source material for the social and ceremonial life of the Choctaw Indians.* Smithsonian Institution, Bureau of American Ethnology, Bulletin 103. Washington, DC: Government Printing Office.

Taylor, J. G. 1982. *Eating, drinking, and visiting in the South: An informal history.* Baton Rouge, LA: Louisiana State University Press.

Thompson, E. T. 1972. The little races. *American Anthropologist* 74:1295-1306.

U.S. Bureau of the Census. 1983a. *1980 census of population: Ancestry of the population by state.* Supplementary Report PC8O-S1-10. Washington, DC: U.S. Department of Commerce.

———. 1983b. "Technical documentation," United States census of population and housing, 1980, Summary Tape File 4, table PA-16 (unpublished computer tape). Washington, DC: U.S. Department of Commerce.

U.S. Department of Agriculture. 1956. *Food consumption of households.* Household Food Consumption Survey 1955, Agricultural Research Service. 5 vols. Washington, DC: Government Printing Office.

———. 1968. *Food consumption of households, spring 1965.* Household Food Consumption Survey, Agricultural Research Service. 5 vols. Washington, DC: Government Printing Office.

U.S. Geological Survey. Various dates. Geographic names information system. (Alphabetical lists of place names appearing on U.S.G.S. topographic sheets, available on microcards or computer print-outs, by state units.) Reston, VA: U.S.G.S., National Mapping Division, Office of Geographic Names.

Voegelin, E. W. 1944. *Mortuary customs of the Shawnee and other eastern tribes.* Prehistory Research Series, vol. 2 no. 4. Indianapolis, IN: Indiana Historical Society.

West, R. C. 1954. The term "bayou" in the United States: A study in the geography of place names. *Annals of the Association of American Geographers* 44:63-74.

Wilhelm, E. J. 1974. The mullein: Plant piscicide of the mountain folk culture. *Geographical Review* 64:235-252.

Williams, M. A. and Dockery, C. 1984. *Marble and log: The history and architecture of Cherokee County, North Carolina.* Raleigh, NC: North Carolina Department of Cultural Resources.

Wilson, C. R., and W. Ferris, eds. 1989. *Encyclopedia of southern culture.* Chapel Hill, NC: University of North Carolina Press.

Wood, P. H. 1974. It was a negro taught them: A new look at African labor in early South Carolina. *Journal of Asian and African Studies* 9:160-189.

Wright, J. L. 1989. Indian cultural contributions. In *Encyclopedia of southern culture,* eds. C. R. Wilson and W. Ferris, 407-409. Chapel Hill, NC: University of North Carolina Press.

Zelinsky, W. 1953. The settlement patterns of Georgia. Ph.D. diss., University of California, Berkeley.

———. 1973. *The cultural geography of the United States.* Englewood Cliffs, NJ: Prentice-Hall.

Material Folk Culture in the Blue Ridge Mountains

Gene Wilhelm

Abstract

This inquiry sought, through the field analysis of many individual structures and other material items, to find types and subtypes that would identify the Blue Ridge material folk culture subregion. Culturally, there is no doubt that the Blue Ridge constitutes an integral subregion of the Upland South. Furthermore, it represents a material culture source area and transition zone which has been somewhat neglected by field investigators, geographers and non-geographers alike.

It is evident after tracing the various types of houses, barns, outbuildings, stores, mills, and some lesser items to their beginnings and following them through their evolution in time and space, that two distinct culture traditions are represented in the Blue Ridge culture complex: the Pennsylvania German-Scotch-Irish and the Chesapeake Tidewater English. In time and with broader experience there was increasing exchange between the two cultures and acceptance of different ideas and material culture. Eventually, a cultural uniformity emerged in the Blue Ridge which we can label "mountain folk culture." A significant part of this field investigation was the recognition and interpretation of vestigial traits making up this new culture complex. For the Blue Ridge mountain culture, with its occupance farms and patterns, became the model for mountain life from the Southern Appalachians to the Ozarks of Arkansas-Missouri.

Key words: Blue Ridge folk culture, Chesapeake Tidewater English, folk culture, Pennsylvania German-Scotch-Irish

Introduction

Specifically, this report is concerned with the material manner of living in the Blue Ridge settlements during the eighteenth and nineteenth centuries. Thus a strong emphasis on folk architectural practices is evident. Such concrete objects as houses, barns, outbuildings, fences, and the like serve the ultimate objectives of the undertaking to find origins, to trace diffusions and changes, and to define the complex material folk culture of the Blue Ridge subregion (fig. 1).

Culture, Form, and Place: Essays in Cultural and Historical Geography, edited by Kent Mathewson, 1993. Geoscience and Man, vol. 32, pp. 197-256. Department of Geography and Anthropology, Louisiana State University, Baton Rouge, LA 70893-6010.

197

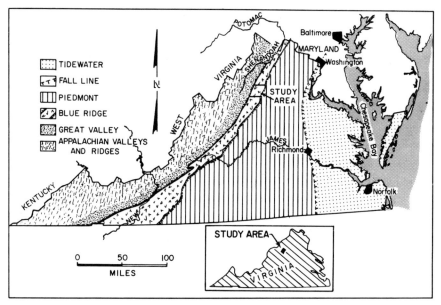

Fig. 1. Virginia main regions.

The basic data are the observations of the archaeological remains of material culture. These data were compiled as field notes, sketch drawings, maps, measurements, and black and white photographs during twenty summer seasons (1963-1982) in the field. Personal data, in turn, were supported by National Park Service photographs and descriptions of mountain folk buildings recorded in the 1920s and 1930s before the establishment of Shenandoah National Park. For detailed accounts of the environmental setting and culture origin of the Blue Ridge landscape, consult Wilhelm (1968, 1973, 1975, 1978, 1982).

The mountain folk were conservative in their ways. Therefore, it was customary for many mountain families to continue to use their original dwellings even after larger, more substantial houses were built. Other mountain families simply added onto their initial dwellings an assortment of appendages in the form of useful rooms. Such common architectural practice in the past allows the field investigator of the present to observe many of these old structures on the Blue Ridge landscape adjoining the study area and to extrapolate similar structures for the study area itself.

Further, these material folk objects best represent the typical rural mountain settler. Other material things, such as tools, implements, furniture, and accessories, are also helpful, and these items supplement the immobile, durable, and much larger mountain folk buildings. Again, because most of the material folk culture is no longer visible in the study area between Front Royal and Waynesboro, Virginia (fig. 2), essential in-

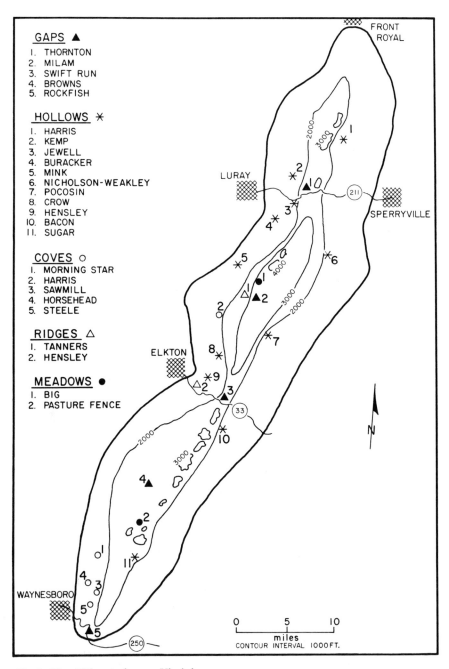

Fig. 2. Blue Ridge study area, Virginia.

formation came from National Park Service files in Shenandoah National Park, local informants, and areal context.

Among the major categories of material folk items found in the eastern part of the United States, typologies of folk houses, barns, outbuildings, and fences have been well established (Kniffen 1965). So has the fact that there were four major centers of folk culture dispersal on the East Coast during the first two centuries of American settlement from whence these types came: New England, southeastern Pennsylvania, the Chesapeake Bay region, and the coastal belt from North Carolina to Georgia (Kniffen and Glassie 1966). It is not the purpose of this study to describe these major cultural source areas, for that task has been accomplished admirably by Kniffen and Glassie. Instead, it is to indicate that the Blue Ridge study area represents a transitional subregion of the Upland South which received material folk culture traits from southeastern Pennsylvania and the Chesapeake Bay region. As will be seen shortly, some subregional traits have been overlooked previously by field investigators, indicating that the Blue Ridge Mountains were far more complex as to folk material than previously assumed.

House Types

Occupation of the Blue Ridge Mountains by initial settlers of predominantly Pennsylvania German and Scotch-Irish origin brought house types, associated farm structures, and building techniques in keeping with traditional European construction practices. For example, the Pennsylvania Germans used horizontal log construction of the type which they had known in the Rhineland region of Europe. This Pennsylvania German log work was characterized "by logs notched near the end, a method that eliminated the overhang and produced a box corner" (Kniffen and Glassie 1966, 59). Spaces between the logs were "chinked" or filled with clay, stones, or wood chips. The logs were hewn for a variety of reasons (Kniffen and Glassie 1966, 59):

> A large log could be handled more easily when reduced in size; a large round log took up interior space and produced an irregular wall that was hard to utilize; and hewn logs were thought to produce a tighter building, more finished in appearance.

The Scotch-Irish, of a stone- or mud-using tradition, saw the practicality of this log construction in timber-rich Pennsylvania and quickly adopted it.

These settlers of German and Scotch-Irish origin took the Pennsylvania German forms of corner-timbering from southeastern Pennsylvania to the Blue Ridge and farther south. This log construction became a symbol of the region.

Glassie (1963, 10) separately and together with Kniffen (Kniffen and Glassie 1966, 59) notes that of the three forms of corner-timbering found in southeastern Pennsylvania (saddle notching, V notching, and full dovetailing), V notching came to predominate to the virtual exclusion of the other forms during the movement east into the Blue Ridge and south through the Valley of Virginia (fig. 3). Further, virtually every log cabin in the mountains of Virginia was constructed supposedly with this type of corner-timbering (Glassie 1963, 10). Also, according to Glassie (1963, 10), full dovetailing is not common outside southeastern Pennsylvania as it was early developed into half dovetailing. However, I have found that at least five different types of corner-timbering are used.

Investigations of surface archaeology in Shenandoah National Park, combined with National Park Service photographs of mountain dwellings taken in the 1920s and 1930s, and personal photographs taken in the Blue Ridge districts adjoining the study area, attest to the fact that at least five different types of corner-timbering were used in the past: saddle notching, V notching, full dovetailing, half dovetailing, and half-log construction. Numerically, saddle notching and V notching characterized about half of the 150 log dwellings examined in the field, although it can never be ascertained accurately what the original proportion of each type was in the study area.

It is the primary function of corner-timbering to lock the logs so that they are held securely in place. Saddle notching, probably the oldest in origin and typologically the simplest, certainly attains that end (Kniffen 1969a, 1). In the Blue Ridge the technique is commonly used on logs left in the round. There are three forms of saddle notching: double notching, in which the notches are on both sides of the log; and single notching, in which the notch will be on either the top or the bottom of the log (fig. 3). All three forms are still found in the Blue Ridge and are confined almost entirely to early, simple dwellings and to barns and other outbuildings. The irregular projection of logs beyond the corners commonly goes with saddle notching.

V notching (fig. 3), according to Kniffen (1969a, 3),

> seems to be derived from the single saddle notch on the bottom of the log, an evolution that took place in Europe prior to its introduction into America. The notch is cut on the underside of the log into a sharp V into which the tapered head of the lower log fits. If the log is squared, the end resembles the gabled end of a house.... In V notching, the ends of the logs are invariably cut off as closely as possible.

Full dovetailing (fig. 3) is the most difficult method of corner-timbering employed in the Blue Ridge or elsewhere for that matter. However, the technique effectively locks, and since the faces of the notch all slope

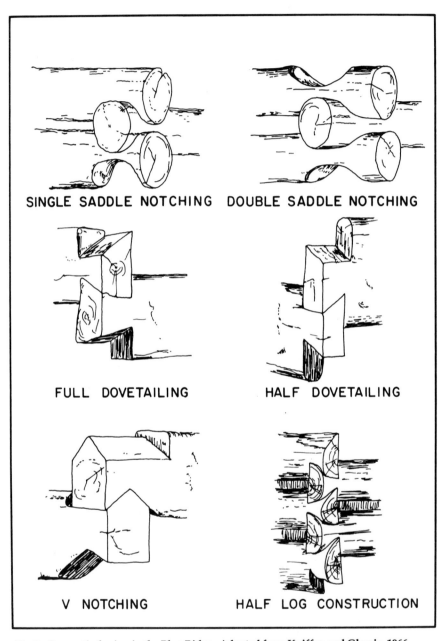

SINGLE SADDLE NOTCHING   DOUBLE SADDLE NOTCHING

FULL DOVETAILING   HALF DOVETAILING

V NOTCHING   HALF LOG CONSTRUCTION

Fig. 3. Corner-timbering in the Blue Ridge. Adapted from Kniffen and Glassie, 1966.

outward, it drains well, thus assuring long use. I have found full dovetailing only on squared timbers in the Blue Ridge, although elsewhere the technique is occasionally used with round logs.

Half dovetailing, on the other hand, differs from full dovetailing "in that the bottom of the notch is flat instead of sloping" (fig. 3). In the Blue Ridge this method is most commonly applied to hewn or squared logs. According to Kniffen (1969a, 3), "the half dovetail is quite as effective as the full dovetail and much easier to make." Probably this fact accounts for its wide use in and adjoining the study area. As Kniffen concludes (1969a, 3): "Close observation of both forms of dovetail jointing in log construction shows that many of them were at least partially sawed rather than completely chopped out." This statement applies to the Blue Ridge as well.

The last form of corner-timbering, half-log construction (fig. 3), is occasionally observed in the Blue Ridge. Actually this is a variant of the preceding types and appears where half logs with flat sides inward are used instead of full logs. The use of half logs appears in the study area on structures of rather recent origin (circa 1890), from a time when available timber was so small that it could not be used if hewn. Usually half-round logs are half dovetailed and sometimes full dovetailed. Characteristic of this variant is its half-moon end appearance.

Corner-timbering receives due stress because it is the most distinguishing variable feature in mountain folk architecture. It is simply insufficient to record log house, barn, or outbuilding, for building with logs is a mode of construction and not a type. In the Blue Ridge a number of different house types may be built of logs, and at the same time any one house type may be found in both log and other construction materials (Kniffen 1969b, 3).

Although diamond and square types of corner-timbering are commonly found in areas east of the Blue Ridge, neither type was recorded in the study area. This further supports the idea that corner-timbering techniques diffused to the Blue Ridge via the Pennsylvania Germans and Scotch-Irish and not by eastern Virginians of English descent. When settlers of English background finally occupied the mountains, they quickly adopted the log construction methods of the former Pennsylvanians, but at the same time clung to their own house types and related structures.

Cabins

According to informants, some initial settlers, after having chosen their land, put up as temporary living quarters a type of shelter used by some hunters today called a "three-sided camp" or "three-sided shelter." This was a crude but simple structure of light poplar poles placed vertically into the ground on three sides. The open (front) face of the camp was higher than the rear so that the pole roof sloped from front to back. Brush and long strips of bark were interwoven between the poles to keep out the elements. This tiny shelter, perhaps eight by eight feet, was particularly important for those families who had little manual labor to build sturdier temporary quarters. I found no existing examples of this shelter in the study area.

The first four-sided structure built by the initial settlers in the Blue Ridge was a temporary one called "pole shack," "pole hut," "pole shelter," or rarely "pole cabin." This formerly common building was low with a shallow pitched roof and was built of round logs, roughly saddle notched, with overhanging ends. Originally this house type had a dirt floor and an external stone chimney. The dwelling could be raised in a day with just a few men; it served admirably as a shelter until a better house could be built (Glassie 1963, 8).

Although not built to last, this single-room log structure was encountered occasionally in the study area outside of Shenandoah National Park between 1963-1982. The eight examples of the pole shack averaged nine by twelve feet, possessed shingle roofs and mud chinking between the round logs, and with one exception, were windowless (fig. 4). If it was retained for any length of time, changes were made to the pole shack, such as adding a wooden floor, adding a window, capping the stone chimney with brick, and clapboarding the gable ends (fig. 5). I discovered one example of a pole shack with hewn, dovetailed logs and an internal brick fireplace, indicating possibly a more recent origin (fig. 6). Consult figure 7 for the distribution of the pole shack.

Fig. 4. Pole shack belonging to Tom Sankford. Photograph taken by the National Park Service, 1944.

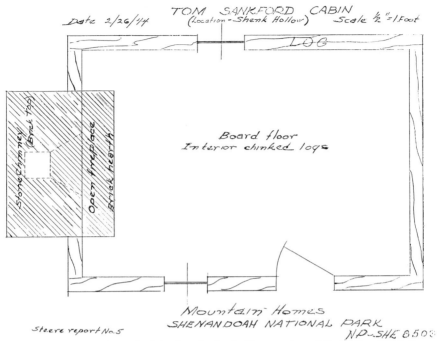

Fig. 5. House plan of Tom Sankford's pole shack. Plan courtesy of the National Park Service, 1944.

Fig. 6. A pole shack with hewn, dovetailed logs and an internal brick fireplace. Owner and exact location unknown. Photograph taken by the National Park Service, 1930.

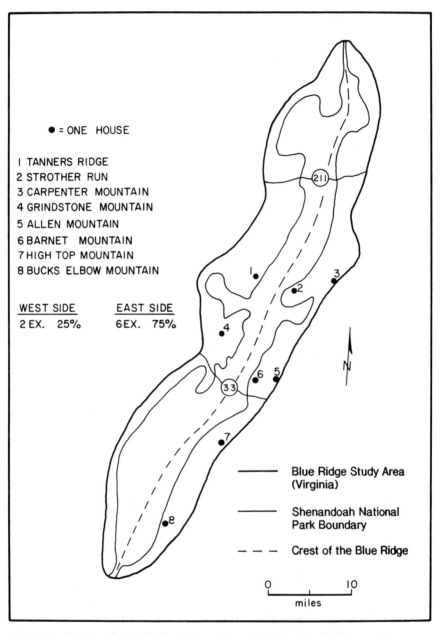

= ONE HOUSE

1 TANNERS RIDGE
2 STROTHER RUN
3 CARPENTER MOUNTAIN
4 GRINDSTONE MOUNTAIN
5 ALLEN MOUNTAIN
6 BARNET MOUNTAIN
7 HIGH TOP MOUNTAIN
8 BUCKS ELBOW MOUNTAIN

WEST SIDE   EAST SIDE
2 EX. 25%   6 EX. 75%

Blue Ridge Study Area
(Virginia)

Shenandoah National
Park Boundary

Crest of the Blue Ridge

0   10
miles

Fig. 7. Distribution of the Pole Shack House Type - 1970. Based on field reconnaissance by the author, 1963-1982.

As Shurtleff (1939) has so admirably shown, the term cabin had several meanings in the English colonies of America; it meant a flimsy hut of boughs and leaves, a mere sleeping-closet or bunk, or a small house cabin. In Ulster, the term cabin meant a dwelling inferior to a cottage, usually built of mud or fieldstone walls and having no chimney. Flimsy cabins, built on a frame of poles thrust into the ground at both ends, were also constructed for temporary summer use in the Ulster hills. In America, the term "log cabin" first appeared in print in 1770 in Botetourt County in the Valley of Virginia (Shurtleff 1939, 25). The term was used in reference to new construction in a Scotch-Irish area of the valley, and thus the Scotch-Irish are credited with inventing the term log cabin.

The Appalachian log cabin, with its characteristic types of corner-timbering, stands as a proper symbol of the meshing of German and Scotch-Irish construction methods in the Blue Ridge Mountains of Virginia. As Glassie stated (1963, 8):

> The Scotch-Irish, having inferior construction modes and few skilled artisans, quickly adopted German horizontal log construction, which utilized skills similar to those of British military, and half-timber construction. The Scotch-Irish did not fully adopt the German house form, but rather made certain changes in accordance with their architectural traditions which were reinforced by the arrival in the mountains of the English in about 1800. The house was constructed on a more square plan and had one large rather than three small rooms. The chimney was moved from the inside, as in German tradition, to the outside, as in British tradition, where it could be more quickly and easily built. The result was . . . a house built upon a British plan using German construction techniques.

A few examples of the German three-room log house remain in the Valley of Virginia, but none was recorded in the study area (Kerkhoff 1962, 2; Terrell 1970, 25-26). On the other hand, the English single-bay house type, commonly found east of the Blue Ridge Mountains, penetrated the eastern side of the study area by the closing of the eighteenth century. Although apparently never common in the mountains, this frame or clapboard over log one story and attic structure has a square floor plan, steep gable roof, external stone chimney at one gable-end, front and rear doors centered in the walls, and often no windows. Frame and clapboarding were common in certain sections of England but a luxury in Ulster due to the lack of timber. Most of the farmhouses and cottages in Ulster were frameless structures of stone or mud walls, covered with a thatched roof laid upon slender rafters (Campbell 1937). Thus the single-bay house type in the Blue Ridge reflects an English mode of construction.

I found evidence of ten examples of the English single-bay house on the eastern side of the Blue Ridge, most of them clustered in the Nicholson-Weakley Hollow district and farther southeast (fig. 8). However, I suspect that this lowland Virginia house type was more widely dispersed at the mouths of eastern hollows in former times than at present, as attested by the many examples of the type still in existence on the adjoining Piedmont (fig. 9).

In the Blue Ridge study area the log cabin varied from a square dwelling averaging about sixteen by sixteen feet to a rectangular house of about eighteen by twenty-two feet. It was almost always one and one-half stories high, but occasionally it attained a full two-story height. The log cabin was usually built about two feet off the ground on a stone foundation and had a wooden floor. A chimney at one gable-end was built of field stone with or without clay mortaring. As Eaton accurately described it (1937, 52):

> The chimney rests firmly upon the ground and the ascent of its stone…seems as natural and as beautiful as the growth of a symmet-

Fig. 8. English single-bay house type at the mouth of Kinsey Run. Photograph taken by the National Park Service, 1930.

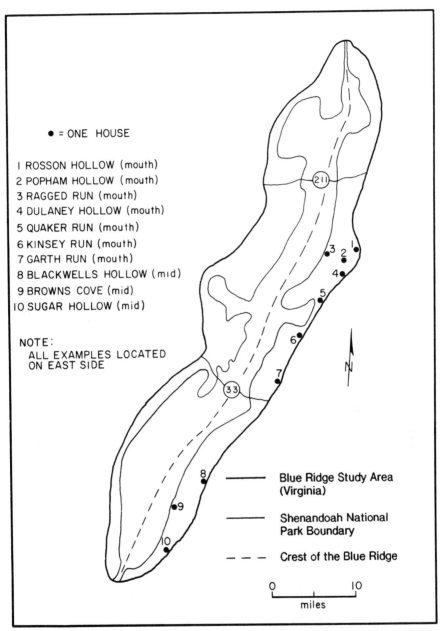

Fig. 9. Distribution of the English single-bay house type - 1970. Based on field reconnaissance by the author, 1963-1982.

rical tree. Its generally harmonious outline is always pleasantly broken by the varying sizes of the stones used, so that the eye follows, not swiftly but in leisurely fashion, the outside angles of the mass with its horizontal lines equally pleasing....No two faces of the stones are alike...but all...give a most satisfying...texture when seen in combination with hewn logs or rough boards.

In certain cases a narrow vertical or horizontal opening was made in the log wall to the right or left of the fireplace. The space was about a foot high and varied in width from a peephole to about a foot. This small opening allowed a shaft of light to enter and cabin dwellers to peek out. Over the one room most log cabins had a ceiling which served the purpose of conserving heat and of providing a loft for storage or sleeping purposes. Access to the loft was usually gained by pegs placed in the log wall, or by a ladder, and even later by steps. The roof was generally lightly framed and covered with shake shingles. If the log cabin plan was based on the Pennsylvania or Ulster fashion, it was distinguished by its rectangular plan and opposed front and rear doors. If it followed the English-Tidewater style, the plan was square and a rear door was usually missing. Occasionally there was a mixture of both plans.

At least thirty log cabins are still standing intact in the study area (fig. 10), most of which occur in the southeastern corner outside Shenandoah National Park, where there are fewer people and disturbances. Some of the log cabins are covered with clapboard or frame siding, while others have additional rooms or extensions. Fourteen examples of V notching, eleven

Fig. 10. A typical example of a one-room log cabin in the Blue Ridge Mountains. Owner and exact location unknown. Photograph taken by the National Park Service, 1935.

of half dovetailing, and five of full dovetailing were recorded in the field (fig. 11).

The number of log cabins recorded in the study area today is not a true representation of the number prior to 1935. After carefully examining the photographs of former dwellings in Shenandoah National Park files, I was able to count 111 log cabins as existing in the park prior to 1940. Most of the photographs contained scant information about location, dimensions, age, history, and ownership of the dwellings. Based on the fact that there were approximately 475 families living in the park area prior to 1930 and that each family had an average of one dwelling (several had two or more), 111 log cabins represent about one-fourth of all dwellings circa 1930. This figure excludes, of course, those log cabins located outside the present boundaries of the park.

The point is that the log cabin quickly succeeded the pole shack as the first permanent log dwelling in the Blue Ridge. Basically differing from the pole shack in its greater size, more sophisticated corner-timbering, and often opposed front and rear doors, the type spread throughout all the six settlement types in the study area, but particularly dominated the hollows, coves, and ridges until recent times. Only in gaps and in the mouths of several hollows did it, in turn, give way to other house types.

Houses

In the minds of the mountain folk a log cabin became a "log house" when significant additions and changes were made to the original dwelling, or when an altogether newer, larger, and more up-to-date house was built with two or more rooms. Although durable, the one-room log cabin was not very large for an average size mountain family of five or six people, thus even during the initial settlement period additions were made onto it. This evolutionary process in construction started simply with a crude pole lean-to added onto the rear, side, or front of the log cabin. The lean-to served many functions, but it was used most commonly as an outside kitchen. A kitchen lean-to was usually attached to the rear of the house and soon further evolved into an enclosed shed, which was well within the British tradition.

The Old Brown House, formerly situated at the head of Weakley Hollow, is an excellent example where enclosed sheds were attached to the rear of the original log house. This one-and-one-half story structure initially had one large room on the first level and an unfinished attic above it. Over the years the large room was subdivided into two smaller rooms and a hallway with an enclosed frame kitchen added to the left rear of the structure (fig. 12). Later a frame shed was joined to the right side of the kitchen to complete a four-room first-floor plan. Eventually the exterior of the entire

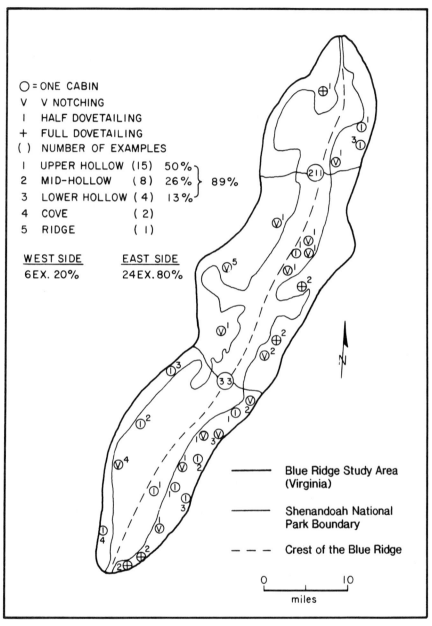

Fig. 11. Distribution of the Log Cabin - 1970. Based on field reconnaissance by the author, 1963-1982.

Fig. 12. Brown house at the foot of Old Rag Mountain. Photograph taken by the National Park Service, 1944.

structure was clapboarded. Alterations in the house design continued until the dwelling was abandoned in the early 1930s, as witnessed by the inclusion of several doors and the boarding up of others. Generally, this dwelling example resembles the common hall and parlor house type found on the Piedmont and in the Virginia Tidewater (fig. 13).

Another common addition to the log dwelling, favored by both the Pennsylvania Germans and Scotch-Irish, was the "ell." Robert Sour's log house, formerly standing in Jewell Hollow, was a rather large (sixteen by twenty-five feet), one-and-one-half story structure (fig. 14). Originally it had a single room with a large, clay-mortared, stone chimney, a single front door, and a loft above it. A stone cellar complemented the original log structure and V notched corner-timbering was used. Next, a frame end addition was joined to the right side of the log dwelling, forming a double-pen, one-and-one-half story structure of two equal units with two front doors and one side chimney. Finally, a frame ell with three doors and a stone chimney was added to the right pen and an L-shaped porch attached to both the house and the ell. The outside of the dwelling was covered at various times by an assortment of wooden materials: clapboards, vertical sheaths, shingles, shakes, and frame (fig. 15).

The mountain folk tried various ways to add a new log pen (room) to an old one (fig. 16). Unlike the frame addition described previously, if an addition of log is made to log, the old and new logs cannot be fitted together. "Thus, a log end addition could not become an integral part of the old house but could only be built as close as possible..." (Glassie 1963, 14). One logical solution was to build onto the end opposite the chimney resulting in a double-pen with end chimney; another solution was to build the log

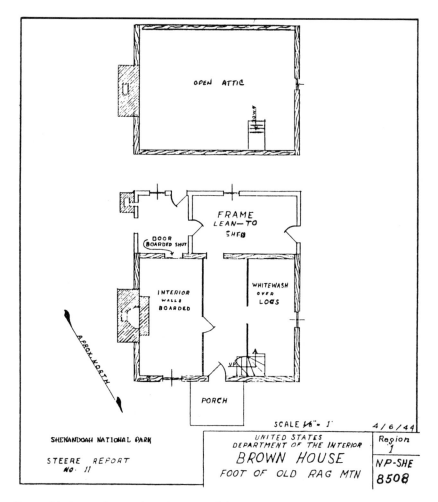

Fig. 13. The Brown house plan. Courtesy of the National Park Service, 1944.

addition onto the chimney end of the old dwelling. The chimney joined the two pens and supplied both with heat. Such a house type is called a "twin-pen" in the Blue Ridge and a "saddlebag" elsewhere (Zelinsky 1953, 175 and Wright 1958). Although formerly more common in the mountains, as depicted by park photographs taken in the 1930s, saddlebag houses with two log pens are now rare in the study area. I failed to discover a single example, although six cases of this house type with log and frame pens were recorded outside of park boundaries. Six other examples were identified, along with their locations, from park photographs (fig. 17).

Another less common solution to the log end addition was the "two pens and a passage" or "breezeway" house, known as "dogtrot" outside of

Fig. 14. Robert Sour's log house formerly located in Jewell Hollow. Photograph taken by the National Park Service, 1943.

the study area. Such folk terms describe the central breezeway or corridor which extended through the house between two pens. The second pen was not built up to the end of the first, but rather was constructed some feet away. Then the two pens were covered by a common roof. "The result was two cabins, each with its own chimney, with an open covered passage between them" (Glassie 1963, 14).

At present the dogtrot is an unknown house type in the study area. Formerly, at least two examples existed in Shenandoah: one at Big Meadows, built around 1800, and the other atop Hazel Mountain. I could find very little information about the first dwelling except that it was called a "breezeway" house and had two pens of equal size and a symmetrical relationship. The other dwelling was listed in a park report as "an unusual architectural specimen," but only a few notes and an accompanying poor photograph were attached. According to the notes the structure was constructed around 1810 and was abandoned long before the creation of Shenandoah National Park (Steere 1936).

Authorities state that the well-defined and dominant form of the dogtrot originated in the southern Tennessee Valley about 1825. Glassie believes that it is actually a subtype of the old hall and parlor house built symmetrically with a central hall in the Southern Tidewater from North Carolina to Georgia. But in "the western areas of higher elevation, these houses were built, when built of log, in two separate units because logs the length of a central hall house — about forty feet — would have been difficult to obtain and work" (Glassie 1968, 96). He earlier believed that the dogtrot bore a remarkable resemblance to the German double-crib barn found throughout the Blue Ridge, which might have been a model for the

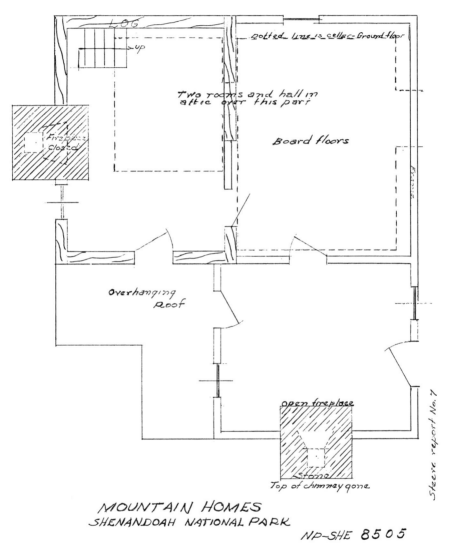

Fig. 15. Robert Sour's house plan. Courtesy of the National Park Service, 1944.

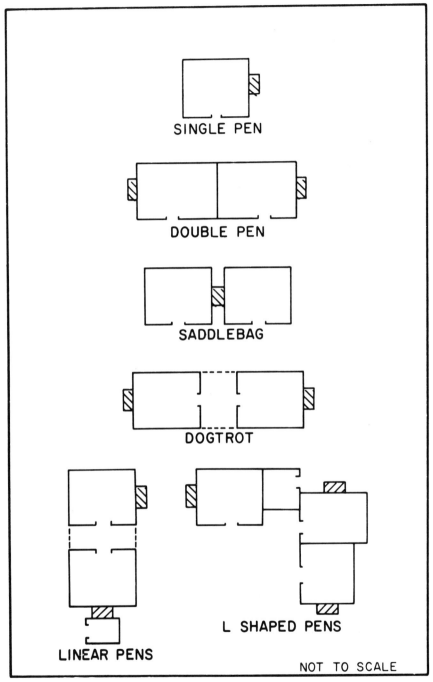

SINGLE PEN

DOUBLE PEN

SADDLEBAG

DOGTROT

LINEAR PENS

L SHAPED PENS

NOT TO SCALE

Fig. 16. Basic mountain folk house plans. Based on field reconnaissance by the author, 1963-1982.

Fig. 17. Saddlebag house type belonging to Rost Nicholson formerly of Nicholson Hollow. Photograph taken by the National Park Service, 1935.

house; he further thought that the house type originated west of the Blue Ridge and diffused into the mountains.

Two examples of any house type are flimsy evidence for indicating origins. Nonetheless, I am suggesting that the dogtrot examples in the study area represent English Tidewater ideas. The English were familiar with the hall and parlor house type in the Tidewater and Piedmont sections of Virginia, where it still can be found today. This cottage of two end-to-end rooms probably inspired the log dogtrot house as Kniffen (1965, 565) suggested. A discrepancy exists between the suggested 1825 time of origin for the dogtrot much farther south and the 1800 to 1810 known dates for the two examples in the study area. Admittedly, the dogtrot form scarcely worked against the major stream of diffusion from north to south, being uncommon north of Tennessee-North Carolina. Glassie, (1968, 99) however, believes that the dogtrot was carried northward at least to the northern North Carolina Piedmont.

Regardless, the Blue Ridge study area is still some 200 air miles farther north. It seems unlikely, therefore, that the dogtrot diffused northward into the Blue Ridge Mountains of Virginia when all other known house types in the study area diffused from Pennsylvania or the Chesapeake Tidewater. I suspect that the dogtrot developed in the Blue Ridge, having been built on the hall and parlor house plan, substituting logs for frame building material, and using Pennsylvania techniques of corner-timbering. Probably the dogtrot was formerly a more common house type in the Blue Ridge. Later it diffused southwestward via the Allegheny Mountains with other mountain culture traits. Presently, dogtrot examples are found in the Alleghenies due west of the study area. Perhaps "facing gable toward gable then roofing over the intervening space is so obvious a solution...that it was surely hit upon many times individually..." (Kniffen 1965, 561). Consult figure 18 for the distribution of the saddlebag and dogtrot house types.

A common solution to the problem of dwelling space in the mountains was to build a new and often larger pen close to the old one, but not always gable-end to gable-end. The Sheldon Dodson dwelling complex formerly situated in Dark Hollow is one such example (fig. 19). The original structure was a small log cabin with crude V notched corner-timbering, built on the typical English Tidewater square plan with front door, two windows, and shingle roof. The cabin lacked a chimney, built-in loft, and stone foundation. The structure was occupied until a larger one was built next to it. The newer, larger log house had a dry stone chimney, stairs to an open loft, and two windows. Although constructed with a rectangular floor plan, the dwelling lacked the opposed front and rear doors typical of the plan. The two units were connected by a roof abutting the chimney. The last constructed pen was similar in floor plan to the unit before it. However, it differed in that the V notched corner-timbering was neater, the gable-end faced away from the gable-end of the other unit, the stone chimney was reinforced with clay mortaring, and the pen had a small stone cellar beneath it. Apparently, the first unit was abandoned with the erection of the last rectangular pen. A boardwalk connected the last two units (fig. 20).

I House Type

The I house type developed in the Chesapeake Tidewater region was patterned closely after English originals (Glassie 1968, 66). The type first appeared in gap settlements in log form in the late eighteenth century. By the early part of the nineteenth century the type had spread to the mouths of the most prosperous hollows and varied in construction material from brick and stone to frame and log. There was seemingly great variation in house plan. Chimneys might be central, inside end, or outside end; lateral and rear sheds, ells, and front and rear porches appeared in mountain examples. But all Blue Ridge I houses had these common attributes: "gables to the side, at least two rooms in length, one room deep, and two full stories in height" (Kniffen 1965, 555). Entrance usually was in the long section. Although diffusing from the east side of the Blue Ridge, the I house became popular not only in the mountain gap and hollow settlements, but also in the Shenandoah Valley. The type apparently also diffused southward along the Shenandoah Valley with the Pennsylvanians.

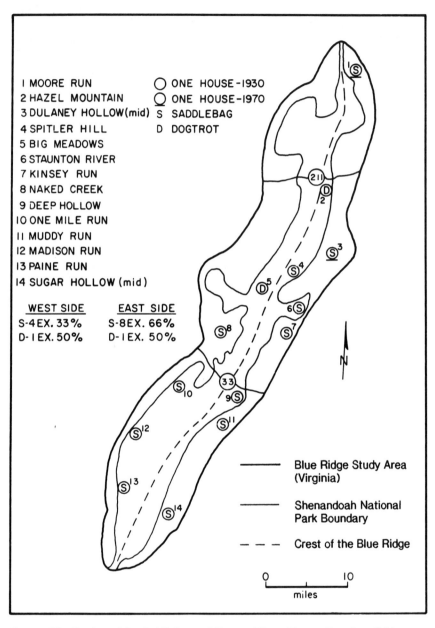

I MOORE RUN
2 HAZEL MOUNTAIN
3 DULANEY HOLLOW(mid)
4 SPITLER HILL
5 BIG MEADOWS
6 STAUNTON RIVER
7 KINSEY RUN
8 NAKED CREEK
9 DEEP HOLLOW
IO ONE MILE RUN
II MUDDY RUN
12 MADISON RUN
13 PAINE RUN
14 SUGAR HOLLOW (mid)

○ ONE HOUSE -1930
Ọ ONE HOUSE -1970
S SADDLEBAG
D DOGTROT

WEST SIDE
S-4 EX. 33%
D- I EX. 50%

EAST SIDE
S-8 EX. 66%
D- I EX. 50%

N

Blue Ridge Study Area
(Virginia)

Shenandoah National
Park Boundary

Crest of the Blue Ridge

0   10
miles

Fig. 18. Distribution of the Saddlebag and Dogtrot House Types. Based on field reconnaissance by the author, 1963-1982.

Fig. 19. Seldon Dodson's linear house complex. Photograph taken by the National Park Service, 1934.

Originally built on a two-room plan with logs, the type in the early nineteenth century came to be constructed with a broad central hall after the Georgian style with sheathing over logs or frame-stone construction.

The Belmont House, built in 1845 near Front Royal, is the epitome of how an affluent mountain family lived during the nineteenth century. This two-and-one-half story dwelling (fig. 21) had an all-brick, long, front section with two inside-end brick chimneys, a large central hall, four rooms, and twelve windows. A two-story-high clapboard over log ell was attached to the right rear of the house, which contained two rooms (up and down) and an inside-end brick chimney. The household kitchen was in the lower room of the ell. According to meager park notes, the Belmont House was owned by the Buck family. The house was part of a large, prosperous farm operating between 1845 and 1875 (fig. 22).

Today there are thirty I houses in the study area, all associated with settlements at the mouths of hollows or in gaps (fig. 23). Based on park photographs of houses in the 1930s, there were probably three times that number then. Still, at present, the I house is the commonest house type immediately surrounding the study area.

Other House Types

An important contribution to the type of log architecture which marks the mountain area was the great variety and large supply of native hardwood

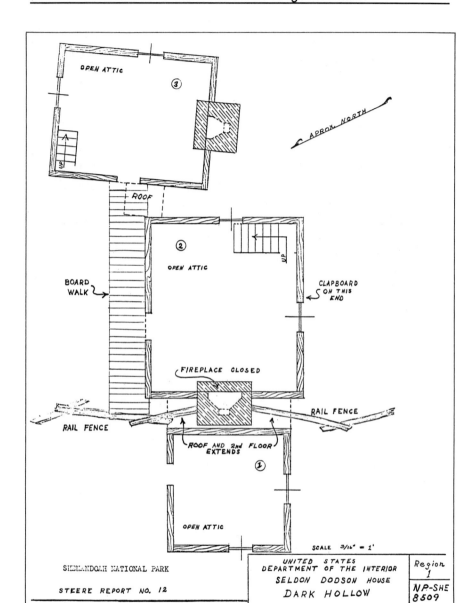

Fig. 20. Plan of Seldon Dodson's linear house conplex. Courtesy of the National Park Ser-evice, 1944.

Fig. 21. Belmont I house built in 1845 near Front Royal. Photograph taken by the National Park Service, 1943.

trees. Among those that were most commonly used were ash, oak, chestnut, hickory, poplar, and locust. The initial settler secured all his materials near his home site and worked them by hand, often supplying every item of construction himself, including the wooden or leather hinges, latches, and fasteners for windows and doors carefully whittled with his own knife (Eaton 1937, 47).

This does not imply, however, that all mountain houses were log structures in the initial settlement period. Both stone and stone-frame structures were built after initial settlement occupance had taken place and finished lumber became readily available. All-stone dwellings were commonly constructed in the Shenandoah Valley during the first half of the eighteenth century by Pennsylvanian German immigrants (Kerkhoff 1962). Toward the end of the third quarter of the eighteenth century the stone house diffused eastward into the gaps of the Blue Ridge Mountains. Although this type was never common and was almost entirely confined to Thornton, Swift Run, and Rockfish Gaps in the study area, at least one excellent example of an all-stone farm complex, the Bower House, was photographically recorded by the National Park Service in the early 1930s before the houses disappeared. How many other all-stone farm complexes existed at one time is unknown. Probably there were some stone dwellings dispersed throughout the main gaps and at mouths of some hollows. The following sketchy description of the Bower complex is based upon limited data gleaned from park files.

The Bower House was the main dwelling and the largest (twenty-eight by thirty feet) building in the farm complex. It was a fine two-and-one-half story structure, all stone, except for a two-story frame front porch and a second story frame rear porch. A shake-shingle roof and two stone

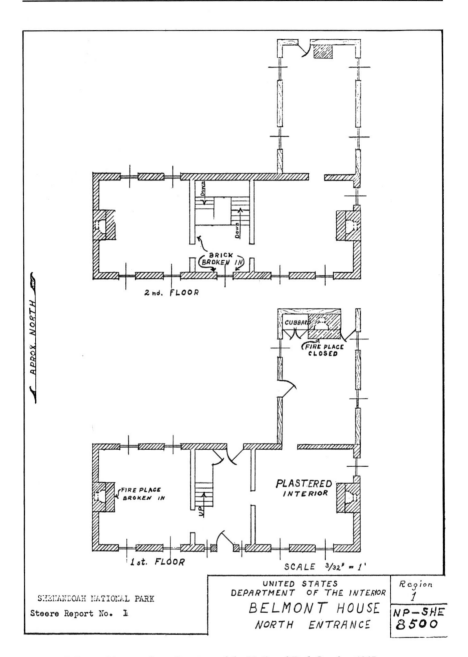

Fig. 22. Belmont I house plan. Courtesy of the National Park Service, 1945.

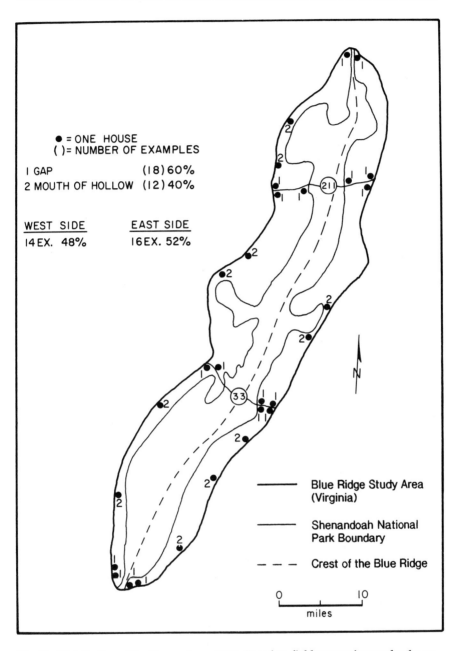

Fig. 23. Distribution of the I house type - 1970. Based on field reconnaissance by the author, 1963-1982.

end chimneys complemented the structure. The stone masonry was reinforced with cement throughout the structure. There are only sketchy details on the floor plan, but overall it resembled the stone blockhouses of the
valley (fig. 24).

Somewhere nearby stood another stone structure called the Bower
Springhouse. Reputed to have been built in 1775, perhaps a few years earlier than the Bower House, by Frank Skinner, this twenty-four-by-sixteen-
foot structure was a fine example of dry stone construction with an added
front lean-to (fig. 25). The ground floor of the two and one-half stories contained an entrenched spring and, coupled with the two-foot-thick stone
walls and oak window bars, this lent the house a close resemblance to the
stone fort dwellings of the valley in the early eighteenth century (fig. 26).
A stone tool house, stone root cellar, and a log and stone single-crib barn
constituted the farm's outbuildings.

The Bower House was located east of the ridge in Thornton Gap and
was later sold to the Barbee family. There were extensive exotic plantings
made on the property by the Barbee family, including a diversified orchard of apple, peach, pear, and plum trees. The farm complex perhaps

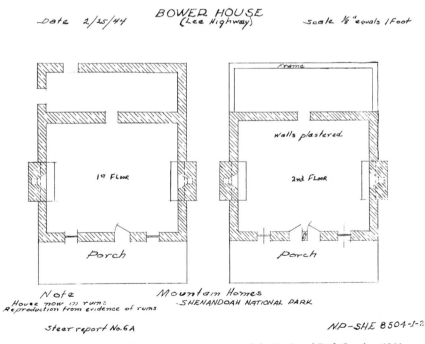

Fig. 24. Floor plan of the Bower house. Courtesy of the National Park Service, 1944.

Fig. 25. Side view of the Bower springhouse. Note the lack of mortaring. Photograph taken by the National Park Service, 1944.

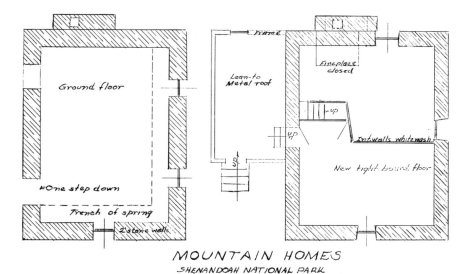

Fig. 26. Floor plan of the Bower springhouse. Courtesy of the National Park Service, 1944.

commanded one of the most outstanding views of the Piedmont in the entire study area. The farm has long since disappeared.

Evidence of a rather unusual house type was found in park files, although details are lacking. Crude sketches depict the George Berry House, a two-and-one-half story stone and frame structure with a stone chimney, which was located at the foot of White Oak Canyon on the eastern slope of the Blue Ridge (fig. 27). This example of an upper frame level overhanging a lower stone level, although unusual construction among house types, is common in mountain outbuildings. The form has perhaps both Western European and British antecedents, and New World source areas in Pennsylvania and New England. The house type is still rarely seen in Tidewater Virginia and apparently diffused into the eastern Blue Ridge with the later arrival of English immigrants. Although several mountain folk called the house type an "overshot" house when viewing the sketches of it, I found no existing example of this type of construction during field reconnaissance (fig. 28).

Barns and Smaller Outbuildings

Investment in mountain outbuildings was small during the initial settlement period. The tardiness of most mountain immigrants in building large, sturdy barns was due to the great expense in time and energy and

Fig. 27. The George Berry overshot house type formerly built near the junction of Cedar Run and the Robertson River. National Park Service, 1935.

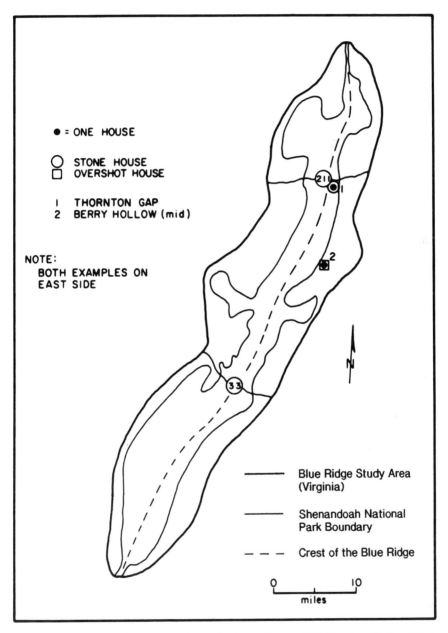

= ONE HOUSE

○ STONE HOUSE
□ OVERSHOT HOUSE

1 THORNTON GAP
2 BERRY HOLLOW (mid)

NOTE:
 BOTH EXAMPLES ON
 EAST SIDE

N

——— Blue Ridge Study Area
(Virginia)

——— Shenandoah National
Park Boundary

– – – Crest of the Blue Ridge

0   10
miles

Fig. 28. Distribution of the stone and overshot house types - 1930. Based on National Park Service data and field reconnaissance by the author, 1963-1982.

to the little need for them. Settlement priorities demanded that mountain families first build their homes, next clear more land for crops, and finally construct small outbuildings as they were needed. At first the settlers did not possess many stock. A typical mountain family, if fortunate, had a cow or horse, a few hogs, and some poultry (chickens and geese). Thus there was little need for large barns. Farm equipment and tools were few and simple, demanding little storage space. Generally, various small out-buildings, such as springhouses, smoke "sheds" or smokehouses, root cel-lars, corn cribs, and chicken houses, were constructed sooner than large barns. The latter finally appeared after material gain was assured and de-mand called for them.

The form and material of construction, number, and physical upkeep of farm outbuildings can be correlated with the economic status of each mountain family. A greater number of buildings, more sophisticated con-struction, and larger size of the barn and house are empirical criteria that indicate greater economic affluence. Today the more prosperous Blue Ridge farmsteads consist of I houses, double-crib barns, and several out-buildings. The I house is usually built in frame or brick, while the barn and smaller outbuildings are constructed of frame, stone, or stone-frame combination. The poorer mountain farmsteads consist of smaller houses and barns (if any exist) and generally fewer outbuildings. Basic log con-struction, although exteriorly altered by various forms of siding, prevails among these farm structures. Most Blue Ridge farmsteads had at least one or two outbuildings before 1930, although there were a few mountain fam-ilies living in single-room dwellings without any outbuildings of any kind.

The first outbuildings of the Blue Ridge settlements, like the house types before them, were constructed of log after the Pennsylvania German fashion (Glassie 1964 and Glassie 1965). However, log outbuildings were usually less carefully constructed than log houses, the logs being left in the round, "unpeeled" (bark), unchinked, and saddle notched. From the an-cient, rectangular construction unit, called a "crib" in the Blue Ridge, there developed "partially in Europe and partially in America, most…of the tra-ditional barn types found today in the Southern Mountains" (Glassie 1965, 21).

The rectangular log construction unit, which was brought into the Blue Ridge Mountains by Pennsylvanians, was easily adapted to the stor-age of maize and became the corn crib found throughout the Southern Highlands. "The corn crib is the same form as the Pennsylvania one-level outbuilding; that is, rectangular with a gable or lean-to roof and the door in one gable-end…"(Glassie 1965, 22).

In time, sheds for stabling were added to the sides of an enlarged rect-angular log unit producing the single-crib barn. As Glassie said (1965, 24):

The single-crib barn is closely related to the corn crib with gear shed but may be distinguished from it by function (the sheds of the barn are used for stabling, the shed attached to the corn crib for the storage of farm equipment), by form (the crib of the barn is a more moderate rectangle than that of the corn crib with gear shed...and may even be square), and by the fact that the crib of the single-crib barn is usually divided into two levels: the lower utilized for corn storage, the upper as a hay loft or "mow," whereas, the crib of the corn crib with gear loft has only one level.

In the study area the single-crib barn diffused throughout all the hollow and cove settlements and even was constructed atop Tanners and Weakley Ridges and in Big Meadows and Pasture Fence. The structure could be varied easily to meet the needs of the individual farmer by adding lean-to's or sheds, and "as a result of this flexibility...it became common ...along the Blue Ridge..." (Glassie 1965, 25). Forty examples were located in the study area. The Pennsylvania one-level outbuilding was the commonest form in the study area and it also served several functions: springhouse, smokehouse, corn crib, and chicken house. Even the pig pen or "hog shed" was a variant of this rectangular, single-level form; it was simply lower in height and lacked flooring. Although not always present, the most distinguishing feature of the single-level log outbuilding was its projecting roof, "constructed on the cantilever principle typical of Pennsylvania German construction. The projecting roof was supported in log buildings by the forward extension of the top log in the wall..." (Glassie 1964, 23).

Occasionally in the Blue Ridge the single crib barn varied into a form of log stable. Photographic records in park files, surface archaeology, and informants indicate that at least twelve cases of the log stable were distributed in the lower parts of Harris, Jewell, Mink, Crow, Bacon, and Sugar Hollows; and in Morning Star (two examples), Harris (two examples), Browns, and Steele Coves (fig. 29). The first level of the rectangular mountain stable was usually divided into three sections: two areas for stabling separated by a walkway which has access to the hay loft above. However, one example in the file varies slightly from this typical form. The first door (left) opens into the corn crib; the next room (right) might have been used for a stable or as a storeroom for items of farm equipment. The log pole ceiling in this room forms the floor of a loft for storing hay. A small shed was added onto the rear end of the structure.

Ten examples of the larger but less common double-crib barn type were discovered during field reconnaissance between 1963 and 1982 at the mouths of Milam (two examples), Swift Run, and Brown Gaps (two examples); and Harris, Buracker, Pocosin, Bacon, and Sugar Hollows (fig. 30). At least six other examples of this type formerly existed in Morning Star

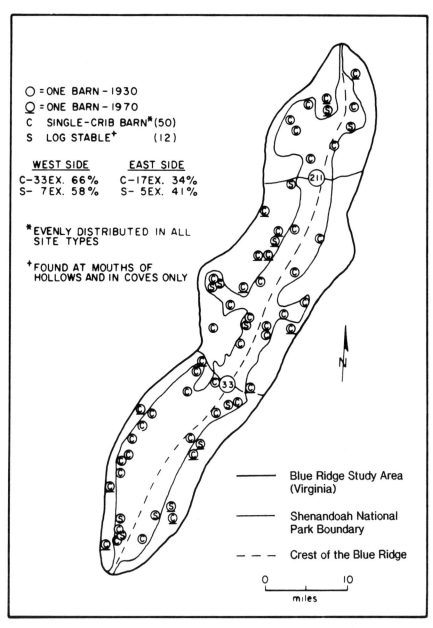

Fig. 29. Distribution of the single-crib barn and the log stable. Based on National Park Service data and field reconnaissance by the author, 1963-1982.

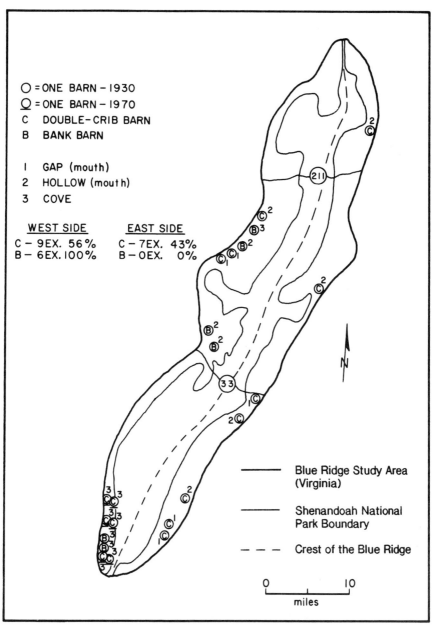

Fig. 30. Distribution of the double-crib and bank barn types - 1970. Based on National Park Service data and field reconnaissance by the author, 1963-1982.

(two), Horsehead (two), and Steele Coves, but since 1930 they have been destroyed or succeeded by other barn types. In the Blue Ridge the double-crib barn is basically two separate cribs facing each other or side by side, separated by a runway and joined by a common roof. In those with cribs facing each other, the doors open into the runway; if the cribs are side by side, the doors open to the front. Sometimes the runway is closed off, and occasionally the double-crib barn is built into an embankment forming two distinct levels plus a loft above each crib. Under the latter conditions the double-crib closely resembles the Pennsylvania bank barn.

The lower level of the great Pennsylvania barn is used for stabling, while the upper level is reached by a ramp and typically has an overhang or forebay in the rear. The upper level is commonly divided into three sections: two hay lofts separated by a threshing floor. This barn type was apparently developed in Pennsylvania by building a log, side by side, double-crib barn on a hillside with a stone basement under it as barns were often built in Switzerland. Interestingly, the examples of both the two-level double-crib barn and the German bank barn indicated above are found one-quarter mile apart on adjoining farms in a gap a few miles south of the study area.

The Pennsylvania bank barn diffused southward in the Shenandoah Valley and penetrated the surrounding mountains. In the Blue Ridge it is presently confined to the western side, six examples being found at the mouths of Buracker, Mink, Crow, and Hensley Hollows, and in Steele Cove (two examples). It should be emphasized that the barn type is common in the valley and can be found on the Piedmont beyond the study area. Although not well suited to small mountain farms, the Pennsylvania barn, usually of small proportions, is commonly found in the Allegheny Mountains and in the Blue Ridge Mountains south of the study area (fig. 31).

The Pennsylvania one-level outbuilding occasionally had a room added above it producing the Pennsylvania two-level outbuilding type. Glassie (1964, 23) claims that this type is the most common outbuilding in the Southern Highlands. This may be true elsewhere, but not in the study area. Only the root cellar was consistently built in two levels in the past (prior to 1930) and is uncommon today. Normally built into a hillside, the root cellar consists of a ground level constructed in stone with an upper level of round log and saddle notched corner-timbering. According to all accounts the root cellar had a wide distribution throughout the hollows of the study area and for that reason the form's distribution is not mapped.

The Tidewater outbuilding was the third and last type to reach the Blue Ridge circa 1800. Having a typical English square floor plan and a pyramidal roof, the type is represented at present by three smokehouses on the eastern side of the study area. One all-stone example is found at the mouth of Sugar Hollow, another clapboard over log example at the mouth

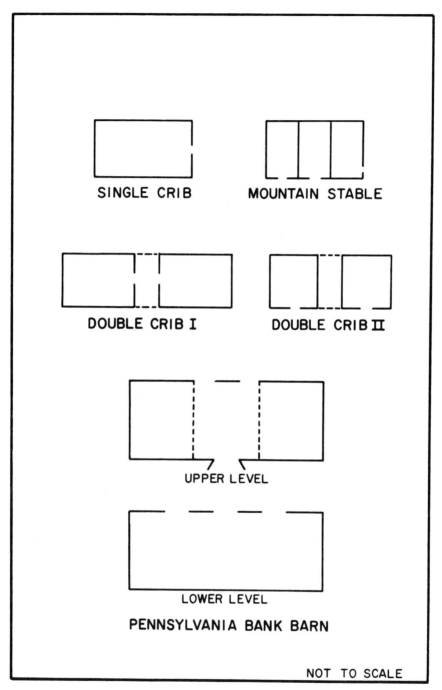

SINGLE CRIB

MOUNTAIN STABLE

DOUBLE CRIB I

DOUBLE CRIB II

UPPER LEVEL

LOWER LEVEL

PENNSYLVANIA BANK BARN

NOT TO SCALE

Fig. 31. Blue Ridge barn types. Based on field reconnaissance by the author, 1963-1982.

of Pocosin Hollow, and a third example of clapboard over log construction near the mouth of Bacon Hollow. Outbuildings are frequently built of stone in the valley and on the Piedmont. Springhouses or milkhouses are built over springs and have water piped through stone troughs (rarely hollowed logs) along one wall. Years ago, before electricity, crocks of milk, butter, eggs, and other perishables were kept cool here, since stone walls were more satisfactory than wood for maintaining the low temperature necessary for preserving dairy products.

Stores

Nearly every major gap and hollow in the Blue Ridge had its general store. Originally constructed with log, all stores conformed to two basic floor plans: 1) a square one-story structure which followed the English style of eastern Virginia, and 2) a rectangular one-story unit which closely resembled other buildings of Pennsylvania German and Scotch-Irish origin. Log stores no longer exist on the landscape, apparently all being succeeded by larger frame structures. Ten examples of the latter were recorded in the study area. Photographic records of others indicate that at least twenty stores were in business circa 1930 (fig. 32).

The English store type pierced the Blue Ridge from Tidewater and Piedmont localities and managed to reach the crests of a few gaps. Fletcher Store (fig. 33), at the base of Pocosin Hollow on the east slope of the Blue Ridge, is a good example of an English store type. It has square floor plan, one and one-half levels, a stone foundation, clapboard over frame, two front entrances on the long side, a front porch and two right-side shed additions.

In busy gaps and hollows, however, this type of store was too small to render sufficient service to its customers. Clearly, larger buildings were needed. Circa 1825, perhaps earlier, the first stores with two levels appeared in log and later in frame. The Ida Valley Grocery (fig. 34), at one time a general store, is an existing example of this type. Ida Valley is at the mouth of Buracker Hollow on the west side of the study area. Fortunately several of these nineteenth century structures still occur on the outside perimeter of the study area. The store typically has large dimensions (twenty by forty feet), two and one-half stories, front entrance and two windows at one of the gable-ends on the first level, and one, large, rectangular room. The second floor is divided into four rooms with six windows; entrance to the second level is by way of outside stairs along the right side of the building. The entire structure is built on several stone and wooden pilings.

Functionally, the mountain store was the hub of the local district and acted as bank and credit house, news center, market place, recreation center, public meeting place, and political forum. As so aptly stated in Clark (1964):

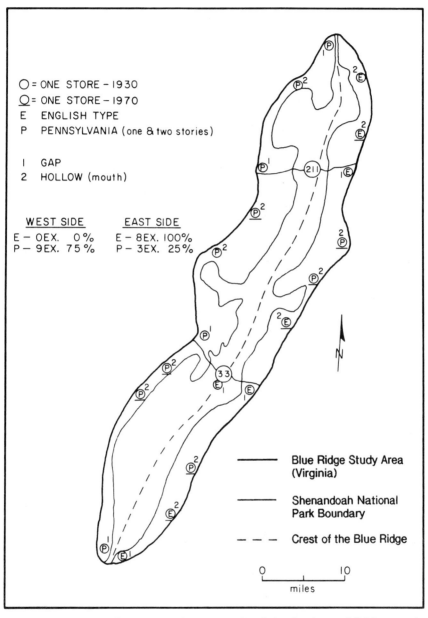

O = ONE STORE – 1930
Q = ONE STORE – 1970
E   ENGLISH TYPE
P   PENNSYLVANIA (one & two stories)

I   GAP
2   HOLLOW (mouth)

WEST SIDE	EAST SIDE
E – 0EX. 0%	E – 8EX. 100%
P – 9EX. 75%	P – 3EX. 25%

N

——— Blue Ridge Study Area
       (Virginia)

——— Shenandoah National
       Park Boundary

– – – Crest of the Blue Ridge

0 _____ 10
        miles

Fig. 32. Distribution of stores. Based on National Park Service data and field reconnaissance by the author, 1963-1982.

Fig. 33. Fletcher store at the base of Pocosin Hollow on the east side of the Blue Ridge is an example of an English store type. Photograph taken by the author in May 1967.

Fig. 34. Ida Valley grocery, an example of a two-level store. Photograph taken by the author in June 1965.

Literally everything from swaddling clothes to coffins, from plow-shares to Christmas candy for the children, from patent medicines to corsets was included in its inventory. The storekeeper was all things to his community, and if his credit practices sometimes smacked of usury, who else would have advanced credit on shaky liens or prom-issory notes secured by unplanted crops...?

Mills and Stills

The mountain term "mill" applies to any device (machinery) which pro-duces an end product through the continuous repetition of some action (e.g., sawing logs into lumber). Mills come in various sizes and complex-ities, ranging from the large water-powered gristmill through the sawmill, and the horse-driven sorghum mill to the hand-powered cider mill.

At least two types of gristmills were erected in the eighteenth century: the overshot-wheel and the horizontal or "tub" wheel. The overshot-wheel variety occurred primarily at the mouths of major hollows on the eastern side of the ridge because of the larger, faster-flowing streams there. Two mills of this type also operated for many years in Thornton and Swift Run Gaps; again both were located on the east slope of the mountains (fig. 35). Various forms of information (photographs, informants, county building permits, and surface archaeology) indicate that at least fifteen gristmills of this type existed in the study area circa 1930. However, only a few of those were still operating at that time. A few of these abandoned structures re-main intact, but years of neglect are causing serious deterioration. Over-shot-wheel gristmills were built of logs in the eighteenth century, but this mode of construction changed to frame and clapboard in the early nine-teenth century. The large overshot wheel was usually made of oak wood, and the sturdy device lasted for years. Wooden machinery gave way to cast iron in the late nineteenth century.

Apparently a few horizontal water wheels set with oblique paddles were used in the study area in the nineteenth century. These were espe-cially used for small farm operations. These wheels were about six feet in diameter and were called "tub wheels" because of the tub-shaped hopper in which the grist was placed. Since the overshot wheel was more effi-cient, the former type was never common and gradually disappeared in the late 1890s. At any rate, I found no archaeological evidence or photo-graphic records of the type in the study area. Nevertheless, according to informants, tub wheels were used in Richards, Pocosin, and Dark Hollows on the eastern side of the ridge.

Just about every overshot-wheel gristmill had an up-and-down saw-mill in proximity to it. The early mountain settlers were, of necessity, lum-bermen. The small sawmill provided the mountain folk with shelter and supplemental income during the agricultural "off season."

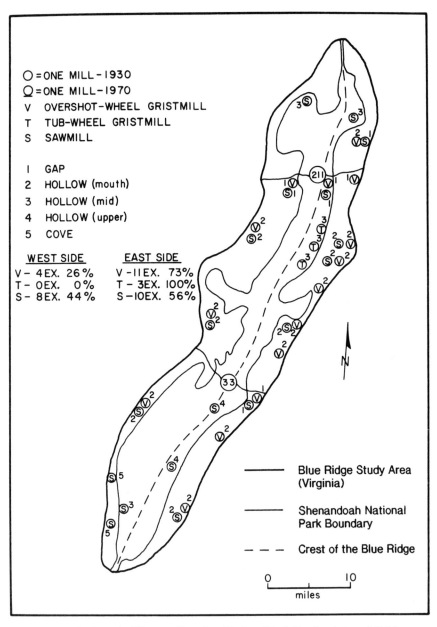

Fig. 35. Distribution of mill types. Based on National Park Service data and field reconnaissance by the author, 1963-1982.

Lumbering and the number of sawmills increased steadily in the nineteenth century until the outbreak of the Civil War. Circular saws appeared after 1850. Large quantities of staves, headings, planks, boards, and shingles were exported to Piedmont and Shenandoah Valley towns. A few hollow and cove farmers operated small sawmills along the streams in the midst of large tracts of timber. After 1865 lumbering became more specialized, that is, a business by itself instead of a side line of farming. It also became more centralized. Less lumber was handled by small local mills and more by a few corporation-owned mills in Piedmont and valley towns. Thus the peak of lumbering activity in the Blue Ridge, between 1880 and 1910, actually had fewer mountain sawmills than before the Civil War. Today because of National Park Service regulations prohibiting the cutting of timber, sawmills are nonexistent. However, several small sawmills powered by diesel engines are found in the Blue Ridge south of Shenandoah National Park.

The accompanying map showing the distribution of eighteen known water-powered sawmills circa 1930 is based on data collected from county building and operating permits (1890-1930), county tax rolls, park files, surface archaeology, and personal interviews. Note the close association of sawmills with gristmills (fig. 35).

Smaller mills, such as those used for the making of sorghum syrup and apple cider, were found in most mountain hollow, cove, and ridge settlements. Their number undoubtedly varied from settlement to settlement, depending on the number of families per settlement, kinds of crops and fruits grown locally, and the like. The making of sorghum syrup entailed the feeding of the butt ends of the plant into the mill, which was powered by a horse, mule, or ox walking a slow circle. The juice crushed out of the sorghum was caught in a pan or tub, poured into an evaporator tray over a wood fire, boiled down to syrup, strained, and put up in jars (Booker 1930, 24-25).

Tree fruits were grown primarily to furnish a drink, frequently to feed to hogs, and only incidentally to eat, for the Blue Ridge mountain folk were prodigious drinkers of a great variety of liquors, both fermented and distilled. Most folk viewed water for drinking purposes with deep suspicion, if not aversion. Mountain folk preferred apple cider above all other fruit drinks. Before the Revolutionary War, a cider commonly was made for home use by pounding the apples with a "stamper" or "presser" in a wooden trough, then placing the pulp in a large splint basket to drain (Fletcher 1950, 212). Cider mills were introduced after the Revolutionary War. Resembling the sorghum mill in appearance and operation, it was composed of a wooden wheel three to four feet in diameter and a foot thick, with a shaft through the center. The wheel revolved in a circle or groove. The apples were placed in this groove and by applying horse power to the shaft the wheel passed over and crushed them to pulp. Then the pulp was placed in a press of crude wooden construction and the cider squeezed from it. In the nineteenth century the wheel and groove were made of cast iron manufactured beyond the Blue Ridge.

Prior to 1930, mint and whiskey "stills" were used by the mountain folk. In fact, whiskey or mountain stills are operating illegally in many parts of the Blue Ridge today.

Distillation of mint oil from the native meadow mint plants was a process known by several mountain families. The oil was used domestically and sold or bartered at mountain stores for flavoring and medicine. The homemade still operated very simply. Water was placed in steam tanks and holes were cut into the upper part of each tank. Barrels were packed full of mint and placed above them. Cooling pipes were then connected to the upper ends of the barrels. A fire was built in the firebox below, enabling steam from the boiling water to rise through the mint, vaporizing the oil from the mint plants and carrying it on through the pipes to the condenser trough. Here, flowing water condensed the steam and oil which then flowed into a large glass jar. The jar had a vertical spout mounted on the side that allowed the weight of the mint oil to force the water up and out, leaving almost pure mint oil behind. Similar stills were used to make birch and pine oils as well.

A similar distillation process was used for the making of whiskey. Scotch-Irish of the early seventeenth century had made "poteen" in small distilleries in their native land of Ulster, and like many other cultural traits, the knowledge of the process was retained by the immigrants to Pennsylvania and the Southern Mountains (fig. 36).

Fence Types

The early practice of allowing livestock to run at large made it necessary for mountain families to fence their croplands, gardens, and orchards. Clearly, fences in the Blue Ridge were erected to keep the livestock out rather than in. Fencing imposed some burden on farmers; fields generally were small and the labor of building and maintaining fences time-consuming. Still, there was plenty of wood and stone material for constructing fences. The first permanent fence type was constructed of wood by interlocking stacked split rails of chestnut or oak at an angle to form what is variously known as the worm, snake, zigzag, or Virginia rail fence. Fence builders "lay the worm with a bottom course of rails and then build up to the desired height." This type became an integral part of the Blue Ridge landscape and has survived to the present in mountainous areas north and south of Shenandoah National Park. One initial problem presented by the snake fence was that of keeping the top rail in place, there-

Fig. 36. A moonshine still found in Steam Hollow in July 1938. Photograph taken by the National Park Service, 1938.

fore the mountain folk stabilized the fence by crossing the tops of two upright stakes and laying the top rail in the angle formed by the crossing (fig. 37). This fence subtype was called the "stake-and-rider." Later, in the declining years of the nineteenth century, two heavy stones were wired together and thrown over the top rail with a stone hanging on either side of the fence. This replaced the stake-and-rider.

Rails were made by splitting logs in halves, quarters, or eighths according to their size. Snake fences were built of rails eight to twelve feet long. The fences generally were about four and one-half feet high, which usually required five or six rails. Between 700 and 800 rails were used to fence an acre, although this figure varied with the terrain. The snake fence was used primarily to mark farm boundaries, outfield enclosures, and the infield. However, the snake fence was unsatisfactory at least on three counts: 1) it was wasteful of land and wood supply; 2) it was easily knocked loose or pushed over by cattle; and 3) it became the haven for unwanted weeds, insects, and snakes.

The apparent successor of the snake fence, in particular in hollows and coves, was the "stake-and-rail" type (fig. 38). Because the snake fence was easily reconstructed, many mountain farmers dismantled it from around the perimeter of the infield and reused it in demarking outfield boundary extensions. This procedure required little in the way of specialized equipment or skills. Then, the farmer re-fenced his infield with stake-and-rail. Being a straight rail fence, this type was more economical in the amount of space it occupied and required less wood than the snake fence.

Fig. 37. Stake-and-rider rail fence near Humpback Rocks. Photograph taken by the author in July 1964.

Fig. 38. Stake-and-rail fence near Afton, Virginia. Photograph taken by the author in May 1966.

However, one disadvantage was that postholes had to be dug; at the same time this bolstered the strength of the fence to withstand greater pressures and abuse.

An uncommon subtype of the stake-and-rail, called the "spike-and-rail" in the Blue Ridge, occasionally was used for infield fencing. Only one post was used, to either side of which the rails were bolted, spiked, or tied alternately (fig. 39).

Another type of fencing, although not nearly as common as the snake or stake-and-rail, appeared after the Civil War in the lower reaches of a

Fig. 39. Spike-and-rail fence near Afton, Virginia. Photograph taken by the author in May 1968.

few gaps and hollows. This was the "post-and-rail" fence. During the winter mountain farmers cut chestnut trees into six foot lengths for posts and into ten foot lengths for rails. The posts were set into the ground approximately ten feet apart, with holes previously cut into them. Rails were inserted into the holes from either side of the post; most post-and-rail fences contained two or three rails, one above the other. Wherever it was found, the fence type was associated with the wealthier mountain farms and commercial gap establishments along public roads.

One last type of split-rail fence, called the "buck" or "pitchpole" fence by the mountain folk, was discovered twice at the south end of the study area. This type had one rail about ten feet long resting in the crotch of two other six-foot-long rails. The two shorter rails crossed and were set firmly into the ground. Pairs of crossed rails were about four feet apart (fig. 40). Since both examples of this fence type were located beside busy mountain

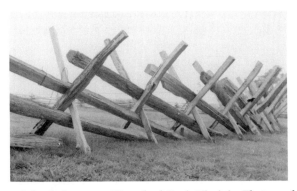

Fig. 40. Buck or pitchpole fence near Humpback Rock, Virginia. Photograph taken by the author in September 1966.

roads, the unusual form seems to have been used for aesthetic rather than functional reasons.

Three other wooden fence types commonly were placed around mountain homes and gardens: the paling, picket, and board fences. The paling fence was used early in the history of the Blue Ridge settlements, and practically always demarcated the garden and dwelling area. In contrast to the paling fence, the picket fence was usually commercially made at a nearby sawmill. Often it was painted, but not always. Finally, the board fence represented a late arrival to the mountains, definitely after the Civil War. Commercially made, the type had aesthetic, prestige, and functional qualities attached to it. It was an expensive fence, thus was found mostly, but not always, in association with the wealthier farmsteads.

Not all pioneer fences in the Blue Ridge were constructed of wood. Stone-wall fences, for example, were widely dispersed and have come to symbolize poverty of soil and agriculture (Raup 1947, 2). That does not seem to be a fair judgment of the Blue Ridge region or of the adjoining Shenandoah Valley where stone-wall fences are commonly seen on some of the most productive farms. In both regions the construction of stone fences served two purposes: 1) to protect and bound the field, and 2) to remove excess stones from it. By clearing his land of these stones and skillfully laying them into well proportioned walls, the farmer accomplished the double purpose of land preparation and permanent fencing.

Two different subtypes of stone-wall fences were constructed in the Blue Ridge. The first generally lined roads, encircled fields, but not pastures, and climbed hillsides; it followed a similar pattern of the largest stones being laid on the surface first with tiers of smaller stones being placed on top of them. Such fences were four feet high and two feet thick. The second subtype was far less common, but when constructed it acted as a wall for barnyards, garden plots, and pastures. Typically, large-sized stones were laid as a base with medium-sized stones placed atop them. Many smaller stones were fitted into holes and pockets throughout the wall. Finally, the wall was "capped" with large, flat stones placed at about a forty-five degree angle. Such walls were clearly intended to confine stock animals, as attested by the five to six feet height and the average two foot thickness of the wall. The nearly vertical capping stones increased the height of the wall and at the same time the heavy superstructure secured the lower part with its weight. Mountain folk also claimed that the tottering appearance deterred cattle from approaching the wall. At times heavy round stones replaced the flat slabs (fig. 41). This stone wall technique is almost an exact duplication of the method followed in Ulster.

The first subtype of stone-wall fence is seen occasionally today with a rail stake-and-rider addition (fig. 42). This innovation dates from the post-Civil War period when cattle raising became more prominent in certain

Fig. 41. Stone-wall fence "capped" with round stones. Photograph taken by the author in May 1969.

Fig. 42. Stone-wall fence with a rail stake-and-rider addition near Afton, Virginia. Photograph taken by the author in May 1969.

mountain districts. The stake-and-rider simply increased the height of the wall by one or two feet.

Another stone formation is observed presently in the mountains and in the adjoining Shenandoah Valley. Circular to oblong piles of stones, averaging ten to fifteen feet in diameter and five to six feet high, are the result of laboriously clearing stones from fields. Nearly every hollow and cove farmstead had at least a few of these stone piles and often many of them (fig. 43).

Fig. 43. **Stone pile near Love, Virginia. Photograph taken by the author in May 1969.**

In summary, as Hart and Mather stated (1957, 9):

The fence, perhaps more than any other single observable item, demarcates the layout of the rural landscape. It is not only an economic and a functional expression, but fully as significant is the fact that it is a manifestation of culture or a mode of life. It exerts a stabilizing influence on land occupancy since it represents more than a single year's commitment to the use of the land. It involves long-range planning, measured at least in terms of a few decades.

Discussion

This inquiry sought, through the field analysis of many individual structures and other material items, to find types and subtypes that would identify the Blue Ridge material folk culture subregion. Culturally, there is no doubt that the Blue Ridge constitutes an integral subregion of the Upland South. Furthermore, it represents a material culture source area and transition zone which has been somewhat neglected by field investigators, geographers and non-geographers alike.

It is evident after tracing the various types of houses, barns, outbuildings, stores, mills, and some lesser items to their beginnings and following them through their evolution in time and space, that two distinct culture traditions are represented in the Blue Ridge culture complex: the Pennsylvania German-Scotch-Irish and the Chesapeake Tidewater English. Likewise, mixture of the two traditions is apparent. For example, often a log cabin was erected along the English square floor plan, using the German technique of corner-timbering, and the Scotch-Irish tradition of good stone masonry for its foundation and chimney. The log cabin, more than any other house type, was the epitome of interculture meshing and eventually became the architectural symbol of the entire Upland South. However, significant cultural, temporal, and spatial differences identify the two culture traditions of the Blue Ridge.

The Pennsylvania and Chesapeake Tidewater regions, heavily bolstered by European antecedents, acted as the two primary dispersal centers for practically all the known material culture in the Blue Ridge. Pennsylvania German-Scotch-Irish immigrants combined culture traits, centering on construction techniques, to produce the single, most impressive, material culture imprint on the Blue Ridge landscape. This heterogeneously new mountain culture, made up of many capable Scotch-Irish stone masons and German carpenters, erected numerous log structures with fine stone chimneys and foundations, and corner-timbering. Actually, the Pennsylvania Germans made two major contributions to the mountain culture: log construction methods and basic barn types, for the principal dissemination of which they depended upon the fast moving Scotch-Irish.

The Pennsylvania architectural log tradition was earlier and stronger, and dominated a broader area of the Blue Ridge Mountains than the later, weaker, and less forceful Chesapeake Tidewater frame and clapboard tradition. The pole shack and log cabin, all four of the common barn types (single-crib, double-crib, log stable, and bank barn), two of the three types of outbuildings (Pennsylvania single and double levels), and two of the three kinds of mountain stores (one-story and two-story) followed the dominant Pennsylvania rectangular floor plan. The mode of construction for all these structures was log with any one of the five different varieties of corner-timbering possible: saddle notching, V notching, full dovetailing, half dovetailing, and half-log construction. All of these forms have European antecedents, but only three of these were employed in the German areas of southeastern Pennsylvania: saddle notching, V notching, and full dovetailing.

It seems that at least one dormant form of corner-timbering brought to America from Europe, half dovetailing, and one deviant form, half-log construction, emerged in the Blue Ridge and diffused south and southwestward in the Appalachian Mountains. The Blue Ridge represents, as of the moment, the oldest region to employ these methods of corner-timbering, since the movement from Pennsylvania along the Allegheny Mountains began later than the initial settlement of the Blue Ridge Mountains.

Further, it is probable that the Blue Ridge acted as a major staging area for other forms of dormant corner-timbering (square notching, half notching, and diamond notching) found in the 1800s on the Piedmont side of the mountains. The English descendants east of the Blue Ridge received the concept of horizontal log construction more by diffusion than by direct migration, and I propose that this diffusion eastward received its impetus from the Blue Ridge Mountains. Unfortunately, hundreds of log structures were destroyed outright or left to decay by the National Park Service and possibly some of these buildings contained the dormant forms of corner-timbering.

Houses, barns, smaller outbuildings, mills, stores, and fences are integral components of any settlement. It follows, therefore, that if the Blue Ridge acted as a staging area for entire settlement types to diffuse throughout the Southern Appalachians (see Wilhelm 1978), then characteristic material elements might have spread with them. However, it is much easier to change a component than an entire settlement pattern as witnessed by Blue Ridge examples. The mountains were the testing ground for adding lean-to's, ells, and sheds to the basic log cabin of rectangular floor plan. All of these additions are well within the British tradition and are commonly found in frame and clapboard, indicating that they were for the most part added after the introduction of milled lumber. The British tradition also was reflected in new mountain house forms, like the double pen, saddlebag, and dogtrot. In still other cases, adjoining but disconnected pens seemed to satisfy the expanding needs of mountain families.

I believe that both the saddlebag and dogtrot house types were developed in the mountains circa 1800, perhaps on a strictly experimental basis, by Tidewater English immigrants familiar with enlarging a single pen into two rooms side by side. Neither house type was common in the Blue Ridge, but early construction suggests that they diffused southwestward via the Allegheny Mountains into the Upland South. The dogtrot reached its peak of occurrence in the southern Tennessee Valley circa 1825, while the saddlebag was abundant in West Virginia and Kentucky before 1840. We clearly need more specific dates of construction for early examples of these types in order to positively pinpoint their area of origin. Perhaps it is already too late.

Chronologically, all structures described in this report, except the German bank barn, probably appeared in the Blue Ridge in the eighteenth century. The bank barn did not appear until circa 1850. All of these types of structures and other material items were still parts of the mountain landscape circa 1930. Pennsylvania pole shacks, log cabins, and log houses (except the dogtrot and I house type), and the Pennsylvania single-crib barn were dominant in the eighteenth century. The log cabin with square floor plan, double pen, single bay, and especially the I house, all of English tradition, became prominent in the nineteenth century. In the twentieth century the I house alone constituted one-fourth of all known and estimated dwellings prior to 1930. Saddlebag houses and double-crib and German bank barns complemented the picture. V notch and half dovetail corner-timbering dominated other construction methods by the early part of the nineteenth century and this situation continued into the present century.

An interesting contrast in the distribution of major structure types of Pennsylvania German-Scotch-Irish and Chesapeake Tidewater English origins is illustrated in table 1. Although the crest of the Blue Ridge Mountains cannot be used as a rigid demarcation line separating two material culture traditions, it is apparent after examining the table that the Pennsylvania German-Scotch-Irish tradition was distributed most prominently on the western side of the ridge. It is recalled that this mixed culture penetrated the mountains from the Shenandoah Valley circa 1730 and domi-

Table 1. Origin, type and distribution of major folk structures, 1930-1983

Origin/Type	No. on West Side of Ridge	%	No. on East Side of Ridge	%
Pennsylvania German-Scotch-Irish				
Pole Shack	2	25	6	75
Single-crib Barn	33	66	17	34
Double-crib Barn	9	56	7	44
Log Stable	7	58	5	42
Bank Barn	6	100	0	0
Pennsylvania Store (one- & two-level)	9	75	3	25
Chesapeake Tidewater English				
Log Cabin*	6	20	24	80
Single Bay House	0	0	10	100
Saddlebag	4	33	8	67
I House	14	48	16	52
English Store	0	0	8	100

Sources: Based on National Park Service photographs and records, and personal field sketches, photographs, and interviews with moutain inhabitants, 1963-1982.

*Log cabin examples are based on the square floor plan only.

nated the region for many years before English immigrants arrived on the eastern slope. This dominant period of Pennsylvania tradition had its overall effect on the mountain landscape, not the least of which was the erection of hundreds of log structures. Most, but not all, of these buildings were located on the western side of the ridge. As seen by examining the table, four major house types are English in origin and were carried from the Chesapeake Tidewater area (single bay and I house types) or developed in the mountains (log cabin and saddlebag) from English lowland models. Two other house types, the rare dogtrot and overshot, were built in the Blue Ridge by English immigrants. The former type developed probably from the hall and parlor house type found in the coastal lowlands, while the latter type diffused intact from New England and possibly the Chesapeake region. On the other hand, the predominant barn, store, outbuilding, and construction types are all traceable to Pennsylvania and the German-Scotch-Irish settlers. Outbuildings are not listed in the table because their numbers and forms lack accurate field accounts. However, it was generally noted that the Pennsylvania one- and two-level outbuildings of rectangular plan outnumbered the English outbuildings of square plan by a wide margin.

The above table shows an apparent anomaly in that the pole shack of Pennsylvania origin was dominant on the east side of the study area. However, there is a simple explanation for six of the eight examples of the type occurring there: all are still active hunting camps located in wild and inaccessible localities outside Shenandoah National Park.

Economic and environmental differences are also used in identifying the two material culture traditions. The log cabin is still seen in mid- and upper hollows of both abandoned and active mountain settlements. This house type represents later settlement in higher, more rugged elevations, and poorer economic conditions The present high proportion of cabins on the east side of the ridge is due to poorer accessibility and more recent settlement. The period circa 1800 marked the closing of the initial settlement period. Many mountain families, mostly of Pennsylvania background, already had been in the region for two generations. Several families were expanding and prospering, especially in the gaps and at the mouths of hollows, and were seeking larger and more prestigious houses. The recently developed English two-pen house types did not fit their needs, but the English I house did. The latter form could accommodate larger, more affluent families. In fact, the I house soon became the status symbol of achievement, whether it was in agriculture, industry, or transmontane business. The less prosperous hollow farmers built I houses of log, while the innkeepers, merchants, and professionals living mostly in gaps imported frame and brick and stone construction materials. The I house was eagerly accepted by the Germans and Scotch-Irish, since the house type not only pierced westward through the mountains, but also diffused more slowly southward from Pennsylvania into the Shenandoah Valley. Thus with the exception of the gap settlement type, there was a declining socio-economic status with elevation, from well-to-do mouth-of-hollow and cove farms to meager subsistence in upper hollows and atop high ridges. Such status was reflected in dwellings and related outbuildings: substantial brick, frame, or stone I houses and large double-crib or bank barns with several smaller outbuildings at the mouths of hollows to single-pen log cabins and small, single-crib outbuildings in upper hollows and along the ridge crests.

One barn type in the Blue Ridge, the Pennsylvania bank barn, was confined entirely to the west side of the ridge. There are several reasons for this distribution. First, the barn was too late in making its appearance in the mountains, circa 1850, to have had a wide distribution. It penetrated the mountains from the Shenandoah Valley side, where it remained dominant. Second, and perhaps more importantly, the bank barn was too large structure to meet the agricultural needs of most mountain farmsteads. The single-crib, log stable, or double-crib barns suited the mountain farmer better. In fact, in upper hollows and along the ridge crests barns were practically nonexistent since stock were free-ranging year-round, and crop storage meager. The only exceptions were the farms in the mouths of hollows and in southwestern coves; there the bank barn was readily accepted because of the spaciousness of the farms. Third, there was a certain regional and national affinity for the bank barn in the nineteenth century. Descendants of English extraction just did not accept the bank barn, probably because they had adequate barn types of their own. However, none of these reached the Blue Ridge to any extent, even though they are found on the Piedmont east of the range. At least prior to the Civil War the bank barn was a distinct component of the Pennsylvania material culture tradition.

An interesting contrast in values and priorities existed in the nineteenth century between barn and house types in the two traditions. The Pennsylvanians had a priority interest in their crops and their livestock; interest in the dwelling was secondary. Actually, several German-Scotch-Irish immigrants from Pennsylvania built bank barns before they built I houses, sometimes several years earlier, as evident from dates of construction. It must be recalled that the I house and the bank barn were both marks of agricultural achievement; still, the barn was built first. On the other hand, immigrants of English extraction customarily built the I house first, and rarely if ever improved the various log or frame outbuildings. Even today it is common to see this contrast in culture values on either side of the Blue Ridge: handsome I houses and bank barns on the west, and attractive I houses with rundown, log outbuildings on the east side. For the descendants of the Tidewater English immigrants the house is more important than the outbuildings and reflects a culture carryover from earlier times when "English" livestock were free to roam while the livestock of the "Pennsylvanians" was receiving close attention, including warm barns in winter and stored feed.

After the Civil War the bank barn did diffuse east onto the Piedmont and is seen there today. South of the study area, along the Blue Ridge Parkway, the barn type is even situated in gaps. Interestingly, I have discovered eight bank barns north of Charlottesville in Albemarle, Greene, and Madison Counties. One carpenter family by the name of Schumacher, a father and two sons, traveled through the region and built the barns between 1868 and 1873. The Schumachers came from Rockingham County in the Shenandoah Valley; exact location is unknown.

Conclusions

House types and their related outbuildings are measures of cultural influence. It is obvious that many mountain folk were materially well-off and apparently satisfied. Of course, economic conditions were relative and varied from settlement to settlement and farmstead to farmstead. I houses, bank barns, numerous smaller outbuildings, and prestigious board fencing attest to the fact that some mountain families attained a degree of affluence. Generally their farms were situated in linear gap settlements where livelihood depended on transmontane travel, or in coves and at the mouths of hollows where the best agricultural land was available. The I house and bank barn were conspicuously absent in upper hollows, meadows, and atop ridges where, unfortunately, agricultural conditions deteriorated with an increase of slope. And so did the economic livelihood of the people. Still, it would be harsh to say that these folk were economically destitute or completely isolated. Even in upper hollows and along ridges, house additions and the construction of outbuildings were commonplace. All mountain families, regardless of economic or geographic position, recognized the better things of life and were determined to attain them. This motivation toward a better life was present even in the upper hollows, as illustrated by the infield-outfield system, the use of terracing, and the construction of various buildings — especially houses — which changed with the attainment of more affluence.

With the exceptions of the Pennsylvania bank barn and the English store and single bay house type (see table 1), most structure types of major significance diffused throughout the mountains. The Pennsylvania one- and two-story stores, for example, reached the east side of the ridge, even though they remained more nearly dominant on the west side. Pennsylvania stores were larger structures than the English type, reflecting more affluence. These stores were accessible to lowland communities and had more customers, and thus greater business than did the smaller, often less accessible English stores. Pennsylvania stores were located in gaps, at the mouths of hollows, and near coves of agricultural importance on the Shenandoah Valley side, and in gaps on the Piedmont side as well. The English store simply arrived in the mountains too late and lacked the status of the already flourishing Pennsylvania stores to spread west of the ridge.

The inference that the two distinctive source areas, Pennsylvania and Chesapeake Tidewater, extended their cultures into the Blue Ridge Mountains is based chiefly on field-observed differences in house, barn, store, and other types of construction. In time and with broader experience there was a greater exchange between the two cultures and acceptance of different ideas and material culture. Eventually, a cultural uniformity emerged in the Blue Ridge which we can label "mountain folk culture." A significant part of the present investigation was the recognition and interpretation of vestigial traits making up this new culture complex. For the Blue Ridge mountain culture, with its occupance forms and patterns, became the model for mountain life from the Southern Appalachians to the Ozarks of Arkansas-Missouri.

Acknowledgments

The author wishes to thank the National Park Service, Shenandoah Natural History Association, Eastern National Park and Monument Association, National Research Council of Canada, Canadian Department of Energy, Mines, and Resources, St. Louis University, McGill University, University of Virginia, and Slippery Rock University for supporting this field investigation with research grants, contracts, and fellowships between 1963 and 1982. Further, the completion of the field research was due in large measure to the splendid assistance rendered by thirteen of my former university students: James Birckhead, Beverly Brunner, Barbara Ellison, Nancy Enlow, Anthony Jones, Joseph Kopfer, Ray O'Brien, Jane Ratcliffe, Glenn Sebastian, Darlene Sweeney, Dean Wells, Evelyn Wessel, and Irene Workiewicz. Finally, the continuous encouragement and support of my wife, Joanne, was invaluable to the success of this venture.

References

Booker, H. 1930. Molasses-making. *Mountain Life and Work* 6:24-5.
Campbell, A. 1937. Notes on the Irish House. *Folkliv* 2-3:205-34.
Clark, T.D. 1964. *Pills, petticoats, and plows.* Norman: University of Oklahoma Press.
Eaton, A.H. 1937. *Handicrafts of the southern highlands.* New York: Russell Sage Foundation.
Fletcher, S.W. 1950. *Pennsylvania agriculture and country life 1640-1840.* Harrisburg: Pennsylvania Historical and Museum Commission.

Glassie, H. 1963. The Appalachian Log Cabin. *Mountain Life and Work* 39:5-14.

———. 1964. The Smaller Outbuildings of the Southern Mountains. *Mountain Life and Work* 40:21-5.

———. 1965. The Old Barns of Appalachia. *Mountain Life and Work* 41:21-30.

———. 1968. *Pattern in the material folk culture of the eastern United States.* Philadelphia: University of Pennsylvania Press.

Hart, J. F., and Mather, E.C. 1957. The American fence. *Landscape* 6:4-9.

Kerkhoff, J.A. 1962. *Old homes of Page County, Virginia.* Luray, Virginia: Launch and Company.

Kniffen, F.B. 1965. Folk housing: Key to diffusion. *Annals of the Association of American Geographers* 55:549-78.

———. 1969a. On corner-timbering. *Pioneer America* 1:1-8.

———. 1969b. On studying pioneer vestiges. *Pioneer America Society Newsletter* 2:3-4.

Kniffen, F.B., and Glassie, H. 1966. Building in wood in the eastern United States: A time-place perspective. *The Geographical Review* 56:40-66.

Raup, H.J. 1947. Fences in the cultural landscape. *Western Folklore* 6:1-12.

Shurtleff, H.B. 1939. *The log cabin myth.* Cambridge, Massachusetts: Harvard University Press.

Steere, E. 1936. *Report on preservation of structures in the Shenandoah National Park.* Luray, Virginia: Shenandoah National Park.

Terrell, I L. 1970. *Old houses in Rockingham County:1750 to 1850.* Verona, Virginia: McClure Printing Company, Inc.

Wilhelm, G. [E. J., Jr.] 1968. *The Blue Ridge: Man and nature in Shenandoah National Park and Blue Ridge Parkway.* Charlottesville, Virginia: The Reynolds Press.

———. 1973. Fire ecology in Shenandoah National Park. *Proceedings of the Annual Tall Timbers Fire Ecology Conference* 12:468-85.

———. 1975. Folk culture history of the Blue Ridge Mountains. *Appalachian Journal* 2:192-222.

———. 1978. Folk settlements in the Blue Ridge Mountains. *Appalachian Journal* 5:204-45.

———. [Jr.] 1982. Shenandoah resettlements. *Pioneer America* 14:15-40.

Wright, M. 1958. Antecedents of the double-pen house type. *Annals of the Association of American Geographers* 48:109-17.

Zelinsky, W. 1953. The log house in Georgia. *The Geographical Review* 43:173-93.

Material Culture and Environmental Change on the Illinois River

Craig E. Colten

Abstract

The Illinois and the section of the Mississippi River immediately to its west have been de-scribed as a hearth for the folk society that harvested these waterways. Evidence to support this claim includes the diversity of material culture associated with the inland river culture, folk terminology for fishing equipment, and the density of people using traditional tools and techniques. An examination of the traditional equipment, the geographic source areas of people working the river, adaptations to environmental change, and subsequent out-migra-tion of the river folk along the Illinois River tends to support this view. A full range of fishing tools was in widespread use and enabled fishermen to land tremendous catches around the turn of the century. Expansion of the fishery hastened the dissemination of the folk culture among many newcomers to the waterway. When faced with deteriorating environmental conditions, the wide range of fishing techniques enabled the folk society to shift from one type of collecting method to another and thereby sustain a moderate fishery. Innovation among the river folk who worked the mussel beds indicates a familiarity with aquatic life and the ability to exploit numerous resources. Declining productivity prompted many of the Illinois River Valley fishing families to migrate to other regions or leave the river. This acted to spread the inland river folk culture throughout the Mississippi River Valley.
Keywords: Material culture, Illinois River, freshwater fishery, mussel gathering.

Introduction

Within the first two decades of the twentieth century, the Illinois River yielded the second highest tonnage of freshwater fish (in 1908) and the largest mussel take per mile in the U.S. (Alvord and Burdick 1915; Dang-lade 1914). The volume of wildlife desired by urban consumers drew an increasing number of men and their families into the river trades. They learned traditional fishing techniques from the small number of commer-cial fishermen and developed methods to collect mussels efficiently. The

Culture, Form and Place: Essays in Cultural and Historical Geography, edited by Kent Mathewson, 1993. Geoscience and Man, vol. 32, pp. 257-274. Department of Geogra-phy and Anthropology, Louisiana State University, Baton Rouge, LA 70893-6010.   257

level of cultural exchange and innovation along the Illinois and middle Mississippi rivers and the eventual movement of fishing families out of the region contributed to the development of a specialized culture hearth for the inland fisheries.

Most discussions of culture regions refer to the expansive territories occupied by settlers of somewhat common ethnic or national origins who developed complexes of agricultural and economic practices that derived from European and North American traditions. Within these broad regions, scholars have recognized smaller more specialized regions (Zelinsky 1973; Mitchell 1978). One aspect of the evolving cultural geography of the Americas that has escaped mapping at a national scale is the existence of the riverine folk culture along the inland waterways. It is somewhat distinct from other culture regions in that is limited to a narrow band of land along the major rivers and their tributaries (and distributaries). The inland river folk culture complex derives from European sources, but leaves a far less permanent impress on the land than do agricultural societies. Without the bonds of land ownership, river folk have been more mobile than their agricultural counterparts and have largely ignored some of the more traditional cultural divides.

Lund (1983) portrays the evolution of the inland fisheries culture as a function of the general westward migration of European settlers (also Glassie 1968). Comeaux (1989a and 1989b) on the other hand postulates that the area where the Mississippi and Illinois rivers merge provided a nurturing area for this specialized culture to evolve. While he acknowledges some direct diffusion, Comeaux notes some patterns at variance with major migration routes of Euro-American settlers. He speculates that some elements may have been transplanted into this region directly from Europe and may not have arrived as part of the westward movement of people and ideas. This notion he supports with linguistic evidence that suggests certain terms for the hoop net leapfrogged directly into the midwest. Based on extensive fieldwork, Comeaux (1989b) suggests that the confluence of the Mississippi and Illinois rivers stands out in terms of the full-blown development of an inland rivers cultural complex and the historical density of individuals engaged in riverine pursuits. What other evidence can be used to examine the presence of a riverine folk culture hearth?

This paper will consider several possibilities. The first area of discussion will examine the rapid expansion of the Illinois River fishery. Thousands of non-fisherfolk entered the river trades during the late nineteenth century, thereby acting to hasten the diffusion of the traditional culture among a cross section of residents of the valley. The musseling trade, which began on the Mississippi River and quickly spread to the Illinois, reflects a high level of interaction between the inhabitants living along the two water courses and a high level of shared innovation. Finally, a review of the impact of environmental change on the Illinois River fishery will document the forces behind the rapid dispersal of fisherfolk from this waterway. Each of these components of the historical development of fishing along the Illinois River tends to support Comeaux's identification of this area as a significant nurturing area for the inland fishery.

The Illinois River Valley

The Illinois River is formed at the convergence of the Des Plaines and Kankakee rivers and flows some 270 miles to Grafton where it empties into the Mississippi (fig. 1). The upper river is a relatively young stream, formed by the overflow of Lake Chicago during the retreat of the most recent glaciation. It is deeply incised and has a narrow floodplain. By contrast, the lower river is underfit and follows an ancient channel of the Mississippi. The floodplain varies in width from 2 to 6 miles and the bottomlands once contained hundreds of acres of lakes and wetlands.

Father Marquette described the lower Illinois and its fauna in the 1680s with typical exploratory wonder:

> We have seen nothing like this river that we enter, as regards its fertility of soil, it prairies and woods; its cattle, elk, deer, wildcats, bustards, swans, ducks, parroquets [sic], and even beaver. There are many small lakes and rivers. That on which we sail is wide, deep, and still, for 65 leagues. (Marquette [1682] 1900)

It was the lower river with its sloughs, lakes, and wetlands that supported the greatest abundance of wildlife. Fish depended on the backwater lakes for breeding areas, and wildfowl fed there during their seasonal migrations. The river supported a diverse and abundant population of freshwater mussels.

Aquatic life had played an important role in the diets of native Americans along the Illinois for more than five millennia. They collected fish from the lakes and consumed the flesh of mussels. The French sought to establish a beaver trade, but found the Illinois valley's fur bearing mammals poor in comparison to those in the Rockies and Canada. Although American Indians traded furs and the French and Euro-American pioneers relied on fish as a dietary supplement, river resources were less important to the colonial settlers than to the native Americans.

Fishing

Commercial fishing on the Illinois reportedly began in 1819 and by 1870 fishermen supplied local fish markets throughout the valley. After trunk

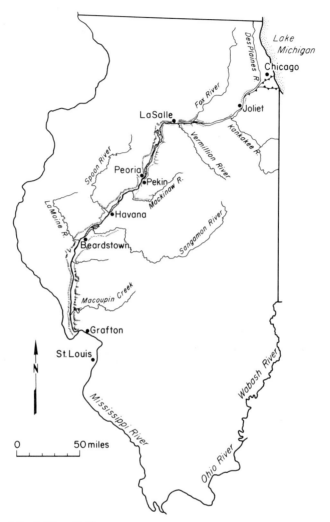

Fig. 1. The Illinois River Valley.

rail lines reached the Illinois River Valley in the 1850s, the potential for interregional trade existed. Transportation linkages in conjunction with the development of the refrigerated boxcar in the 1870s produced the means for long-distance shipment, and the growth of ethnic/religious ghettos in urban centers provided the market for the inland fishery (Comeaux 1972; Pisani 1984). Catholics required fish on Fridays and throughout the Lenten season, while Jewish dietary codes called for the consumption of "scaled" fish. The changing demography of industrial cities produced a steady demand for inland fish. For example, the introduction of the "German carp" to the Illinois in the 1880s and their rapid propagation enabled Illinois fishermen to cater to Jewish foodways. Most rail shipments from Havana, the principal distribution point along the Illinois River, were destined for New York and Chicago (Alford and Burdick 1915).

From a relatively small scale local fishery in the 1870s, fishing on the Illinois grew into a lively business by the early twentieth century. The fishing towns of Liverpool and Browning reflect the rapid growth and expansion in the number of fishermen. Only 3 individuals listed their occupations as fishermen in Liverpool in 1870, but the total rose to 35 by 1910 (McGimsey et al. 1985). Bath experienced a similar rise from 4 fishermen in 1870 to 65 in 1910 (U.S. Census 1870/1910). In 1908 over half of the state's 2,500 fishermen worked the Illinois, and the catch reflected the sharp increase in manpower. Fishermen sold over 6,000,000 pounds of fish through the markets of the valley in 1894. By 1908, the total exceeded 23,000,000 pounds —a peak that has since to be equaled (Alvord and Burdick 1915).

Seines were well established on the Illinois River during the period of rapid expansion. The introduction of seine fishing can be traced to the first commercial fishery on the Illinois River. In 1819 seven fishermen, including two Frenchmen, moved their fishing operation to Peoria. They used seines to work the waters of Peoria Lake. They dried their own fish for sale. Several were still living in the area three decades later (Drown 1850).

Hoop nets were also widely used during the rapid expansion of the fishery. By 1894 Illinois had the largest number of hoop nets in the country (Comeaux 1989b). Lund suggests hoop nets diffused into the Illinois River from Lake Michigan before 1890 (Lund 1983, 259). Comeaux, however, has presented evidence that hoop nets were established in the Mississippi valley before 1870. Given the known route of diffusion of seining into the Illinois valley and the linguistic differences employed on inland rivers and the Great Lakes, it is plausible to argue hoop nets followed the same route. Comeaux speculates that an anonymous English fisherman may have been responsible for introducing the hoop nets to the inland rivers (Comeaux 1989b). Perhaps not coincidentally, one of the first fishermen in Liverpool, Illinois, was of English descent (U.S. Census 1870-1910).

A review of U.S. Census manuscript forms was inconclusive in settling which route of diffusion introduced hoop nets to Illinois. Birthplaces of men engaged in river trades (fishing, musseling, boat making, fish market operator, and boatman) were tabulated for two small river towns known as important fishing communities (fig. 2). Between the years 1870 and 1910, no single source area outside of Illinois served as a major contributor; and migrants from the source areas could have followed routes either through the Great Lakes or along the Ohio River. Nevertheless, the significance of the high proportion of Illinois-born river workers suggests

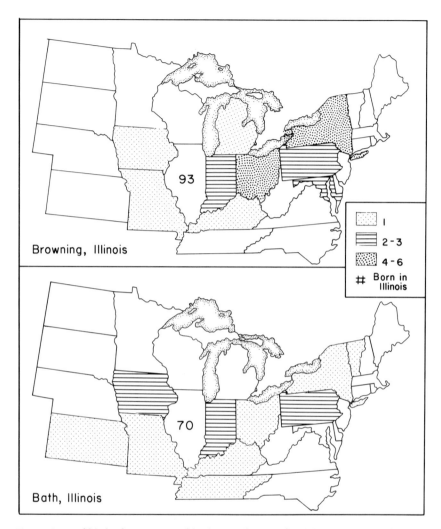

Fig. 2. State of birth of men engaged in river trades, 1870/1910, in Browning and Bath, Illinois. These men were indicated in U.S. Census manuscript records as those who reported working as fishermen, mussel gatherers, boat makers, fishmarket operators, and boatmen. The number in Illinois indicates the sum of river tradesmen born in Illinois. *Source:* U.S.Census decennial reports from 1870 to 1910.

that the dissemination of skills and fishing techniques occurred between experienced river workers and novices. Most new workers came from the farms, mines, railroads, and factories rather than as migrants from outside the region. Thus, the rapid growth of the fishing industry along the Illnois River served to expand the number of individuals familiar with traditional fishing techniques.

A full complex of fishing techniques and associated skills reached a high level of both diversity and sophistication along the Illinois. Using traditional techniques, fishermen worked the backwater lakes with seines to collect the majority of their catch (Richardson 1921). Seining required crews and the Dixon Fish Market of Peoria kept men on the payroll throughout the year (fig. 3; Dixon 1989). In winter they would cut long tracks in the ice to drag the seines into shallow, spring-fed pools where ice had not formed. Smaller markets operated a system comparable to share cropping to ensure a supply of fish. Fishermen used boats and nets owned by the market in exchange for a share of the catch (Walton 1987). Fishing with seines was also carried out as a family operation. The Woodruffs, for example, made a living from Peoria Lake (fig. 4). The patriarch of the clan had worked up and down the river during the 1870s, then settled near Peoria and taught his sons the ways of the river. This family's annual round included market hunting in the fall and spring, and ice cutting during the winter months. (Woodruff 1871; Woodruff 1987).

The motorized johnboat has been a mainstay of Illinois River fishermen since around 1910 (Vertrees 1913). The broad, flat-bottomed craft enables the fishermen to work out on the gunwales without capsizing (see fig. 8). It also holds a large load and is easily crafted and customized by the fishermen. Skiffs and launches were used most frequently by seining crews. Skiffs, which have a shallow keel, hold a line when rowed and the larger launches generally were steam-driven and provided the power necessary to haul loaded "live boxes" (figs. 3 and 4).

Fig. 3. The Dixon Fish Market near Peoria, Illinois. A fishing crew sits in front of the floating market. Two steam-powered launches are tied up to the right and a "live box" is beached in front of the boats. Courtesy Dixon Fisheries.

Hoop nets were an important tool used by the individual fishermen. Hand-tied cotton twine was attached to a series of hoops with funnels, or throats (fig. 5; see Comeaux 1989b). To preserve the twine, the nets would be dipped in tar—usually every two weeks. An individual fisherman would set dozens of these nets in the river. Extensive alteration of the natural setting prompted greater use of hoop nets during the twentieth century. As farmers erected levees and drained nearly half of the wetlands between 1900 and 1930 (Thompson n.d.), they eliminated essential spawning areas and many of the backwater lakes where seining took place. Crew fishing dwindled and hoopnets took on greater importance. In 1931,

Fig. 4. Seine haul is displayed by Woodruff brothers on Peoria Lake, ca. 1927. The small boat on the left is a skiff propelled by oars. A semi-submerged "live box" is held in position by poles pushed into the lake bed. Courtesy Donald Woodruff.

Fig. 5. A mid-sized Illinois hoopnet, ca. 1965. Courtesy Illinois Natural History Survey.

there were only 66 seines in use on the Illinois as opposed to over 6,000 hoopnets (U.S. Dept. of Commerce 1932, 400-1). By 1950, the hoopnet catch exceeded the value of the more efficient seine (Starrett and Parr 1950, 13). The Dixon Fisheries halted seining altogether in 1967, although limited seine fishing occurs in highly controlled situations today. The hoopnet, however, still finds widespread use among the few remaining independent fishermen.

The fishing crews worked on the water and many lived there as well. Cabinboats, as they are known in Illinois, once lined the waterfront of Havana, the center of the commercial fishery (fig. 6). The linear arrangement of rooms set on a barge was generally topped by an arched roof (Lund 1989), although examples of these hipped-roof cabinboats in Havana suggest some stylistic borrowing from the shotgun house type. Families rowed or towed their cabinboats to fishing areas during the summer and towed them back to town for the winter. During the off season, the owners would pull them on shore, caulk and tar the hulls, and await spring floods to refloat them (Easley 1987). The cabinboat offered considerable mobility for the river family, but it was not uncommon for cabinboat owners to eventually drag them on shore and use them as the core for a land-based house (fig. 7). The decline in fishery and other aspects of modernization (i.e. automobiles) have acted to eliminate a striking component of the riverfront landscape.

Fishing on the Illinois River has declined dramatically over the last half century and has continued to drop, while the catch from the Mississippi River has stabilized in recent years. The Illinois catch has fallen from nearly 6 million pounds in 1950 to less than a million pounds in 1980 (Sparks 1984). The primary factor has been the elimination of backwater areas. Pollution has played a significant role as well. The effects of urban

Fig. 6. Cabinboats tied up along the waterfront at Havana, Illinois, ca. 1909. Courtesy Lake County Museum.

Fig. 7. Cabinboat converted to a land-based dwelling. Courtesy Donald Woodruff.

and industrial sewage have reduced both the food and oxygen supply of the river. Among principal commercial fish, only carp can survive in the polluted conditions. Even so, they seldom reach full size and therefore do not support a commercial fishery.

Despite the decline in aquatic life, a few fishermen still work the Illinois river. Fish markets, familiar fixtures in most of these communities, now rely more on farm-raised catfish and saltwater fish. However, the fishermen generally travel to the nearby Mississippi River to extract and transport their catch from the larger waterway (Sparks 1984). The decline in productivity has contributed to outmigration of fishermen and thereby contributed to both the dissolution and diffusion of the inland river culture.

Musseling

Collecting freshwater mussels from the Illinois River was another trade that experienced a rapid growth shortly after the turn of the century and enjoyed a brief period of intensive activity. Prior to 1891, there was only limited mussel gathering. Occasional word would spread through the inland rivers that a valuable pearl had been discovered. This would spark short-lived "pearl fevers." Fishermen and farmers alike would wade along the shallow bars, collecting mussels by hand. They would search for a pearl and then discard the undesirable shell and meat (Vertrees 1913). During the 1870s, local entrepreneurs shipped limited quantities of shells to Europe for use in button making (Danglade 1914).

In 1891, John Boepple introduced a drill bit that spawned a domestic button industry based in Muscatine, Iowa. This innovation redirected subsequent mussel-gathering efforts. His enterprise, in conjunction with several other button factories, inspired the growth of an extensive mussel-gathering industry on the inland rivers. As Muscatine became a button-making center, "clam diggers" fanned out along the Mississippi River in search of beds of the suddenly valuable mussel shells (Scarpino 1985). Within a decade, the intensive collecting had eliminated the beds near Muscatine and gatherers ventured into adjoining rivers in search of more plentiful supplies (Coker 1919, 46). They entered the Illinois River Valley in force in 1907 (Danglade 1914). Census records indicate that the combined number of mussel gatherers in Pearl and Kampsville grew from zero in 1900 to 144 by 1910 (U.S. Census 1900 and 1910). By 1910 there were over 2,600 boats engaged in the mussel trade on the Illinois River. Most were concentrated in the area from Peoria Lake to the mouth of the river (Danglade 1914).

Commercial mussel gathering required more efficient means than wading and hand gathering. This involved the development of special equipment. The crowfoot bar, introduced from the Mississippi, enabled clammers to work deeper beds and collect extensive areas in relatively short periods of time. The crowfoot was a 14-foot-long bar with about 150 metal hooks (fig. 8). Fishermen used an underwater sail, known as a "mule" (fig. 9), to propel their boats across the mussel beds. When dropped in the river, the canvas sail filled with the current and pulled the

Fig. 8. A mussel fisherman on the lower Illinois River, ca. 1910. Crowfoot bar is positioned on supports attached to the sides of a motorized johnboat. Courtesy Marshall County Historical Society.

Fig. 9. The clammers' "mule" was made of a piece of heavy canvas, weighted with a piece of lead pipe sewn into the lower hem. A wooden dowl in the upper hem provided buoyancy. When lowered into the river and controlled by lines held by the mussel gatherer, it filled with the current and towed the boat and the crowfoot bar downstream. Drawing by Kathrine Hammersley.

crowfoot bar slowly across the mussel beds. Mussels, feeding with their shells open, reflexively clamped shut on the multi-barbed hooks on the crowfoot bar (Fig. 10). An average daily catch was somewhat less than 500 pounds (Coker 1919, 52).

In areas where there was no current, mussel gatherers used the "dip net." First developed on Peoria Lake in 1911, the dip net consists of a long metal or wooden handle with a rake-like attachment at the end (fig. 11). When the open-mouthed rake is dragged across the lake bottom, the attached net collects any shells that are lifted from the bottom (Coker 1919, 53-4). An efficient worker could haul in 1,000 pounds a day in 1912 (Danglade 1914, 14).

When their johnboats were filled, gatherers returned to their camps and steamed the shells open (fig. 12). They would search the meat for pearls and sort the shells according to species. Shell buyers, under con-

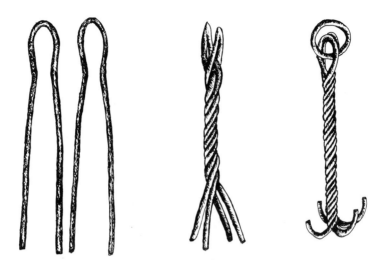

Fig. 10. Traditional crowfoot hooks consisted of two pieces of heavy gauge wire twisted to form a hook five to six inches in length. Drawing by Kathrine Hammersley.

tract to the various button manufacturers, traveled the river and purchased shells from the workers in the riverside camps.

There were fifteen button factories on the Illinois River during the early years of collecting (fig. 13). Most of the Illinois operations merely cut "blanks" or unfinished disks from the shells and then shipped them to the finishing plants in Muscatine. Workers used hollow drill bits to cut numerous blanks from a single shell and received wages based on the number of pieces they cut (Boyd 1987).

Mussel gathering and button manufacturing declined as rapidly as it grew. By 1912, there were reports that shell beds were declining or dying off. This was partly due to overfishing, but also to pollution of the waterway. In 1900 Chicago diverted its untreated sewage into the Illinois River in an attempt to protect its own drinking water supply. A wedge of severe pollution gradually pushed downstream as far as the important mussel beds near Peoria and Beardstown. The tainted water from Chicago and industrial cities along the Illinois wiped out the important commercial species of mussels. The number of species fell from approximately forty in the three major pools at the turn of the century to about twenty by 1966 (Starrett 1971). Many of the gatherers moved to other rivers where more plentiful supplies existed. Others simply drifted to other trades or placed a greater reliance on fishing. Although limited gathering continued, large-scale musseling disappeared by 1930. Only 82 boats reported having crowfoot bars in 1931 (U.S. Dept. of Commerce 1932). The last blank factory closed in 1948 as plastic replaced nacre as a raw material for buttons (Boyd 1987).

Fig. 11. Along stretches of the river without current, mussel gatherers working from their johnboats used the dip net to rake up shells from the river bed. From Coker 1919.

Fig. 12. Mussel gatherers set up camps on the river banks near the richest mussel beds. They steamed the shells open and then sorted them into piles in anticipation of the arrival of the buyers. Courtesy E. E. Van Fossen.

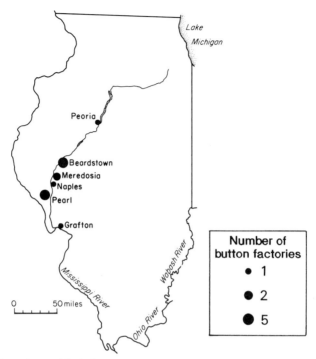

Fig. 13. Fifteen button blank factories operated on the Illinois River in 1913. Only one of the factories, at Pearl, produced finished buttons. After Danglade 1914.

In the 1960s a revival of musseling took place. Spurred by an expansion of the Japanese cultured pearl industry, rivermen returned to the water with their crowfoot bars (Starrett 1971). Most collecting today, however, is done by divers who scour the river bottom and leave few legal-sized shells behind. The shells are steamed open and shipped to Japan where bits of shell are shaped into tiny balls. These "seeds" are placed in saltwater oysters and become the core of a cultured pearl. Over 730 tons of shells were taken from the Illinois in 1985. However, as during earlier episodes of resource exploitation, supplies are dwindling.

The Significance of the Illinois River Fishery

Several observations deserve emphasis. First, fisherfolk in the Illinois River Valley used traditional tools and methods. Fishing techniques brought from Europe long served local fishermen and spread rapidly as outsiders entered the folk occupations. This pool of knowledge had lain more or less dormant until outside economic opportunities drew numbers of farmers and town dwellers into the river trades. The ability of the river people, both "old" and "new," to meet the demands of the urban fish markets argues for a rapid dissemination of local knowledge and oral traditions across ethnic and cultural boundaries.

These rapid cultural disseminations and innovations underwrote the high concentrations of river folk and a vital river culture in this region. The development of specialized mussel gathering equipment on the Mississippi and Illinois rivers attests to a people who were keenly aware of the habits and habitats of aquatic life. The eventual diffusion of the crowfoot bar and the dip net to locations as distant as central Tennessee, Minnesota, and central Arkansas charts the movements of these people.

Adaptation to changing environmental conditions also illustrates the diversity of tools and techniques available to the Illinois River folk society. The elimination of the backwater lakes caused a sharp decline in the use of seines and crew fishing activity. Fishermen turned to the river and more individual means of resource collection, namely the hoopnet. In terms of mussel gathering, new tools were developed to fit different environmental settings—such as the dip net on the currentless lakes. Without a fully developed set of tools and techniques, this folk society would not have been as adaptable in the face of adverse environmental changes.

Finally, the intense but short-lived periods of resource exploitation undoubtedly contributed to the diffusion of fishing technology throughout the inland river system. As the Illinois River's productivity increased, it drew in men from the farms and towns who sought different sources of income. When the productivity declined due to environmental change, they either returned to their old trades or sought better fishing grounds. The Illinois country exported many experienced fishermen and thereby played an important role in spreading the inland river culture.

Acknowledgements

This research was made possible in part by a grant from the National Endowment for the Humanities. Elaine Rangel compiled most of the manuscript census information; Julie Snider prepared the maps; and Kathrine Hammersley drafted the illustrations of museling gear. I would like to express my gratitude for their contributions.

References

Alvord, J. W. and Burdick, C. B. 1915. Report of the rivers and lakes commission on the Illinois River and its bottom lands. Springfield, IL: Illinois Rivers and Lakes Commission.

Boyd, J. 1987. Tape-recorded interview, Meredosia, IL. Harvesting the river oral history project, Illinois State Museum, Springfield, IL.

Coker, R. E. 1919. *Freshwater mussels and mussel industries of the United States.* U. S. Department of Commerce, Bureau of Fisheries Bulletin V. 36. Washington, DC.

Comeaux, M. L. 1989a. Hook and line fishing in the Mississippi River system. *Material Culture* 21(1):23-45.

———. 1989b. Use of hoopnets in the Mississippi River Basin. *Journal of Cultural Geography* 10(1):75-87

———. 1972. *Atchafalaya swamp life: Settlement and folk occupations.* Geoscience and Man, vol. 2. Baton Rouge, LA: School of Geoscience, Louisiana State University.

Danglade, E. 1914. *The mussel resources of the Illinois River.* U. S. Department of Commerce, Bureau of Fisheries, Document No. 804. Washington, DC.

Dixon, D. 1989. Personal communication, East Peoria, IL.

Drown, S. D. 1850. *Drown's record and historical view of Peoria, 1851.* Peoria: E. O. Woodcock.

Easley, L. 1987. Tape-recorded interview, Meredosia, IL. Harvesting the river oral history project, Illinois State Museum, Springfield, IL.

Glassie, H. 1968. *Pattern in the material folk culture of the eastern United States.* Philadelphia: University of Pennsylvania Press.

Lund, J. 1983. Fishing as a folk occupation in the lower Ohio valley. Ph.D. diss., Indiana University. Bloomington, IN.

———. 1989. Nomadic architecture: The river houseboat in the Ohio valley. In *The old traditional way of life,* eds. R. E. Walls, and G. H. Schoemaker. Bloomington, IN: Trickster Press.

Marquette, J. (1682) 1900. Voyages of Marquette. In *The Jesuit Relations* 59: 109-163. Cleveland: Burrows Brothers.

McGimsey, C. R., Schroeder, E. K., and Hajic, E. R. 1985. A geological assessment and cultural resource survey of the proposed flood control levee and borrow areas: Liverpool, Illinois. Technical report prepared for the U. S. Army Corps of Engineers, Illinois State Museum, Springfield, IL.

Mitchell, R. D. 1978. The formation of early American cultural regions: An interpretation. In *European settlement and development in North America,* ed. J. P. Gibson, 66-90. Toronto: University of Toronto Press.

Pisani, D. J. 1984. Fish culture and the dawn of concern over water pollution in the United States. *Environmental Review* 8:117-31.

Richardson, R. E. 1921. The small and bottom fauna of the middle and lower Illinois River and its connecting lakes. *Illinois Natural History Survey Bulletin* 13(15): 363-522.

Scarpino, P. V. 1985. The great river: An environmental history of the upper Mississippi, 1890-1950. Columbia: University of Missouri Press.

Sparks, R. E. 1984. The role of contaminants in the decline of the Illinois River: Implications for the upper Mississippi. In *Contaminants in the upper Mississippi River*. Proceedings of the 15th annual meeting of the Mississippi River Research Consortium, eds. J. G. Wiener, R. V. Anderson, and D. R. McConville. Boston: Butterworth.

Starrett, W. C. 1971. A survey of mussels of the Illinois River: A polluted stream. *Illinois Natural History Survey Bulletin*, 30(5):267-403.

Starrett, W. C. and Parr, S. A. 1951. *Commercial fisheries of Illinois rivers: A statistical report for 1950*. Illinois Natural History Survey, Biological Notes No. 25. Urbana, IL.

Thompson, J. n.d. From carp to corn: An historical geography of land drainage in the lower Illinois valley, 1890-1930. Unpublished manuscript.

U.S. Department of Commerce, Bureau of Fisheries. 1932. *Fisheries industries of the United States, 1932*. Washington, DC.

U.S. Census. 1870-1910. Population census manuscript forms. Illinois State Archives. Springfield, IL.

Vertrees, H. H. 1913. *Pearls and pearling*. New York: Fur News Publishing Company.

Walton, L. 1987. Tape-recorded interview, Browning, IL. Harvesting the River oral history project, Illinois State Museum, Springfield, IL.

Woodruff, G. 1871. Diary. In the possession of Donald Woodruff, Joliet, IL.

Woodruff, D. 1987. Personal communication, Joliet, IL.

Zelinsky, W. 1973. *The cultural geography of the United States*. Englewood Cliffs, NJ: Prentice-Hall.

The Marigold (Tagetes *spp.*) and
the "Cult of the Dead" in Puebla-Tlaxcala

James J. Parsons

Abstract

All Saints' and All Souls' Days, November 1 and 2, are major dates on the Mexican calendar of fiestas when golden-flowered marigolds (*Tagetes* spp.) are used in profusion to decorate home altars and cemeteries, welcoming the "return" of dead relatives. Two separate species of the marigold, native to the Meso-American highlands and taken into cultivation and improved by pre-Columbian peoples, are involved. The symbolism of this most Mexican of flowering annuals as related to the Days of the Dead celebrations in rural Puebla and Tlaxcala, as well as the diffusion of these showy garden composites to other parts of the world, is the subject of this contribution.

Key Words: Days of the Dead, marigold, Mexico, Puebla, *Tagetes*, Tlaxcala.

The Meso-American highlands of Mexico and Guatemala are a major world center of floral diversity that has provided a significant number of ornamental plants familiar to modern gardeners. Dahlias, zinnias, poinsettias, morning glories, cosmos, plumerias, salvias, and marigolds, among other showy flowers, were collected and often taken into cultivation by indigenous peoples in pre-Columbian times. Here I want to look especially at the golden flowered marigold, *Tagetes* spp., (*cempoalxóchitl* in Nahuatl) and its traditional ceremonial and symbolic role in the celebration of one of the major occasions on the crowded Mexican calendar of fiestas. In this I have been motivated in part by a recent study by the University of Pittsburgh anthropologist Hugo Nutini (1988), *Todos Santos and the Cult of the Dead in Rural Tlaxcala*. This led me to visit that state and neighboring Puebla to observe and photograph this event which, although it has counterparts throughout the country, seems to be especially colorful and expressive in the predominantly Indian villages of that area.

Culture, Form, and Place: Essays in Cultural and Historical Geography, edited by Kent Mathewson, 1993. Geoscience and Man, vol. 32, pp. 275-286. Department of Geography and Anthropology, Louisiana State University, Baton Rouge, LA 70893-6010.

275

Flowers and Flower-gardening Among the Aztecs

The passion for flowers among the native peoples of New Spain was much commented on by the earliest Europeans. The accounts of early chroniclers such as Torquemada ([1615] 1975), Durán ([1575-81] 1971), and Sahagún ([1590] 1975), as well as the botanist and *protomédico* Francisco Hernández ([ca. 1570] 1959), confirm in detail the importance of flowers in Aztec everyday life. José de Acosta, who knew both Peru and Mexico, wrote at the end of the sixteenth century that the Indians were "*muy amigos de las flores, y en Nueva España más que en cualquier parte del mundo.*" (Acosta 1940, 301) Wreaths, crowns, or garlands of flowers were worn as personal adornment. People of status are often depicted as carrying a flower or flowers in their hands. Diego Durán, writing about 1580, observed that "they find gladness and joy in spending the entire day smelling a little flower or bouquet made of different kinds of flowers; their gifts are accompanied by them; they relieve the tedium of a journey with flowers." (Durán 1971, 238).

The great lord Montezuma was reported to be a connoisseur of flowers. His gardens and those of lesser Aztec chieftains, perhaps the world's first botanical gardens (as at Tenochtitlán, Chapultepec, Texcoco and Oaxtepec), were compared favorably to the finest in sixteenth century Europe and may even have inspired some of them. One measured two leagues in circumference and was elaborately landscaped with roads, terraces, pools of fresh water, and always a grove of the sacred Mexican bald cypress (*Taxodium mucronatum*) or *ahuehuete*. The stately native magnolia (*Talauma mexicana*) was another characteristic marker of such places (Nuttall 1921; Langman 1956; Paso y Troncoso 1988). The abandonment and disappearance of these remarkable pleasure gardens was one of the great tragedies of the Conquest.

Cortez and his followers were greeted with garlands of flowers en route to Tenochtitlán; initially at the Totonac town of Cempoala (or "marigold," literally "twenty" in Nahuatl, as in twenty-petaled flower), inland from Vera Cruz, where blossoms and green branches were strewn in their path as was the custom with honored guests. Bernal Diaz describes the tumultous entry into Tlaxcala where "the streets and roof-tops were packed with men and women who carried great bouquets of many colors and good fragrance which they gave to Cortez and the soldiers (as he said) with great affection and humility." The native marketplaces were regularly festooned with flowers. Certain towns like Xochimilco (="flower garden") with its *chinampas* or floating gardens and Ocuituco in modern Morelos were especially renowned for their flowers. Marigolds, dahlias, zinnias, tiger lilies, and other colorful blooms were grown to be paid as tribute, often in the form of floral offerings (*guirnaldas*). Some, like plumeria (frangipani) and tuberose (*Polyanthes* spp., *nardo*), attracted attention especially for their fragrance and these, along with the marigold, had important funerary associations. Their ceremonial role even extended to warfare. Several early chroniclers called attention to the formalized, ritualistic tournaments or "flower battles" (*xochiyaoytl*) that Aztec warriors fought with their neighbors as they sought to capture prisoners for sacrifice.

Some flowers were reserved for royalty. Those with yellow color seem to have been held in special esteem by the sun-worshipping Aztecs. Both the native peoples and the Spaniards after them were inclined to attribute fanciful medicinal values to virtually all plants with showy inflorescences, the more handsome ones often tending to be seen as the more efficacious. A few, like *Datura* spp. or angel's trumpet, were prized for their hallucinogenic properties. Quite aside from its esthetic appeal the marigold was also valued as a medicinal and dye plant, while its strong scented foliage was recognized as effective in discouraging garden pests. It was, as it is today, planted along milpa borders or between crop rows for this purpose. Its roots contain recently identified compounds that are lethal to many strains of root parasites or nematodes (fig. 1).

Fig. 1. Harvesting marigold blooms for the cemetery at Zacatelco, Tlaxcala. The plants are pulled up by the roots, which are later cut off.

The "Dias de los Muertos"

The Mexicans of today have lost none of their reverence and passion for flowers. Their knowledge of and love for them is clearly an heritage from the past (Heyden 1983). Elaborate flower displays remain one of the most important and visible aspects of their fiestas. In many parts of the country there are celebrations devoted wholly to flowers. There may be carpets of petals in the streets, as in Ixtapalapa and Puebla during Holy Week or at Huamantla (Tlaxcala) in August, crosses of flowers on buildings under construction, and displays of lilies at Easter, poinsettias (*nochebuenas*) at Christmas, bouvardia on San Juan's Day, or the offerings of flowers to the Virgin by children in May. But no floral celebration is more impressive or widespread than that on the Dias de los Muertos on November 1 and 2 of each year, perhaps the most Mexican of all holidays.

While two distinct celebrations are involved according to the church calendar, they are in fact joined as one in the Days of the Dead. Preparations for the festive event are often elaborate and costly. Early on All Saints' Day, November 1, flower-decked home altars are built and decorated with mementos and perhaps photos of the dead relatives who will make their annual brief visit, along with generous offerings of their favorite foods. Trails of marigold petals (*caminos de petales*) may be laid in the street to direct the returning dead to the living room altars where the *ofrendas* of food and drink await them (fig. 2). Traditionally, these are items indigenous to Mexico: amaranth cakes, chilis, mole, avocados, turkey soup, tamales, corn tortillas, refried beans, and almost always generous *vasos* of tequila or mescal and pulque beer. While all of these oblations are more for adults, deceased younger family members may be lured by sweets or a treasured toy or firecrackers, which children always enjoy. In Puebla, traditional *pan de muertos* (*hojalabras*) and candied sweet potatoes (*camotes de Santa Clara*) are much in evidence. Among the flowers, the bright yellow and orange marigolds are especially represented.

The grim iconography associated with the Dias de los Muertos — candy skulls and coffins, skeleton puppets, the gruesomely illustrated "*calaveras*" newssheets (with satirical verses lampooning prominent persons and politicians) — often creates mild shock or even revulsion for those of us raised in a culture which denies and rejects death. But it provides Mexicans a way of underscoring the ultimate equality of rich and poor, of breaking down the barrier between classes. The celebration may superficially suggest Halloween, even to a ritualized begging that is reminiscent of "trick or treat," but it is a legitimately Mexican celebration and there are no witches. Despite nearly 500 years of missionary effort, "Heaven" and "Hell" in the Christian sense of reward for good and punishment for evil in this life are not easily accepted. Intercourse between the living and the dead is natural, everyday, and quite unmystical (Anonymous 1987;

Fig. 2. Trail of pine needles and marigold blooms leading to a community altar and *ofrenda* at San Miguel Canoa, Puebla.

Strump Green 1976). Halloween, on the other hand, is a gringo import and those who wish to celebrate it run the risk of being seen as slavish imitators of the North American way.

All Souls' Day, November 2, usually begins with a ritualized tolling of the church bells. It is a day reserved for festive family gatherings at the local cemetery where graves are cleared and decorated with floral designs and arrangements. In the Puebla and Tlaxcala villages, and even in the pantheons of the central cities, the conspicuous radiance of the marigolds, their stems cut short and planted in freshly stirred soil, is dominant. Other flowers employed, although to a much lesser extent, include the gaudy, cherry-red cockscomb (*Celosia cristata, moco de pavo*), the South American amaranth or love-lies-bleeding (*Amarantus caudatus, cresta de gallo*) and the delicate white baby's breath (*Gypsophila* spp., *nubes*), sprays of which are used to decorate the graves of children. Gladiolas, chrysanthemums and carnations are also encountered. All of these, except the amaranth and marigolds, are of Old World origin.

Since graves are tended and flowers offered, it is easy for North Americans to see this as a kind of Decoration Day. But tending of graves is only incidental to visiting them (fig. 3). It is a time of family reunion and communion. The participants do not sit around looking woebegone and

Fig. 3. Todos Santos cemetery crowd at San Bernardino Tlaxcalacingo, Puebla.

contemplative. There is no hint of seance and apparently very little prayer. The family is present, neat and well-groomed, the dead are present, and that's all. If it looks like a large party with some graveside tippling, it is. But to the celebrants all the spirits are not in the bottles. Friendly ghosts hover everywhere. They are lively and convivial. It is all one, today and tomorrow, the living and the dead. It is carnival time, with picnics, lots of flowers, traditional foods, candies, incense burning, street vendors, mariachi bands, and dancing, a joyous and utterly unpretentious welcome of friendly departed souls, returned for the moment for reunion. It is also a reaffirmation of sorts of the concept of the nuclear family (Scheffler 1971).

The nature of this observance of All Saints' and All Souls' days, following one upon the other, varies in detail and intensity from place to place in contemporary Mexico (Brandes 1988, 88-109; Anonymous 1987). Among the best known of such celebrations are the candlelight procession of flower-bedecked boats at Janitzio on Lake Patzcuaro, the festivities at Misquic, a barrio of Xochimilco, and in certain places in Morelos and Oaxaca. Each village has its distinctive tradition, including the *ofrenda* or offering of food and drink at home altars for dead members of the family who are believed to return for an annual visit on Todos Santos. But in almost all cases the marigold reigns supreme, the traditional and symbolic bloom of the fiesta.

Marigolds and Marigolds

Tagetes (*Compositae*) is a genus comprising some thirty species, mostly with showy golden flowers and pungent leaves. Their natural range extends from the southwestern United States to Argentina with the greatest diversity in south-central Mexico. Already in 1570 Hernández (1959, 2:218-221) could list Nahuatl names for seven different varieties. It is generally accepted that both *Tagetes erecta* and *Tagetes patula* had been selected and improved from simple, single flowered stock to the larger-headed, tufted forms in pre-Columbian times. Both are said to be unknown outside of cultivation or semi-cultivation except as garden escapes (Kaplan 1980). The Spaniards marveled at the conspicuous orange and yellow flowers that they found in the hands of Indian plant collectors and breeders. Their use in ceremonies for the dead apparently goes back to pre-Conquest times, as indicated by the large marigold inflorescences alternating with small ears of maize in a garland about the neck of a figure on an archaeological funeral urn from the Valley of Mexico (Kaplan 1980).

It often has been stated, although without clear authority, that marigold seeds were sent back to Spain with the first ships returning with the news of Cortez's conquests. From there they somehow became established on the North African coast in time to have been collected and brought back to peninsular Spain from Tunisia in 1535 by the conquering troops of Charles V. From this time came the misleading name "African marigold," which is still applied to *T. erecta*. This term appears as early as 1576 in the *Plantarum* of Matthias De Lobel (*flos africanus maior simplici*). He figures both *T. patula* and single and double forms of *T. erecta* and states that marigolds were growing spontaneously (sic) on the banks of the Rio Tagus (Kaplan 1980).

T. *patula*, a lower-growing species of cultivated marigold, is known to us in one form as a border plant with small, tufted, yellow and orange flowers that are often streaked with mahogany red. It is widely held to have been introduced into France in 1573 from where it was carried to England to become known as the "French marigold," a name it still confusingly retains. On the other hand *T. patula* has been identified by Kaplan (1980) in the 1542 herbal of Leonhart Fuchs, which illustrates both a single and a double form. It is here that the term *Tagetes*, of doubtful derivation but later adopted by Linnaeus, is first employed. The use of *indica* as part of the Latin name for the plants by Fuchs as well as later herbalists (e.g. Jerome Bock 1550 and William Turner 1551) underscores the then current misconception that India was the place of origin of *Tagetes*. In French it is still *fleur d'Inde*. The terminological confusion is acknowledged in John Gerard's 1597 *Historie of Plants* when he notes that the so-called "African marigold" was sometimes vulgarly referred to as the "French marigold." And the editor of the magnificent new edition of the *Florilegium* of Basilius Besler, a folio of 367 color plates of flower paintings from a German garden about 1613, says that the "Aztec or African marigold," as Besler labeled *T. erecta*, arrived later than *T. patula* in the Old World, probably at the end of the sixteenth century (Aymonin 1987, 407-408).

What we can say is that the French and African types, with chromosomes of 24 and 48 respectively, are beyond doubt of Mexican origin and that both were well developed ornamentals, probably with funerary roles, prior to their sixteenth century establishment in the Old World. But the precise time and manner of their spread will probably always remain uncertain. An early English account (Tusser 1577) describes the humble "Mary's gold" as "the follower of the sunne...sown in gardens as well as the potte as for the decking of garlands, beautifying of nosegays and to be worn in the bosom."

A third species of *Tagetes*, frequently available in public markets for its hallucinogenic and presumed medicinal values but apparently not cultivated, is described in the de la Cruz-Badiano herbal of 1552 as *Tagetes lucida* (*yauhtli*), a name it still carries. Still another, the resin-exuding *T. minuta*, sometimes used in seasoning, is considered a noxious weed in the warmer parts of the United States (Neher 1968).

The confusion regarding *Tagetes* has been much aggravated by its similarity with the Old World calendula (*Calendula oficinalis*) or "pot marigold," a sacred flower of East Asian origin that in Europe found an early role both as a medicinal and as a spice. As a yellow food dye it provided a substitute for turmeric and the costly saffron. The calendula, in fact, was the original "marigold" and that is still the first meaning of "marigold" listed in the Oxford Dictionary. An early English term for *Tagetes* was "goldflower." Associated in some manner with the Virgin Mary, it was transformed to "Mary's gold" or "marigold." In Spanish it is usually "*clavel de Indias*" (carnation of the Indies), in German "*ringelblume*" (curly flower).

The prominence of the marigold in the ritual and everyday life of India and parts of Southeast Asia raises interesting questions. It is most readily associated with the symbolic significance of the color yellow in that part of the world, as described some forty years ago by David Sopher (1950). Much earlier George Watt (1889-1896) had noted that the prominence of the marigold in Indian ritual seemed to coincide with the areas of early Portuguese influence there and he postulated an introduction by them. Today sacred bulls are said to walk through the Benares bazaar with wreaths of American marigolds around their necks while flower stalls near the public ghats where the dead are cremated are reported to sell millions of them. In Nepal the flowers are a conspicuous element of the markets where they are sold to be strung as house decorations at certain festivals. In Thailand beds of marigolds fill the grounds of the Grand Palace, one of Buddhism's most magnificent monasteries, and street hawkers fashion garlands of the orange-yellow blooms for offerings to be placed at the foot of the statue of Buddha together with incense and fruit. One recent observer, describing a harvest festival in the Kulu valley of northwest India, noted that the ubiquitous marigolds were almost exactly the same color as maize and chili peppers (two other New World introductions) and speculated that these might have been purposefully selected to match that of the marigolds (Neher 1968).

A possible pre-Columbian presence of *Tagetes* in India has even been suggested. It is included in a list of such candidate useful plants in a recent provocative paper by Johannessen and Parker (1989). However, its easy confusion in the often shadowy early literature of the subcontinent with the calendula and other like-appearing composites, may well explain early reports of its presence. Given the almost complete absence of archaeological evidence, the time and manner of the diffusion of such non-food plants is fraught with difficulties and will almost always remain a question.

The Marigold in the United States

Tagetes arrived in the United States soon after the Revolution when great stores of ornamentals and orchard stock were sent from English and

Dutch nurseries for North American gardens. Half a century ago the W. Atlee Burpee Company of Philadelphia, a major factor in the seed business, instituted a spirited campaign to popularize the marigold in the face of declining demand for the then top-selling sweet pea, at the time threatened by a spreading root rot (Kraft 1963). Through selection, crossings, and induced polyploidy, the Burpee Company developed many new forms, including both white and odorless varieties and non-reproducing "mules" from hybrids of *T. erecta* and *T. patula*. Breeding for resistance to bacterial wilt has been a recent goal. The current Burpee catalogue lists nearly fifty different marigolds, most of which are patented. The literature of the Marigold Society of America mentions as many named cultivars again, and more are being developed each year, the number of days from seed to flower ranging from fifty to ninety. Major categories include "shaggy chrysanthemum hybrids," double- and single-head "carnation types," and "dwarfs."

The long and at times emotional crusade of the Burpee organization to have the marigold named the official national floral emblem was lost to those who championed the rose. The campaign had been carried to the halls of Congress where legislators were provided with boutonnieres of the finest blooms. The lobbyists for grass, the corn tassel, and the carnation as well as the rose were faced down in formal hearings. But the marigold bill authored by Senator Everett Dirkson (R-Illinois) and Representative William Curtin (R-Pennsylvania) failed to find the necessary support (White 1958, Kraft 1963). The Burpee company continues to give special attention to *Tagetes erecta*, careful always to call it "the American marigold" or "America's favorite flower" in its promotional literature. To the Marigold Society of America, established in 1978, it is "the international friendship flower."

Flowering annuals have cycles of popularity much like fashions. Once it was the morning glory, then the sweet pea, the snapdragon and the nasturtium. In more recent years the marigold has led the list (Kraft 1963). Only zinnias and petunias, two other annuals of New World origin (from Mexico and Chile respectively), approached *Tagetes* in popularity until the late arrival of impatiens from New Guinea and Southeast Asia. Among the top vegetables in the U.S. nursery trade, it is also a clean sweep for the Americas, with tomatoes, green beans, corn, and green peppers being one, two, three, and four. One may well ask: Where would the world be without us?

Conclusion

As for the marigold in Mexico (*cempoalxóchitl, cempoalsúchil*), it appears to be well out in front, in part because of its wide acceptance and use in the observances of the Dias de los Muertos. In addition, it has found a growing commercial market as an ingredient in poultry feed to pigment broilers' skins and egg yokes. The blossoms of *T. erecta* are harvested on a substantial scale in the states of Sinaloa, Guanajuato, and Puebla by several companies from which carotenoids (saponified xanthophyll concentrates) are produced for large-scale chicken operations both in Mexico and in the United States (Saucedo 1989). Mexican housewives particularly appreciate the intensified golden colors that such feed stock induces.

But it is the colorful home altar and cemetery decorations so characteristic of those first two days of November, All Saints' and All Souls' Days, that this distinctive contribution of Mexico to the world of flowers really comes into its own, appreciated for its beauty, its *mexicanidad*, and as a reminder of the transitory nature of human life. For Octavio Paz (1961, 52-53) it is in such fiestas that the Mexican opens up, participates, and communes with their fellows and with the values that give meaning to their existence. "It is significant," he has written," that a country as sorrowful as ours should have so many and such joyous fiestas…. Without them we would explode…. For we Mexicans death is not the natural end of life but one phase of an infinite cycle, a cosmic process that repeats itself continuously." No celebration, save perhaps Holy Week, retains such a firm grip on the Mexican imagination, even in the age of television. And the marigold is its symbol. It provides a classic example of the syncretism of pre-Columbian and Spanish ways that has been the product of the "encounter" of New World and Old World cultures whose quincentennial we celebrated in 1992.

References

Acosta, J. de. 1940. *Historia natura y moral de las Indias*. Mexico: Fondo de Cultura Económica (written before 1590).

Anonymous. 1987. *Los dias de muertos, una costumbre mexicana*. Mexico: GV Editores.

Aymonin, G., ed. 1987. *The Besler florilegeum: Plants for the four seasons*. New York: Harry Adams.

Bock, J. 1550. *De Stirpuim*. Strassburg.

Brandes, S. 1988. *Power and persuasion: Fiestas and social control in rural Mexico*. University of Pennsylvania Press.

Cruz, M. de la. 1959. *The de la Cruz-Badiano Aztec herbal of 1522*. Baltimore: The Maya Society.

Durán, D. 1971. *The book of the gods and rites and the Aztec calendar*. University of Oklahoma Press (written 1575-81)

Hernández, F. 1959. *Historia natural de Nueva España*. 7 vols. Mexico: Universidad Nacional Autonóma (written ca. 1570).

Heyden, D. 1983. *Mitología y simbolismo de la flor en el Mexico prehispánico.* Mexico: Universidad Nacional Autonóma.

Johannessen, C. and Parker, A. Z. 1989. European crop plants in Asia prior to European contact. *Yearbook 1988, Conference of Latin Americanist Geographers* 14:14-19.

Kaplan, L. 1980. Historical and ethnobotanical aspects of the domestication of *Tagetes. Economic Botany* 14:200-202.

Kraft, K. 1963. *Garden to order.* Garden City: Doubleday.

Langman, I. 1956. Botanical gardens in ancient Mexico. *Missouri Botanical Garden Bulletin* 44:17-31.

Neher, R. T. 1968. The ethnobotany of *Tagetes. Economic Botany* 22:317-325.

Nutini, H. 1988. *Todos Santos in rural Tlaxcala, a syncretic, expressive and symbolic analysis of the Cult of the Dead.* Princeton, NJ: Princeton University Press.

Nuttall, Z. 1921. Los jardines del antiguo Mexico. *Memoria de la Sociedad Científica Antonio Alzate* 43:593-608.

Paso y Troncoso, F. del. 1988. La botánica entre los Nahuas y otros estudios. In *Jardines botánicos de Anáhuac*, Pilar Máynez, ed. Mexico: Secretaria de Educacion Publica.

Paz, O. 1961. *The labyrinth of solitude, life and thought in Mexico.* New York: Grove Press.

Sahagún, B. de. 1975. *Historia general de la cosas de Nueva España.* Mexico: Editorial Porrua (written about 1590).

Saucedo, F. 1989. Industrias Alcosa, S.A., Mexico. Personal communication.

Scheffler, L. 1976. La celebración del dia de muertos en San Juan Totolac, Tlaxcala. *Boletín del Departamento de Tradiciones Popular* 3:91-103.

Sopher, D. 1950. Turmeric in the color symbolism of southern India and the Pacific Islands. M.A. thesis, Department of Geography, University of California, Berkeley.

Strump Green, J. 1980. The Day of the Dead in Oaxaca Mexico, an historical inquiry. In *Death and dying, views from many cultures*, ed. Richard Kalish, 56-71. Farmingdale, N.Y.: Baywood Publishing.

Torquemada, J. de. 1975. *Monarquía indiana.* 7 vols. Mexico: Universidad Nacional Autonóma (written about 1615).

Turner, W. 1551. *A new herball.* London: Mierdman.

Tusser, T. 1577. Gardeners' labyrinth. London.

Watt, G. 1889-1896. *A dictionary of the economic products of India.* 7 vols. London: W.H. Allen.

White, K. 1958. *Onward and upward in the garden.* New York: Farrar-Strauss-Giroux.

Culture in Place: Costa Rica's Italian Agricultural Colony

Clifton V. Dixon

Abstract

In 1951, 117 Italian families immigrated to the headwaters of the Rio General in southern Costa Rica. They based their future on a 10,000 ha land grant and the trust that the Pan American Highway would be routed through their settlement. Even though the highway never came, the foundation for a foreign agricultural colony was nevertheless established. Despite limited access to the colony, four decades of foreign agricultural activities transformed the region into one of Costa Rica's richest agricultural cantons. The Italian culture presence on the landscape is also manifest in place names, diet, language, house types and settlement patterns. Geographical reinterpretations of twentieth century foreign agricultural colonies in Latin America may provide insight into alternative land use practices for the remaining settlement frontiers in Latin America.

Key words: agricultural colonization, Costa Rica, Italian emigrants, settlement geography

> *Pioneering today is not a mere farming venture but a field of social and engineering and agricultural experimentation. It is not a mere extension of farm population but a thrust of an entire civilization with all its qualities — a new form of nation building.* (Isaiah Bowman 1931, 46)

> *The agricultural pioneer still creates a distinct type of life and thought. He has a large measure of imagination, independence and self-reliance trying to improve his position and future and not depending on job and wage from day to day. (He) will leave a lasting imprint on the land* (Isaiah Bowman, 1927, 264)

Culture, Form, and Place: Essays in Cultural and Historical Geography, edited by Kent Mathewson, 1993. Geoscience and Man, vol. 32, pp. 287-309. Department of Geography and Anthropology, Louisiana State University, Baton Rouge, LA 70893-6010.

Agricultural Colonization in Latin America

For those geographers inspired by, or fortunate enough to have studied with Fred Kniffen and Robert West at LSU, Bowman's thoughts echo the importance still placed on understanding the culture history of agricultural pioneers and the places they create. Reflecting the theme of this volume, this paper examines the culture, the form, and the place of an Italian agricultural colony within Costa Rica's national landscape.

Foreign agricultural colonization forges a unique association between people and the land. Implicit within this association is the process of culture creating place. In agricultural colonization, the impact of culture becomes most evident in the uncouplings of the familiar from their former groundings, and their recombinations in new environmental contexts in which old behaviors are not precisely duplicated. The simple facts of migration and settlement in relatively primitive circumstances often circumscribe the cultural baggage pioneers transfer from old to new homelands. In new habitats, colonists discover that ecological perceptions along with other preconceptions are often challenged. The successes and failures of agricultural colonists become historical markers in their cultural landscapes.

As a distinctive association of humans and the land, the foreign agricultural colony has long attracted the attention of geographers (Bowman 1931; Minkel 1967; Dozier 1969). Settlement geographers have followed the various colonization attempts with a keen interest in: the process of occupying pioneer areas (Eidt 1971; Crist and Nissly 1973); inventories of land use detail (Augelli 1958b; Eidt 1962); the environmental impacts of agricultural colonization (Hiraoka 1977; Schumann and Partridge, 1989); the economic roles of such settlements (Augelli 1958a; Crist 1983); and the effectiveness of foreign colonies as instruments of settlement and the causes of their successes and failures (Eidt 1964; Stewart 1968; Moran 1989). For the cultural geographer, however, immigrant agricultural colonization provides an additional complex of cultural patterns in place (Stewart 1963).

During the twentieth century nearly every Latin American nation attempted to strengthen weak political borders and extend the realm of its national economy by establishing foreign agricultural colonies within sparsely populated regions of their territories. Colonists came from many parts of the world. Some colonies survived the hardships inherent in pioneer settlement, but the majority failed. Over the past 140 years there have been many attempts at colonizing underdeveloped areas of Costa Rica with immigrant colonists (Salazar 1962; Sandner 1962; Hall 1985; Augelli 1987). In southern Costa Rica, the Italian agricultural colonization project stands out as one of these few successes. The focus of this paper is on the cultural milieu of settlement patterns, agricultural history, house types, and diet of Italian colonists living in relative isolation on Costa Rica's southern frontier.

Italian Settlement: History, Flow and Patterns

Following the Japanese attack on Pearl Harbor in 1941, the Pan American Highway suddenly assumed a new and strategic role in the military defense of the hemisphere. This reenforced ongoing efforts to link the Central American nations with a single highway network. Anxious to close a number of gaps in the highway system, in 1943 the United States appropriated 20 million dollars to complete the section between Costa Rica and Panama. The United States projected a route which was to proceed in an almost straight, southeasterly direction along the northern slope of the Pacific coastal mountains to Sabalito, where it was to cross the border into Panama at La Union (fig. 1).

At this same time, Costa Rica became increasingly interested in colonizing the Sabalito region, an area which had hitherto been outside of the effectively-occupied national territory and was gradually becoming settled by Panamanian squatters drifting across the unmarked boundary. By 1951, the first colonists arrived: they were Italians. A defeated Italy had just emerged from WWII with an army of unemployed workers. Keenly open to new possibilities, a small group of disenchanted Italians was per-

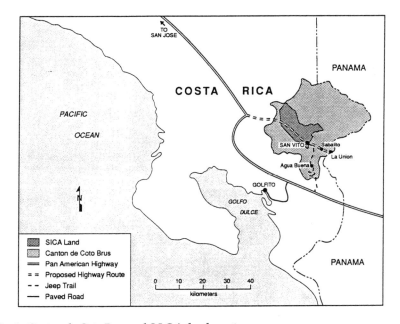

Fig. 1. Canton de Coto Brus and S.I.C.A. land grant.

suaded to redirect its future on a 10,000-hectare land grant near Sabalito, in the *canton* of Coto Brus (Weizmann 1987).

Under terms set forth by the Costa Rican Government and the Italian Society of Agricultural Colonization (S.I.C.A.), 250 to 300 Italian families would be deeded 10- to 20-hectare plots inside the S.I.C.A. parcel (fig. 1). Their passage from Italy to Golfito would be paid for by S.I.C.A.. Once in Costa Rica, the colonists would be provided with a home, agricultural tools, and seeds. S.I.C.A. was also responsible for clearing the land, building roads, deciding upon settlement nuclei, and assisting in preparing harvests for national and international markets. Colonists would not begin to repay S.I.C.A. until after ten years. The pace began slowly. Within the colony's first six years, only 117 families arrived in Coto Brus. During the next two years only a few more families would join them. They came from all over Italy and although most of them had been farm laborers (32.3%), there were also a number of mechanics, carpenters, and others with skills needed for the project (Masing 1964, 53-58).

It was also during these formative years that the colonists saw most of their plans erode when the Pan-American Highway was rerouted along a southern-lowland route (fig. 1). As a result of this change, their plans to participate in external agricultural markets were largely frustrated. Moreover, Golfito, their nearest market center was inaccessible during the rainy season. Even today, there is no improved-surface all-weather road from Coto Brus to Golfito. In one particularly rugged part (south of Agua Buena) the road drops 950 meters in less than 7 kilometers. Isolation proved to be the key obstacle to their prosperity. Within ten years after the first colonists arrived, S.I.C.A. was bankrupt and the prospects of success appeared bleak. A few disenchanted Italian families returned to Europe, others moved to San Jose. However, those who remained in Cotos Brus laid the groundwork for what would become one of Costa Rica's most prosperous agricultural cantons outside the Mesa Central or the domains of the fruit companies (Hall 1985, 120).

Today, the canton of Coto Brus ranks as one of the leading agricultural centers in Costa Rica. The canton's transition from tropical forest to agriculturally productive land occurred faster than in any other frontier region in Costa Rica (Hall 1985, 121). The Costa Rican government and S.I.C.A. had two major objectives in creating the land grant. The most fundamental objective was to colonize the "empty" spaces of southern Costa Rica with European farmers. It was hoped that by granting favorable conditions to new immigrants, Costa Rica could attract agriculturalists with "moderate ambitions"; that is, Costa Rica wanted people of perseverance and industry, good character, sufficient intelligence, and dedication to a peaceful existence. The government hoped that European farmers would teach local farmers better agricultural methods and new soil and resource conservation practices (S.I.C.A. 1955; Masing 1964, 48-51).

The Italian land grant lay just a few kilometers to the west of the tiny settlement of Sabalito. In 1952, Sabalito was the principal settlement nucleus of Coto Brus. The community had roughly fifty inhabitants, which included Costa Rican *campesinos*, Panamanian squatters, and engineers surveying for the Pan American Highway. Collectively, they had fewer than ten rough-timber structures and houses. The community's only connection to the lowland port of Golfito was by trail. The first Italian community, San Vito de Java, was named after Vito Sansonetti, the project's director (fig. 2). By 1991, San Vito was the largest community (approximately 8,000) in Coto Brus (37,000). Its successes as an urban center eclipsed the potential growth of the older Hispanic settlements of Sabalito, Agua Buena, and La Union (M.E.H. 1991).

The area chosen as the site for the San Vito colony is a rugged altiplano of loamy sandstone. In many places there is a mantle of heavily dissected volcanic ash. In 1950 the canton's vegetation was primarily tropical moist forest. Situated at 1,200 m, the area's salubrious climate varies little in temperature, ranging between 16° C and 19° C throughoutthe year. The area receives an average of 4,000 mm of precipitation concentrated during the summer months. Thus the rainfall regime is almost monsoonal, with less than 20% of the annual budget coming during the winter. The seasonal rainfall, coinciding with the end of the summer growing season, has always presented problems for colonists attempting to haul their harvests to market on the region's unimproved roads.

In May of 1952, nine Italian men arrived in Golfito and ascended the mountain path to Agua Buena, thus initiating the settlement process that would leave its cultural imprint throughout the region (Weizmann 1987). From Agua Buena they cut a trail along an abandoned Indian path to the settlement site which would become San Vito (fig. 2). There, their first shelters were tents. A few months earlier, S.I.C.A. had dispatched a small group of Nicaraguan laborers to the area to begin clearing the land. When the Italians arrived, the pace of clearing the land accelerated and the foundations for settlement of the southern frontier of Costa Rica was laid.

The first Italian colonists (27 families) arrived in San Vito on Christmas Eve of 1952. By the end of the following year, S.I.C.A. had settled 108 colonists around San Vito (Masing 1964, 100; Weizmann 1987). The area's first sawmill was in place by 1952 and was located in San Vito. The mill's location prompted Italian colonists to settle near town (Cole 1963) (figs. 3, 4, and 5). As this was the only sawmill in the canton, Costa Rican migrants took advantage of its location and initially settled near the eastern border of the S.I.C.A. tract. Within three years, a hardware and grocery store opened, an electrical generator was in place and piped water ran to every

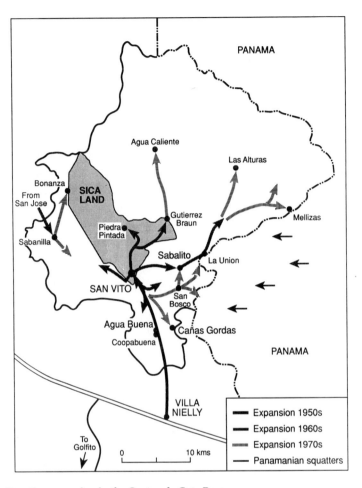

Fig. 2. Frontier expansion in the Canton de Coto Brus.

house in San Vito. Thus began the rapid growth of San Vito. At first, the Costa Ricans squatting on S.I.C.A. land were viewed as a problem. The situation was accepted though, as it became evident that Costa Ricans would be needed as farm laborers if commercial agriculture was to become profitable.

Throughout the 1950s, most settlement in Coto Brus was focused around San Vito and was initiated by Italians. Within the first decade of Italian colonization (1951-1962), Italian colonists and S.I.C.A. realized that without improved all-season roads connecting settlements within the canton and without an improved road linking the colony to the major Costa Rican markets, the colonization project would not succeed as planned.

Fig. 3. Italian settlement at San Vito, Coto Brus (1954).

Fig. 4. Italian settlement at San Vito, Coto Brus (1955).

During this time, colonists were generating income from coffee, but they had been unable to repay S.I.C.A. as planned, and therefore S.I.C.A. was not generating a profit. In 1962, there were still no roads, and S.I.C.A. had exhausted its funds. Before the year's end the company was dissolved and Italian colonists were no longer arriving in Coto Brus. However, approximately 280 Italians had settled there, and the Italian cultural milieu had been firmly established in San Vito.

During the next decade, settlement frontiers expanded eastward to the Panamanian border and northward into the S.I.C.A. land grant (fig. 2). These further frontier expansions were the work of a growing number of new landless Costa Rican farmers immigrating to Coto Brus and eager to settle new lands beyond the Italian frontier. Frontier expansion since the 1970s has focused upon a northward push into the foothills of the Talamancan Ranges coupled with a pattern of infilling and intensification of population growth in the triangle formed between San Vito, La Union, and Cañas Gordas (D. G. Cole, pers. comm., Cañas Gordas, 1990; Sansonetti 1990). The steady influx of Costa Rican settlers has rapidly expanded the canton's agricultural frontiers. However, the non-Italian colonists have adopted relatively few of the Italians' cultural and settlement traits, thus leaving the Italian nucleus of San Vito as the center of Italian culture (figs. 2 and 6).

Agricultural History

S.I.C.A.'s goal was to settle the colony (and Coto Brus) with a commercial agricultural economy as its base. Given the problem of rain-damaged roads at the end of the growing season and S.I.C.A.'s inability to market its perishable produce, the Italian colonists turned to the production of coffee. They saw coffee as the only crop which could meet high transportation costs and assure the producer a profit. Moreover, coffee thrived in the region's precipitation regime and acidic soils. Initially, the Italian colonists were unfamiliar with coffee growing. They soon learned the necessary production methods from neighboring Costa Ricans who included it in their subsistence agricultural plots. Promise of high yields became apparent after the first harvests. As long as coffee prices remained high, the product also promised a high rate of return in a relatively short time with little effort. Little attention was given to growing anything but coffee. Under contract agreements established by S.I.C.A., the prescription for a 20-hectare farm was: 4 hectares of commercial coffee, sugar cane, or cacao; 8 hectares of pasture; 7 hectares of "cereals" (corn, beans, and rice) for home and market; and 1 hectare of marketable vegetables. The Costa Rican government had hoped that the Hispanic colonists in southern Costa Rica would adopt this seemingly Old World agroecosystem (S.I.C.A. 1955, 3).

Fig. 5. Italian settlement at San Vito, Coto Brus (1957).

Fig. 6. Main street of San Vito, Coto Brus (1965).

The model, however, was never effective as long as the colony remained relatively isolated.

Today, approximately 58% of the cleared area in Coto Brus is in coffee monoculture (M.A.G. 1990). Provided the farmer has a large enough area under production (more than 8 hectares), coffee, in spite of fluctuating prices which continue to creep downwards, is still lucrative. The Italian colonists, along with their Costa Rican counterparts, who converted all or most of their land to coffee, have been able to weather the decline of coffee prices. Today, there are a few prosperous colonists in San Vito and land prices are almost as high as those in the Meseta Central of Costa Rica (C.N.P. 1990).

A strategy of coffee monoculture is not without ecological problems (Borbon 1984; Boucher 1983). Coffee growers have to contend with increasing plant specific leaf blight, soil nematodes, and herbivores. In the initial phase of the colonization project, the Costa Rican Government stated that one of S.I.C.A.'s objectives was to have the Italian colonists assist in establishing a better environmental ethic among Costa Rican peasants. S.I.C.A.'s farm model stressing diversification was part of the attempt to meet this challenge (D. G. Cole, pers. comm. Cañas Gordas, 1990; Masing 1964, 179-181). It was not until 1970, however, that some Italian colonists began to consider the potential benefits of small farm polyculture. It is difficult to pinpoint just what led to their shift from coffee farming. Certainly the dwindling cost of coffee coupled with the increasing cost of sustained high-yield production was a factor. But also the colony and region had matured. San Vito had a settled urban population with a growing local market. Roads were now passable during all seasons because all-terrain vehicles were improved and many farmers had jeeps. With a small, but expanding, local market and the potential for an external market, Italians took the lead in removing some of their coffee and shifting to dairy cattle, some others began small vegetable plots for truck farming, and others established plant and flower nurseries. The trend has been spreading to their *Tico* (native born Costa Ricans) neighbors.

Field work conducted by the author in 1985 and 1991 focused upon land use and activities on farms ranging from 2 to 30 hectares in size in the San Vito area. Within the study area it has been possible to measure and map over 300 farms and record the changes Italian and *Tico* coffee growers are making. Field investigations focused upon recording the percentage of land devoted to: 1) coffee growing, 2) farming an assortment of vegetables, and 3) pasture. An interesting pattern emerges when one examines the length of time the farmer has had his land in the present mix of land use activities (fig. 7; table 1).

Initial settlers, both the Italians and *Ticos*, promptly focused upon coffee as a commercial and economic mainstay crop. Every colonist who en-

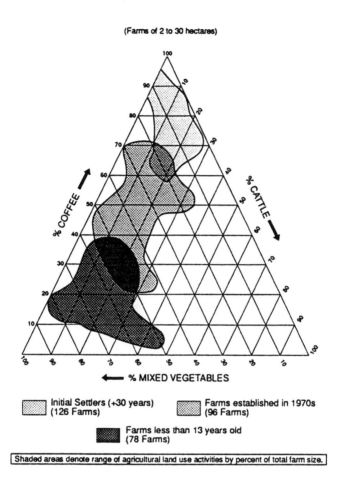

(Farms of 2 to 30 hectares)

% COFFEE

% CATTLE

◄── % MIXED VEGETABLES

Initial Settlers (+30 years)
(126 Farms)

Farms established in 1970s
(96 Farms)

Farms less than 13 years old
(78 Farms)

Shaded areas denote range of agricultural land use activities by percent of total farm size.

Fig. 7. Coto Brus small farm land use.

tered Coto Brus in the 1950s and early 1960s still maintains at least 60% of his land in coffee monoculture. Of these farmers, 87% have more than 85% of their land devoted entirely to coffee. Eleven percent of them have dairies, and 6% produce vegetables in large-scale home gardens. But the average percentage of total land in coffee is 83% for all farms established before 1970. Coffee is grown under shade provided by *Musa* (plantain and banana), *Erythrina, Inga,* and *Gliricidia* trees. Most often, the fruit of the *Musa* is consumed on the farm and only on occasion is it sold. *Erythrina, Inga,* and *Gliricidia* are leguminous, nitrogen-fixing trees. Farmers prune

Table 1. Coto Brus small farms land use

Farm age	Percentage of farm land in:			Total farms[1]
	Coffee	Pasture	Vegetables	
Initial settlers 1951-1969	83	11	6	126 (42%)
Established 1970-1979	51	12	37	96 (32%)
Less than 13 years old	28	20	52	78 (26%)
Total				300

[1]Three hundred small farm systems (2 to 30 ha farms) were inventoried within a 20-km radius of San Vito, between 1985 and 1990.

these shade trees during the dry season and mulch the cuttings for a nitrogen enriching soil additive.

Coffee *fincas* require abundant temporary help during the harvest (early fall). The remainder of the year is devoted to periodic weeding, mulching, pruning, and applications of agrochemicals (herbicides, fungicides, insecticides, and fertilizers). Coffee agroecosystems require a highly structured maintenance program which is both time consuming and expensive.

Farms established in the 1970s represent a continued migration to Coto Brus by *Ticos* who took advantage of the roads, towns, and coffee processing *beneficios* built by pioneer settlers and S.I.C.A. Initially, the majority (75% and greater) of the agricultural land on these small farms was devoted to coffee, continuing the practice of coffee monoculture that had been established by Italians just a decade earlier (Vito Sansonetti, pers. comm., 1990; M.A.G. 1970-1989). However, by 1992, these farms had decreased their coffee dependence to 51% of their total land in use. A partial explanation for the decrease in land in coffee and the movement to a more diversified agroecosystem is the fact that these farmers began following trends established by younger farmers who began farming in Coto Brus after 1980. Many of these new farms (less than 13 years old) are run by the first generation of Costa Rican-born Italian farmers. These farm systems maintain less of a dependence upon coffee and have established a more diversified agroecosystem than their pioneer parents (table 1). These young farmers are conscious of the ecological problems created by crop monoculture and unchecked agrochemical applications.

For example, they experiment with polycultural systems and alleopathic plants, practice intensive cultivation on terraced slopes, and test bean-mulch rotations (locally referred to as *frijol tapado*) which enable them to maintain sustained-yield cropping with little agrochemical input. Second-generation Italian farmers are taking the lead in initiating these agricultural changes and their *Tico* neighbors of the same generation are acutely interested in the Italians' success and are steadily adopting similar polycultural practices. Although farms established since 1980 only represent 26% of the sample, the number of small farms maintaining highly diversified agricultural systems should continue to increase.

Excited about their agricultural futures, many of these next generation Italian farmers organized a local environmental movement (APREN-ABRUS) aimed at stopping local deforestation and maintaining sustainable agroecosystems. Already they have begun reforestation projects along the Río Coto Brus. Young Italians also teach fundamental courses in ecology and resource management at the San Vito high school and these classes are the only exposure young Costa Ricans in the area have to environmental education. Most farms in Coto Brus reflect the initial directions of Italian colonists in isolation, that is they grow coffee and lots of it. But Italians and their *Tico* neighbors appear to be reestablishing the pioneer spirit with new directions in agriculture. The geographer Carolyn Hall (1985, 120-121) recognizes that, of the numerous foreign agricultural colonies established in Costa Rica, only two were significantly successful. The Mennonites of the cloud forests of Monte Verde established dairying activities when they settled their land. The initial Italian colonists were successful with coffee and it appears that their descendants will continue to be successful despite whatever happens to national coffee production. Apparently, the emerging-generation Italian colonist is forging the future look and use of the landscapes of Coto Brus. Ironically, Italians are finally meeting one of S.I.C.A.'s initial objectives, that being to transfer Italian (European) agricultural management systems and land use ethics to Hispanic Central America. It has taken forty years for these agricultural systems to develop in situ. Although S.I.C.A. collapsed, it now appears that its objectives will survive.

House Types

In his presidential address to the Association of American Geographers, Professor Kniffen (1965) focused attention on the importance of folk housing as a key to interpreting the cultural landscape and the role of diffusion in creating such cultural places. Kniffen and those he has inspired have demonstrated that house types are an important element of the cultural baggage people transport to new regions of settlement. Housing is a basic fact of human geography; it reflects cultural heritage, current fashion, and functional needs. These relationships are most evident in contexts where plant and animal husbandry are dominant pursuits. Folk house types on the pioneer fringe of tropical Latin America are signatures of human adaptation to climate, resourcefulness with limited tools and materials, and the functional needs of a pioneer farmer. The house serves as a home, barn, storage shelter, and retreat from daily labor.

When Italians arrived in Golfito in 1951, they immediately sensed the strangeness of their new home. They had left the Mediterranean climate for the hot humid tropics. They were embarking upon a life as farmers and would soon be growing seeds unfamiliar to them. Every aspect of their future would have to be built one step at a time and the first step was to build a shelter and home.

The original houses of the Italian colonists were unlike any other house found in frontier Coto Brus (fig. 8). Moreover, there is nothing distinctly Italian about the Italians' houses. The model for their houses was borrowed from the architectural styles of the American-owned fruit company housing at Golfito (fig. 9). In Golfito the Italians saw how the fruit company adapted style and function in housing to the harsh environmental demands of the tropics. According to Vito Sansonetti (pers. comm., 1990), S.I.C.A. had no plan for non-agricultural landscape development. Vito and other Italian colonists lament that they appropriated the fruit company house style even though the design was simple to construct, utilized native building materials (tropical hardwoods), and was ideally suited to the functional needs of the pioneer farming family.

Most Italian houses in Coto Brus follow the basic style of the lean-to (fig. 10), the foursquare (fig. 8), the overlap shed, and the Costa Rican three roof (Field 1968). All of these house styles are found in Golfito. Most Italian houses were placed on stilts. Their rationale was that houses placed upon stilts provide more sheltered area from seasonal rains (under a small roof). Initially, the ground floor was left open and subsequently enclosed when time and materials were available. It was commonly used as a *bodega*, or a place to keep jeeps, tractors, farm animals, and tools dry during tropical showers. The second floor provided living quarters, bedrooms, and an indoor kitchen. Detached kitchens are common among *Ticos* and Guaymi Indians living in Coto Brus. Porches were common among the Italians.

Italians built their homes of mill-cut rough timber and corrugated metal roofing, both of which were abundant in the colony. The present-day Italian landscape of Coto Brus is characterized by a continued adoption of the folk houses the Italians brought to the area (fig. 11). Variations on the basic design are more widespread after forty years of cultural isolation; but the center of Italian folk design remains within a few kilometers of its original center at San Vito.

Diet

Diet and food preferences also mark a sharp contrast between Italians and *Ticos* in Coto Brus. Even though Italians and *Ticos* have lived in the same

Fig. 8. Italian Colonist House Type, San Vito (1955).

Fig. 9. American Fruit Company house type, Golfito (built circa 1950).

Fig. 10. First Italian house built in San Vito (1952).

Fig. 11. Pioneer home built in 1953 (photo date 1990).

communities for more than three decades, there has been little acceptance of each other's diets. The mainstay of the *Tico* diet is rice and beans, while Italians prefer macaroni and pasta and almost never eat rice and beans. The Italian's preference for Mediterranean foods also includes a passion for *chiconi, achicoria,* parsley, zucchini, brussel sprouts, *finocchi,* lettuce, and grapes.

Componential analyses of traditional *Tico* and Italian diets also indicates that Italians consume a more balanced diet (Nietschmann 1967). Italians eat more salads, green vegetables, meat, and dairy products than do their *Tico* neighbors. Passing through numerous household kitchens in Coto Brus and sampling a variety of foods makes it evident that Italians employ many more spices and tomato-based sauces than do *Ticos*. Not surprisingly, each of the two culture groups claims to abhor the other's diet, foods, and manner of preparation.

The Italian's predilection for these and other Old World foods is easily seen in their kitchen gardens where they attempt to raise many of their traditional foods. Italians maintain small kitchen gardens (generally less than 1,000 m²) which are almost always an assemblage of ornamental (48%), food (36%), and medicinal (8%) plants.[1] There is nothing fundamentally different between *Tico* and Italian gardens. Gardens function as a source for fresh fruits and vegetables, but ornamental and shade plants always dominate the species diversity. Italians, however, do attempt to grow more, and greater varieties of, cooking herbs than do their *Tico* neighbors.

In the mid-1950s, when the Italian colony was at its zenith, there were more than 100 families with kitchen gardens. In 1991, there were only 21 Italian kitchen gardens. These remaining gardens represent the vestigial cultural elements of dietary preference that all Italian colonists in Coto Brus have shared (Vito Sansonetti, pers. comm., 1990). Cooking herbs found in Italian gardens include: oregano, basil, thyme, parsley, and garlic. For the most part, Italians use these herbs for personal consumption and occasionally sell them to the two Italian restaurants in San Vito. Italians attempt to grow a large variety and quantity of cooking vegetables such as cabbage, tomatoes, carrots, green beans, and leafy greens. The canton's warm-wet climate and numerous herbivorous pests have prevented many Italians from being successful at growing enough vegetables to meet their demands. Some Italians have always had to rely upon Italian merchants in San Vito to supply them with the exotic food items they are unable to produce.

Throughout the growth and development of San Vito as the urban and marketing center of Coto Brus, the Italians have always dominated and controlled the small collection of businesses. Aside from owning the local grocery and butcher shop, cinema, hardware and furniture store, gas station, and hotel, Italians also operate the town's bakery and pasta shop, and the two Italian restaurant-pizzerias. San Vito's two Italian restaurants are rustic in that they have only a few tables, simple furnishings, and the stove and kitchen function for both the restaurant and the proprietor's home, which is attached to the rear of the building. The restaurants serve a complete Italian menu including: spaghetti, lasagna, *gnocchi*, *orechietti*, ravioli, and pizza. The restaurants are popular meeting places for Italians, and every night a few Italians sit around the tables speaking Italian and creating what is essentially a home-kitchen atmosphere (while at adjacent tables, Spanish speaking *Ticos* are left out of the conversation). These nightly gatherings also further strengthen the bond between the surviving Italian colonists and help to accentuate the little separatism that exists between the Italians and *Ticos*.

Cheeses for Italian dishes are produced at a local Italian dairy. The bakeries sell both Italian- and *Tico*-style baked goods. The Italian style pastries include *queque borracho*, *bignes*, *sabaglioni*, and *pan amarillo*. Typical Mediterranean drinks served by the Italians include *café expresso* and *capuccino* to which anise is sometimes added. Traditional Italian food ways perpetuate ethnic socialization and identification and thus assist in maintaining Coto Brus's unique sense of place.

Culture in Place

Although the Italian population has dwindled to less than 300, its cultural presence is strong. The settlers have an Italian community center *(Dante Ailigheri)* directly across from the site of San Vito's first Roman Catholic church. At the cultural center they keep the colony's *recuerdos*, such as its first shortwave radio, photos of pioneer life, and an Italian language library with current copies of Italy's versions of *Life* and *Town and Country* magazines. Every Sunday many *Ticos* visit the center and watch a 15-minute video on San Vito's history. Italian is taught in the local elementary school to all children, both *Tico* and Italian. Italian place names range from San Vito to streets in San Vito named after Christopher Columbus, Amerigo Vespucci, and Marco Polo.

Almost all of San Vito's businesses and shops are owned by first and second generation Italian families (fig. 12). In fact some families also own stores in San Jose. Many of the Italian families can afford to return to Italy periodically or visit the United States. They send their children to European or American colleges and it appears that Costa Rica's Italians maintain a much broader view of the world than most Costa Ricans. Reflecting upon Bowman's thoughts which stemmed from a lifetime of observations of pioneer landscapes, one sees that the Italian agricultural pioneers in Coto Brus created a distinct type of life and thought. Their process of maintaining Italian culture and creating form in the landscape was prima-

Fig. 12. Main street San Vito, 1990 (photo taken at same point as figure 3).

rily the result of the Italians' independence, imagination, and self-reliance. They were young families who were successful at improving their future prospects, and such efforts have left a lasting imprint on the land (fig. 13) (Bowman 1957).

Rethinking Pioneer Agricultural Colonization

Throughout much of Middle America, rapid deforestation and quickly eroding soils have become the norm. The quality of most farm land is being degraded. As a result, whenever possible, farmers are quick to move. The theme of settlement geography has always been focused upon the pioneer fringes. However, there are few undeveloped settlement fringes remaining in Middle America and those remaining areas are characterized as marginal lands or fragile ecosystems. Generally, such areas are not suitable for sustained-yield agriculture; yet these areas are inevitably the next agricultural frontiers.

Concomitant with the present-day expansion of agricultural frontiers in Middle America has been the shift from the European agricultural colonist to the wave of increasing numbers of landless *campesinos* abandoning

Fig. 13. Monument to Italian colonists, San Vito 1990.

failed agricultural landscapes, escaping war-plagued regions, and suffering from economic adversity. These "Fourth World" settlers have become the next wave of agricultural "colonists" in tropical America. Unlike the agricultural colonists earlier in this century, these migrants typically do not have a master land use plan, government support, financial backing or a unifying cultural presence. Already it is evident that the success of these migrants will depend upon their developing sustained-yield agroecosystems and their quest for a harmonious ecological balance with the natural environment (Schumann and Partridge 1989).

The pioneering works of geographers studying pioneer agricultural colonies in Latin America may be the key to discovering alternative agricultural systems adapted to or developed within frontier fringes. Since the 1920s, there have been numerous geographical studies focused upon agricultural colonization in Latin America (Minkel 1967; Dixon 1992). Few of these studies, however, focus on the potential of non-Hispanic pioneer land use systems as exemplars for the new migrant colonists in Latin America.

Perhaps the time has come to rethink studies of pioneer agricultural colonization. It is time to reexamine the geographical literature on tropical colonization and revisit foreign agricultural colonization sites to focus specifically upon the quest for identifying managed ecosystems which may serve as land use models for future agricultural frontiers. The potential value of such research is evident in southern Costa Rica. The Italian colony in San Vito may serve as one possible model for sustainable agro-ecosystems within some parts of the tropics. Many of the pioneers of this system, such as Vito Sansonetti, are still alive. San Vito has persisted in spite of relative isolation and declining coffee prices. It also stands out as a node of distinctive culture firmly in place in southern Costa Rica.

Acknowledgment

Field work was conducted in 1985 and 1990 with research funds provided by the Organization for Tropical Studies and the College of Arts and Sciences, Memphis State University. Bill Manger assisted in collecting data in 1990.

Note

1. Garden surveys included twenty-three Italian house kitchen gardens. Gardens were inventoried for species diversity and economic use of plants.

References

Augelli, J. P. 1987. Costa Rica's frontier legacy. *The Geographical Review* 77(1): 1-16.

——. 1958a. Cultural and economic changes of Bastos, a Japanese colony on Brazil's Paulista frontier. *Annals of the Association of American Geographers* 48(1):3-19.

——. 1958b. The Latvians of Varpa, a foreign colony on the Brazilian pioneer fringe. *Geographical Review* 48(3): 365-387.

Borbon, M. O. 1984. *Descripción Ecológica Población Uso de Tierra Producción de Café en Coto Brus*. San José, Costa Rica: Ministerio de Agricultura y Ganaderia and Oficina del Café.

Boucher, D. H. 1983. Coffee. In *Costa Rican natural history*, ed. D. H. Janzen, 66-72. Chicago: University of Chicago Press.

Bowman, I. 1931. *The pioneer fringe*. American Geographical Society, Special Publication 13. New York.

——. 1957. Settlement by the modern pioneer. In *Geography in the twentieth century*, ed. G. Taylor, 248-266. New York: Philosophical Library.

C.N.P. (Consejo Nacional de Productores). 1990. *Estadísticas Agropecuario de Coto Brus*. San Vito, Costa Rica: Government Document.

Cole, D. G. 1963. Italian colonist in Costa Rica. *Americas* 15(6): 38-41.

Crist, R. E. 1983. Westward thrusts of the pioneer zone in Venezuela: A half century of economic development along the Llanos-Andes border. *American Journal of Economics and Sociology* 42(4): 451-462.

Crist, R. E. and Nissly, C. 1973. *East from the Andes: Pioneer settlements in the South American heartland.* Gainesville: University of Florida Press.

Dixon, C. V. 1992. Cartobibliography of twentieth century foreign agricultural sites in Latin America. Unpublished Manuscript. Memphis, TN.

Dozier, C. L. 1969. *Land development and colonization in Latin America: Case studies of Peru, Bolivia, and Mexico.* New York: Frederick A. Praeger.

Eidt, R. C. 1962. Pioneer settlement in eastern Peru. *Annals of the Association of American Geographers* 52(3): 255-278.

——. 1964. Comparative problems and techniques in tropical and semitropical pioneer settlement: Colombia, Peru and Argentina. *Association of Pacific Coast Geographers Yearbook* 26:37-41.

——. 1971. *Pioneer settlement in northeast Argentina.* Madison: University of Wisconsin Press.

Field, C. 1968. Housing in the pioneer landscape. In *Land and life in the tropics*, 29-37. San José, Costa Rica: Organization for Tropical Studies.

Hall, C. 1985. *Costa Rica: A geographical interpretation in historical perspective.* Dellplain Latin American Studies, No. 17. Boulder, CO: Westview Press.

Hiraoka, M. 1977. Landscape change in a pioneer region: The eastern Bolivian example. In *Man, culture, and settlement*, eds. R. C. Eidt, K. N. Singh, and R. P. B. Singh, 69-81. Kalyani Publishers Research Publication No. 17. New Delhi.

Kniffen, F. B. 1965. Folk housing: Key to diffusion. *Annals of the Association of American Geographers* 55(4): 549-577.

M.A.G. (Ministerio de Agricultura y Ganadería). 1970-1989. *Informe Resúmen de Agrícola en Coto Brus.* San Vito, Costa Rica: Government Document.

——. 1990. *Informe de Daños y Perdidas, Coto Brus.* San Vito, Costa Rica: Government Document.

Masing, U. 1964. Foreign agricultural colonies in Costa Rica: An analysis of foreign colonization in a tropical environment. Ph.D. Diss., University of Florida, Gainesville.

M.E.H. (Ministerio de Económica y Hacienda). 1991. *Estadística de Costa Rica. Dirección General de Estadística y Censos.* San José, Costa Rica: Impreso en Casa Gráfica.

Minkel, C. W. 1967. Programs of agricultural colonization and settlement in Central America. *Revista Geografica* 66:19-52.

Moran, E. F. 1989. Adaption and maladaption in newly settled areas. In *The human ecology of tropical land settlement in Latin America*, eds. D. A. Schumann and W.L. Partridge, 43-85. Boulder: Westview Press.

Nietschmann, B. Q. 1967. Food consumption in San Vito and vicinity. In *Tropical land utilization: The Costa Rican example*, 55-60. San José, Costa Rica: Organization for Tropical Studies.

Salazar, N. 1962. *Tierras y Colonización en Costa Rica*. Serie Tess de Grado y Ensayos no. 15. San José, Costa Rica: Editorial Universitaria, Universidad de Costa Rica.

Sandner, G. 1962. *Investigaciones Geográficas: La Colonización Agrícola en Costa Rica*, 2 vols. San José, Costa Rica: Instituto Geográfico de Costa Rica.

Schumann, D. A. and Partridge, W. L. 1989. *The human ecology of tropical land settlement in Latin America*. Boulder: Westview Press.

S.I.C.A. (Sociedad Italiana de Colonización Agrícola). 1955. *Un Esperimento di Colonizzazione en Costa Rica*. Rome: Tipografia Editrice Italia.

Stewart, N. 1968. Some problems in the development of agricultural colonization in the Andean Oriente. *Professional Geographer* 20(1):33-38.

———. 1963. Foreign agricultural colonization as a study in cultural geography. *Professional Geographer* 15(5): 1-5.

Weizmann, H. G. 1987. *Emigrantes a la Conquista de la Selva: Estudio de una Colonización en Costa Rica, San Vito de Java*. San José, Costa Rica: Privately published.

Morphologic Patterns of Resort Evolution along the Gulf of Mexico

Klaus J. Meyer-Arendt

Abstract

Coastal resorts around the Gulf of Mexico exhibit great variability in urban morphology. Although physical geography may partly explain regional variations, cultural-historical factors are of greater importance. Changes in urban morphologies may be correlated with development stages in conceptual models of resort evolution. Such models serve to explain historical trends, present variations, and future development conflicts.

Key words: coastal resorts, Gulf of Mexico, historic tourism, urban morphology

Introduction: Modeling Resort Evolution

Seaside resorts have been studied in terms of both historical evolution and urban form (morphology), but few studies have integrated these two research approaches. Since seaside recreation is an element of popular culture, it should follow that the component parts of resorts reflect the dictates of prevailing fashions — perhaps limited by technological constraints — at the time of development. Thus resort evolution is hypothesized to entail sequential stacking of popular culture overlays upon the seaside landscape. Many, if not most, of the elements of historical popular culture are ephemeral and last only until they are replaced by the next fad. More substantial material elements, however, such as fishing piers, boardwalks and ornate beach hotels, may persist in the landscape because of enduring popularity, or simple durability, despite being out of style. Thus, there is an unevenness to the evolving morphology of seaside resorts that involves the more structural components of coastal recreation along with the faddish artifacts that quickly come and go.

Culture, Form, and Place: Essays in Cultural and Historical Geography, edited by Kent Mathewson, 1993. Geoscience and Man, vol. 32, pp. 311-323. Department of Geography and Anthropology, Louisiana State University, Baton Rouge, LA 70893-6010.

Seaside resorts, can be viewed as complexes of popular culture arti-facts. As such, they undergo "life-cycles" not unlike new products intro-duced into the popular culture marketplace, such as slinkies, pet rocks, Cabbage Patch dolls, Batman T-shirts, and Teenage Mutant Ninja Turtle paraphernalia. In marketing, whether it is for new products or tourist des-tinations, this "product life cycle" takes on a bell-shaped curve. Although the evolutionary nature of resorts has been recognized for several decades (Christaller 1963; Gilbert 1939; 1949; Wolfe 1952; 1962), it was not until Butler (1980) proposed his own S-curve adaptation of the product life cy-cle that a useful theoretical framework for understanding resort develop-ment was provided. Imbedded in the Butler model, as in the product life cycle model, is an implied upper limit to growth. In terms of resort devel-opment, this invokes the quantifiably elusive concept of carrying capacity. In turn, the evolution of urban resort morphology is dependent upon sev-eral variables, including time, environment (sustainability of the physical resource base), and popular culture (evolving preferences of material cul-ture and sustainability of the cultural resource base).

The urban morphology of tourist destinations has long been recog-nized as distinctive when compared with other urban types (Gilbert 1939, Jones 1933, Wolfe 1952). Land use zonation at seaside resorts was not sys-tematically modelled until Barrett's (1958) comprehensive work on coastal resorts of the United Kingdom. Barrett's model of "theoretical accommo-dation zones" (fig. 1) identified a zone of "frontal amenities" in which tour-ists and tourist facilities congregate. With distance from the central beachfront, the intensity of tourism-related activities decreases. Stansfield (1971), comparing English and northeast U.S. resorts, found a similar pat-tern and identified a "recreational business district" (RBD), which has be-

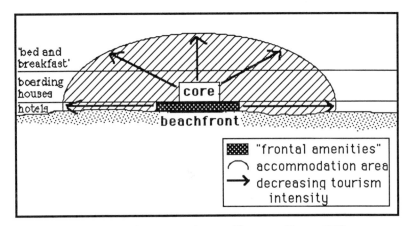

Fig. 1. Theoretical accommodation zones in a seaside resort. (Barrett 1958)

come an integral component of subsequent models (Lavery 1971) and case studies (Pigram 1977, Taylor 1975) of resort morphology.

In an effort to incorporate the cultural-historical component into morphological aspects of coastal development, both conceptual as well as morphological models of resort evolution were devised (figs. 2 and 3). These models, based upon research at eight tourist destinations around the entire Gulf of Mexico (fig. 4) (Meyer-Arendt 1987), are particularly applicable to the longer-settled (and recreationally-developed) central Gulf Coast. At least four stages of resort evolution are identified: exploration, infrastructural development, settlement expansion, and maturation (see fig. 2). If levels of recreational demand remain high enough to warrant higher density development, a fifth stage — land use intensification — may be entered prior to reaching carrying capacity. Although some resorts became infrastructurally developed earlier than others, the latter stages of expansion, maturation, and land use intensification all took place in the post-World War II era and closely coincided. In terms of material popular culture and resort morphology, we must look at the landscape impacts of the boom periods.

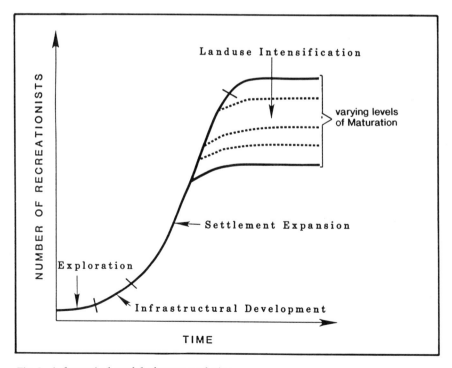

Fig. 2. A theoretical model of resort evolution.

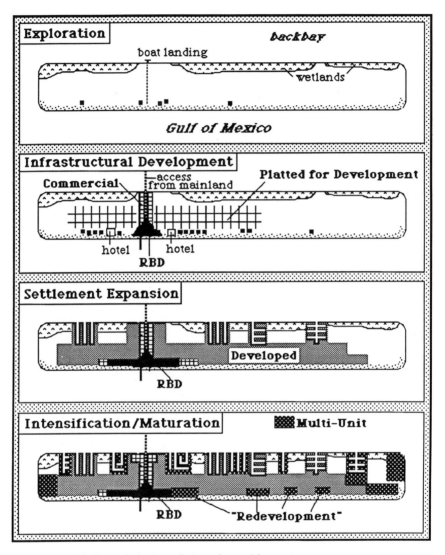

Fig. 3. A model of morphologic evolution of a seaside resort.

Exploration

Before the Civil War, the Gulf Coast urban elites began to establish summer residences and frequent lodging facilities along nearby sheltered shorelines. This was in response to the popularization of swimming, bathing, and "taking in" sea breezes, and facilitated by the onset of rail and steamship transportation. New Orleanians seasonally migrated to the shores of Mississippi Sound and Lake Pontchartrain (Sullivan 1988). Mo-

Fig. 4. Gulf of Mexico resorts selected for study.

bilians preferred the eastern shore of Mobile Bay and Houstonians were drawn to Galveston Bay. With few exceptions, the wave-washed, hurricane-prone coast of the Gulf of Mexico was generally avoided by all but the "explorer" class (Cohen 1972) of summer recreationists during this period. The infrastructural development stage, in which recreation-seekers were drawn to the coast for reasons of health or pleasure, was postponed on the open Gulf until after the Civil War. Access was provided by steamship or railroad, and a central tourist focus was usually provided in the form of a hotel or dance pavilion built by speculative entrepreneurs. In cases where pre-existing fishing or port towns antedate recreational discovery of the beachfront, the patterns remain essentially similar because the initial settlement focus of these towns (e.g. Tecolutla, Galveston, Grand Isle, and Dauphin Island) was away from the beach. The initial locus of recreation was at the point on the beach closest to the core of the pre-existing settlement.

Infrastructural Development

The tourism potential of an area was quickly recognized by patterns established in the exploration stage, and infrastructural development soon followed. Tourist-oriented businesses and lodging facilities were opened, and bridge or causeway linkages to the beach were built. A typical pattern is for an entrepreneur (one or more individuals, corporations, or even local governments) to acquire a chunk of real estate, construct a commercial enterprise such as a combination hotel-restaurant — perhaps with bathhouses and/or a fishing pier — and plat out a vacation home subdivision. This speculative activity is often initiated prior to easy access and followed by privately-funded highway and/or bridge construction. With provision of highway access, an RBD replete with one or perhaps two beach hotels becomes morphologically defined about the point of closest beach access, and subsequent commercial clustering leads to its gradual enlargement (fig. 5). Commercial establishments also begin to line the beach access highway, and summer cottages are built along the shorefront extending outward from the RBD. Beach subdivisions, although platted, exhibit little actual development in this stage. Geologically unstable and physically less desirable property (e.g. shorelines near tidal inlets, backbarrier wetlands) also remain relatively undisturbed during this early development stage.

Fig. 5. **Beach approach and recreational business district at Pensacola Beach. Note cottage development at lower right.**

Settlement Expansion

Once the seeds of infrastructure have been planted, settlement expansion can take place. This completes the transformation from a landscape little impacted by human activity to a complete recreational landscape. All land use zones experience growth during the expansion phase, particularly the RBD, strip commercial areas along the access and beach highways, and the residential zones. Along the beachfront, the RBD zone expands laterally from its original core as more hotels, motels, and recreation-oriented businesses are constructed (fig. 6). The remainder of the beachfront, save perhaps for less stable inlet-flanking beaches and overwash zones, becomes filled in with summer homes. The better-drained central sections of the resort area, site of the initial subdivision plats, are subject to extensive vacation home construction. The dredging and filling of wetlands increases, especially if little property remains available for development in other zones of the island, and demand for private boat docking facilities is high.

Very discrete zones of land use characterize this stage of resort evolution: 1) the RBD is the zone of the concentration of most recreation businesses and lodging facilities; 2) additional commercial development flanks the approach highway, the distal ends of the RBD, and perhaps

Fig. 6. Linear beachfront sprawl resulting from recreational development, near Progreso, Yucatán.

strips along the beach highway; and 3) vacation housing, both beach- and backbay-oriented, comprises the remainder of resort development. As the land suitable for development is filled, the settlement expansion phase is complete and resort growth levels off into a stage of maturation.

Land use Intensification

Residential development in resorts dating to the 1960s or before consisted almost exclusively of detached single-family units, but since about 1970 multi-unit structures, including townhouses and condominiums, have become more prevalent. If more intensive, i.e. high-rise, forms of land use become adopted during the active settlement expansion stage, the number of potential housing units per unit area will increase. The varying degrees of land use intensification do not constitute a requisite stage of resort evolution, but rather reflect a high sustained recreational demand (either real or perceived by developers), which in turn will modify the pre-existing resort morphology.

Land use intensification can occur by means of two primary mechanisms: 1) the introduction of higher density forms of land use during the active settlement expansion phase, which has the effect of continually raising the theoretical carrying capacity, prolonging the settlement expansion stage, and thereby delaying onset of the maturation stage; or 2) "redevelopment," in which a pre-existing form of land use is replaced by one of higher density. The first mechanism is reflected in the landscape by condominiums and multi-unit structures occupying distal beachfront zones and remaining undeveloped wetlands (fig. 7). Although state and federal legislation in the United States placed increasing restrictions on development in wetlands beginning in the 1970s, condominium developers nonetheless are still able to placate regulatory agencies by various means (such as leaving a strip of wetlands at the land-water interface).

Contemporaneous with the multi-unit construction in the formerly less desirable sectors of the island, pressures for redevelopment of older (and prime) real estate mount. Older commercial structures and beachfront cottages become replaced by high-rise hotels and condominiums as rising property taxes force cottage owners to sell to developers who then consolidate small properties and lobby for variances to existing zoning laws. Land use intensification can also be stimulated by destructive hurricanes which instantly remove older, low-density forms of land use (e.g. beach cottages) and subsequently facilitate the transfer of property to such high-rise developers. The net result is that severe storms may increase levels of recreational development rather than decrease them. Hurricane Frederic in 1979 stimulated such redevelopment at Gulf Shores, Alabama, for example.

Fig. 7. Land use intensification at Ft. Myers Beach. Wetlands removal in progress at right was halted by legislative action.

The two mechanisms of land use intensification lead to two differing morphologic responses in the landscape. The first, whereby land use intensification is a continuation of the settlement expansion process, continues the pattern of discrete land use zonation already established. The redevelopment mechanism, however, leads to a hodge-podge of land uses that often stimulates public protests against continued development. In theory, the process of redevelopment may continue until only multi-unit structures occupy the island, but increasing public opposition to destruction of an earlier, idyllic resort landscape coupled with federal and state wetlands preservation efforts often result in legislation limiting the amount of further development. Such legislation both defines an arbitrary carrying capacity for the specific resort and also freezes in situ the rampant morphologic transformations so characteristic of the land use intensification stage. Thus, vestiges of relict resort landscapes are often preserved amongst the towering symbols of modern resort landscapes.

Maturation

In the proposed final stage of resort evolution, a level of maturation is reached. All potentially developable land has been developed, either low-density or high-density, and equilibrium conditions have been reached.

Except perhaps for replacement construction, no new construction is taking place, and levels of visitation by recreationists and tourists have stabilized.

The development level at which maturation sets in depends upon a variety of factors including market demand, land use regulation, and environmental regulation. Assuming sustained market demand, areal expansion will continue until political or physical growth boundaries are reached. Even less suitable micro-environments such as wetlands and unstable shorelines bordering tidal inlets are subject to development if sufficient demand exists and no prohibitive laws have yet been implemented. A low-demand resort such as Grand Isle (fig. 8) has reached the maturation stage prior to extensive wetland modification or land use intensification, while Fort Myers Beach has reached that level prematurely because wetlands and zoning legislation abruptly halted active land use intensification processes (fig. 9).

Applicability of the Resort Morphology Model

Although the proposed resort morphology model does not adequately model the new, self-contained resort complexes, it is useful in documenting the evolution of established resorts and predicting uncontrolled future

Fig. 8. Grand Isle, a low-intensity, mature resort. Note beach nourishment project in progress in 1984.

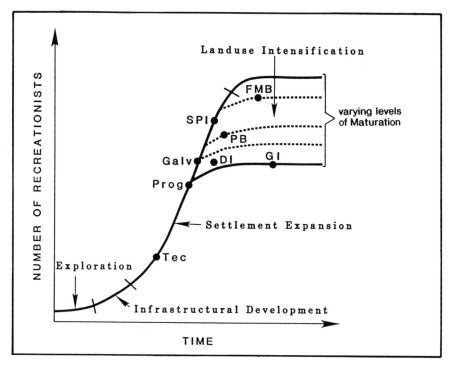

Fig. 9. Stage of resort development at the study sites. (see Fig. 3 for key)

courses of evolution. If a particular resort exhibits sustained recreational demand, as in southern Florida, then all development stages can be expected to occur. Planning agencies must then decide at what level of land use intensification resort development should be slowed. By setting an arbitrary cap on levels of development and levels of tourism, a resort can be steered into a maturation level both profitable for vested interests and still appealing to tourists and recreationists. Sanibel Island, Florida, may be a good example of this process.

In a more historical sense, the Gulf of Mexico resorts examined in this study fit the S-curve conceptual model on the basis of their individual morphologies coupled with growth-visitation data (fig. 9). The two Mexican resort areas (Tecolutla, Veracruz, and Progreso, Yucatán) are still in a settlement expansion stage. Since 1987, high-rise hotel construction has begun near Progreso, thereby launching resort evolution into the land use intensification stage. In spite of a poor Mexican economy, recreational demand by a Mérida hinterland is still increasing. The two Texas resorts are in a land use intensification stage, but more as part of the latter settlement expansion stage. Both Galveston Island and South Padre Island still have sufficient space into which to expand, and visitation levels are still increasing. But whether market demand exists to occupy the Texas-size supply of high-rises is questionable, especially at remote South Padre Island (fig. 10). The two Florida resorts are at maturation levels, but at differing levels of land use intensity. The maturation level at Fort Myers Beach has now been arbitrarily frozen, and at Pensacola Beach, residents and planning authorities are grappling with deciding at what levels to freeze development. Grand Isle and Dauphin Island have both suffered from negative environmental images, and the resulting low recreational demand has led the two resorts into a low-density maturation level.

Acknowledgements

This paper, based upon data initially presented at the 84th annual meetings of the Association of American Geographers in Phoenix, April 7-10, 1988, and at the LSU Culture, Form, and Place Symposium February 23-25, 1990, is partially derived from work supported by the National Science Foundation under Grant No. SES-8507500. Any opinions, findings, and conclusions or recommendations expressed are those of the author and do not necessarily reflect the views of the National Science Foundation.

Fig. 10. South Padre Island, a high-intensity resort with much vacant space for potential expansion.

References

Barrett, J. A. 1958. *The seaside resort towns of England and Wales.* Ph.D. diss., Department of Geography, London University, London.

Butler, R. W. 1980. The concept of a tourist area cycle of evolution: Implications for management of resources. *Canadian Geographer* 24:5-12

Christaller, W. 1963. Some considerations of tourism location in Europe: The peripheral regions — underdeveloped countries — recreation areas. *Regional Science Association Papers, XII Land Congress,* 95-105

Cohen, E. 1972. Toward a sociology of international tourism. *Social Research* 39:164-182

Gilbert, E. W. 1939. The growth of inland and seaside health resorts in England. *Scottish Geographical Magazine* 55:16-35

——. 1949. The growth of Brighton. *Geographical Journal* 114:30-52

Jones, S. B. 1933. Mining and tourist towns in the Canadian Rockies. *Economic Geography* 9:368-378

Lavery, P. 1971. *Recreational geography.* New York: Wiley and Sons.

Meyer-Arendt, K. J. 1987. *Resort evolution along the Gulf of Mexico littoral: Historical, morphological, and environmental aspects.* Ph.D. diss. Department of Geography and Anthropology, Louisiana State University, Baton Rouge.

Pigram, J. J. 1977 Beach resort morphology. *Habitat International* 2:525-541

Stansfield, C. A., Jr. 1971. The nature of seafront development and social status of seaside resorts. *Society and Leisure* 4:117-148.

Sullivan, C. L. 1988. *Hurricanes of the Mississippi Gulf Coast, 1717 to present.* Biloxi, MS: Gulf Publishing Company.

Taylor, V. 1975. The recreation business district: A component of the East London urban morphology. *South African Geographer* 5:139-144.

Wolfe, R. I. 1952. Wasaga Beach — The divorce from the geographic environment. *Canadian Geographer* 2:57-66.

——. 1962. The summer resorts of Ontario in the nineteenth century. *Ontario History* 54:149-161.

Landscape Transformation in Ontario's Norfolk Sand Plain

Samuel R. Sheldon

Abstract

During the early decades of the twentieth century Ontario's Norfolk Sand Plain changed from a minor "dust bowl" to one of the wealthiest agricultural regions in the province. Two factors are of paramount importance in explaining the dramatic landscape transformation that occurred between 1900 and 1930. First, a comprehensive reforestation program initiated shortly after the turn of the century succeeded in stabilizing soil conditions and making rural residents cognizant of sound conservation practices. Second, flue-cured (or "Virginia leaf") tobacco was introduced to the area in 1923. The light-textured soils of the Norfolk Sand Plain proved ideally suited to the cultivation of Virginia leaf, and by the late 1920s a highly productive tobacco culture was in place throughout the region.

Key words: flue-cured tobacco, land degradation, Norfolk Sand Plain, reforestation, St. Williams Forestry Station

Introduction

Ontario's rural economy has a long and variegated history. The livelihood of its country residents has, at one time or another, been directly linked to subsistence agriculture, commercial lumbering, and a variety of market-oriented crops. Nowhere in Ontario have the contours of a fluctuating rural economy been more visible than in the Norfolk Sand Plain, a physiographic region comprising some 1,200 square miles in the province's southeastern sector (fig. 1). During the early decades of the twentieth century, this triangular-shaped region (which adjoins Lake Erie and includes most of the former Norfolk County, the eastern end of Elgin County, and small portions of Brant and Oxford Counties) was transformed from the poorest to one of the wealthiest agricultural landscapes in the province. The same land described as "worthless" for farming in 1900 sustained one

Culture, Form, and Place: Essays in Cultural and Historical Geography, edited by Kent Mathewson, 1993. Geoscience and Man, vol. 32, pp. 325-344. Department of Geography and Anthropology, Louisiana State University, Baton Rouge, LA 70893-6010.

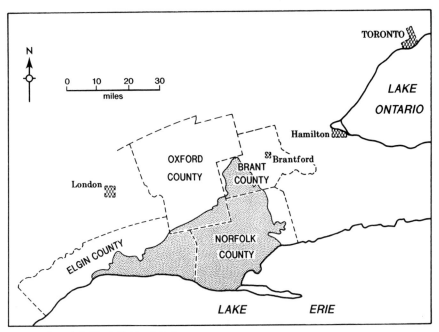

Fig. 1. Ontario's Norfolk Sand Plain

of Canada's most profitable agricultural endeavors by 1930. This paper details the factors effecting the Norfolk Sand Plain's dramatic transformation between 1900 and 1930.

The Physical Setting

The roller coaster fortunes of Norfolk Sand Plain residents are attributable, in part, to the productive capacity of the region's soils. Soil composition, in turn, is largely a consequence of the last glacial period. During the Wisconsin phase, southern Ontario was covered by continental ice and glacial meltwaters. As the ice sheet receded, eroded sediments carried by streams from adjacent highlands were deposited in large shallow lakes that formed south of the glacier in the vicinity of present-day Lake Erie. These sands mixed with lake clay beds to form the soils upon which most of Ontario's crops are produced. The sand-clay mix varies in different sections of Ontario. For example, sand deposits are less evident in Ontario's southwestern section. There, the soils are dominated by clays and loams. At the turn of the century these "heavy" soils supported a flourishing rural economy in Essex and Kent Counties dominated by the production of dark tobacco used in cigars and pipes. In contrast, sands and silts were deposited in much greater quantity in south central Ontario. They reach thicknesses in excess of sixty-five feet in places (Presant and Acton 1984, 12). They currently constitute the dominant surface material throughout the Norfolk Sand Plain, with over 80% of the region's soils classified as sand or sandy loam (Chapman and Putnam 1966, 87).

Several soil types are associated with the Norfolk Sand Plain. Among these, the Fox series is particularly noteworthy. It is widely distributed and well suited for the cultivation of flue-cured tobacco. Fox series soils predominate in the northern and western parts of the sand plain. They are typically well-drained and have deep, mature profiles. In the southeastern section the sand layer thins and moisture is held closer to the surface, resulting in a poorly drained soil classified as Watrin sand. Plainfield sand is also commonplace throughout the Norfolk Sand Plain. A course, well-drained soil, it is more lightly textured than the Fox series types, has a shallower profile, and is notable for its susceptibility to blowing and drifting. The inherent fertility of the Norfolk Sand Plain's sandy soils is low. They contain little organic content, tend to be droughty, and nutrients are rapidly leached out of the upper horizons. They are also easily eroded by wind if regularly cultivated and left unprotected.

Pre-settlement survey maps and early travelers' accounts of vegetation on the Norfolk Sand Plain depict an area of diverse forest cover dominated by stands of white pine and oak. Sugar maple, beech, and mixed Southern hardwoods prevailed on the best soils, while soft maple and elm occupied similar but poorly drained soils, particularly on elevated lands between watersheds. Oak associations ("oak openings") were common in the sandier areas. White pine grew in stands on the better drained soils. In general, the eastern half of the Norfolk Sand Plain had a higher proportion of broad-leaved hardwood trees while pine obtained in the west. The pine forests were particularly significant because of their size and quality. In his seminal work detailing the North American assault on Canadian forests, A.R.M. Lower (1938, 119) writes:

> Some of the largest pine trees on record and some of the heaviest stands of pine per acre were originally to be found in that part of Upper Canada lying along Lake Erie...westward from the Niagara River, the country contiguous to the lake shore contains many sandy tracts of little use for agriculture, but able apparently to grow pine to perfection.

Hotchkiss (1898, 20), in his history of North America's lumber and forest industries notes that, "in the region embraced by the counties of Haldimand, Norfold, Brant, and Elgin, pine quality has never been exceeded by that of any other section of the continent." This includes the pines that grew on the Norfolk Sand Plain.

One of the first descriptions of Norfolk Sand Plain vegetation was penned by a Reverend J. Proudfoot. During the course of his travels through the region in the early 1800s, Proudfoot made the following observations:

> Left Mr. Lalor's (on Otter Creek) this morning in a waggon which we engaged to take us 18 miles for $2. Upon leaving his house we entered upon the sandy ridges which extend over the remainder of Bayham. The part of Houghton through which the Talbot Street runs and the whole of Middleton, the timber is all pine not very heavy but closely set; now and then we saw a little hard-wood. The soil is the worst I have seen. The small clearings which we passed begun to be covered with pine and were fast relapsing to the domain of the forest. While we were at Sovereign's tavern (Delhi) there was a man going to Vittoria with a waggon and two horses, and he took us for $1. The road is all down hill. At first it was oak plains, where the soil is sandy but good for wheat, then pine flats, where we saw some of the handsomest pine trees I have ever seen (London and Middlesex Historical Society n.d., 25).

Although trees dominated the landscape it is obvious from Proudfoot's account that not all of the Norfolk Sand Plain was covered with forest. Indeed, after journeying to Long Point, one early nineteenth century traveler commented:

> When I first visited this part of the Province the sudden change which took place in the aspect of nature seemed like magic. The soil became light and sandy, the forests had dwindled away, and natural groves and copses met the eye in their stead. The fields were beautifully level, and the uncultivated lands had more the appearance of a pleasure-ground than of a wilderness. The trees being few in number, and distributed in beautiful clumps, did not at all suggest the idea of a forest (Howison 1821, cited in Ladell and Ladell 1986, 149).

Early Settlement and Deforestation

The exploitation of Norfolk's pine-oak forests was probably inevitable as settlers pushed into the region beginning in the 1790s. At the onset they practiced mixed farming and grazed cattle on the oak plains. In the eyes of the pioneer farmer, the surrounding forest was perceived as a barrier to sustenance and success; it stood between him and the establishment of his farm. Not surprisingly, trees were felled as rapidly as possible in order to clear land and plant crops. Clearing the land proved to be a long and arduous task. Most farmers were considered fortunate if they opened up more than a few acres annually. One of the initial settlers clearing in the Norfolk County township of Windham recounted the difficulties of forest clearing in southern Ontario:

When I commenced here I laid out to clear about ten acres a year, and I guess I averaged about that much. There was pure timber scattered all over the hull lot. In some places it was 'sap-pine,' an' stood thick on the ground, an' in other places it was big white pine, some of which was four feet, or over, in diameter. No man who never had any experience in clearin' pine land forty or fifty years ago, knows anything about the amount of labor involved in the undertaking (Owen 1898, 243-44).

A description of Norfolk County in 1851 provides insights on both the sheer number of man-hours required to clear the native vegetation and pioneer attitudes regarding the forest.

In some localities the preparation of lumber engrosses more of the attention of the settlers than agricultural operations, and is likely to do so till the pine woods are exhausted, which, at the rate the destruction of the forests is now carried on, is likely to be the case in a few years; this, however, is not much to be regretted, as the improvement and cultivation of the land, and consequent enrichment of the district must necessarily follow (Smith ca. 1851, 118-119).

Sawmills appeared and quickly spread across the pioneer landscape to meet local demand for wood products. One of the first settlers in Langton, a small farm community near the center of the Norfolk Sand Plain, described the region as a "booming place...one with trees everywhere, especially white pine, and numerous sawmills and very little cleared land" (Moore 1985).

The use of woodlands for local needs gave way to commercial forestry beginning about 1830. Pine became a major trade item as professional loggers moved into the area to supply timber for British markets and the expanding provincial plank road network. Even more important was the seemingly insatiable demand for forestry products in the United States. Tariffs on logs and unplaned lumber were eliminated under terms of the 1854 Reciprocity Treaty between Canada and the U.S. The subsequent "free trade" era accelerated U.S. imports of Canadian forest products. Norfolk's proximity to U.S. markets and improved transport systems fostered the emergence of a number of coastal "boom towns" on Lake Erie's north shore. Port Burwell in eastern Elgin County became one of the most successful. Located at the mouth of the Big Otter Creek, Port Burwell was initially surveyed in 1830. By mid-century a dozen water-powered sawmills were floating logs downstream to Port Burwell. Larger, steam-operated mills capable of cutting 40,000 feet of lumber a day began operations in Port Burwell after 1850. In 1851, a twenty-five-mile-long plank and gravel road was completed from Port Burwell inland to Ingersoll. It quickly became the major north-south trunkline through the western part of the Norfolk Sand Plain. Timber and produce previously moved by water could now be transported to Lake Erie by land as well. During the heyday of the lumber boom, as many as ten schooners loaded wood products in the Port Burwell harbor at the same time. In 1859, over 8,400,000 feet of sawed timber, 3,142,500 shingles, and 949 cords of shingle wood were loaded onto 193 vessels at the port (Haggan 1976, 5-6).

Commercial forestry in the sand plain peaked around 1880. By the 1890s it was virtually nonexistent. Despite its brevity, the lumber industry had a profound impact on the Norfolk Sand Plain. In less than 50 years the townships of the region lost roughly two-thirds of their forest cover (table 1). By 1900 the pine-oak forests that had dominated the landscape a century earlier had been reduced to about 15-20% of the total land area (Ontario Department of Planning and Development 1953, 4). Deforestation led to generalized environmental degradation. The loss of woodlands altered the run off/percolation ratio, accelerating soil erosion. Springs and creeks dried up; stream and river levels fluctuated widely. Less vegetation increased summer droughts and allowed winter snow cover to be blown from fields, drifting across highways. Rural residents were faced with shortages of fuelwood and timber for building and fencing (Kelly 1974, 3-4).

Table 1. The percentage of wooded land remaining in townships of the Norfolk Sand Plain, 1851-1891

Township	1851	1891
Bayham (Elgin)	77.8	26.1
Burford (Brant)	65.9	16.4
Charlotteville (Norfolk)	69.2	31.7
Houghton (Norfolk)	87.8	35.9
Malahide (Elgin)	74.5	23.3
Middleton (Norfolk)	89.6	36.5
Norwich South (Oxford)	78.3	22.9
Oakland (Brant)	n.a.	n.a.
Walsingham North (Norfolk)	81.9	31.0
Walsingham South (Norfolk)	89.6	34.9
Windham (Norfolk)	71.4	26.1
Average:	78.6	28.5

Source: Estimated from Census of Canada figures (Dominion Bureau of Statistics 1882-1933).

Post-Forestry Developments

With the decline of commercial forestry, agriculture resurfaced as the primary economic activity on the Norfolk Sand Plain. During the early phases of the forestry era, wheat farming remained profitable, but neglected. After the 1850s, however, the center of wheat production shifted westward to the soil rich prairie provinces. Rural residents cultivating and harvesting a variety of crops (including wheat, corn, rye, and peas) on the sand plain during the 1870s, 1880s, and 1890s discovered that the loss of woodlands increased the subsistence challenge. The light-textured, sandy soils proved easy to work, but the humus that developed under centuries of forest cover and enhanced soil fertility was quickly exhausted when regular cropping practices were employed. As wind ablation increased, agricultural yields declined. One contemporary farmer summarized the frustration of working the land when he remarked, "I sow 10 bushels of rye to get 5 back" (MacLaren 1983, 13). As substantial areas of the Norfolk Sand Plain turned to desert and farming deteriorated to the subsistence level, country folk abandoned the region in increasing numbers after 1880.

Norfolk County, a political subdivision comprising a sizable portion of the Norfolk Sand Plain (and which currently constitutes the western half of the Regional Municipality of Haldimand-Norfolk), experienced a demographic decline between 1881 and 1921 that was typical of the sand plain. By 1881 slightly more then one-half of the county's land was cleared and cropped to fall and spring wheat, barley, rye, oats, and corn (Ontario Agricultural Commission 1881, Appendix B). Twenty-four percent of the area remained timbered, but approximately seventy percent of Norfolk's 634 square miles was covered with sand, sandy loam, and gravelly soils (Harcourt and Ruhnke 1928, 5). By 1900, so much of Norfolk's land was depleted of plant nutrients or severely wind eroded that twenty percent of the county was considered unfit for general agriculture (Hall 1952, 42). Environmental degradation was most severe in South Walsingham township. In 1901 the Provincial Director of Forestry noted that approximately forty percent of South Walsingham's total area (21,640 of 54,000 acres) was classified as "wasteland" (Provincial Director of Forestry 1902, 26). Not surprisingly, farm abandonment in Norfolk County became commonplace after 1880. The rural population was 28,618 in 1881. It dropped to 22,741 in 1901, and bottomed out at 18,423 in 1921 (a decline of almost ten percent per decade) (Hilborn 1970, 83).

The remaining farmers scratched a meager living sowing various field crops and raising pigs and poultry. Farm houses and outbuildings went unpainted and unrepaired, many farmers were unable to pay taxes, and the rural economy slipped into deep depression. By 1900 Norfolk County was one of the poorest agricultural areas in Canada. It was described as a "desert," where roads were plowed of sand during the summer months, "roving deeds" were essential because the soil moved about so freely, and, as a local joke had it, any rabbit crossing a hundred-acre farm had to pack his lunch. A long-time resident of the region summarized conditions in the Norfolk Sand Plain during the early years of the twentieth century as follows:

> Most of the district was worthless sand waste. The area was covered with sand dunes similar to snow drifts in winter, and the land was almost incapable of producing a living for the inhabitants, the farms selling for a few dollars an acre, if a farmer could get rid of his farm at all (Streefkerk 1984, 1) (figs. 2 and 3).

The Landscape Transformation

The environmental degradation that had characterized the Norfolk Sand Plain in the decades before and immediately after 1900 was largely reversed by the time of the onset of the Great Depression. By 1930 the sand plain was experiencing a settlement renaissance. Farms which sold for ten dollars an acre in 1920 were selling for ten times that a decade later.

One measure of the rapid changes occurring during this period can be gleaned from the memoirs of Ford A. Stinson, Head of the Agriculture Canada Research Station at Delhi from 1935 to 1949. Stinson recalls that:

> There was a little farm of about 30 acres (near Delhi) that was real blow sand. It was drifting, and there was sand piled up....I thought, 'goodness sakes, I should buy that land and see if I couldn't plant some trees or something to nail down the sand.' But they wanted $300, and I didn't have $300. A few years later I had $300, but they wanted $3,000 then, and well, I didn't have $3,000. Then, the next time I asked, they wanted $30,000. So that's the way it was — there was lots and lots of land that you could buy in Norfolk for $10 an acre, if you had $10 (Tobacco History Museum display 1989).

Two factors largely explain the Norfolk Sand Plain's transformation from a "dust bowl" into a prosperous farming region. First, in response to the rapid topsoil loss following deforestation, the provincial government established a forestry station in southern Norfolk County at St. Williams in 1908. Second, flue-cured (or "Virginia leaf") tobacco was introduced to the sand plain in 1923. Within a decade it emerged as the region's economic mainstay.

Establishing a forestry station was one outgrowth of Ontario's conservation movement that dated back to the middle of the nineteenth century. As early as the 1860s the Board of Agriculture of Upper Canada and the *Canadian Agriculturalist* published a series of articles detailing the negative impact of deforestation on the environment. By the 1870s, farmers began

Fig. 2. Scene at the border of the sand plain in Charlotteville Township, southern Norfolk County. Photo taken in 1905.

Fig. 3. Abandoned farmstead in Charlotteville Township, ca. 1910.

to see the consequences of overclearing and the need to regenerate woodlands. In 1871 the Ontario legislature passed an "Act to encourage the planting of trees upon the highways in the Province," and the 1879 report of the Fruit Growers Association of Ontario argued that:

> The Fruit Growers Association need to put forth their best efforts to husband our Dominion and Provincial resources in their timber limits — to carefully instruct the farming community how much depends on the judicious planting of forest trees, their presence producing abundant rainfall, preserving and distributing moisture, and thereby forming a preventative against drought and devastating floods (Zavitz 1908-09, 1).

By the end of the century, forest preservation had emerged as a central theme in maintaining Ontario's environmental integrity. As Kelly (1974, 10) notes in his summary of the conservation ethic that prevailed throughout the province during the late 1800s:

> An image of a reforested agricultural southern Ontario was formulated during the last two decades of the nineteenth century. Large blocks of forest were envisioned, located on the larger areas of land too sandy or rocky for cultivation and on the major heights of land. The highways were to be lined with shade trees. Several farm woodlots together would clothe the summits and steeper slopes of hills. Every farm would have at least a ten acre woodlot and a grid of fieldside plantings would shelter the crops. Small groves would shelter the farm houses and be scattered through the permanent pastures, and thickets would snake across the countryside, marking and protecting the banks of water courses.

After 1900 the local newspapers, regional journals, and government reports promoting revitalization of degraded landscapes in southern Ontario increasingly emphasized reforestation of waste and abandoned lands. Academic institutions also entered the fray. The "Ontario Agricultural and Experimental Union," a loosely-knit consortium of faculty and students at the Ontario Agricultural College at Guelph, passed a resolution at their annual meeting in 1902 that stated, in part:

> The Experimental Union, recognizing the urgent necessity for action in the reforesting of the wastelands throughout Old Ontario, would recommend that the Department of Crown Lands be requested to provide material sufficient to reforest areas sufficiently large to provide forest conditions in typical situations throughout Ontario, the Union undertaking to supervise the distribution (Zavitz 1964, 3).

Ontario's "wastelands" became the subject of extensive research by Edmund John Zavitz, widely known as the "father of reforestation in Ontario." Zavitz developed an interest in forestry while studying for a B.A. degree at McMaster University. After receiving an M.S. degree in forestry from the University of Michigan in 1905, Zavitz was appointed Lecturer in Forestry at the Ontario Agricultural College (O.A.C.) at Guelph. Zavitz later became Deputy Minister of Forestry in the Provincial Department of Lands and Forests, and served as Chief Forester for the province of Ontario until his retirement in 1953.

When Zavitz joined the O.A.C. staff, he was assigned the responsibilities of developing an on-campus forest nursery to supply trees for reforestation, and surveying the barren areas adjacent to Lake Erie. He visited the Norfolk Sand Plain numerous times between 1905-1907 and reported his findings in a published memorandum entitled *Reforestation of Waste Lands in Southern Ontario* in 1908. Zavitz identified Norfolk County as one of the most seriously degraded in Ontario, and he outlined the procedures by which the county's blow sand areas could be reforested. Zavitz' recommendations were apparently influenced by the pioneering reforestation efforts of a few Norfolk residents. One "pioneer" was a St. Williams businessman named Walter F. McCall who used local timber in his sawmill and furniture factory. The mill was located at the edge of a large sand dune that in earlier years had been heavily wooded. McCall witnessed firsthand the deforestation wrought by his business operation, and in 1905 he embarked on a personal crusade to reverse the process. During the spring of that year he planted a row of saplings adjacent to his sawmill.

Walter McCall's attempts to plant trees in the sand attracted the interest of Lieutenant Colonel Arthur C. Pratt, an old friend of McCall's. Pratt had been elected to the Provincial Legislature in 1905, and as a lifelong resident of the region, he knew the dramatic landscape changes that had taken place in Norfolk. Moreover, he believed county soils could once again support a forest vegetation. He recalled that:

> As a youth I had rambled all over south Norfolk. On my fathers farm in North Walsingham we still had some of the massive pine trees that were the pride of Norfolk lumbermen. In every township were stands of virgin timber, including the great White Pine, which was king of them all. As I grew up, I saw these great trees gradually disappear....I knew that our land in Norfolk would grow pine, and we had plenty of suitable nursery soils in the waste sandy land that remained after the lumbermen were through with their work. I talked with John Backus, Alex McCall, Walter and Bruce McCall and others. All were agreed that we should have reforestation and that Norfolk was ideal for nursery work (Pearce n.d., 121-122).

Impressed with McCall's attempts to convert Norfolk's blow sand into woodlots, Pratt broached the idea of reforesting the region to the Provincial legislature in 1905, 1906, and again in 1907, but no action was taken. About this time, however, Pratt and McCall were able to enlist the support of Zavitz. The two men took Zavitz through the sand dunes to the mill site to see the juxtaposition of barren land and incipient reforestation. Zavitz incorporated much of what he witnessed into his 1908 memorandum. Zavitz submitted a formal reforestation program to Pratt, and Pratt placed it before a session of the Ontario legislature. In 1908 the legislature approved the plan. Later that year, the Provincial government bought one hundred acres of land (at $10 per acre) in South Walsingham Township for a tree nursery. Pratt recalled the events leading up to the Ontario legislature's approval of the reforestation as follows:

> When the budget debate got under way in 1908, I gave the house some history of the early days in Norfolk, of the great pine that the early settlers found; of the tall trees from Norfolk forests that went for masts to the British Navy. Finally, Hon. Frank Cochrane, who was now Minister of Lands and Forests, agreed to come with me to see the conditions in Norfolk first hand. We traveled for miles over sandy land, some of which had fine timber growth, and the Minister was amazed at what he saw. Two hours after our return to Toronto, the Minister phoned to tell me that an order-in-council would be passed to provide $5,000 to take up the land options and to start work on the project (Pearce n.d., 122).

The land was mostly submarginal, in a part of southern Norfolk County dotted with vacant farmsteads that had been selling for as little as $5 an acre. In government hands, the site became known as Provincial Forest Station No. 1, St. Williams.

During its initial years, the main function of the St. Williams Forestry Farm was to foster reforestation in Norfolk and adjoining counties. The station's small staff began their efforts in the spring of 1909. They scattered brush on the ground to halt blowing sand, planted over 350,000 seedlings, sodded sandy areas contiguous to the station, and established a rudimentary system of windbreaks. By 1920 seedling production at St. Williams had increased to 3,000,000, and their inventory stood at 1,178,139 trees, representing thirty different species (Mutrie 1988, 68). This included a number of non-indigenous conifers such as Scots pine, red pine, and jack pine. Hundreds of thousands of seedlings were distributed free of charge to area residents. St. Williams staff members traveled to surrounding communities to demonstrate proper planting techniques and convince the local citizenry that timber could be grown successfully on "desert" lands. While planting small pines on sandy lands was initially ridiculed by many farmers, the positive results soon gained the active support of the local populace. By 1919 almost three and one-half million saplings had been distributed to residents of Norfolk and surrounding counties. Many private land owners established woodlots on the waste portions of their farms (Coons 1981, 19). These woodlots initially took the form of copses of pine trees and other conifers on dunes to stabilize the sand hills.

Throughout the 1910s and 1920s the station experimented with different species, spacings, and mixtures of trees to discover which tree combinations were best suited to the region's sandy soils (fig. 4). Windbreaks planted at the forestry farm as an example of how erosion could be abated had a notable effect on local farmers. After it was discovered that the light soils of the Norfolk Sand Plain could produce marketable tobacco, reforestation efforts at St. Williams shifted from providing planting stock for woodlots to establishing windbreaks. Farmers quickly saw that wind breaks and shelter belts not only slowed top soil loss, but also reduced abrasive damage to their new crop (fig. 5).

The reforestation and land reclamation programs instituted by the St. Williams Station quickly bore fruit. By 1930 most of the blow sand in Norfolk County and vicinity was under control. Rows of trees serving as windbreaks and shelter belts dotted the landscape, and farmers employed a variety of soil conservation practices (fig. 6). Small, privately owned woodlots (or "plantations") quickly spread throughout the region. By the 1950s Norfolk County had 5,000 to 6,000 acres in woodlots largely planted in red, white, and Scots pine. This acreage represented slightly more than half the area originally estimated to be wasteland in the county (Hilborn 1970, 82). Thus, in only a few decades, the conservation practices promoted by the forestry officials and adopted by local farmers succeeded in reversing a century's worth of land degradation and neglect.

Fig. 4. Woodlot of red and white pine planted in 1910 at the St. Williams Forest Station.

Fig. 5. Pine windbreak sheltering tobacco crop, Norfolk County.

Fig. 6. Tree-lined rural road in Charlotteville Township, ca. 1940.

The Advent of Tobacco

The second catalyst to dramatically alter the rural landscape of the Norfolk Sand Plain after 1900 was the introduction of flue-cured tobacco. The sand plains' light-textured soils had proven ill-suited to the sustained cultivation of cereal grains and row crops. Traditional Ontario farming practices that succeeded on heavier soils, such as fall plowing, spring disking for seedbeds, and cultivating row crops after each summer rain to maintain a "dust mulch," only served to enhance wind and water erosion and destroy organic matter in the region's sandy soils. The derelict farms that appeared with increasing regularity made Norfolk County, in the words of one contemporary observer, a "source of official embarrassment" (Stinson 1989, n.p.).

The Norfolk Sand Plains potential for growing flue-cured tobacco was first recognized by a soil specialist from Greenville County, South Carolina. In 1917, Henry Freeman moved to Ottawa to work as a soil chemist for the Dominion Experimental Farms. In response to a request from a Norfolk County fruit farm administrator for a soil analysis, Freeman went to the small community of Lynedoch during the spring of 1919 to collect soil samples. Freeman's analysis suggested that the sandy soil was well suited for tobacco cultivation, despite its low fertility. In 1920 and 1921 experimental plots of burley tobacco were raised in the Lynedoch area under Freeman's supervision. The crops proved successful, but the burley market all but disappeared in 1921 when the price per pound dropped from 50¢ to 10¢ (Pearce, n.d. 134). Freeman decided to turn his attention to flue-cured tobacco. The worldwide increase in cigarette smoking that occurred during and after World War I had fostered a renewed interest in the milder and more finely textured "Virginia leaf" tobacco. During the summer of 1923 Freeman and an American associate produced and harvested their first commercial crop of Virginia leaf on about twenty-five acres of land. Years later one of the growers who worked for Freeman recounted the birth of Norfolk County's flue-cured tobacco industry:

> That first crop provided a real thrill for all of us. We had a perfect growing season and the plants ripened beautifully....farm neighbors around Lynedoch watched as the smoke rose from the flues in the four kilns. They did not hesitate to call the experiment a hazardous and foolhardy one. But when the harvest was in and the crop was safely stored in the pack barn, and buyers pronounced it a fine quality of leaf and paid a good price for it, the tobacco fever took hold and soon many growers were flocking to buy up cheap land (Stinson 1989, n.p.).

The Norfolk Sand Plain proved ideal for growing tobacco because well-drained soils ranging in texture from sandy to sandy loam produce the highest quality Virginia leaf. Drainage is particularly important in that the tobacco plant does not tolerate "wet feet." Well-drained open soils permit good aeration, allowing rapid and healthy root growth and early maturity. Moreover, tobacco is a heat-loving crop that does best on sandy surfaces where rapidly drained soils dry out quickly and retain their warmth (Sheidow 1989).

The discovery that the Norfolk Sand Plain could produce tobacco on soils thought to be of little economic value quickly attracted growers from eastern Canada, the southeastern United States, and Europe. By the mid-1920s, the same area that had been a "source of official embarrassment" was experiencing a "green gold rush." Hundreds of outsiders were lured by the prospect of producing a high value cash crop on land purchased for a pittance. This influx of migrants helped reverse a long-standing depopulation trend in the Norfolk Sand Plain. Population in the sand plain townships peaked in 1881 and declined until the early 1920s. By 1931, however, the area experienced a demographic revival that continued into the 1950s (table 2). Land values also skyrocketed with the tobacco boom. It was not uncommon to see the same location in North or South Walsingham Township jump from $5 or $10 an acre as "wasteland" in 1923 to over $1,500 an acre as tobacco land a year or two later.

One measure of the agricultural revolution that swept through the Norfolk Sand Plain after 1923 can be gleaned from a comparison of crop acreage changes between 1921 and 1931. During this period the region's eleven townships collectively experienced an absolute decline in the

Table 2. Population change in Norfolk Sand Plain townships, 1881-1931

Township (County)	1881	1901	1921	1931
Bayham (Elgin))	4,649	3,771	3,438	3,510
Burford (Brant)	5,466	4,512	4,126	3,836
Charlotteville (Norfolk)	4,416	3,464	2,750	3,289
Houghton (Norfolk)	2,071	2,035	1,304	1,444
Malahide (Elgin)	4,415	3,795	3,191	3,045
Middleton (Norfolk)	3,514	2,591	2,057	2,505
Northwich South (Oxford)	3,360	2,664	2,092	2,378
Oakland (Brant)	939	745	889	857
Walsingham North (Norfolk)	5,819	2,359	1,482	2,047
Walsingham South (Norfolk)	—	2,012	1,547	1,710
Windham (Norfolk)	4,913	3,884	3,259	3,677
Population totals:	39,562	31,832	26,135	28,298
Population increase/decrease	—	-7,730	-5,679	+2,163
Percentage increase/decrease	—	-20	-18	+8

Source: Census of Canada data for 1881, 1901, 1921, and 1931 (Dominion Bureau of Statistics 1882-1933).

amount of land devoted to a variety of farm commodities. Indeed, every crop grown on the Norfolk Sand Plain in 1921 was produced on less acreage in 1931. During the same ten year period the land devoted to tobacco growing expanded from zero to over 15,000 acres. By 1932, just under 850 farms produced 26,000,000 pounds of Virginia leaf on 26,000 acres in what became known as the "New Belt" (the "Old Belt" coinciding with portions of Essex and Kent Counties where burley and dark tobacco were dominant) (Musgrave 1934, 284).

Tobacco cultivation diffused rapidly throughout the Norfolk Sand Plain despite some initial problems. Perhaps the greatest danger confronting the fledgling industry was southern Ontario's relatively short growing season. Frost losses were serious enough during the mid to late 1920s that some tobacco men believed the only areas suitable for Virginia leaf were those immediately inland of Lake Erie. The risk of frost loss was greatly reduced by changing tobacco varieties and switching to priming after 1931. In recent years, frost loss has been further reduced by encouraging earlier ripening via changes in fertilization, varieties, and irrigation techniques. Winds also posed difficulties for the pioneer tobacco growers of the Norfolk Sand Plain. Strong on-shore winds passing over the region's lighter soils created blow sands that frequently smothered young plants or exposed plant roots. In 1929, a particularly fierce sandstorm destroyed most of the young tobacco crop and the windswept landscape yielded one of the worst harvests on record. Farmers minimized wind damage by placing hay and brush between rows of tobacco until windbreaks grew to sufficient heights. To restore organic matter to the soil, tobacco men often bought loads of barnyard manure from local farmers strapped for cash. Many growers reasoned that applying large quantities of night soil to the same land year after year would permit high yields on an annual basis. They quickly learned, however, that tobacco mosaic, a virus disease capable of overwintering in the ground, could ruin an entire crop.

Tobacco cultivation on the Norfolk Sand Plain survived the difficulties presented by a limited growing season, desiccating winds, and disease. As the industry flourished, so too did the local populace. The coming of Virginia leaf tobacco created a new chapter in the economic history of the sand plain counties. It was a history marked by prosperous farms, conspicuous consumption, and an optimism previously absent in the area. Throughout the countryside farm houses were refurbished and repainted, derelict buildings were replaced by new ones, fences were mended, and machines appeared with increasing frequency on the landscape. In addition to the direct cash flow accruing to farmers, tobacco stimulated the growth of new banks, stores, real estate offices, and many other businesses. Small enterprises specifically geared to serve the needs of tobacco farmers were established in communities the length and breadth of the sand plain. Welding shops, earth moving companies, greenhouse builders, and drainage contractors were but a few of the businesses founded in response to tobacco farming. The growing commercial value of Virginia leaf also led to the creation of an experimental substation in 1933. Located on the outskirts of Delhi, the federally funded research unit was charged with the responsibility of providing scientific assistance to the tobacco industry.

Expanding flue-cured acreage resulted in substantial increases in property tax assessments, and increased tax revenues converted Norfolk's sand roads into gravelled by-ways and eventually into an extensive network of blacktopped rural roads. Finally, the tobacco "revolution" sparked the growth of the region's towns and villages. Delhi, the self-proclaimed "heart of the tobacco belt," experienced a near four-fold increase in residents between 1920 and 1940. In Norfolk County, where environmental degradation and population decline had been most pronounced at the turn of the century, the number of residents increased by almost 20% between 1921 and 1931 (Dominion Bureau of Statistics, Seventh Census of Canada 1931, 727).

Conclusions

The landscape changes that unfolded on the Norfolk Sand Plain during the first three decades of the twentieth century represent one of the most remarkable environmental transformations in Canadian history. By 1930 the abandoned farms and blow sand of an earlier era had been supplanted by one of the wealthiest agricultural landscapes in the country. Looking back in 1969, an editorial written for the London, Ontario, *Free Press* remarked that the introduction of flue-cured tobacco "transformed the useless sandy soil of southwestern Ontario farms into a rich and flourishing enterprise" (*Free Press* 1969, 6). One of the leading tobacco growers of the period once boasted that there were more flashy automobiles and bottles of good whiskey in Norfolk County and surroundings than in any other farming district in North America. If true, the advent of high priced vehicles and expensive liquor throughout the Norfolk Sand Plain can be attributed to the remarkable reforestation effort launched in 1908 and to the introduction of flue-cured tobacco in 1923.

Underwriting this perceived and actual prosperity was the conjunction of two somewhat contradictory impulses. The conservationist-inspired reforestation program initiated in 1908 showed the remaining farmers how to reverse the process of landscape degradation. The introduction of "bright-leaf" tobacco in 1923 coupled with the 1920s consumer society's market forces and mentality, showed both locals and newcomers how to make money as never before.

References

Chapman, L. J., and Putnam, D. F. 1966. *The physiography of Southern Ontario*. Toronto: University of Toronto Press.

Coons, C. F. 1981. *Reforestation on private lands in Ontario*. Forest Resources Group, Armson Private Land Forestry Review.

Dominion Bureau of Statistics. 1882-1933. *Second to seventh census of Canada, 1881-1931*. Ottawa.

Free Press (London, Ontario). 1969. July 18 editorial, p. 6.

Haggan, I. 1976. *A history of Port Burwell*. Port Burwell, Ontario: Personally typed notes.

Hall, R. B., Jr. 1952. *The introduction of flue-cured tobacco as a commercial crop in Norfolk County*. PhD. diss., University of Michigan, Ann Arbor, Michigan.

Harcourt, R., and Ruhnke, G. H. 1928. *Tobacco soils in Norfolk County*. Guelph, Ontario: Ontario Department of Agriculture.

Hilborn, W. H. 1970. *Forests and forestry of the Norfolk Sand Plain*. Masters thesis, University of Western Ontario, London, Ontario.

Hotchkiss, G. W. 1898. *History of the lumber and forest industry of the Northwest*. Chicago: G. W. Hotchkiss and Co.

Howison, J. 1821. *Sketches of upper Canada*. Edinburgh: Oliver and Boyd.

Kelly, K. 1974. Damaged and efficient landscapes in rural and southern Ontario 1880-1900. *Ontario History* 66:1-14.

Ladell, J., and Ladell, M. 1986. *Inheritance: Ontario's century farms past and present*. Toronto: Dundurn Press.

London and Middlesex Historical Society. n.d. *Transactions*, Part VIII. London, Ontario.

Lower, A.R.M. 1938. *The North American assault on the Canadian forest: A history of the lumber trade between Canada and the United States*. Toronto: Ryerson Press.

MacLaren, D. 1983. Magic of tabacco. *The Canadian Tobacco Grower* 31:13ff.

Moore, D. 1985. Interview conducted by personnel of the Tobacco History Museum (Delhi), December 13.

Musgrave, J. E. T. 1934. Canadian tobacco. *Canadian Geographical Review* 6:277-290.

Mutrie, R. R. 1988. *St. Williams: The history*. Simcoe, Ontario: Second Avenue Printing.

Ontario Agricultural Commission. 1881. *The soil, climate, topographic features, cultivable area and products of, and the progress and conditions of husbandry in the Province of Canada*, Vol. II, App. B. Toronto: C. Blacklett Robinson.

Ontario Department of Planning and Development. 1953. *Big Creek conservation report - 1953*. Toronto.

Owen, E.A. 1898. *Pioneer sketches of Long Point Settlement.* Toronto: William Briggs.

Pearce, B. n.d. *Norfolk's reforestation story.* Historical Highlights of Norfolk County. Simcoe, Ontario: Second Avenue Printing.

Presant, E. W., and Acton, C. J. 1984. *Soils of the regional municipality of Haldimand-Norfolk.* Department of Land Resource Sciences Report No. 57. Guelph, Ontario.

Provincial Director of Forestry. 1902. *Annual report of the Director of Forestry for the Province of Ontario, 1900-1901,* Vol. 34, Part 1. Toronto: L. K. Cameron.

Sheidow, N. 1989. Personal interview conducted October 19.

Smith, W. H. ca. 1851. *Canada: Past, present and future,* Vol. 1. Toronto: Maclear.

Stinson, F. 1989. Personal correspondence dated October 16.

Streekkert, L. 1984. *The effects of the tobacco industry: A study of Delhi, Aylmer, and Tillsonburg.* Monograph.

Tobacco History Museum (Delhi). 1989. July display.

Zavitz, E. J. 1908/09. *Fifty years of reforestation in Ontario.* Toronto: Ontario Department of Lands and Forests.

——. 1964. *Recollections, 1875-1964.* Toronto: Ontario Department of Lands and Forests.

Mind and Matter in Cultural Geography

James M. Blaut

Abstract

Cultural geography in the Kniffen tradition is particularly interested in the material land-scape and material culture. This approach has been criticized from various subjectivist points of view. The most important and famous example is Hartshorne's critique in *The Nature of Ge-ography*. The present paper refutes Hartshorne's arguments and also offers a brief rejoinder to other subjectivist critiques of more recent times. All such critiques are based in an inade-quate appreciation of the importance of space-time process, history, and culture theory.
Key Words: geography, Hartshorne, Kniffen, matter, mind, space

A couple of years ago I went to London. The occasion was an Institute of British Geographers conference entitled "New Directions in Cultural Ge-ography." I had been invited to give one of the papers. It developed that I was the only cultural geographer at this conference on "New Directions in Cultural Geography" who spoke in favor of the main tradition in our field. This is, of course, what most people call the "Sauer tradition," although I prefer to call it the "Sauer-Kniffen tradition." Almost everyone at that con-ference was into something very different: "post-modernism," "post-in-dustrialism," "post-Fordism," "post-Marxism," post-this-ism, post-that-ism. I was, if anything, a post-Sauerist, that is, a Kniffenite.

Now it often happens that the student of a great man goes forth into the world proclaiming the great man's doctrines and gets them all wrong. David Lowenthal was in the audience when I spoke, and Lowenthal, who studied under Sauer, probably thinks of himself as a post-Sauerist and perhaps even as a Kniffenite, since he has an interest in the cultural land-scape. But David Lowenthal, whom I respect very much, is into mind, not matter. He is about as deep into the human mind as Sauer was deep into the material landscape. Lowenthal is an epistemologist. Sauer was an ecol-

Culture, Form, and Place: Essays in Cultural and Historical Geography, edited by Kent Mathewson, 1993. Geoscience and Man, vol. 32, pp. 345-356. Department of Geogra-phy and Anthropology, Louisiana State University, Baton Rouge, LA 70893-6010.

ogist. Lowenthal thinks about time; Sauer thought about evolution. And so on. I do not mean to insult David Lowenthal. My point is that many newer approaches in cultural geography can claim to be rooted in the Sauer-Kniffen tradition, but they may only be fruits of that tradition, better yet wind-blown seeds, borne to places far distant from Berkeley and Baton Rouge. It is possible that my ideas are as distant from the Sauer-Kniffen tradition as are the ideas of Lowenthal and the London post-modernists (Philo 1988), but I doubt it. The issue is very straightforward. It is a question of mind versus matter.

Doubtless some of you are saying to yourselves, "Aha, this fellow Jim Blaut is about to proclaim the virtues of *materialism*. Dialectical materialism. Cultural materialism. Whatever." Of course, it would be laughable to describe the views of Sauer and Kniffen as materialistic in these senses. And I am not a dialectical or cultural materialist. I'm an American Pragmatist, in the intellectual line of Dewey, Mead, and Morris, strongly influenced also by the closely related process philosophy of Whitehead. I have been a pragmatist since the age of six when I began attending Progressive Schools which follow Dewey's philosophy that teaches that the best form of learning is direct experience, activity, hands-on work with the material world. I read the philosophical writings of Dewey, Mead, Morris, and Whitehead in college, and I was fairly clear about my own views before I ever encountered geography.

This autobiographical comment is necessary to my argument. As an undergraduate geography major at the University of Chicago I was told two very different things. First: it is of scientific and practical importance to study the way real human beings use, transform, and fashion things out of the material earth. Second: the science which studies these questions is a science of mind, not matter. Figure that one out. I listened to Derwent Whittlesey lecture about how geography is a science of space. Of course, as a pragmatist, I was well aware that space does not exist apart from time. Nobody has ever isolated pure space. Physical science since Einstein has accepted the inseparable unity of process, of space-time. Needless to say, I decided that this spatial metaphysicalism was plain nonsense. Besides, was it not obvious that we geographers study, as subject matter, concrete, substantial, material things, not some will-o'-the-wisp called "space" (Blaut 1961)? I studied with Robert Platt and learned much that was important about method and about Latin America, but Platt, in his zeal to destroy the monster of environmental determinism, insisted that the human mind is unpredictable, capricious (Platt 1948a, 1948b). For Platt, therefore, we study geographical facts as the product of mind, but mind remains in essence unexplained.

Then I was introduced to Richard Hartshorne's (1939) book *The Nature of Geography*. Every graduate student was required to read this book and as an undergraduate I was intrigued enough to read it myself, although I was warned that it was "hard." It wasn't hard for me because I was a pragmatist. Transparently, the emperor had no clothes. Hartshorne was trying to show that (1) geography is a science of space, and (2) space, like time, is an internal property of the mind, an "*Anschauung*," and not a property of the material world. Therefore, in essence, one can have a science of pure space because the mind divides things up into the spatial, the temporal, the causal, etcetera. What was the evidence for this? No evidence, just the mighty authority of the philosopher Immanuel Kant (Hartshorne [1939] 1961, 134-42). Said Hartshorne, following Kant, spatiality is not in the material world. Hartshorne was unaware that Immanuel Kant's most disastrous error was to take everything knowable out of the material world and put it inside the mind, leaving the material world essentially uninhabited (Rorty 1979). The "thing in itself" apparently does not exist. Matter is a mental construct.

I have to say something now about the historical context. The Kantian view that there are chorological, spatial sciences, grounded in the mental *Anschauung* of space, was of no real interest to geographers throughout most of the 19th century. Their focus was the material world, the environment, "man's relationship to the environment," and so on. Probably there were two main reasons for this. One was the monist, holist, Romantic movement, with its Nature Philosophies, themselves really a form of ecology gone wild. Secondly, the Kantian notion was just very hard to take seriously in empirical science and could not be helpful to geography. Some years ago I went through the methodological literature of 19th century Germany, and found hardly any mention of Kant before the 1880s. The Kantian theory was revived by Hettner, Marthe, Gerland, and some others, late in the century. The reason, in my view, was the crisis in German geography of that period. In the 1890s in Germany, as in the 1930s in the United States, the legitimacy of geography as a university discipline was under attack. Careers were at risk. Physical geography had left human geography far behind: what was to be its role? The study of human-environment relations was becoming discredited for two reasons: the evident mysticism of the Ritter-Humboldt-nature-philosophical idea of landscapes as organic unities, and the difficulty of studying human-environment relations without falling into environmental determinism. At the same time, this was the period of the "return to Kant," Neo-Kantianism. The Neo-Kantians were rescuing social science and psychology from dangerous materialism by putting them back into the mind: they were sciences of "spirit," not "nature." Take this one step farther and you have put geography back into the mind. For Hettner (1905a, 1905b), the "nature of geography" was demonstrated by the philosophical arguments of Kant. For this time and place, these arguments were widely persuasive because

Kant enjoyed high prestige. Geography's legitimacy could not be questioned because the "nature of geography" was *transcendental*.

Hartshorne then popularized this view in the United States. It became terribly influential because it seemed to defend geography from the attacks being made upon its legitimacy. But this is a thin reed. If you don't believe in Kantian philosophy, you don't believe in geography. According to Hartshorne in *The Nature of Geography* — he improved his view somewhat in a later book (Hartshorne 1959) — geography studies the "where" of things, their distribution (that is, areal differentiation), their combined distributions in regions.[1] Other sciences study the things themselves. Geography therefore has no subject matter of its own. No "thing." No object. No *material*.

If I had time, I would pause at this point to discuss the tortured way Carl Sauer (1925, 1935) dealt with this problem of distinctive subject matter. He knew the German literature, and he borrowed a lot of the Neo-Kantian terminology. But Sauer was interested in the material landscape, and in human ecology writ large (see Leighly 1987). Evidently he was persuaded by one of the Neo-Kantian arguments: geography cannot be a science of man-environment relationships because "relationships" are intangible, not real. Also, he argued, correctly, "man-environment relationships" always seemed to translate as "environmental influences." I incline to the view that Sauer returned to the older idea of regions or landscapes as entities: if not really organic entities, nonetheless real enough to serve as the "objects," the units of subject matter, for geography (Sauer 1925, 316, 321). I'm not sure about this interpretation. I *am* sure that Sauer had no truck with the kind of thinking which cuts us off from our roots in the material earth. Actually, for a pragmatist, and for followers of nearly all modern philosophies of science, you can't separate "object" from "relationship" (Blaut 1962). Empirically observable relations are processes. Objects are processes. Everything is process.

Sauer and Kniffen are strongly attacked in *The Nature of Geography*. The thrust of the attack is their concern with the material landscape. Hartshorne understood very clearly that the Sauer tradition in cultural geography was, in 1939, the main alternative to the Hettnerian view of human geography which Hartshorne was projecting. Environmentalistic focus on "man-environment relations," in the Davis-Semple-Barrows tradition, was no longer very popular in front-rank universities. The focus on the material landscape and human use and production of the landscape was therefore the main antagonist. I think, though I cannot prove, that *The Nature of Geography* was written mainly as an answer to Sauer's *Morphology of Landscape* (1925) and to Kniffen's methodological focus on material culture (Kniffen 1936, Kniffen et al 1937).[2] The attack on Kniffen (Hartshorne [1939] 1961, 222, 228-234) is probably the most vitriolic of many attacks which Hartshorne makes upon geographers who don't toe the Hettnerian line. Let us look at it more closely.

The Nature of Geography is like a morality play. Hartshorne relates to us the true nature of geography and its true line of descent from Kant to Hettner to Hettner's followers. The true geographers are the Hettnerians, believers in the doctrine that geography is a science of space with no material subject matter of its own, and that its job is to study the areal differences and similarities of just about anything that is areally differentiated. Opposing these true geographers are the deviationists, plotting to divert geography from its grand historical trajectory (chapter 3 of *The Nature of Geography*, for instance, is entitled "Deviations from the Course of Historical Development"). The deviationists insist that geography *does* have a definite body of subject matter, a definite kind of *thing*, of *object*, to study; that it is a science of real processes, not abstract mental space. Hartshorne is well aware that, in 1939, the really dangerous deviationists are those whom he calls the "landscape purists." Why so? I will express the matter as follows.

The real alternative to Neo-Kantian Hettnerism was a view of human geography as the field which focuses on the human use of the earth, and which claims that the processes involved in the human use of the earth constitute a body of subject matter the study of which is our responsibility. Now there are two traditional ways to translate that phrase "the human use of the earth." One is to choose language which focuses on *activity*. The other, language which focuses on the *product*, that is, material culture and the cultural landscape. The difference is a matter of language and, in practice, of research interest. Some of us prefer to study environmental behavior; others, material culture. The behavior produces material culture. Material culture is a product of the behavior. No problem. Now it happens that, in 1939, the study of activity was tarred with the brush of environmentalism; this was the study of "environmental relationships." Moreover, those who studied land-use activity had little help from psychology or the other social sciences in the devising of non-environmentalistic explanations for these activities. Psychology in particular had not yet really discovered the existence of the material environment (Stea and Blaut 1973). A final difficulty was the error of thinking of a relationship in Newtonian terms as an unreal predicate: the human being and the environment are real, but the relationships between them are unreal or they are somehow in our mind, not in the world. At any rate, the relational view was no great threat to Hettnerism in 1939. Quite the opposite was the case with the view which saw our responsibility as the study of the human use of the earth with focus on its tangible, material aspect. This was the heresy which Hartshorne called "landscape purism." The arch-heretics in the United States, and therefore the main targets of Hartshorne's inquisition, were Sauer, who talked about the cultural landscape, and Kniffen, who talked about material culture.

Hartshorne's quite lengthy attack on Kniffen (Hartshorne [1939] 1961, 222, 228-234) focussed almost exclusively on Kniffen's brief comments during a 1936 round-table discussion of problems in cultural geography (Kniffen et al 1937; the critique also embraced Kniffen 1936). Kniffen had said, in relatively few words, that he felt the core of cultural geography, its "responsibility," should be the study of the important elements of material culture in the landscape, and he described this study as being rather close to cultural anthropology. For anyone who is literate in anthropology, and in culture theory, and for anyone who reads Kniffen's empirical writings, it is quite clear that Kniffen here is stating that we must explain the material patterns we observe in terms of culture theory. Hartshorne however ignored the penumbra of meaning, with its invocation of a powerful body of explanatory theory, and focussed his attack on the simple assertion that we should concentrate our attention on material culture in the landscape. He then argued roughly as follows. Culture, he said, is immaterial. It is, he said, "ideas" (pp. 201, 233, 234). If we study the elements of material culture we are studying only the reflections of culture, not culture itself. This could have become a rather powerful critique of culture theory, which in those days said very little about ideas, but in fact Hartshorne was saying something altogether different. He said ideas are studied by other social sciences, therefore the products of those ideas are the property of the other social sciences — not of cultural geography. This comes straight from Kant (recall Kant's comment in *Physische Geographie* to the effect that systematic science studies the crocodile; geography merely tells you where to find the crocodile. This is quoted approvingly in Hartshorne [1939] 1961, 135). According to Hartshorne, geography does not study culture-as-idea but rather studies the areal patterns created by culture. Geography *is* idea: the idea of space. For Kniffen, nothing would be more absurd than to study the elements of material culture and not look for their causes, and also their effects, in culture.

Hartshorne next attacks Kniffen on the grounds that Kniffen's supposed "limitation" — it is in reality merely a statement of responsibility, in no way a "limitation" — would exclude the study of the areal patterns of non-material culture. This criticism is grounded in the Hettner doctrine that geography studies areal distributions and patterns regardless of what it is that is areally distributed (provided only that there is a difference from place to place). This criticism neglects a terribly important principle, one which has been forgotten not only by Hartshorne but by a great many location theorists in more recent times. The problem is what I call the fallacy of the white spaces on the map (Blaut 1971). It is very wrong to imagine that a distribution of any human fact is a distribution in pure space, not in earth-space with tangible properties. The white spaces on the map do not signify nothingness. They signify the earth's surface. The paper itself may be an isotropic plane but the message communicated is one of abstraction from a real landscape. Kniffen, however, would have given a different reply. Distribution of non-material culture is important to the geographer if it is a sign of the regional differentiation of culture. In that case it most certainly should not be neglected. Here I introduce an anecdote. When I went to study with Kniffen I was very much interested in folk music and I wrote the draft of a paper on the cultural geography of American folk music, why we needed to study it and how we might proceed. I never finished that paper, and Kniffen bugged me about it for years. He was very disappointed that I didn't finish the paper. Folk music is non-material for the most part but Kniffen would never consider excluding such non-material elements from our purview as geographers.

The last of Hartshorne's several attacks was a double-barreled shot at those who waste their time studying things that are small. Size, for Hartshorne, equals significance. He was following a familiar theme, used previously against microgeographers like Robert Platt, but it served also to attack those, like Kniffen, who studied small things in the landscape, things like houses. Hartshorne in essence dismisses the idea that small things are significant in themselves and insists that we certainly have the right to study small things like folk houses — here a condescending nod to Kniffen — but really we should do so only to build toward an understanding of areal differentiation, that is, an understanding not of material form but of location.

When I arrived at LSU as a graduate student, I knew about Hartshorne's attack on Kniffen and I was very anxious to hear Kniffen's response. I have to digress for a moment now to say something about the reason I came to study under Fred Kniffen. I had decided to specialize on peasant agriculture, and Robert Platt had something to do with that decision, but the Chicago department as a whole was so stodgy, so Hettnerian, so given to description, not explanation, that I decided to quit geography and learn something useful: to study tropical agriculture in Trinidad, then perhaps go into anthropology. Luckily, I ran into Andrew Clark just before leaving for Trinidad and he told me that I had given up on geography much too hastily. I should consider going to LSU, where people had respect for culture theory, for folk society, for anthropology, for intensive, ecological, non-locational approaches, and where I could also study subtropical agriculture on the side. I took his advice and after a year in Trinidad came here to LSU, just about the best decision that I ever made. But I had no interest in settlement forms. And my interests as a whole were vastly different from Kniffen's. Yet he guided me nonetheless. He educated me. And his view of cultural geography became my own — again warning you that the student of a great teacher often goes forth proclaiming the great man's doctrines and gets them all wrong.

I will now try to give you Kniffen's answer to Hartshorne's attack as I understood it then and understand it now. First of all: Cultural geography is concerned with the systems and processes involved in human interaction with the material environment. This is indeed a study of human-environment relationships provided that we understand relationships to be real, observable, material processes, principally processes of human action, the thoughts behind human action, and the effects of human action. Some of these effects are hard material things, concretized processes: material culture and human imprints on the environment. Other effects are matters of locational behavior: behavior which does not *make* material things but *moves* things, people, and ideas. Still other effects are ephemeral, or non-substantial, like geographical folk songs, or material in a special sense like geographical paintings and poems.

Some cultural geographers study the hard items, houses, settlements, bridges, tools, and the like. Others of us — today we tend to call ourselves cultural ecologists, having sloughed off the environmentalism of Barrows-era "human ecology" — study particularly the soft processes involved in human activity in the environment, not neglecting the hard concretions like crops, terraces, tools, houses, and the rest. Both these kinds of cultural geographer deal with systems of processes which are real, and which few non-geographers consider it their responsibility to study. We can call this, if we wish to, "distinctive subject matter."

Do we study these processes *spatially*? We study them wherever they take us. We study their form. We study the causes of their existence and form. Their functions in culture. Their evolution through time. Their movements in space. Cultural geography is a peculiarly "spatial science" in one respect only: many of the processual units that we deal with are *huge*. They are things like villages, culture regions, nation-states, long-distance diffusions. To make a picture of these huge slabs of space-time (borrowing Whitehead's terminology) you need to make a map, or at least get a snapshot from very high up in the sky. Geography tends to deal with spatially large processes and is a spatial science precisely in this sense. It is a spatio-temporal science. But many of the processes which we study are *not* spatially large. A house. A three-year-old child making a landscape out of toys (Blaut and Stea 1971, 1974; Blaut 1987a, 1987b). A piece of written text. And so on. Size is not significance.

A pause here to insert another personal note. My dissertation dealt with an entirely non-spatial problem, the cultural ecology of Chinese market-gardening in Singapore. Most of the research took place on tiny farms. Locational patterns were only of secondary interest. My concern was process. In the introductory chapter I extolled the virtues of a human-ecological approach, like the one I was using. Fred Kniffen had no objections to any of this: not to my use of the ecological approach, not to my focus on micro-microgeography, not to my lack of interest in space. When I came back from the field he asked me simply, "what have you found out about the historical evolution of this farming system?" I had not even considered that problem. So I dove into libraries and added an evolutionary dimension to my thesis. Evolutionary questions led to questions of diffusion and technological change. My horizons broadened.

For Kniffen, explanation is the heart of our work. We describe bits of reality, but description is not enough. Explanation takes us in two directions, both of which are matters of scientific theory, and anyone who says that Kniffen's approach is non-theoretical or anti-theoretical (see Philo 1988) simply does not understand this kind of cultural geography (Blaut 1977, 348-349). One direction is into culture. Here we ask: What is the reason why this process occurs as it does? And what is its significance? This is a matter of connecting the geographical fact to other cultural facts, as causes and as effects. But explanation at this level tends to entrap us in functionalist circles. The more crucial explanations are the large questions of historical change: of cultural evolution.

For Kniffen's kind of cultural geography, every single fact is thought of in a context of large-scale historical processes, that is, evolutionary processes. Some geographers interpret Kniffen's very wholesome skepticism about evolutionary schemata, and particularly about economic determinism, as a rejection of the evolutionary approach (Philo 1988). This is false for two reasons. First, cultural geography is essentially historical, and secondly it is historical in the sense that searches for reasons, for explanations, for evolutionary patterns. This is not evolutionism in the old sense but it is an evolutionary perspective nonetheless.

We are coming to the bottom line. Fred Kniffen's approach to cultural geography is ecological, a study of the processes by which humans use the earth. These processes are material in the sense that they are empirically observable. All of them have a more narrowly material dimension, because human-environment interaction concretizes into material things, like food, tools, and houses. Cultural geography, therefore, *does* have a central focus on material culture. It analyzes the major elements of material culture as material facts, and it connects them backward and forward into the rest of culture. It explains them, or tries to, both functionally and — much more important — historically. There are other approaches, and they have validity. But it is scientifically improper to flail at Kniffen's sort of cultural geography and claim that somehow "it isn't geography." While it is easy to laugh off this sort of charge, the fact is that it has important negative effects. Those who were persuaded by Hartshorne's arguments in *The Nature of Geography* were apt to turn toward other sorts of geographical work, not all of it very useful.

I do not wish to criticize any current approach to cultural geography in the same narrow-minded way that Hartshorne criticized Kniffen. Yet, in some of this new writing, there is more than an echo of the morality play *The Nature of Geography*. I am referring to the "post-this-ism" and "post-that-ism" to which I alluded at the beginning of this paper. Denis Cosgrove (1989, 571) and some others rather arrogantly describe it as "the new cultural geography," making no secret of their contempt for "the old cultural geography." I have not looked at this work in detail, but the following comments seem valid.

The essence of this new approach seems to be to force cultural geography back into the mind and out of the environment. The key questions seem to concern the way humans construct cognitions of the environment. The material environment itself is rather consistently ignored. Constable's painting of a rural landscape is more important than the landscape depicted. Cultural evolution is of little or no interest. Culture history seems to enter in only in a very Eurocentric and elitist way. "Culture" is spelled with a capital "C."[3]

Now I comment on all of this as a cultural geographer whose research is much more concerned with the human mind than with the landscape, and I am not about to criticize any cultural geographer who wants to study matters of psychology and subjectivity. Personally, I will not follow these people into the virtually solipsistic position in which some of them now place themselves.[4] If these new cultural geographers want to study what they call "the invention of tradition" I will not object so long as they do not deny the reality of genuine tradition. These are personal reactions to a line of thinking which I do not find to be very productive. But that's a personal opinion and I could be wrong. What must be criticized is the way some practitioners of "the new cultural geography" consider it to be a *replacement* for "the old cultural geography."

The kind of cultural geography which Kniffen personifies does not ignore mind. But it holds to a view of mind which places it within culture as a whole, and within cultural evolution, and within the material world.

Notes

1. Hartshorne did not himself perceive that his Kantian view of geography as the science, not of time, not of process, but of space, reduced it to the study of the "where" of things, the analysis and comparison of locations, distributions. In Hartshorne [1939] 1961, compare pages 127-129, 134-5, and 370-371. Also see Blaut 1961.

2. Hartshorne's critique of Sauer and Kniffen in *The Nature of Geography* is much lengthier and much more emphatic than his critiques of other North American geographers and their points of view.

3. Phrasing borrowed from Kent Mathewson. Two reports on the London conference on "New Directions in Cultural Geography" (discussed at the beginning of this paper) suggest the post-modern tack of the "new cultural geographers." According to Kofman (1988, 86), "we have clearly rejected structuralism, grand theory, the economic, and an interest in the conceptualisation of causality." (Kofman's report is entitled "Is there a cultural geography beyond the fragments?") Philo (1988), agreeing with Kofman, writes of "the reluctance of contributors at the conference to speculate on 'grand theoretical' matters" (p. 181). Conceding that there was not much concern at the conference with material culture and none with the "homely phenomena"of houses, barns, and the like, Philo tries nonetheless to associate Kniffen with the new approach, claiming that Kniffen didn't like generalizations and "most contributors would share Kniffen's interest in studying...fairs, carnivals and conferences where all sorts of rules can be bent and maybe even broken" (idem). All is whimsy.

4. For instance, Cosgrove (1989, 567-568) writes about "space as symbol" as though space were not out there all along; and about the "relativity of meaning within a discourse of endless possible meanings," such that "all meaning... [is] unstable," as though humans did not form definite judgements about meaning and put those judgements to good practical use. Notice in particular this comment: "Concepts like landscape have been subjected to detailed deconstruction over the past decade" (567).

References

Blaut, J. 1961. Space and process. *The Professional Geographer* 8(4): 1-7.

———. 1962. Object and relationship. *The Professional Geographer* 9(6): 1-7.

———. 1971. Space, structure, and maps. *Tijdschrift voor Economische en Social Geographie* 62:1-4.

———. 1977.Two views of diffusion. *Annals of the Association of American Geographers* 67:343-349.

———. 1987a. Place perception in perspective. *Journal of Environmental Psychology*, 7(4): 297-306.

———. 1987b. Notes toward a theory of mapping behavior. *Children's Environments Quarterly* 4(4): 27-34.

Blaut J, and Stea, D. 1971. Studies of geographic learning. *Annals of the Association of American Geographers* 61:387-393.

———. 1974. Mapping at the age of three. *Journal of Geography* 73(7): 5-9.

Cosgrove, D. 1989. A terrain of metaphor: Cultural geography 1988-89. *Progress in Human Geography* 13(4): 566-75.

Hartshorne, R. [1939] 1961. *The nature of geography: A critical survey of current thought in light of the past*, rev. ed. Originally published in *Annals of the Association of American Geographers*, vol. 39, nos. 3 and 4, 1939. References are to the revised 1961 ed. Lancaster, PA: Association of American Geographers.

——. 1959. *Perspective on the nature of geography*. Chicago: Rand McNally for the Association of American Geographers.

Hettner, A. 1905a. Das System der Wissenschaften. *Preussische Jahrbücher* 122:251-277.

——. 1905b. Das Wesen und die Methoden der Geographie. *Geographische Zeitschrift* 11:545-564,615-629,671-686.

Kniffen, F. B. 1936. Louisiana house types. *Annals of the Association of American Geographers* 26:179-93.

Kniffen, F. B., et al. 1937. Round table on problems in cultural geography. *Annals of the Association of American Geographers* 27:155-75.

Kofman, E. 1988. Is there a cultural geography beyond the fragments? (Report of a conference on new directions in cultural geography organised by the Social Geography Study Group, University College London, 1-3 September 1987). *Area* 20(1): 85-87.

Leighly, J. 1987. Ecology as metaphor: Carl Sauer and human ecology. *The Professional Geographer* 39:405-412.

Philo, C. 1988. New directions in cultural geography: A conference of the Social Geography Study Group of the Institute of British Geographers, University College London, 1-3 September 1987. *Journal of Historical Geography* 14:178-181.

Platt, R. 1948a. Determinism in geography. *Annals of the Association of American Geographers* 38:126-32.

——. 1948b. Environmentalism versus geography. *American Journal of Sociology* 53:351-358.

Rorty, R. 1979. *Philosophy and the mirror of nature*. Princeton: Princeton University Press.

Sauer, C. 1925. The morphology of landscape. *University of California Publications in Geography* 2:19-53.

——. 1935. Cultural geography. In: *Encyclopedia of the Social Sciences* 6:621-624.

Stea, D. and Blaut, J. 1973. Notes toward a developmental theory of spatial learning. In *Image and environment: Cognitive mapping and spatial behavior*, eds. R. Downs and D. Stea, 51-62. Chicago: Aldine.

THE GEOSCIENCE AND MAN SERIES

Human Geography

The American South, edited by Richard L. Nostrand and Sam B. Hilliard. Vol. 25, 1988, 167 p., $25.00

Cultural Diffusion and Landscapes: Selections by Fred B. Kniffen, edited by H. Jesse Walker and Randall A. Detro. Vol. 27, 1990, 80 p., $22.00

Culture, Form and Place: Essays in Cultural and Historical Geography, edited by Kent Mathewson. Vol. 31, 1993, 376 p., $24.95.

Historical Geography of Latin America: Papers in Honor of Robert C. West, edited by William V. Davidson and James J. Parsons. Vol. 21, 1980, 163 p., $14.00

Man and Cultural Heritage: Papers in Honor of Fred B. Kniffen, edited by H. J. Walker and William G. Haag. Vol. 5, 1974, 236 p., $12.50

Man and Environment in the Lower Mississippi Valley, edited by Sam B. Hilliard. Vol. 19, 1978, 165 p., $12.00

Person, Place and Thing: Interpretative and Empirical Essays in Cultural Geography, edited by Shue Tuck Wong. Vol. 31, 1992, 440 p., $24.95

Pioneers of Modern Geography: Translations Pertaining to German Geographers of the Late Nineteen and Early Twentieth Centuries, translated and edited by Robert C. West. Vol. 28, 1990, 200 p., $30.00.

Place: Experience and Symbol, edited by Miles Richardson. Vol. 24, 1984, 80 p., $10.00

The Uneven Landscape: Geographical Studies in Post-Reform China, edited by Gregory Veeck. Vol. 30, 1991, 276 p., $14.95

In production: **Aboriginal and Colonial Mining in Spanish America**, edited by Alan K. Craig and Robert C. West. Vol. 33.

Physical Geography

Research Techniques in Coastal Environments, edited by H. J. Walker. Vol. 18, 1977, 320 p., $18.00

The Mississippi River Delta: Legal-Geomorphologic Evaluation of Historic Shoreline Changes, David Joel Morgan. Vol. 16, 1977, 196 p., $15.00

Coastal Resources, edited by H. J. Walker. Vol. 12, 1973, 127 p., $6.00

Grasslands Ecology: A Symposium, edited by R. H. Kesel. Vol. 10, 1975, 50 p., $9.50

Anthropology and Archaeology

The Poverty Point Culture, by Clarence H. Webb. Vol. 17, 1982, 2 ed. rev., 86 p., $25.00.

The Poverty Point Culture: Local Manifestations, Subsistence Practices, and Trade Networks, edited by Kathleen M. Byrd. Vol. 29, 1991, 203 p., $35.00.

Tojolabal Maya: Ethnographic and Linguistic Approaches, edited by M. Jill Brody and John S. Thomas. Vol. 26, 1988, 74 p., $18.00

Historical Archaeology of the Eastern United States: Papers from the R. J. Russell Symposium, edited by Robert W. Neuman. Vol. 23, 1983, 69 p., $10.00

Traces of Prehistory: Papers in Honor of William G. Haag, edited by Frederick H. West and Robert W. Neuman. Vol. 22, 1981, 134 p., $14.00

THE FRED B. KNIFFEN CULTURAL LABORATORY MONOGRAPH SERIES

Louisiana's Remarkable French Vernacular Architecture, by Jay D. Edwards. No. 1, 1988, 36 p. Reprint to be announced.

Historic Louisiana Nails: Aids to the Dating of Old Houses, by Jay D. Edwards and Tom Wells. No. 2, 88 p., $18.00.

Forthcoming: The Historic Maps of Louisiana: An Annotated Bibliography, compiled by Joyce Nelson and Anne Stanton. No. 3.

DIGITIZED COUNTY BOUNDARY FILES

China County Boundaries Files, by Nina S. Lam. In Atlas*Graphics, and Arc/Info. $150.00

Historical United States County Boundary Files (1850-1970), by Carville Earle and Changyong Cao. In Atlas*Graphics. $250.00

Pakistan Boundary Files, Philippines Boundary Files, or Vietnam Boundary Files, by Russell Hires and Gregory Veeck. In Atlas*Graphics. $50 per country.

VIDEOTAPE

Bringing the Past Alive: Conversations between Bill Haag and George Quimby on WPA Archaeology in Louisiana. 2 hours. $20.00

OTHER WORKS FROM
GEOSCIENCE PUBLICATIONS

Human Geography

Atlas of Louisiana: A Guide for Students, by Milton B. Newton, Jr. 1972, 200 p. $12.00

Atlas of Louisiana Surnames of French and Spanish Origin, by Robert Cooper West. 1986, 212 p. $37.50

Environment and Culture, compiled by H. J. Walker and M. B. Newton, Jr. 1978, 259 p. $5.00

Journal of John Landreth Surveyor: An Expedition to the Gulf Coast, November 15, 1818-May 19, 1819, edited by Milton B. Newton, Jr. l985, 204 p. $20.00 Also available in hard cover, $30.00.

Plantation Traits in the New World, edited by R. E. Chardon, 1983, 126 p. $8.00

Physical Geography

Climatic Perspective of Louisiana Floods 1982-1983, edited by Robert A. Muller and Gregory E. Faiers. 1984, 48 p. $4.00

New Orleans Weather 1961-1980: A Climatology by Means of Synoptic Weather Types, by Robert A. Muller and James E. Willis. 1983, 70 p. $8.00

LINGUISTICS JOURNAL

The Journal of Mayan Linguistics, edited by M. Jill Brody. Write for rates.

mélanges

(All mélanges $3.00.)

Archaeological Assessment of Coastal Louisiana, by Robert W. Neuman. No. 11, 1977, 44 p.

Country and Small Town Stores of Louisiana: Legacy of the Greek Revival and the Frontier, by Linda Pulliam and M. B. Newton, Jr. No. 7, 1973, 11 p.

Current Interest and Research in Coastal Marine Geography, compiled by H. J. Walker and Robert F. Haswell. No. 8, 1973, 26 p.

The Lake St. Agnes Site: A Multi-Component Occupation of Avoyelles Parish, Louisiana, by Alan Toth. No. 13, 1979, 51 p.

Louisiana House Types: A Field Guide, by Milton B. Newton, Jr. No. 2, 1971, 18 p.

Louisiana in North American Prehistory, by William G. Haag. No. 1, 1971, 45 p.

Publications from Coastal and Marine Research at Louisiana State University, compiled by H. J. Walker. No. 6, 1972, 32 p.

Recent Geological History of Timbalier Bay Area and Adjacent Continental Shelf, by James P. Morgan. No. 9, 1974, 17 p.

Reconstructing the Forest Primeval, West Feliciana Parish, by Hazel R. Delcourt. No. 10, 1975, 14 p.

The Spanish Moss Folk Industry of Louisiana, by Fred B. Kniffen and Malcolm L. Comeaux. No. 12, 1979, 19 p.

Stewards of the Past, by Charles R. McGimsey III, Hester A. Davis, and Carol Chapman. No. 4, 1972, 21 p.

All books are paperbound unless otherwise indicated.

For orders or information, contact:
GEOSCIENCE PUBLICATIONS
Department of Geography and Anthropology
Louisiana State University
P.O. Box 16010
Baton Rouge, LA 70893

FAX: 504-388-2912   **Bitnet: GAWILC @ LSUVM.SNCC.LSU.EDU**